THE SELF CONCEPT

THE SELF CONCEPT

A Critical Survey
of Pertinent Research Literature

by

RUTH C. WYLIE
Sarah Lawrence College

UNIVERSITY OF NEBRASKA PRESS
LINCOLN

Copyright © 1961 by the University of Nebraska Press.
Library of Congress catalog card number 61-8377.
Manufactured in the United States of America.

First printing: February 1961
Second printing: November 1961
Third printing: January 1967
Fourth printing: April 1970

To My Mother

Preface

Some years ago, I became interested in the current trend toward rapprochement between personality theories and general behavior theories, and in the beginning which had been made in applying experimental and psychometric methods to the testing of some personality theories. One of the systems I examined from this viewpoint was self-concept theory, and I hoped to formulate some research of relevance to this and other personality theories which emphasize constructs concerning the self. As a background for such an undertaking, I began to examine the pertinent theoretical and empirical literature. It soon became obvious that this literature was growing in chaotic profusion, and could profit from some sort of evaluative, organized summary.

At the outset I intended to limit myself to a critical summary of the available studies. However, appropriate comprehensive criteria for evaluation were not available in any one place, and so a major part of my task became the accumulation and systematic presentation of such criteria. Although there is much useful material in the methodological literature of experimental and psychometric psychology, the setting up of suitable criteria was not an entirely simple, straightforward job of compilation and application of ready-made standards. In fact, in the development of my own thinking, reflection on the basic rationale of research design and measurement in this particular area has proved to be the most interesting and potentially valuable aspect of the preparation of this book. I hope that these ideas, as well as the particularized criticisms and substantive overviews, will prove useful to graduate students and researchers who are interested in this and related topics. I believe that there are important lessons to be learned in exploring the issues involved in research in this area.

When this book was in various stages of preparation, several persons read substantial portions of the manuscript, or all of it. Thanks to these interested and perceptive critics, the accuracy, clarity, and comprehensiveness of the book are much greater than they otherwise would have been. These persons are: Katherine E. Baker, Robert R. Blake, Mary Evans

Collins, Lee J. Cronbach, Frank J. Dudek, Marshall R. Jones, Jane S. Mouton, James T. Russell, William Stephenson, and Georgiana R. Wylie. Throughout the preparation of the book I received especially valuable support and encouragement from Katherine E. Baker, Mary Evans Collins, and Georgiana R. Wylie.

Correspondence with a number of the authors cited in the book clarified certain questions I had about their theoretical or empirical work. Many of these correspondents encouraged me to feel that this arduous task needed doing. There are also numerous friends and colleagues with whom I have had helpful, informal conversations during the time when this book was being prepared. I wish to thank all of these persons collectively for their encouragement, kind cooperation, and contributions to my thought. Of course I must take final responsibility myself for any shortcomings of accuracy or interpretation in the book.

Thanks are also due to Shehbal Erdeniz and Vivian McCraven for their part in the search for titles, and to Edith Spoley who did the major part of the typing.

The publisher and the author wish to express their gratitude to the copyright owners listed below for permission to quote from their publications. *Acta Sociologica,* American Psychological Association, Inc., Appleton-Century-Crofts, Inc., Basic Books, Duke University Press, D. Van Nostrand Co., Inc., *Educational and Psychological Measurement,* Houghton Mifflin Co., Inc., *Human Relations, Journal of Clinical Psychology, Journal of Counseling Psychology, Journal of Projective Techniques,* Journal Press, *Journal of Social Issues,* Ohio State University Press, *Personnel and Guidance Journal,* The Ronald Press Co., School of Aviation Medicine, United States Air Force, University of Chicago Press, and Yale University Press.

Part of the cost of the literature search, the critical reading, and the writing of this book was defrayed by funds from Grant No. M-1822 from the National Institute of Mental Health. The author wishes to thank that agency for making it possible to carry out this work.

RUTH C. WYLIE

Contents

Chapter I. Introduction 1

A. A Brief Historical Overview of Interest in Constructs Concerning the Self 1

B. Purpose and Scope of the Book 2

Chapter II. Phenomenological Theories and Problems of Research Design 6

A. Phenomenal and Nonphenomenal Variables: Measurement Problems Stemming from Ambiguities in Their Relative Roles 6

B. Research Designs Appropriate for Tests of Phenomenological Personality Theories 8
    1. Existential Psychology 9
    2. Nomological Scientific Psychology 10
        a. Observable Consequents 11
        b. Inferred Constructs 11
        c. Observable Antecedents 13

C. General Vagueness of the Theories 21

Chapter III. The Measurement of Phenomenological Constructs ... 23

A. An Analysis of Problems in Measuring Phenomenological Constructs 23
    1. The Problem of Construct Validity 23
    2. Recommendations; Summary 38

B. Specific Measures Used in This Area: A Descriptive Survey and Analysis of Construct Validity and Reliability 39
    1. Instruments for Measuring Phenomenal Self-Regard .. 40
        a. Q Sorts, with Special Reference to Butler and Haigh's Items 41
        b. Rating Scales, Questionnaires, Adjective Check Lists 65
        c. Coding Plans for Interview Materials 107
    2. Instruments Purporting to Index Aspects of the Phenomenal Self besides Self-Regard 110

Chapter IV. Studies Purporting to Relate the Phenomenal Self to
    Other Variables and/or to Test Some Aspect of Self-Concept
    Theory 114

A. An Analysis of Problems of Research Design 114
B. An Introductory Orientation to Empirical Categories of
    Studies to Be Reviewed 118
C. Summaries and Criticisms of Studies, Grouped in Empirical
    Categories 119
    1. Development of the Self Concept 119
    2. Parent-Child Interaction and the Self Concept 121
    3. Social Interaction (Other than Parent-Child) and the
        Self Concept 136
        a. Sex and Role as Related to Self Concept 137
        b. Peer Interaction and the Self Concept 149
        c. Self Concepts and Friendship Choice 150
        d. Self-Regard and Susceptibility to Persuasion 153
    4. Body Characteristics and the Self Concept 159
    5. Effects of Counseling or Psychotherapy on the Self
        Concept 161
        a. Counseled Ss Compared to Noncounseled Ss 166
        b. Therapy Success or Duration of Therapy Correlated
            with Self-Concept Changes 169
        c. Changes in Counseled Ss 174
        d. Studies of Single Cases 177
        e. Miscellaneous 181
    6. Effects of Lobotomy on the Self Concept 183
    7. Effects of Experimentally Induced Success or Failure on
        the Self Concept 184
        a. Experiments in Which S's Personality Characteris-
            tics Are Devaluated 186
        b. Experiments in Which Ss Were Made to Fail on
            Experimental Tasks 189
    8. Learning and the Self Concept 199
        a. Influence of Learning in the Development of the
            Self Concept 199
        b. The Influence of the Self Concept on Learning 200
    9. Relationships between "Adjustment" and Self-Regard . 202
        a. Self Concepts of Ss with Varying Degrees of Diag-
            nosed Pathology 205

      b(1) Teacher, Authority, and Peer Ratings of Be-
            havior Presumably Relevant to Adjustment . . 218
      b(2) Other Observable Behaviors Presumably Related
            to Adjustment 221
     c. Projectives for Measuring Adjustment 226
     d. Self-Report Instruments as Indices of Adjustment . 229
  10. Acceptance of Self and Acceptance of Others 235
     a. Cross-Sectional R-R Correlations 235
     b. Covariation of Self-Acceptance and Acceptance of
        Others as a Function of Time and/or a Third Vari-
        able 238
  11. Self-Esteem and Authoritarianism and/or Ethnocentrism 240
  12. Self Concept and Level of Aspiration Behavior (LA) . 243
     a. [Self—Ideal] Discrepancies, Self-Acceptance, Self-
        Adequacy, and LA Behavior 245
     b. Limited Self-Evaluation and LA Behavior 247
     c. Nonphenomenal Self-Regard and LA Behavior . . 248

Chapter V. Operational Definitions of the Nonphenomenal Self and
Its Relationships to Other Variables 250

A. General Problems of Construct Validity 250

B. Survey of Specific Measures Used in This Area and of Studies
   Relating the Nonphenomenal Self to Other Variables 251
    1. TAT and Other Picture-judging and Story-telling Tech-
       niques 252
    2. Rorschach Scores (Other than Fisher's Scores Purport-
       ing to Index "Body Image") 262
    3. Various Indices of "Body Image" 263
     a. Aniseikonic Lenses 264
     b. Distorted Pictures 265
     c. Rorschach Barrier Scores 266

C. Summary Comments on Studies Involving the Unconscious
   Self Concept 274

Chapter VI. Studies Concerned with the "Insightfulness" of the Self
Concept 275

A. Introduction 275

B. Varieties of Operational Definitions 276
  1. Discrepancy Scores 276
  2. Insightfulness of *S* Directly Inferred by an Observer .. 278
  3. Insightfulness of *S* Inferred from a Specially Devised
    Self-Insight Test 279
C. Construct Validity of [Self—Other] Discrepancy Measures
  of Insight 279
  1. *S*'s Self-Reports 279
  2. *O*'s Reports on *S* 284
D. Errors of Method in Relating Insight to a Dependent Variable 285
E. Summary of Studies Relating Insight to a Dependent Variable 286
  1a. Adjustment Inferred from *S*'s Self-Report 286
  1b. Adjustment Inferred from an External Observer's Re-
    port 290
  1c. Adjustment Inferred from a Combination of *S*'s Self-
    Reports and an External Observer's Diagnosis 293
  1d. Adjustment Inferred from *S*'s Having Undergone Psy-
    chotherapy 294
  2. Adjustment Inferred from Defensive Behavior 295
  3. Adjustment Inferred from Psychotherapeutic Com-
    petence 302
  4. Adjustment Inferred from Vocational Success 303
F. Conclusions Concerning the Relationship of Insight to Adjustment 304
G. Descriptive Facts about the Occurrence of Insight 306

Chapter VII. Conclusions and Implications 317

Bibliography 325

Supplemental Bibliography 349

Index 369

Tables

Table I. Sets of Self-descriptive *Q*-Sort Items   61

Table II. Questionnaires, Adjective Check Lists, Rating Scales for Indexing Self-Regard   86

Table III. Specific Evaluation Instruments   97

Table IV. Indices of the Nonphenomenal Self Concept   259

I

Introduction

In psychological discussions the word "self" has been used in many different ways. Two chief meanings emerge, however: the self as subject or agent, and the self as the individual who is known to himself (English & English, 1958). The words "self concept" have come into common use to refer to the second meaning, and it is with the self concept that this book is concerned.

Early in the history of American psychology, there was considerable interest in the self. For example, William James (1890) accorded this topic an important place in his psychological thinking, and to a certain extent the study of the self was pursued by introspectionists (Calkins, 1915).

During the second, third, and fourth decades of the twentieth century, constructs concerning the self did not receive much attention from the behaviorist and functionalist psychologies which were dominating the American scene. As Hilgard (1949) points out, the introspectionists were unable to handle the self, and of course such a "mentalistic" construct as the self concept was anathema to behaviorists. Meanwhile the psychodynamic postulates which were being developed by Freudians and neo-Freudians necessarily implied a self referent in order to make them plausible and understandable. For at least two reasons these theories did not immediately bring constructs concerning the self to the forefront of American psychology. First of all, Freud himself, in his early theorizing, strongly emphasized the role of the id, and he did not explicitly formalize a self construct nor assign the closely related ego functions much importance, relatively speaking. Secondly, his theory was being denied or ignored by many American general psychologists who found it lacking in rigor, in susceptibility of empirical test, and in compatibility with the theoretical models then in favor.

Recently, however, there has been a marked proliferation of self theories, traceable to a number of influences: In his later writings, Freud himself assigned greater importance to ego development and functioning, and of course the neo-Freudians stressed the importance of the self picture and the ego-ideal. At the same time, American psychologists who were beginning to work in clinical areas found behavioristic models apparently too limited to account for the phenomena they were observing, and they were ready to entertain psychoanalytic ideas, particularly of the revised variety. Since their interests were somewhat different from those of students of the general experimental psychology of cognition and motivation, the clinicians may have felt less need for neat, philosophically sophisticated, operationally circumscribed theorizing. They may have been less distressed to depart from such theorizing in their search for conceptual schema to account for their observations.

Throughout this period the functionalists never gave up introspective methods, and the Gestalt psychologists injected their phenomenological methods and theories into the stream of general psychology. Meanwhile, the possibility of an operational behaviorism involving complex cognitive and motivational intervening variables was being explored within the domain of general psychology. All of these facts implied the possibility of fusing general psychological theories of cognition and motivation with the psychoanalytic or psychodynamic theories originating in the clinic. And so we find that all the theories of personality which have been put forth within the last two decades assign importance to a phenomenal and/or nonphenomenal self concept with cognitive and motivational attributes.

Although there was much writing of such theories during the 1940s and 1950s, there was very little empirical work done prior to 1949. Since that time, however, there has been an increasingly large output of investigations, and it is with the review of this empirical literature that the present book is concerned.

B. PURPOSE AND SCOPE OF THE BOOK

The purpose of this book is to review critically the recent research literature in the area of "self psychology." So far as the present writer knows, no comprehensive overview of these studies has been published.

The domain to be surveyed is broadly conceived to include studies of pertinence to a wide variety of theories which accord an important or even central role to the self concept (e.g., Adler, 1924; Angyal, 1941; Freud, 1950; Fromm, 1939; Horney, 1937; Lecky, 1945; Lynd, 1958; Maslow, 1954; Mead, 1934; McClelland, 1951; Rogers, 1951a; Snygg & Combs, 1949; Sullivan, 1947). Some of these theorists (e.g., Lecky, Rogers, and Snygg & Combs) have been called phenomenological theorists because of their stress on the role of the conscious self concept in determining a person's behavior. In the present review, major emphasis is given to studies which pertain to this conscious self concept, sometimes called the phenomenal self. To a lesser degree, attention is also given to investigations concerned with nonphenomenal constructs, e.g., the unconscious self concept.

When one reads the empirical literature pertaining to self-concept theories, one finds that a bewildering array of hypotheses, measuring instruments, and research designs has been used. As a consequence, one cannot prepare a simple synthesis of the established results. In view of this situation, it seemed necessary to broaden the goals of this overview. They are (1) to make an analysis of the requirements for adequate measurement and research design in this area; (2) to point out the limitations in method which recur frequently in the studies reviewed; (3) to summarize what appear to be reasonably safe conclusions after allowing for these limitations in method; (4) to bring out what is needed by way of future research.

The theories are in many ways ambiguous, incomplete, and overlapping, and no one theory has received a large amount of systematic empirical exploration. Therefore the book is organized in terms of measurement and research design problems, and clusters of empirical studies, rather than around the framework of any one theory. Reference to theoretical ideas will be made when discussing proposed operational definitions of constructs and empirical tests of principles, and we shall draw some conclusions concerning the extent to which the principles of various theorists seem to have been explored and supported.

Since we are dealing mainly with phenomenological theories, we need to consider whether any special problems of research design are involved in making appropriate tests of such theories. This question is considered in Chapter II.

An examination of empirical studies makes it apparent that ambiguities in the measuring instruments can be traced partially to inadequacies in the theorists' definitions of their terms. We cannot attempt in this book systematically to review, compare, criticize, or put in order the various nonoperational definitions in common use.[1] However, the general problem of defining terms in phenomenological theories will be considered at length in Chapter III. Also some nonoperational definitions will be recorded and discussed in Chapter III when we try to evaluate the construct validity of those instruments which researchers have used in an effort to define these concepts operationally.

Chapter IV presents studies which bear on hypotheses "derived" from self-concept theory. In these researches some aspect of the phenomenal self concept is related to theoretically relevant variables. Because of the limitations of the theories mentioned above, it seemed best to group these investigations into categories according to what was actually available rather than according to any a priori arrangement of theoretical relevance. In general the investigations belong in one or more of the following major categories:

(a) studies which are concerned with the influence of antecedent factors upon the consequent phenomenal self concept;

(b) studies which are concerned with the influence of the antecedent phenomenal self concept upon consequent behaviors;

(c) studies which are concerned with correlations between the phenomenal self concept and theoretically relevant variables, without specifying the direction of the hypothesized antecedent-consequent relationship.

As we said above, the major discussion of measurement problems will center around operational definitions of phenomenal constructs. But, since even phenomenological personality theorists implicitly or explicitly admit nonphenomenological constructs (e.g., the unconscious self concept), measurement problems concerned with these constructs will be considered at the beginning of Chapter V, on the nonphenomenal self, and Chapter VI, on insight.

Chapter V is concerned not only with definition of the unconscious self concept, but also with studies purporting to relate aspects of the unconscious self concept to variables of theoretical relevance.

---

[1]For extensive listing of such terms the reader is referred to Symonds (1951), Chein (1944), English and English (1958), Hall and Lindzey (1957), Combs and Soper (1957), and Rogers (1951a).

It is implicitly or explicitly assumed by all theorists that the self concept is not entirely "realistic," and that lack of "realism" may have psychodynamic significance and important behavioral consequences. To the degree that a person's self concept is realistic, he is said to have "insight" into himself. Chapter VI first considers the general problems which one encounters when attempting to define this kind of insight. It then reviews the various operational definitions in common use, and the studies relating insight to theoretically relevant variables.

In selecting studies to be reviewed, some limiting criteria had to be established. From one viewpoint, any investigation in which S makes a report about himself, say on a personality inventory or in an interview, might be regarded as suitable for inclusion in this survey. However, we shall restrict ourselves mainly to studies which appear to have received at least some of their inspiration from self theories. Most of the publications which are reviewed here appeared between 1949 and 1958. Some studies of an earlier date and some which appeared in 1959 are also included. Doctoral dissertations are listed in the bibliography for the sake of completeness, and they may be referred to occasionally. But since they were studied mostly through the Dissertation Abstracts rather than in the original, there was, in many cases, insufficient information on which to base salient evaluations.

In Chapter VII, we shall try to summarize the main implications of the detailed facts and evaluations presented in Chapters II through VI. We shall try to appraise both theory and method, to see what we have found which may be useful for future conceptualizing and empirical work.

II

Phenomenological Theories and Problems of Research Design

A. Phenomenal and Nonphenomenal Variables: Measurement Problems Stemming from Ambiguities in Their Relative Roles

As is well known, self-concept theorists believe that one cannot understand and predict human behavior without knowledge of S's conscious perceptions of his environment, and of his self as he sees it in relation to the environment. Because of this central role accorded to conscious perceptions, cognitions, and feelings, these theorists have often been labeled "phenomenological."

Not all writers have consistently reserved the term "phenomenology" to refer to "the study of direct awareness," but we shall use the term with that meaning only. Most workers refer to a continuum of clarity in the phenomenal or conscious field, including the phenomenal self, and we shall apply the word phenomenal to all aspects of that continuum. On the other hand, attitudes, knowledge, motivations, and perceptions which are hypothesized to be definitely unconscious, we shall call "nonphenomenal."

Like all psychologists who deal with inferred variables, phenomenological personality theorists face many difficult problems in defining terms and achieving appropriate observable indices for their constructs. In Chapter III we shall be concerned with a detailed analysis of these difficulties, and shall try to outline the requirements for achieving appropriate measurement of phenomenological constructs. We shall see that many of the measurement problems are not new, nor unique to this area, but that researchers have not paid sufficient attention to previous relevant analyses, or to parallel kinds of problems already discovered by workers in other fields of psychology. In addition, we must note that in some ways we face uniquely difficult problems in achieving valid measurement of the constructs of the phenomenologist.

Some of the most crucial difficulties seem to center around the degree to which self-concept theorists wish to be, and can fruitfully be, consistently phenomenological. Many examples of this unresolved dilemma can be found in the writings of phenomenological theorists. As one illustration we have chosen some quotations from Rogers's publications. At some points he seems to imply that *only* when a feeling or item of information about the self or environment comes at least dimly into awareness will it influence behavior. "The self-concept or self-structure may be thought of as an organized configuration of perceptions of the self which are admissible to awareness. It is composed of such elements as the perceptions of one's characteristics and abilities; the percepts and concepts of the self in relation to others and to the environment; the value qualities which are perceived as associated with experiences and objects; and goals and ideals which are perceived as having positive or negative valence" (Rogers, 1951a, p. 136). "This configuration . . . as Raimy says . . . 'serves to regulate behavior and may serve to account for uniformities in personality'" (Rogers, 1951a, p. 191). "As long as the self-Gestalt is firmly organized, and no contradictory material is even dimly perceived, then positive self-feelings may exist, the self may be seen as worthy and acceptable, and conscious tension is minimal. Behavior is consistent with the organized hypotheses and concepts of the self-structure" (Rogers, 1951a, p. 191). "[Although the individual whose self concept is incongruent with reality may be vulnerable], the extent to which he dimly perceives these incongruences and discrepancies is a measure of his internal tension and determines the amount of defensive behavior" (Rogers, 1951a, pp. 191-192). However, it becomes obvious in other places that processes such as drives, unconscious motivation, repression, and denial are at least tacitly assumed to occur and to determine behavior, even though it is never clearly specified how such nonphenomenological constructs are to be articulated into the theoretical system. For example, "He may have some experiences which are inconsistent with this perception, but he either denies these experiences to awareness or symbolizes them in such a way that they are consistent with his general picture" (Rogers, 1951b, p. 321). "While these concepts are nonverbal, and may not be present in consciousness, this is no barrier to their functioning as guiding principles" (Rogers, 1951a, p. 498). In general, the problems and limitations of phenomenological theorizing have not been faced squarely by proponents of self-concept theories. (See Smith's [1950] criticisms of phenomenological theories, and Snygg & Combs's [1950] rejoinder.)

In the face of this situation, most empirical workers have initiated their studies by circumventing these confusing issues. They have said, in effect, "Let us see how much of the variance in Ss' behavior on X, Y, Z ... we can account for on the basis of variance in Ss' self-report responses on instruments A, B, C .... We shall offer an interpretation of our findings based on the assumption that the self-report responses correlate with the other behaviors because Ss' phenomenal fields, as tapped by our measures A, B, C, have determined Ss' behaviors on X, Y, Z. We recognize that processes or attributes of which S is unaware may also be affecting his self-report responses and other behaviors. Some of these factors of which S is unaware may be relevant to our theory, some may not be. In any case we can face the problems of alternate interpretations, and of unaccounted-for variance at some future time."

Now we may grant that a researcher is not obligated to perfect his own or someone else's theory before attempting to test some aspect of it. However, careful scrutiny of empirical studies makes one conclude that measurement in this field is chaotic partly because these issues have not been explicitly recognized and systematically handled.

A review like the present one is not the appropriate place for a frontal attack on basic problems in phenomenological theory-building. Therefore we too shall bypass theoretical questions concerning nonphenomenal determinants in Ss' general behaviors. We shall take as our point of departure the fact that these theorists do specify that S's phenomenal field "determines" at least a great deal, if not all, of his general behavior. The latter tenet implies that, regardless of how the questions of nonphenomenal determinants may eventually be conceptualized, we must develop instruments which *do* validly index Ss' phenomenal fields, especially their phenomenal selves. Only then can we relate such responses to the other behavior of S which is allegedly a function of the phenomenal field.

B. RESEARCH DESIGNS APPROPRIATE FOR TESTS OF PHENOMENOLOGICAL PERSONALITY THEORIES

In addition to the problems of obtaining valid measures of the phenomenal self, there is the question as to what kinds of research design are appropriate for testing phenomenological theories, especially phenom-enological personality theories.

Confusion and differences of opinion may be found in the literature concerning this matter.

1. EXISTENTIAL PSYCHOLOGY

The discussions of methodology later in this section, and in the entire book, are based upon the assumption that the scientific method can be fruitfully used to test phenomenological personality theories in order to establish nomological (i.e., general scientific) laws. With some possible exceptions, the statements of Rogers, Lewin, Freud, and the neo-Freudians seem to imply acceptance of this assumption. Recently, however, some personality theorists have been turning to existential psychology, which criticizes the assumptions and methods of modern behavioral science (May, 1958).

Existentialists point out that modern science is concerned with finding methods of isolating factors and observing them from an "allegedly de-tached" base, and with selecting for investigation those phenomena which can be reduced to abstract general laws. As a result, according to the existentialists, the laws formulated have little relation to the person in his unique, changing, concrete world of experience. Not only does scientific method fail to do justice to the data, but it tends to hide rather than reveal what is going on in the person, since we try to see the person in terms of our scientific concepts. While existentialists "do not rule out the study of dynamisms, drives and patterns of behavior . . . they hold that these cannot be understood in any given person except in the context of the over-arching fact that here is a person who happens *to exist, to be,* and if we do not keep this in mind, all else we know about this person will lose its meaning" (May, 1958, p. 12).

There is also a second way in which the beliefs of existential psychol-ogists apparently differ from the views of other psychologists. Existen-tialists seem to feel that it is possible and necessary for the observer to become directly aware of the conscious world of the subject. In this connection, they deplore the influence upon psychology of the historical dichotomy between subject and object in Western thought. May writes (1958, p. 38), ". . . *the grasping of the being of the other person occurs on a quite different level from our knowledge of specific things about him."* And on pages 55-56 he says, ". . . *being together* means *being to-*

gether in the same world" and ". . . the other person's world . . . cannot be understood as an external collection of objects which we view from the outside (in which case we never really understand it)."

Some of the psychologists whose work appears in the present volume have moved toward acceptance of the existentialist view (e.g., Leary and Stephenson).

This book is not the place to evaluate the existentialist position. We are concerned with research methods and results, and these, with a few possible exceptions, appear to stem from the following two assumptions: (1) There *is* value in using modern scientific method to establish nomological laws. (2) Psychological processes occurring inside an organism cannot be directly observed, but must be inferred from observable behavior, in combination with other observables.

2. NOMOLOGICAL SCIENTIFIC PSYCHOLOGY

Returning to those who do seek nomological laws, we find differences of opinion as to the scientific methodological requirements of phenomenological theory. Some persons feel that the methodological requirements of phenomenological theory are peculiar to that type of theory. That is, they feel that the scientific methods of the phenomenologist *must* differ from those which can be used and are appropriate to testing other kinds of psychological theory. (See Spence, 1944.)

In view of this unresolved controversy, we may profitably spend some time analyzing the situation in an attempt to determine the methodological possibilities and requirements which are appropriate to phenomenological personality theories.

We assume that theoretical propositions in psychology are always of the *if-then* variety, in which observable behavior is predicted or explained as a function of relevant variables that are external to the subject and/or characteristic of the subject.

Most psychologists would probably agree that a complete science of behavior must eventually determine which classes of observable antecedents are relevant, and must eventually include all classes of relevant antecedents in its behavior laws. At present we are far from this point, and the typical psychological theorist is aiming toward a more restricted set of laws which are not intended to cover all the important *if-then* possibilities. Such restricted intentions are characteristic of phenomenologists as well as of other theorists.

Our problem is to analyze the *if-then* sequence to find which research designs provide appropriate tests of phenomenological theories. One possibility is that some basically unique approach to the formulation and testing of *if-then* propositions is implied by phenomenological personality theory. We are also interested in determining the relationship between the designs which have actually been used and the sorts of conclusions which can be safely drawn.

Let us work backwards through the *if-then* sequence, beginning with the behavior consequents referred to by *"then."*

a. Observable Consequents

On the consequent side, psychological theorists differ from one another in two respects: (a) Different theorists prefer to study different kinds of consequent behavior variables. (b) Their views differ as to what ways of classifying behavior variables will be most fruitful or convenient.

As will be pointed out in Chapter III, self-concept theorists seem bound to make much use of verbal behavior, but they are by no means restricted to verbal behavior. Some hypotheses of phenomenological personality theorists contain consequent responses from the areas of perception, learning, and motivation. Social behavior categories and psychiatric behavior categories are also often used as consequent variables. As yet there is no systematic plan in phenomenological personality theories for establishing fruitful behavior categories. In any event, observable behaviors of some kind, classified in some specifiable manner, must be the consequents in a scientific psychology, no matter what the school of thought. This requirement applies to phenomenological theorists, insofar as they aspire to be scientific.

b. Inferred Constructs

Preceding the observable, consequent behaviors most psychologists find it necessary to insert inferred variables or theoretical constructs into the predictive "equation." Views differ as to the kinds of constructs which will be most fruitful in developing a behavior science. For example, Hebb prefers neurophysiological constructs, Hull mathematical intervening variables, and Gestalt psychologists phenomenal field constructs. The phenomenological personality theorists, of course, find such inferred variables essential to their theorizing too. As we have already pointed out, many of their inferred variables are phenomenal, but these theorists also use nonphenomenal constructs such as unconscious cognitions.

In any case, from the point of view of theory building, the theoretical constructs or inferred variables of the phenomenological personality theorist fulfill the same role as any other sort of theoretical construct. That is, these constructs are introduced to help explain behavior variations which occur under constant external stimulation, and similarities of behavior which occur under varying external stimulating conditions. And like the theoretical constructs in any theory, those of the phenomenological personality theorist must be defined in terms of relationships between observables if they are to be scientifically useful.

Heider (1959) has recently discussed inferred constructs and their relationship to observable antecedents and consequents, with reference to Lewin's theory. His views may be applicable to other phenomenal theorists as well. Heider says that Lewin's concern with inferred constructs is greater than is the concern of behaviorists. This does not mean, however, that Lewin ignored, either theoretically or experimentally, the observed antecedents and consequents to which inferred variables are anchored. Heider writes (1959, p. 5), "[Lewin's] primary concern is with what goes on in this life space; that is where he expects to find the relevant variables, the nodal points which he expects to follow exact laws without exceptions. In contrast to Lewin's concern with the life space, psychology today often considers input and output as the primary object of study; true enough, there are also intervening variables, but they play only an ancillary role. The psychologist deals with them somewhat reluctantly and then only because otherwise the relations between input and output become unmanageable.

"For Lewin these so-called intervening variables are the focus from the start, and input and output are relegated to a secondary role; they form the tools for observation which make it possible for us to get a glimpse of the processes in the life space which are the ultimate object of observation."

In short, although the phenomenologist may assign greater importance to his inferred constructs, the methodological requirement of anchoring constructs to observable antecedents and consequents is the same for phenomenological theory as for any other.

c. Observable Antecedents

On the antecedent side it is common in psychological theorizing to divide the observables into several classes:

1) observable characteristics of the environment, or stimuli
   a) contemporary environmental conditions or stimuli
   b) past environmental conditions or stimuli
2) observable characteristics of the subject
   a) contemporary observable characteristics of S
   b) past observable characteristics of S

As on the behavioral (consequent) side, theorists may differ with respect to the following points:

1. what kinds of antecedent variables they postulate as probably being important to study

2. what classification scheme they believe will prove to be the most fruitful one to apply to antecedent variables

Contemporary Stimulus Antecedents. Let us consider contemporary environmental conditions or stimuli first. Behaviorists, Gestalt psychologists, and phenomenological personality theorists have all assigned importance to contemporary "stimuli." Problems arise in the definition of "stimulus." To some it has seemed that this is one point at which the appropriate method for phenomenological personality theory becomes unique (e.g., Spence, 1944).

The argument on that point goes as follows: The phenomenological personality theorist has made it clear that he is interested in the "stimulus" from self or from the environment *as the subject sees it,* rather than being concerned with the "stimulus" as it is physicalistically defined. This means that the "stimulus" *must* be inferred from S's response. The necessity of defining stimuli by means of response inferences seems to imply that the phenomenologist must employ R-R (response-response) designs instead of the more usual S-R (stimulus-response) designs.

An overview of the studies actually done in the area of self-concept theory quickly reveals that R-R designs are, indeed, the most common. What does this situation imply?

1. Can one unequivocally infer cause-effect sequences from such R-R correlational designs? The answer is clearly negative. If phenomenological personality theorists are limited by the nature of their theory to con-

temporary response-response correlations, their theory can never lead to predictive or explanatory, cause-effect *if-then* laws.

2. Does the fact that stimuli must be response-inferred by phenomenological theorists necessarily restrict these theorists to response-response correlational designs, so that they will never be able to state cause-effect relationships in the same sense as the behaviorist does?

Verplanck has offered an analysis of the "stimulus" which is helpful in putting this problem of the phenomenologist into the perspective of general psychological methodology.

Verplanck (1954) has outlined four definitions for stimulus: Stimulus I is a part of the environment or a change in part of the environment. Stimulus II adds to Stimulus I the qualification that the environmental change becomes a stimulus only when a response of some kind is produced. Stimulus III refers to a class of environmental events which cannot be identified independently of the observation of lawful activity of the organism. This is Skinner's "stimulus" term. Stimulus IV adds to Stimulus II hypothetical or inferential stimuli such as the movement-produced stimuli of Guthrie, or of Dollard and Miller. Verplanck remarks (p. 286), "Such inference-backward to quasi-independent variables in behavior seems to be characteristic of the work of many behavior theorists . . . . It is not impertinent to ask whether since this is so regularly the case, will it ever be possible to develop a science of behavior in which laws relating data-language stimuli to data-language responses can be found. Is it necessarily the case that 'stimuli' become response-inferred concepts, bearing no necessary relationship to what is put in front of the organism?"

Verplanck's analysis makes it clear that the phenomenological theorist is not unique in having difficulties in defining his antecedents in terms of data language. Stimuli are, it seems, response-inferred constructs in all sorts of psychological theories. Thus no fundamentally new methodological problems for phenomenology seem to be implied by our analysis of the antecedent up to this point.

Let us carry the analysis further, however. First let us note, as Jessor (1956) has pointed out, that "stimulus" characteristics can be defined (inferred) from the responses made by two classes of persons. (1) The experimenter defines the stimulus through his own observing responses, and such defining observations can presumably be repeated by other experimenters. In this instance we say that the stimulus is defined in data language. Let us call the experimenter-response-inferred stimulus $Stim_E$.

(2) The "stimulus" values which variations in $Stim_E$ have for the subject must be inferred from the subject's perceptual responses. Let us call the stimulus as inferred from the subject's response $Stim_S$. One way of looking at classical perception experiments is to say that we relate $Stim_E$ (stimulus as defined by the experimenter's response) to $Stim_S$ (stimulus as inferred from the subject's response). Both psychophysicists and Gestalt psychologists have done many experiments of this sort. It is obvious that we usually call them "stimulus-response" experiments. Although the antecedent is response-inferred, it is called "stimulus" because it is inferred from the experimenter's, not the subject's, response. We certainly have here a situation in which both the antecedent ($Stim_E$) and the consequent (subject's response, from which $Stim_S$ is inferred) can be given in data language.

Consider now that the behavioristic psychologist has actually established "stimulus"-response laws of the sort just described, e.g., he has obtained S's subjective brightness responses to a series of light stimuli of measured energy value. Now he is in a position to go on to use $Stim_E$ in further experiments, involving other predicted behavioral consequents in which he is theoretically interested. For example, he can present S with one value of $Stim_E$ and condition him to give a galvanic skin response to it. From learning theory he predicts that, if he presents other values of $Stim_E$, the generalization of the galvanic skin response will follow a gradient of similarity along the $Stim_E$ dimension. He feels that it is sensible to make the prediction partly on the basis of the already established function which relates $Stim_E$ to $Stim_S$. If his prediction is confirmed, he feels that he has another "stimulus"-response (cause-effect) law. Only to the extent that he has carried out such procedures can he correctly speak of cause-effect relationships between independently defined stimuli and responses.

How does this apply to the questions in which the phenomenologist is interested? Typically the Gestalt psychologist interested in perception has not carried his procedure beyond the first kind of "stimulus"-response experiment, establishing relationships between $Stim_E$ patterns and $Stim_S$, as inferred from S's verbal response. There is nothing in his theoretical orientation which would prevent him from going on to the second kind of experiment described above, however.

A hypothetical example will illustrate how necessary it can be to establish a $Stim_E$ — $Stim_S$ relationship before trying to predict relationships between $Stim_E$ and other behaviors. Suppose the experimenter has established a discriminative GSR to patterns containing curved lines as contrasted to patterns containing only straight lines. To test generalization he presents two parallel straight lines with radiating additional straight lines. $Stim_E$ is defined in terms of the E's responses in preparing and measuring the stimulus pattern of straight lines. S gives a GSR to the straight line pattern. Why? To explain or predict S's behavior in this instance one must utilize $Stim_S$, *not* $Stim_E$, i.e., one needs to know that the S would say these parallel lines ($Stim_E$) look curved to him ($Stim_S$). If that had been established prior to the conditioning experiment, one could, as in the case of the brightness conditioning experiment, say that one had demonstrated cause-effect relationships between independently defined stimuli and responses. And in this case it would be particularly pertinent to use $Stim_S$ as the basis of prediction.

But what about the phenomenological personality theorist? Insofar as he is interested in the subject's phenomenal view of the *environment,* it seems that the logic of the perception experiments would apply to him. The difference lies in the practical difficulties in implementing this logic. These difficulties seem to be greater for the phenomenological personality theorist.

First of all, there are probably greater practical problems in establishing useful $Stim_E$ categories for the sorts of complex environmental patterns in which the phenomenological personality theorist is interested. Secondly, the practical difficulties of making the experimenter's stimulus-defining responses public and repeatable may be greater, due to the complexity of the environmental patterns which seem theoretically relevant (e.g., parental treatments of the subject). And of course the practical difficulties of systematically presenting various values of any $Stim_E$ category would be much greater for the phenomenological personality theorist than for the psychophysicist or for the Gestalt psychologist who is interested in perception. Nevertheless, such studies should be undertaken. Nothing about the theory necessarily implies that such studies are theoretically irrelevant or impossible in principle.

When we turn to the second kind of experiment in which $Stim_E$ antecedents (and therefore $Stim_S$) are related to theoretically relevant responses of the subject, we find again that the practical difficulties are greater for the phenomenological personality theorist. We can explain

this most easily by referring back to the classical perceptual situation described earlier.

In the case of the visual perception experiments, the experimenter assumes that the $Stim_E$—$Stim_S$ law which he established for one or a few subjects will describe what holds true for any other S who can be independently demonstrated to have normal vision. Thus the experimenter feels safe in going on to the conditioning experiment using other subjects than those on whom the $Stim_E$—$Stim_S$ relationship was originally established, so long as he has reason to believe that the new subjects have normal vision.

The situation of the phenomenological personality theorist is typically much more complex in this regard. For one thing, individual differences may be much greater and may occur more commonly in the $Stim_E$—$Stim_S$ relationships of the complex sort which interest the phenomenological personality theorist. Furthermore it is not clear how one can set up general criteria (comparable to the establishment of Ss' visual normality prior to the conditioning experiment), by which one can know that the $Stim_E$—$Stim_S$ function obtained on one subject will quite probably apply to another subject. It seems, therefore, that the phenomenological theorist must use the same subject in exploring the $Stim_E$—$Stim_S$ relationship that he uses in a further study which tests an hypothesis about the relationship between $Stim_E$ (therefore $Stim_S$) and a theoretically relevant response.

For example, the experimenter might first establish that Stimulus Person 1 ($Stim_{E1}$) and Stimulus Person 2 ($Stim_{E2}$) are regarded by the subject as respectively a friend of his ($Stim_{S1}$) and a mere acquaintance ($Stim_{S2}$). The experimenter could then test the hypothesis that a subject's self-rating behavior on a stated instrument is more affected by evaluations of him which allegedly come from Person 1 (friend) than by evaluations of him which allegedly come from Person 2 (acquaintance). One can not safely assume that the same actual stimulus persons, $Stim_{E1}$ and $Stim_{E2}$, would be viewed as friend and acquaintance by another S. Therefore the $Stim_E$—$Stim_S$ relationship would have to be separately established for the second subject before going on to test the hypothesis with him.

To take another example, the experimenter may tell all his Ss that the puzzles he is giving them are an intelligence test ($Stim_E$). He would like to assume that each S does indeed view these tasks as an intelligence test ($Stim_S$). Perhaps each subject's $Stim_S$ will not be so unique as in the previous example about the friend and the acquaintance. However, one can predict S's behavior (say his change in self-evaluation after experimentally induced failure) only if one knows how S regards the tasks, and S's view of the tasks can be ascertained only by a separate $Stim_E$—$Stim_S$ determination.

But this again seems to be a matter of practical complications rather than of different logical requirements for the methods which are appropriate to testing phenomenological personality theories. The self-evaluation problem just outlined seems to be comparable to the situation one encounters in perception studies which use value-related words. To get stimulus words which S values to a greater or lesser degree, one must determine for each individual S and for each word to be used, the relationship between the $Stim_E$ (Word) and $Stim_S$ (Value Response). One then would predict the relationship of S's perceptual responses to $Stim_S$.

Contemporary Characteristics of the Subject. Thus far we have been concerned with contemporary stimuli or environmental factors external to the subject. We turn now to the question of contemporary characteristics of the subject. Here it seems that the situation of the phenomenological personality theorist becomes most complicated.

The behaviorist, if he wishes to, can enter into his *if-then* statements observable characteristics of the subject such as age, sex, IQ, or hormone level. Such variables are consistent with an objective, behavioristic approach. The phenomenologist, on the other hand, if he is consistently phenomenological, should restrict himself to the *subject's view* of his own characteristics. Actually the phenomenological personality theorist is not consistently phenomenological. Therefore his first difficulties lie in specifying theoretically how he intends to articulate these nonphenomenal variables into his system. On the observational (methodological) side, his problems and requirements in dealing with nonphenomenal variables are the same as those of any psychological theorist.

What methodological problems arise in designing studies which involve S's self-report on his self concept as an antecedent? Is this a different situation from that of exploring how the subject views other persons in his environment, and then entering such phenomenal views into further predictions of S's behavior? The experimenter cannot present to or withhold from the subject the "stimulus" (i.e., the subject's own actual characteristic) as he (the experimenter) wishes. It seems to be extremely difficult to develop $Stim_E$ concerning the subject's characteristics which may have corresponding $Stim_S$ value for the subject. In a sense the situation resembles that of the reports the subject may make on his visual field when he is lying in the dark, i.e., the experimenter has no way of making his own observations on the "stimulus" conditions immediately responsible for the subject's reported experience. The instructions which the experimenter gives to the subject in a self-concept experiment are not the stimuli which elicit the self concept. They are merely cues which elicit S's verbal reports of his self concept, the latter being itself elicited by other "stimuli" (characteristics of the S) which are often largely inaccessible to the experimenter's observation. Thus, if our laws call for a self-concept variable as an antecedent, we are reduced to response-response correlational designs where both responses are obtained from the subject in the same study. In such a case, although a plausible cause-effect inference may be made, we can never claim to have demonstrated a cause-effect relationship unequivocally.

This point has sometimes been said to differentiate phenomenological personality theory from general behavior theory. However, we find that a somewhat parallel situation holds true in behavior theory. In the learning equations of Hull, for example, individual or species differences in subject characteristics are to appear as constants. Logically, no unequivocal cause-effect inference can be drawn relating such constants, as antecedents, to behavioral consequents. Nevertheless, the Hullian would feel justified in determining and using these constants to the extent that they improved the predictiveness of his equation.

Is there a basic difference between phenomenological and behavior theorists with regard to the use of "subject characteristics" in predicting S's behavior? At first it may seem that the S's characteristic is objectively determined by the behaviorist experimenter, while it is inferred from the S's response by the phenomenological theorist. That is, S's characteristics are inferred from E's responses in the case of behaviorism, but from S's responses in the case of the phenomenological personality theorist. For example, the behaviorist might use S's IQ as one variable in his hypothesis about S's learning behavior, while the phenomenological personality theorist may use S's estimate of how intelligent he is. Deeper analysis of such comparisons shows that S's responses are part of the defining of his own characteristics in either case, however. That is, E's "objective" measure of S's IQ would of course depend partly upon E's observing responses, but S's responses to the test also form part of the basis for the objective measure.

It would seem, then, that a clear-cut logical distinction cannot be made between phenomenal and behavior theorists in terms of the operations used for measuring S's objective, as contrasted to self-perceived, characteristics. In either case, unequivocal cause-effect inferences are not justified, simply on the grounds of a correlation between S's objective characteristic *(or S's* self concept of his characteristic) and other responses of S.

In any design correlating a contemporary characteristic of S ("objectively" or "subjectively" determined) with a "consequent" behavior of S, there is much danger of artifactual contamination between the two measures being correlated. Probably such contamination has occurred frequently and is more difficult to avoid in the studies of the phenomenal personality theorist than in studies of behaviorists. This merely implies the need for greater precaution in establishing operationally independent measures for the "antecedent" response *(S's* self concept) and the "consequent" response. It does not seem to imply that a fundamental difference in research design is required.

Past Environmental Conditions, Stimuli, or Subject Characteristics. Thus far we have said nothing about designs which involve past environmental conditions, stimuli, or subject characteristics. Phenomenological personality theorists have often been labelled "ahistorical," with the implication that historical or genetic studies involving past antecedents for present behavior are inappropriate to these theories. However, a study of theories such as Rogers's, for example, shows that they are by no means ahistorical. For example, statements are made about the influence of parental treatment, or of psychotherapy upon the self concept. Therefore, genetic research is in order. An overview of the studies reviewed in this volume shows that researchers who were interested in historical propositions have typically used R-R research designs in which two contemporaneous responses are correlated. For example, the young adult's current view of his parents' opinions of him is correlated with his present report of his self concept. Such a design is an inappropriate expedient for exploring the influence of the parents' earlier opinions upon the child's self concept. The design may yield interesting exploratory information on S's current views of parent and self, but it does not test an historical hypothesis in which the researcher was primarily interested.

The problems of defining past antecedent environmental or past subject characteristics in historical studies are in principle the same as those we have already discussed in connection with defining contemporaneous antecedent environmental or subject characteristics. Therefore we shall not repeat our analysis here.

In sum, it appears that practical difficulties in planning and executing appropriate and rigorous research designs are greater for the phenomenological personality theorist than for the general experimental psychologist. In principle, however, the *if-then* statements of phenomenological personality theory involve the same classes of variables and do not imply fundamentally different research designs from those required by any psychological theory.

It seems that R-R (response-response) correlations are necessary for testing certain phenomenological propositions, and that such R-R designs cannot support unequivocal cause-effect inferences. Even in this respect, the phenomenological theory poses no fundamentally new problems, since analogous types of design are necessary to test certain aspects of any behavior theory. There is great possibility of artifactual contamination in the R-R designs of phenomenological personality theory, so special cautions are needed to rule out such artifacts.

Although phenomenological personality theory is supposed by some to be entirely ahistorical, this is not a correct assumption. Since phenomenological personality theory includes historical (genetic) propositions, designs are appropriate here in which past antecedents are related to present consequents.

C. GENERAL VAGUENESS OF THE THEORIES

Another characteristic of currently formulated phenomenological theory which poses problems for research designers has already been touched upon, but deserves a more general expression. We refer to the ambiguity with which these theoretical views are expressed.

The basic constructs as defined in the writings of these theorists frequently seem to point to no clear empirical referents. Thus it is no wonder that a wide array of "operational definitions" of some of these constructs has been devised by various experimenters. And by the same token it is understandable that some constructs have received no empirical exploration.

Sometimes these theories have been expressed in terms of a series of "laws" or "postulates" relating the inadequately defined constructs. Such a form leads one to search for determinateness and internal consistency in the set of statements. However, the shape of the function, the range over which the relationship is supposed to hold, or the manner of interaction between joint determining factors is typically not specified. It appears to the present writer that there are occasional contradictions between one proposition and another, but it is often impossible to be sure. As a consequence of these ambiguities, directional hypotheses are not always clearly implied, and plausible interpretations of trends which go against the predicted direction are often possible.

III

The Measurement of
Phenomenological Constructs

A. An Analysis of Problems in Measuring
Phenomenological Constructs

Throughout this section we shall discuss problems common to measuring any or all aspects of the phenomenal field, including the phenomenal self. Later on, some of the more specific constructs, e.g., self-esteem and self-consistency, will be more specifically considered. All of the general comments to be made in the immediately following paragraphs will be applicable to the evaluation of the specific instruments when they are discussed.

1. *The Problem of Construct Validity*

Problems of measuring the phenomenal field may be seen as essentially those of establishing "construct validity," in Cronbach and Meehl's (1955) sense of this term. Construct validity is necessary because self-concept theories explicitly require that we measure a stated class of variables, Ss' conscious processes; and, by definition, Ss' phenomenal fields are private and beyond direct observation by the experimenter. It is *not* sufficient to demonstrate that one's self-concept measures have "predictive" or "concurrent" validity in the sense that an MMPI scale, for example, may be shown to discriminate nosological categories without an explanation of why the association between MMPI scores and diagnostic labels is obtained.

In order to index constructs involving Ss' phenomenal fields, E must use some form of self-report response made by S as a basis for his inferences. In practice this self-report behavior has usually taken the form of a verbal response or some sort of choice response when S is instructed to indicate specified conscious processes. These methods seem to be the only kinds appropriate to this type of construct. That is, if we obtain motor, autonomic, or projective test responses from S without telling him of our intent to infer his conscious processes, we have no way of knowing whether such responses reflect conscious or unconscious cognitions and feelings.

We would like to assume that S's self-report responses are determined by his phenomenal field. However, we know that it would be naive to take this for granted, since it is obvious that such responses may also be influenced by (a) S's intent to select what he wishes to reveal to the E; (b) S's intent to say that he has attitudes or perceptions which he does not have; (c) S's response habits, particularly those involving introspection and the use of language; (d) a host of situational and methodological factors which may not only induce variations in (a), (b), and (c), but may exert other more superficial influences on the responses obtained.

We mentioned above that self-concept theorists could profit by examining and applying relevant analyses made by psychologists working in other areas. For example, the difficulties and requirements encountered in measuring the phenomenal field seem to be similar to those already encountered, and to some extent analyzed, by experimental psychologists working in the field of perception. Garner, Hake, and Eriksen (1956) have noted the fundamental problem of identifying the influence of *perceptual* processes on responses made in perceptual experiments (as opposed to other influences on response availability and production). We may find it useful in our present discussion of processes influencing Ss' self-concept reports to draw analogies with their analysis of processes influencing Ss' perceptual responses. Before going into details of this sort, however, we need to remind ourselves of pertinent general methodological requirements for establishing construct validity, as these have been stated by Garner, Hake, and Eriksen (1956), by Cronbach and Meehl (1955), and by Campbell and Fiske (1959), among others.

Garner, Hake, and Eriksen have pointed out that

> the necessary condition which makes possible the determination of particular characteristics of any concept (including the concept of perception) is the use of what have been called converging operations. Converging operations may be thought of as any set of two or more experimental operations which allow the selection

or elimination of alternative hypotheses or concepts which could explain an experimental result. They are called converging operations because they are not perfectly correlated and thus can converge on a single concept (1956, pp. 150-151).

In Cronbach and Meehl (1955) and Campbell and Fiske (1959) we find what amounts to more particularized specifications for appropriate "converging operations" for establishing the construct validity of measuring instruments:

(1) We may make observational, including mathematical, analyses of the measuring process to determine what variables other than the construct in question might be influencing our results (Cronbach & Meehl, 1955).

(2) We may ascertain that there are intercorrelations among measures presumed to index the same construct (Cronbach & Meehl, 1955). Campbell and Fiske (1959) in their discussion of trait validity, state an addititonal specification along this line. (In paraphrasing their ideas, we shall use the word "construct" instead of their word "trait.") Using the word "method" to refer to variations in instrument form or procedure for collecting data, they point out that data from a given method can be used to infer different constructs (e.g., the questionnaire form can be used to reveal self-esteem or to reveal test anxiety). On the other hand, different methods can purport to measure the same construct (e.g., either a questionnaire or an interview might reveal self-esteem). They give the following specifications concerning correlations between scores obtained from differing methods which purport to measure the same construct: (a) Ideally such correlations should exceed correlations between scores which are obtained by a given method, but which purport to index different constructs. (b) Such correlations should exceed correlations between scores which are obtained by different methods and which purport to index different constructs. (Humphreys has recently argued that the specification stated under [a] is desirable, but not necessary. He believes that "the degree of importance to be attached to it is simply a function of the number of different methods that can be used to measure the trait" [Humphreys, 1960, p. 86].)

(3) It is pertinent to make internal item analyses and factor analyses of an instrument to determine how many basic processes must be postulated to account for response variance on the instrument as a

whole (Cronbach & Meehl, 1955). We may include here the following related, but more limited, statement of Campbell and Fiske. They specify that correlations between scores obtained from a given method which purports to measure the same construct should exceed: (a) correlations between scores which are obtained by a given method but which purport to index different constructs; (b) correlations between scores which are obtained by different methods and which purport to index different constructs; (c) correlations between scores which are obtained by different methods but which purport to index the same construct.

(4) Cronbach and Meehl (1955) have suggested that, in the absence of suitable external validating criteria, we may examine results obtained from studies in which responses on the instrument in question are related to other stimulus and response variables. That is, we may design a study on the basis of certain theoretical premises coupled with an assumption concerning the construct validity of the instrument we are using to measure one of the variables. Positive findings from such a study offer support simultaneously to the construct validity of the instrument and to the theory behind the study. In general, such investigations would involve (a) successful prediction of group differences, and (b) studies of predicted changes over occasions (especially after controlled experimental intervention). We must bear in mind, however, that such findings offer ambiguous support at best, since the ratio of unknown to known variables does not preclude alternate interpretations. We are not, therefore, warranted in bypassing validating procedures of the types (1)-(3) above. The appearance of face validity of our instruments coupled with studies of type (4) will never suffice to establish the construct validity of a newly devised instrument.

Thus far the requirements we have stated are applicable to the study and measurement of any sort of construct, and we have indicated particular similarity to the problems of psychologists studying perceptual processes. However, we face an additional problem not encountered by psychologists studying perception. In the case of a perception experiment, E usually is dealing with S's response to a stimulus, the properties of which can be agreed upon by a number of observers. Therefore, insofar as S's reports agreed with E's independent knowledge of stimulus attributes, E can establish that S's verbal report is most probably validly indexing his percept. If S's report does *not* reveal that he has seen the stimulus characteristics E expects, E is faced with an ambiguous situation, thus: (a)

S may be missing something, or experiencing something different from other observers who have examined the stimulus under comparable conditions, but his report is nevertheless a valid index of what *he* is seeing; *or* (b) S may be withholding what he sees, or may not have the necessary verbal skills to report accurately, etc. (i.e., his report is *not* a valid index of his percept). The self-concept researcher, although dealing with phenomenal fields in much the same way as the perception experimenter, has the disadvantage of having no way of independently checking S's reports, since there is no immediate stimulus and hence no way of getting agreement of other observers about what S should presumably be experiencing under specified conditions. So the self-concept researcher's method problems are much more complicated than those of the experimental psychologist studying perception.

Now let us apply these specifications to the question of the construct validity of the self-theorists' instruments for indexing Ss' phenomenal fields, to discover to what degree such validity has been established.

(1) ANALYSIS OF IRRELEVANT RESPONSE DETERMINERS

What kinds of observational and mathematical analyses of the measuring process have been made to ascertain what variables other than the construct in question (the phenomenal field) may be determining the observed responses?

Social Desirability

So-called Social Desirability has come in for more study than any other possibly irrelevant or contaminating variable (Edwards, 1957). Edwards has developed a scaling procedure by which each item in a self-report instrument may be assigned a Social Desirability value. Ss other than the judges involved in the scaling procedure are then asked to describe themselves in terms of the self-report instrument, and the proportion of these Ss "endorsing" each item (i.e., saying that the item describes them) may be determined. Thus it is possible to find out whether Ss tend to attribute Socially Desirable characteristics to themselves. Several studies of this type have been done, utilizing various self-report instruments (Edwards, 1957; Kenny, 1956). As a result it is well established that high correlations are found between mean probability of endorsement of self-report items and their independently scaled Social Desirability values.

No way has been worked out, however, to determine in what cases and under what circumstances the Social Desirability variable distorts individual self-reports away from validity in reflecting S's phenomenal field. That is, the fact that a self-report response can be fairly reliably predicted on the basis of its scaled Social Desirability value does not necessarily disprove its validity as an indicator of S's conscious self concept.

Cowen and Tongas (1959) thought that reported discrepancies between S's Self concept and his Ideal Self concept might be free of the influence of Social Desirability. In their study they used the Bills-Vance-McLean Index of Adjustment and Values, which requires S to rate himself on a five-point scale with reference to each of forty-nine adjectives (items). (See Section B below for a description of this instrument). In agreement with Edwards's studies, they found that the mean of the Self ratings which Ss assigned to an item was associated with that item's independently scaled Social Desirability value. That is, there was a high correlation across the forty-nine items between the item mean Self ratings and item Social Desirability values. They also found that item mean Ideal Self ratings correlated highly with item Social Desirability values. They computed a discrepancy value for each item by subtracting the mean Self rating from the mean Ideal Self rating. This discrepancy did *not* correlate across the forty-nine items with the scaled Social Desirability values of the items. We note that this zero correlation would necessarily have to occur, since the item mean Self ratings and item mean Ideal Self ratings were each so highly correlated with item Social Desirability values. Moreover, this zero correlation does not warrant the inference that particular "Self Concept minus Ideal Self" discrepancies *within individuals* are free of the Social Desirability influence. Neither does the zero correlation warrant the inference that *individual differences in total* "Self Concept minus Ideal Self" discrepancies are free of the Social Desirability influence. This is so because the treatment of the data was in terms of *item means* and discrepancies between item means rather than in terms of individual Ss' total discrepancy scores, or individual Ss' particular item discrepancies. Therefore their findings do not support their conclusion that reported discrepancies between Self concept and Ideal Self might, in contrast to reports on either aspect taken alone, be considered to be free of the influence of the Social Desirability factor.

One must conclude that the problem of the influence of Social Desirability on the validity of S's self-report concerning discrepancies between Self concept and Ideal Self remains unsettled.

Recently questions have been raised as to whether Social Desirability, as operationally defined by Edwards's instructions, reflects the "social approval" value of a trait as much as the label Social Desirability may imply. DeSoto, Kuethe, and Bosley (1959) asked three groups of college students to respond to thirty-nine MMPI items which are included in Edwards's Social Desirability scale. These items had been keyed by Edwards, according to the unanimous agreement of ten judges as to their Social Desirability or Social Undesirability. In the present study, one group followed Edwards's Social Desirability instructions (judge the trait in terms of whether you consider it desirable or undesirable in others). The second group followed "social approval" instructions (the trait is desirable if you tend to like or admire a person more if he has the trait). The third group followed "personal well-being" instructions (the trait is desirable if you tend to think that a person is more well off if you know he has the trait). Majority agreement of the student judges with the Social Desirability values assigned by Edwards's original judges was obtained: (a) for 35 out of 39 items answered under "well-being" instructions; (b) for 30 out of 39 items answered under Edwards's Social Desirability instructions; (c) for 23 out of 39 items answered under "social approval" instructions. These results suggest that Edwards's Social Desirability values may reflect Ss' judgments of the "well-being" indicated by an item rather than the "social approval value" of the item.

The conclusions of Kogan, Quinn, Ax, and Ripley (1957) seem to agree with those of DeSoto *et al.,* although the methods used in the two studies differed to an unknown extent. In the Kogan investigation, each of six clinicians sorted 96 items twice: once along a Social Desirability dimension and once along an emotional Health-Sickness dimension. The six Social Desirability sorts were averaged into a single Mean Social Desirability sort, and the six Health-Sickness sorts were similarly averaged into a Mean Health-Sickness sort. The correlation between these two Mean arrays was $+.89$. Since Kogan *et al.* have not stated the exact instructions by which they defined the Health-Sickness dimension for their judges, we cannot tell how similar their Health-Sickness dimension is to the "well-being" dimension of DeSoto *et al.* (The Q items used by Kogan *et al.* are described in Table I below.)

A third study concerning the possible overlap between adjustment and Social Desirability is that of Wiener, Blumberg, Segman, and Cooper (1959). The 100 items used by Butler and Haigh (1954) were Q sorted by 28 clinical psychologists to indicate how a "well-adjusted" person would sort the items when describing himself. (No definition of "adjustment" was given the sorters.) The intragroup correlation among the 28 sorts was +.75. Mean Adjustment values were computed for each item by combining the values assigned to the item by each of the psychologists. Sixteen other clinical psychologists sorted these items along a continuum of "social desirability," i.e., the degree to which "you think *people in general* would consider that trait or behavior socially desirable or socially undesirable" (Wiener *et al.,* 1959, p. 316). The intragroup correlation for Social Desirability was +.62. Again, a mean Social Desirability value was obtained for each item. The correlation across items between the mean Adjustment and mean Social Desirability scale scores was +.88. Although this study uses items and instructions which differ from those of the two studies described immediately above, it seems that it is offering support for the same general proposition: Persons in our culture see Social Desirability as having much in common with health-sickness, personal well-being, and/or maladjustment. In Wiener's study which we have just described, 21 college student Ss also sorted the items under the "adjustment" instructions. Mean item values for Adjustment obtained from their sorts were correlated with mean item values for Adjustment obtained from the clinical psychologists' sorts. The *r,* across the 100 items, was +.95. This suggests that the use of student judges in the DeSoto study and of clinician judges in the Kogan study does not make it impossible to compare them with each other, so far as differences in the type of subject are concerned.

Even if we could say how extensively Social Desirability invalidates self-reports as indices of the phenomenal self, we could not specify in the light of present knowledge what the nature of the invalidating influence is.

Before closing this discussion of Social Desirability, we should note parenthetically that there is another validity question which we have not considered here, because it is not relevant to a discussion of S's phenomenal field. That question is: To what extent does Social Desirability distort S's self-report away from the report which qualified objective observers would make about S's behavior characteristics? Parts of the study by Kogan *et al.* (1957) are pertinent to this question.

Content Areas

Another possible factor which may be related in part to "Social Approval" is the influence of areas of item content. Perhaps it is more socially acceptable to reveal oneself in certain areas than others, even when the factor of the self-favorability of individual item reports is held constant across content areas. Or perhaps areas of item content may be differentially revealed, even with item self-favorability constant, because they are more or less salient to S's self-esteem. This idea receives some suggestive support from the findings of Jourard and Lasakow (1958), whose Ss reported that they voluntarily disclosed themselves to others more freely in certain areas than in other areas. For example, they reported that they revealed more about their attitudes, opinions, tastes, and interests than about their personality or body characteristics. (See also Jourard, 1958.)

Known Identity of S

A number of investigators have taken the precaution to assure S's anonymity, on the theory that this would increase the validity of S's self-report as an index of his phenomenal field. While there is reason to believe that this is a desirable control (Davids, 1955), the influence of this factor on the availability of valid responses in self-report tests covered by this review has not been specifically demonstrated. Many investigators have not taken this precaution.

Lack of Rapport

It is a truism that rapport with the experimenter must affect the accuracy and completeness of S's report of his conscious self concept. However, no one has specifically demonstrated the influence of this factor, and in many studies where data have been taken by group procedures no particular means for establishing rapport have been described. Of indirect relevance to this issue are the findings of Jourard and Lasakow (1958), obtained from a questionnaire on which Ss described the persons to whom they voluntarily disclosed themselves in everyday life. Significant differences were found in frequency of self-disclosure directed toward varying classes of persons (e.g., there was more reported self-disclosure toward Mother than toward Father, more toward Spouse than toward Same Sex Friend). These results may indicate the role of rapport in self-disclosure, although other factors could be operating as well. More directly pertinent is the finding of a significant correlation between Ss' reports of how much they like their parents and their reports of how much they disclosed of themselves to their parents. (See also Jourard, 1958.)

Instrument Form

Under the heading of form we are concerned with whether the instrument consists of rating scales, ranking procedures, inventory questions requiring Yes or No answers, or adjective check lists requiring dichotomous choices. In addition we are concerned with the variations and refinements within these general kinds of forms. For example, there may be special sources of irrelevant response determiners respectively associated with semantic differential scales, linear rating scales, and rating scales with descriptive words at each point. Workers using these forms of instruments in other fields of psychology have called attention to pertinent methodological precautions which help one to avoid some irrelevant response determiners, e.g., acquiescence response sets, halo effect, the tendency to check one end or one range of a scale predominantly or exclusively (Cronbach, 1946, 1950).

Young, Holtzman, and Bryant (1954) have demonstrated that the positive or negative tone of contextual items can affect the average rating assigned to a given item within the context. Their findings suggest another aspect of form which should be controlled in self-concept indices.

The effects of any of these aspects of form upon the validity of the particular self-report instruments utilized in the presently reviewed researches has not been explicitly demonstrated, however. Moreover, a surprisingly large number of investigators have failed even to attempt such controls, indicating no recognition of their possible usefulness.

Many researchers obtain separate scores for ideal self, actual self, social self, etc. by eliciting repeated responses on the same instrument, or by selective scoring of subgroups of items from one instrument. In studies of this kind we have no basis for estimating the influence of response sets induced by the form of the instrument, or by the fact that all items or instructions were reacted to in one sitting.

Degree of Restriction of S's Response

The freedom of response allowed the S is evidently a pertinent determinant of self-report responses, as it is of responses in perception experiments. For example, if we allow S to give a free, unstructured report about his self concept, in a manner comparable to the Gestalt psychologists' techniques in eliciting reports from Ss in perceptual experiments, we may be unable to classify or quantify Ss' responses in a way necessary to relate the response index to other items in the "nomological net." Wylie (1957), for example, found that open-ended essays describing one's self and one's ideals for one's own conduct were not codable for a number of the characteristics on which she had data from other instruments. Ss' failure to mention certain characteristics on the essays occurred despite the fact that these characteristics had been shown by other investigators to be important parts of the self concept, in the opinion of Ss who were similar in many ways to those used by Wylie (Diller, 1954). We have said above that willingness to disclose oneself may vary with different content areas of self-disclosure (Jourard & Lasakow, 1958). This suggests one reason why open-ended self-reports may omit important aspects of the self concept.

On the other hand, when Ss' mode of reporting is circumscribed, as by a semantic differential technique, Q sort, or any kind of inventory or rating scale, especially one of the forced-choice variety, one has no way of knowing to what extent the external limits imposed by the measuring instrument prevent S from giving an accurate report of his conscious cognition or feelings. We are reminded here of the point made by Eriksen (1956) in connection with an operational analysis of "subception": The fact that a galvanic skin response was given along with an incorrect report of the visual stimulus may indicate *not* unconscious perception, but the fact that the range of responses which E permitted S to give did not include a means for him to specify his percept in all its relevant, but subtle, aspects. Few studies in the self-concept area have addressed themselves specifically to these important methodological difficulties. However, one study has shown that normal and abnormal Ss, when given free choice in a Q-sort setting, produce sorts more nearly U-shaped than normal (Jones, 1956). This of course implies that investigations using the conventional Q-sort procedure, which requires Ss to produce a quasi-normal distribution of item placements, have introduced some distortion into their instruments. Edwards (1957, p. 60) has reported that Ss sometimes express frustration when using his forced-choice PPS inventory. This may be due to thwarting of S's desires to put himself in a socially desirable light (since the items are paired according to their scaled Social Desirability value). However, it may also be due to the frustration of having to represent the phenomenal field with an incongruent instrument. Supporting the latter interpretation are the findings of Levonian, Comrey, Levy, and Procter (1959). They factor-analyzed each of the fifteen PPS scales, but found no large factors which were identifiable along the lines of the fifteen major variables scored in the test. The correlations were low between items supposed to measure the same variables. They believe that this may be mainly due to the forced-choice form of the PPS, which encourages unreliability of response because it requires S to choose between two statements which seem to him to be equally self-descriptive (or to be equally inappropriate as self-descriptions). They feel that such difficult choices may easily lead to a negative attitude, which promotes carelessness and unreliability. In their view, item form should make it possible for the respondent to express himself and his position as exactly as possible. If S's self-report is distorted away from his conscious self picture because of the Social Desirability influence, one should try to take this variable into account in some other way than by forced choice.

Set or Expectation

The effect of set or expectation has been found in perceptual experiments to influence Ss' responses, perhaps partly by way of influencing perceptual processes as such, but quite probably by way of influencing response availability to some degree without necessarily altering perceptual processes. As it is well known from general experimental psychology that manipulating instructions may induce changes in set or expectation, the influence of instructions may pertinently be considered here. There have been marked variations from study to study in the particular directions given to S to define a concept which was assigned the same label (e.g., ideal self). No one has systematically studied the influence of such variations upon self-report responses in self-concept studies. Sometimes within the work of a single investigator, there appears to be a wide gap between what S is literally told, and the set which E infers he has induced in S. For example, Cohen (1959; and with Stotland et al., 1957) sometimes asked his Ss to mark his instrument as "a person" would act or feel, and sometimes as "I" would act or feel. But he infers that in either case the individual is revealing his *own* self concept (or ideal self).[1] Experimental

---

[1] Personal communication, January 5, 1959.

demonstration of the equivalence of such differently worded instructions is lacking. In fact, certain investigators using other measuring instruments have demonstrated that reliably differing responses are obtained when the two types of instructions are responded to by the same Ss (Arnold & Walter, 1957, using the Rotter Incomplete Sentences Blank).

Response Frequency

The frequency of making a response in the past has been shown to be related to response availability in perceptual experiments. We may find it pertinent to seek for analogies here, too, in the measurement of the phenomenal field through self-report techniques. With meanings held as constant as possible, to what extent would variations in the familiarity of words furnished to S on check lists or rating scales affect their probability of endorsement, the probability of choice of one member of a pair of items, or the scale value S assigns an item to express his self concept? To what extent will free answer self-reports be a function of the ease with which certain common words or cliché phrases come to mind? This problem in constructing instruments remains virtually untouched. Wylie found that open-ended essays describing the self (used in her 1957 study) gave the coder a strong impression of Ss' cliché-proneness. Using a Q-sort technique, Taylor (1955) found markedly increasing congruence between self and ideal on repeated testing over a short time-interval. Quite plausibly this could be an example of the influence on S's responses of increasing familiarity with the response items, since no therapy or other theoretically relevant variable was known to have intervened which might have changed the phenomenal self as such. We must conclude, however, that there has been no formal study of the possible influence of response familiarity upon the validity of a self-report technique for revealing Ss' phenomenal fields; and that no means of minimizing the influence of this variable has been developed.

Scoring and Statistical Procedures

Finally, as part of the search for the influence of irrelevant variables on our measuring process, we need to examine our scoring and statistical procedures to determine whether they may be affecting our findings in misleading ways. The most serious and frequently occurring difficulties seem to be those associated with two-part indices, e.g., self-minus-ideal discrepancies, "insight," and stability of self concept (i.e., positive self concept minus negative self concept). Two-part indices have been widely used without sufficient prior exploration of such pertinent questions as the following: How much variance is contributed by each part to variance in scores on the dual index? How much is independently contributed by each part to the correlation between the dual index and theory-relevant behavior? By any standard for relevant construct validity, is the dual index superior to a "simpler" score? For example, would the level of self-regard experienced by the S be expressed just as effectively by a direct report of self-acceptance as it is by an experimenter's derived discrepancy score obtained from two of S's reports? Or, alternately, might one infer the level of self-regard from the "actual self" report alone? Is the apparently simpler "actual self" score really less complex than the [Self—Ideal] discrepancy, or does its use imply that we are obtaining another kind of dual index, one part of which may be nonphenomenal? That is, in assigning a self-regard value to a self score, are we in fact assuming a discrepancy between S's phenomenal self and a cultural norm which S may or may not have accepted as his phenomenal ideal for himself?

Much space throughout the book will be devoted to a detailed analysis of the problems associated with dual indices, as they recur again and again in connection with the particular instruments and studies reviewed. Our general conclusion here will be that insufficient attention to these problems has led many investigators to interpret their findings in psychological terms which are more complicated than the operations warrant, or are in other ways inappropriate to the measure used.[2]

(2) INTERCORRELATIONS AMONG MEASURES PRESUMED TO MEASURE THE SAME CONSTRUCT

When we survey self-concept measures from the viewpoint of our second criterion, "intercorrelations among measures presumed to measure

---

[2]Since writing this chapter, the author has read Cronbach's chapter in Taguiri and Petrullo (1958), which treats the general case of "dyadic" indices using the example of social perception for detailed illustrative purposes. The present author agrees with Cronbach's suggestion that such dyadic indices be avoided in all fields of psychology until our knowledge of the simpler ones is more fully developed. Cronbach also gives a suggested method of procedure in re the development and use of such indices.

the same construct," we find that this standard has only rarely been applied, even to a limited degree. Certainly no investigator has satisfied Campbell and Fiske's requirement to demonstrate that the correlation between scores which are obtained by different methods but which purport to measure the same construct should exceed (a) correlations between scores which are obtained by a given method but which purport to index different constructs, and (b) correlations between scores which are obtained by different methods and which purport to measure different constructs. This is a minimum requirement to assure that construct, not method variance, is making the major contribution to variance in the scores.

(3) INTERNAL FACTOR ANALYSIS

So far as our third criterion is concerned, few persons have internally factor-analyzed their instruments to throw light on the number of basic processes which must be postulated to account for response variance. Of course the fact that factors have been obtained would not reveal whether any of the factors represent subregions of the phenomenal field. However, such a procedure might help us to see that our a priori guesses as to the number of variables involved was accurate or erroneous. It might also help to make more obvious the presence of some irrelevant variables.

(4) PREDICTABLE RELATION OF ALLEGED SELF-CONCEPT MEASURES TO OTHER VARIABLES

So far as most of the investigations surveyed here are concerned, the only evidence which might be adduced for the construct validity of their self-concept measures is that implied by Cronbach and Meehl's fourth criterion — positive findings in studies relating alleged self-concept measures to some other variables in a manner predicted by self theory. Since most investigators have proceeded to use their self-concept instruments for such studies without systematically applying any of the other previously mentioned forms of analysis, the results of their studies can be considered to support, rather than to demonstrate unambiguously, the construct validity of their self-concept measures. At present no general conclusion can be drawn concerning any one instrument or type of instrument, because the array of such studies is too widely scattered across instruments. The reader is referred to ensuing sections for details on this type of study.

2. *Recommendations; Summary*

Many of the specific points made in the preceding paragraphs may be viewed as special cases of the general question: To what extent does method variance (broadly conceived) account for response variance on indices purporting to index S's phenomenal field?

A minimum program of constructive procedures needed in future research includes the following steps.

(1) In the design and use of instruments and the derivation and treatment of scores, researchers should systematically introduce all those controls which have been demonstrated to be important in similar research areas. These controls should be included until further direct information can be gathered by steps (2) and (3).

(2) These controlled variables should be experimentally studied as independent variables, in order to determine their effects, if any, upon behaviors measured in this particular research area. Ultimately the information gained from these experiments should be applied to the further refinement of the instruments used in this area.

(3) Correlation matrices should be produced in which method and inferred construct are systematically varied. From such matrices one can explore the discriminant construct validity of a given method for tapping a given construct.

To summarize the argument made thus far in regard to the problem of construct validity of instruments purporting to measure the phenomenal field, especially the phenomenal self: At present it is not clear whether builders of phenomenal personality theories wish to find and/or can find a systematic way to articulate nonphenomenological determinants of behavior into their theories. In any event, it is clear that the phenomenal field, especially the phenomenal self in its various aspects, is considered by them to be a major determinant of S's behavior. Therefore researchers who intend their work to test phenomenal theories must assume the burden of trying to develop instruments which have suitable, known construct validity for indexing the phenomenal field, especially the phenomenal self. They should not be content with empirical or face validity for self-report or other measures they use. By comparison with the analysis of similar problems encountered in experimental studies of perceptual processes, various sorts of irrelevant influences which might determine S's responses on E's indices of the phenomenal self have been discussed. In addition, some of the irrelevant influences of E's inappropriate statistical treatment of the data have been considered. Recommendations for future research have been sketched.

It is concluded that no investigator to date has satisfactorily conceptualized or coped with these difficult measurement problems. Quite a few have indicated that they make no claims for this sort of construct validity and are content to "let the reader beware," as it were.

B. Specific Measures Used in This Area: A Descriptive Survey and Analysis of Construct Validity and Reliability

In the preceding section we have considered the general problems of measuring the phenomenal self (i.e., self concept). We turn now to descriptions and analyses of the specific instruments which have been used to index the phenomenal self. This detailed information should be useful to researchers and to those who wish to evaluate critically the results of studies in the area of self-concept theory.

To anticipate the conclusions from such an approach, we may state a few generalizations: One finds that a very wide range of instruments has been used to measure various aspects of the phenomenal self, most of them having been used in only one study. Many of the articles give incomplete descriptions of the instruments or no real description at all, and no publicly available source is given for the reader to follow up, should he wish to know more about specific instructions, item content, and the like. Consequently it is difficult or impossible for the critical reader to make any confident inferences as to what variables might be influencing Ss' responses. In the majority of studies no reliability estimates are given, and those that are presented are mostly of the split-half or interjudge variety, giving no indication of stability on retest. The problem of any kind of validity is often bypassed entirely, being substituted for by assumptions of face validity, or reliance on the reader to infer what he will from whatever statement of operations is given. Sometimes inappropriate (i.e., theoretically irrelevant or inconsistent) validity criteria are offered, e.g., another's judgment of S, or S's school achievement. Some of the instruments consist of items chosen for a stated purpose, e.g., to tap S's picture of his school behavior, to reveal S's self picture in the area of Murray's needs, to represent Cattell's factors. In many instances item choice is not explicitly rationalized, however. It is as if the implicit assumption was made that particular item contents may safely be used interchangeably to measure the self-concept variables appearing in the hypotheses of phenomenological theorists. This assumption is far from being demonstrated, and in fact there is evidence against it.

1. *Instruments for Measuring Phenomenal Self-Regard*

The most commonly studied class of aspects of the phenomenal self includes such attitudes as self-satisfaction, self-acceptance, self-esteem, self-favorability, congruence between self and ideal self, and discrepancies between self and ideal self. All these terms are not synonymous, even in the literary sense. For some authors, self-acceptance means respecting one's self, including one's admitted faults, while self-esteem or congruence between self and ideal self means being proud of one's self or evaluating one's attributes highly. In fact to some theorists, optimum self-esteem or self-satisfaction is manifested by moderately small (rather than by very small or zero) discrepancies between S's descriptions of self and ideal self on Q sorts, rating scales, or adjective check lists. That is, self-acceptance is presumed by some to be the conscious (realistic) recognition of some falling short of the ideal.

If these terms had more clearly differentiated literary meanings and correspondingly differentiated operational definitions, it would be desirable to classify our discussion of the instruments according to the construct involved (e.g., self-esteem as contrasted to self-acceptance). However, the terms are so intertwined and overlapping in the literature that the constructs must be discussed as a group. Therefore we shall organize our discussion of the instruments according to the experimental and statistical procedures involved in obtaining a score.

This section of Chapter III will be devoted to instruments which purport to measure an over-all or very general evaluative attitude toward self. For convenience of discussion we shall use the words "self-regard" or "self-regarding attitudes" as generic terms to include self-satisfaction, self-acceptance, self-esteem, self-favorability, congruence between self and ideal self, and discrepancies between self and ideal self. If the authors have specifically labelled their instruments or the inferences they are drawing from their scores, this will be indicated in the text.

For purposes of clarity, the following conventions will be observed in regard to language usage. Unless otherwise indicated, self means S's view of his actual self or real self, i.e., his concept of himself as he actually is. When referring to self indices obtained from a particular instrument, we shall capitalize the word Self. Unless otherwise indicated, the word ideal refers to S's view of his ideal self, his concept of the kind of person he would like to be. When referring to ideal (or ideal self) indices obtained from a particular instrument, we shall capitalize the words Ideal (or Ideal Self). When "self sorts" are correlated with "ideal sorts" (as explained immediately below, under Q sorts), we shall refer in a general discussion of this kind of score to self-ideal correlations, or to self-ideal congruence. The expression self-ideal will *not* be used to refer to the person's ideal self. When indices of self-regard are obtained by subtracting self ratings from ideal self ratings, these will always be referred to as [Self — Ideal] discrepancies (to be read "Self minus Ideal discrepancies"). Occasionally the general idea of such discrepancies will be referred to as self-minus-ideal discrepancies.

We turn now to a description and evaluation of the various instruments which have been used to index self-regarding attitudes of a very general kind. In addition to lack of agreement among literary definitions, we shall find that there is a wide variety in the instruments which have been used as operational definitions of these terms.

a. Q Sorts, with Special Reference to Butler and Haigh's Items

General Description of Q-Sort Procedure

One of the most commonly used techniques for assessing phenomenal self-regard is the Q sort or slight modifications thereof (Stephenson, 1935). In the typical application of this technique a large number of personality-descriptive items are sorted by S into nine piles which are arranged on a continuum according to the degree to which they are characteristic of S's self. S is forced by the instructions to place specified numbers of items in each pile so as to yield a quasi-normal distribution of items. S then sorts the same items once more into nine piles which are arranged on a continuum according to the degree to which they are characteristic of his ideal for himself. Again, the instructions force him to produce a quasi-normal distribution of the items.

Each item in the self-description may be assigned a value from one to nine, according to the pile in which S has chosen to put it. Correspondingly, each item in the ideal sort may be assigned a value from one to nine, according to the pile in which S has chosen to put it. For the individual S, a correlation coefficient may then be computed between the pile values of the items, as sorted by that S to describe his self, and the pile values of the same items, as sorted to describe his ideal self. Pearson r may be used because the forced sorting procedure has resulted in both distributions being quasi-normal. Such a correlation coefficient between placement values assigned by a single S is usually called a self-ideal correlation, or self-ideal r, and these are the labels we shall use throughout our discussion. The self-ideal correlation may be considered to be a score for the S, and from the magnitude of that score the degree of that S's self-regard is inferred.

It should be pointed out parenthetically that Q-sort correlational techniques may be used to relate other sets of descriptions than S's self-description and his ideal self-description. For example, S could be asked to sort the same items according to another set of instructions such as "how I *should* be," or "how my friends regard me," or "how my mother wishes I were." A correlation coefficient for an individual S can be computed between item placement values for any two sorts of the same items. For example, if S's ideal self sort is correlated with his sort done under the instructions "how my mother wishes I were," one could infer the degree of agreement between the S's personal ideal for himself and the ideal he feels his mother holds for him. Or the item placement values assigned by one S may be correlated with the item placement values assigned by any other S (e.g., S_1's self-sort may be correlated with S_2's self-sort to infer the degree of similarity in the self concepts of the two subjects).[3]

---

[3]Mowrer (1953b) has suggested that the Q technique as defined by Stephenson is a loose designation for a number of distinct though functionally related procedures which need to be more precisely defined. He and Cattell (in Mowrer, 1953a) have said that there are three series of fundamentals among which the relations of correlation can be established in psychology: organisms, behavioral performances of any kind, and occasions. On Mowrer's modified and expanded version of Cattell's covariation chart, showing correlation techniques in terms of these three dimensions, self-ideal correlations are regarded as examples of Q technique in Cattell's and Mowrer's restricted sense (i.e., correlation of results obtained from two or more persons taking many tests on one occasion). To make this classification, the person sorting items under "self" instructions is considered to be a psychologically different person from himself sorting items under "ideal" instructions. The correlation of a self-sort before therapy with a self-sort after therapy is separately classified as O technique (correlation of the results obtained from one person taking many tests [items] on two or more occasions).

Scores Based on Objectively Judged Ideals

To return to measures of self-regard, we should note that there is another less frequently used way of obtaining a self-regard score from an individual S's self-descriptive Q sort. In this alternate procedure one compares the pile number of each statement, as S has sorted it, with the independently judged self-favorability (social desirability or positive tone) of each item. This type of score introduces a possible theoretical confusion. To be consistently phenomenological, a self-concept theorist must be concerned with the relationship between S's phenomenal self and his phenomenal ideal self, rather than relating S's phenomenal self to an objective judgment or cultural stereotype of the ideal person. Of course S's idiosyncratic ideal self may overlap considerably or entirely with the culturally accepted view of an ideal person. In later sections of the book considerable evidence of this overlap will be presented. If this is the case, results from the use of the individual and cultural ideal will be highly similar. Nevertheless it is not empirically safe to assume that individual Ss' phenomenal ideals for themselves are equivalent to culturally accepted standards for the ideal person. And if Ss do vary from one another with respect to the coincidence between the phenomenal ideal self and the cultural norm, scores based on objectively judged ideals cannot be interpreted in a theoretically consistent way from S to S.

We need systematic research involving items which are separated according to (a) whether or not there is a cultural norm; (b) whether or not S has a personal phenomenal ideal; (c) the extent to which the cultural norm and S's phenomenal ideal coincide.

It may turn out that one can, in some instances, predict behavior better when one uses a score in which E evaluates S's self-report in terms of an objectively judged cultural norm, rather than in terms of S's reported phenomenal ideal self. However, such empirical validity is not equivalent to the construct validity one attempts to attain by comparing S's self-report with his report of his ideal self. Also, such superior empirical validity, if attained, would raise important theoretical questions for self-concept theorists, i.e., it might suggest that the importance of the phenomenal self in predicting behavior has been overemphasized.

Butler and Haigh's Self-Referent Items, Procedure and Assumptions

The set of Q-sort items which has been most extensively used as an index of self-regard is the group of one hundred self-referent statements employed in the research on nondirective psychotherapy described in Rogers and Dymond (1954). This instrument will therefore be given the most detailed discussion, with the understanding that most of the comments made are generally applicable to the Q-sort techniques which will be more briefly considered later.

The Butler and Haigh items were to be sorted into nine piles, either according to the degree they were "like me," or (in another sort) according to the degree "I would most like within myself to be," or (in a third sort) according to the degree to which they characterize the "ordinary person." As is usually true in Q-sort work, S was forced to assign a certain number of items to each of the piles so that a quasi-normal distribution resulted.

Butler and Haigh (1954, p. 55) state that the use of forced sorting, and of the self-ideal correlation as an index of self-regard, was based on the following assumptions: (1) The self concept consists of (a) an organized conceptual pattern of the "I" or "me," together with (b) the values attached to these concepts. (2) This pattern of organizations can be mirrored respectively in terms of (a) ordinal scale placements of the statements according to the degree they are "like me," and (b) ordinal scale placements of the statements according to the degree to which they are like "I wish to be", and in terms of (c) discrepancies between the scale value assigned to an item on the self dimension, as contrasted to the ideal-self dimension.

The items used in the instrument were an "accidental" (rather than random) sample of statements from "available therapeutic protocols," reworded for clarity (Butler & Haigh, 1954, p. 57). Most but not all of the items appear on pages 78 and 275-276 of the Rogers and Dymond book (1954). They are mostly very general assertions, not situationally specified, such as: I am shy, confused, a failure, disturbed, hopeless, unreliable, worthless, optimistic, impulsive, rational, poised, tolerant.

Sampling of Test Item Universes

We have, of course, no way of knowing how representative these statements may be of a total imaginary universe of self-concept characteristics. Presumably they are all statements which refer to attributes of some importance to the self concept, since they were gleaned from remarks made spontaneously in nondirective therapy.

Some investigators have selected items which are known or thought to represent specified trait or need constructs, e.g., factorially described personality characteristics, rationally defined need systems such as Murray's, etc. But the question can be asked: Are the operations of factor analysis, or the types of observation leading to the formulation of Murray's list of needs appropriate to defining a universe of *phenomenal* self-characteristics?

Difficulties in defining and sampling appropriate item universes are by no means unique to Butler and Haigh's procedure. Mowrer (1953b, p. 358) points out that, "whereas much attention has been given to the logic of sampling universes or populations of persons, little attention has been given to sampling theory where test or occasions universes are concerned . . . [and] the results obtained by the use of these [e.g., Q and O] techniques may vary widely with the nature of the universe of statements (or trait names) from which items are selected." Cronbach and Gleser (1953) point out that general similarity (e.g., between self and ideal) can be inferred only if we have some way of knowing that our self-concept measure samples all or a large proportion of the significant dimensions of the phenomenal self.

Stephenson (1953) considered the problems of identifying an appropriate universe of statements for any given purpose, and of drawing representative samples of items for Q sorting. He presents some arguments in favor of building "structured" samples (somewhat analogous to the stratified samples of persons taken by opinion surveyors), rather than drawing "random samples."

Brunswik (1956) has argued that such sampling is of equal importance to the more usual sampling of populations of persons. He has presented a conceptual analysis of the way in which psychological research designs should be elaborated to include both kinds of sampling. Results of studies which follow such elaborated designs will have what he calls "ecological generality" as well as "population generality." In this reference he gives selected examples from the history of experimental psychology to show the transition which has been taking place from the "classical" one-variable design (in which only population sampling is involved), to the more "representative" designs (which systematically utilize both kinds of sampling). He contends that stimulus or test-item sampling has been used in practice more than it has been explicitly accepted or analyzed in discussions of method. His writing attempts not only to synthesize all types of design under one conceptual framework, but also to obtain explicit acceptance of the more "representative designs."

Thus we see that problems of item sampling have received some theoretical consideration. Both theoretical and empirical difficulties remain to be resolved, however.

Dymond's Adjustment Score for the Butler and Haigh Items

Dymond (1954a) found that trained clinical psychologists could agree well that 37 of the characteristics were ones which a "well-adjusted" person should say are at least somewhat "like me"; that another 37 of them were ones which a "well-adjusted" person should say are at least somewhat "unlike me"; and that 26 items were unclassifiable as indicating "adjustment." (All the items which apparently are nowhere listed in the book fall into this third category.) She obtained an adjustment score by finding how many of the 74 items relevant to adjustment are placed on the "like me" or "unlike me" side of the distribution, as respectively appropriate. Dymond, of course, does not imply that the adjustment score necessarily reflects S's phenomenal picture of his own clinically defined adjustment, since he was not instructed to use this dimension as a basis for sorting. As stated above, it is the size of the self-ideal correlation which is assumed to index "self-dissatisfaction," i.e., maladjustment as personally experienced by S.

In a study described earlier (Wiener *et al.*, 1959) 28 clinical psychologists sorted the Butler and Haigh items to describe how they thought "a well-adjusted person would sort these cards." Mean Adjustment values were obtained for each item. Then the 37 items most like the well-adjusted person and the 37 items least like the well-adjusted person were determined. Only 33 of the 37 "most adjusted" items and 29 out of the 37 "least adjusted" items were common to the lists compiled by Dymond and by Wiener *et al.* Of the 26 items found by Dymond to be irrelevant to adjustment, twelve were judged in Wiener's study to be reliably assigned to the adjusted or maladjusted side of the continuum. Weiner *et al.* conclude (p. 320): ". . . the failure to find greater consistency of item placement with the two methods of judgment raises some question about the need to investigate further the problem of establishing an Adjustment scale by either method."

Reliability

Various kinds of questions should be asked concerning the consistency and reliability of the possible measures obtainable from this or from any Q-sorting procedure. In the Q sort we have several levels from which we could obtain quantitative data. These may be arranged in order of increasing complexity as follows: (1) individual item placements; (2) scores based on sorts made under a single set of instructions (e.g., self-sort, *or* ideal-sort *or* average-other-person-sort); Dymond's adjustment score applied to the self-sort would be an illustration; (3) scores which consist of intraindividual correlations obtained between sorts (e.g., self-ideal correlations). We shall now consider problems of reliability and consistency which one encounters at each of these levels of complexity, respectively.

At the most molecular level one may pay attention to the individual item placements made by S. Which items discriminate significantly between individual Ss at any one time? To what extent is each given item assigned the same pile number by the same S from time to time with no known systematic influence intervening between test and retest?

Moving toward more global measures, we should consider indices based on a single sort (e.g., Dymond's adjustment score based on the self-sort). Do these scores discriminate significant individual differences at any given testing time? How stable does the rank ordering of individuals remain over time, with no known systematic influence intervening between test and retest? Of pertinence to group studies is the question whether the mean score of the control (nontreated) group remains stable over time, which it might do even though the rank order of individuals changed considerably. Are there empirical or logical grounds on which sets of items constituting equivalent halves or alternate forms could be chosen or constructed? (If there were, the problem of split-half reliability might be seen as midway in complexity between that of individual item consistency and the test-retest reliability of a complete self-sorting score.) The existence of rationally devised alternate forms would be helpful in appraising test-retest reliability of scores based on a single sort, since the retest would be free of specific memory influences.

A different order of question involving single sorts concerns the size of the test-retest self-self correlation or of the test-retest ideal-ideal correlation. Here we are trying to find out the consistency of a given individual's self (or ideal) sort over time. The issue is of great importance for the evaluation of studies reporting group trends in the self-ideal correlation as a measure of change over time. One needs to know whether those changes that do occur in self-ideal *r*s are due to shifts in self-sort, to shifts in ideal-sort, or to shifts in both.

The most complex type of score is the one typically employed in *Q*-sort studies, namely the *r* obtained between two sorts made by the same *S* under two sets of instructions (e.g., the self-ideal correlation). If we consider the self-ideal *r* obtained from each *S* as a "test score," we need to know the following: (a) Do such scores yield significant individual differences at any one testing time? (b) To what degree is the rank order of such scores stable over time? (c) As stated above, what are the respective contributions of self-self consistency and ideal-ideal consistency to the reliability in rank orders of self-ideal correlations over time? (d) To what extent are the mean scores of specified groups consistent over time, with no known systematic influence intervening?

Now let us see how far the published information takes us in answering the kinds of questions about reliability and consistency which we have just outlined. So far as the separate items are concerned, no information seems to be available on the Butler and Haigh or any other *Q*-sorting instrument. Nor have there been empirical explorations of the pertinent questions concerning scores based on single sorts (e.g., Dymond's adjustment score on the self-sort). There was no attempt to establish equivalent halves or alternate forms of the Butler and Haigh set of items.

It has not been generally discussed in published sources whether or not it is theoretically possible to establish alternate forms for *Q* sorting; and if it is possible, by what criteria such forms could be developed. Presumably one would need to have a clear idea of the conceptual universe from which items are drawn in order to approach the development of alternate forms rationally, and Butler and Haigh have not defined their universe in a specified, conceptual way.

Recently Hilden (1958) has suggested that alternate forms might be made up by drawing sets of items at random from a specified universe. It seems worthwhile to digress temporarily from our discussion of the Butler and Haigh items to consider Hilden's rationale and procedure, since this matter of general importance has not been specifically dealt with by Butler and Haigh.

From the Thorndike Century Senior Dictionary Hilden drew every word of a specified difficulty level which was suitable for formulating a

statement about human reactions. For each word in this universe he composed a sentence appropriate for use in Q sorting. These sentences (items) constitute what he calls the Universe of Personal Concepts (UPC). By means of a table of random numbers he drew twenty sets of fifty items each from the serially listed sentences of the UPC. This procedure meant of course that there was some overlap of items from set to set; and approximately six hundred items were used in no set.

As an empirical check on the equivalence of these randomly drawn sets, four graduate students made twenty self-sorts, then twenty ideal-sorts, using the twenty sets. Then they sorted all 1575 sentences in the UPC for self and for ideal. Since Hilden's procedure did not involve matching items (sentences), he had no rationale for intercorrelating the various self-sorts of a given S (or intercorrelating the various ideal-sorts of a given S) to determine whether alternate forms yielded comparable self-sorts (or comparable ideal-sorts). However, he could see whether the mean of a given S's twenty self-ideal correlations differed significantly from that S's self-ideal correlation obtained from the Universe of Personal Constructs. (This of course leads us into a discussion of reliability and consistency of the most complex of the scoring levels outlined above.) In the case of each of the four Ss, there was no significant difference between the mean of the twenty self-ideal correlations obtained from the twenty sets of items and the S's self-ideal correlation from the UPC. This suggests that the sets were essentially equivalent with respect to the degree to which self-ideal correlations obtained from them represented the specified universe; and that deviations from set to set could be attributed to sampling error.

What light do the results shed on the capacity of the sets to discriminate differences among Ss in self-ideal r? Inspection reveals that on nineteen out of twenty sets, Subject C's self-ideal r was lower than that of any of the other three Ss, as was his self-ideal r on the UPC. Subjects A, B, and D had quite similar self-ideal rs on the UPC ($+.76$, $+.71$, and $+.76$ respectively). These three Ss also tended to fall close to one another in the self-ideal rs obtained from each set and to exchange rank orders vis-à-vis one another on succeeding sets. This suggests that each separate set of sentences may be capable of discriminating significant differences between individuals. It of course does not provide a basis for deciding how large a difference between two Ss must be on a given set in order to indicate a true (UPC) difference between the self-ideal correlations of the two Ss.

It seems to the present writer that it would be appropriate for other investigators interested in Q sorting to follow up the rationale and procedures of Hilden. The attempt to specify the universe more clearly would have advantages in addition to its usefulness in establishing alternate forms. The development of alternate forms of known degree of empirical equivalence would be very helpful in studies requiring "before and after" or even more frequent test repetition. This is true because it seems highly likely that memory or other factors associated with retesting as such can affect self-ideal correlations (see Taylor, 1955). (As an alternative to Hilden's procedure for constructing alternate forms, test constructors might wish to apply Cureton's suggestions which are described below, pages 99-100.)

We return now to a consideration of the consistency and reliability of the self-ideal rs obtained from the Butler and Haigh items. We shall enumerate the findings respectively pertinent to questions (a) through (d) outlined above.

(a) We do find that both client Ss and control Ss exhibited significant individual differences in self-ideal rs within their respective groups. This indicates that the self-ideal r, considered as a test score, was discriminating in some way among individuals.

(b) The Rogers and Dymond book gives no information on the stability across time of Ss' rank order with respect to self-ideal correlations. However, the present writer was able to compute a test-retest *rho* for the sixteen control cases whose initial and follow-up rs are tabled on page 66 of Rogers and Dymond (1954). The obtained value was +.78.

(c) We have no direct way of knowing the respective contributions of self-sorts and ideal-sorts to this *rho* of +.78. The following data suggest very obliquely that self-sorts, being less consistent across time than are ideal-sorts, must play the greater role in lowering a *rho* between two sets of self-ideal correlations across time. For clients who waited sixty days for therapy, the correlations between initial and pretherapy self-sorts ranged from +.57 to +.78; for ideal-sorts from +.56 to +.90. Five of the ideal-ideal correlations exceeded the highest self-self correlation, implying that ideal-sorts may have greater consistency over time.

(d) Finally we note that there is some information on the stability of group mean self-ideal rs across time. The control group of Ss who did not have counseling, but who volunteered for "research on personality," showed a mean initial self-ideal r of $+.58$, as compared to a mean follow-up r of $+.59$. The times between initial and follow-up testing varied from S to S because testing times for each control S were made to correspond with his matched experimental (counseled) counterpart. The client group showed a mean self-ideal r of $-.01$ both in the initial test and in the test following a sixty-day pretherapy waiting period.

Construct Validity

The construct validity of a Q-sort instrument for indexing S's phenomenal self may be viewed from two aspects: (a) its usefulness as an index of S's phenomenal self-regard; and (b) the degree to which it reveals "organization" or "patterning" in the S's phenomenal field. Since the latter question has been assigned much importance by self-concept theorists, we shall discuss it first, and shall return shortly to the main issue of this section, the measurement of phenomenal self-regard.

INDEX OF ORGANIZATION WITHIN THE PHENOMENAL SELF. In self-concept theory, much importance has been assigned to the Gestalt, patterned, or integrated character of the self concept. This is undoubtedly one of the reasons why Q sorts have appealed to investigators of this theoretical bent, since obviously many items can be included and they are arranged by S into a "pattern." For example, Mowrer (1953b, p. 374) says that correlations between sorts obtained from one person on two (or more) occasions are "admirably suited in theory to show personality changes (especially of an organizational kind)." Butler and Haigh (1954, p. 62) speculate, "In brief, certain patterns of the self-ideal Gestalt may be discovered to indicate certain patterns or types of personality integration."

However, we must raise serious questions as to the construct validity of this kind of instrument, at least as it is presently "scored," to mirror "organization" within the self concept. When we apply our specifications for checking construct validity, we note several crucial difficulties, which will be explained in the following paragraphs.

Let us begin with an analysis of the self-sort alone (as contrasted to the more complex self-ideal correlation).

In general we need to note two alternate possibilities for choice of items to be included in a sorting instrument. First we may choose items varying along an evaluative dimension. (For the sake of simplicity let us assume for the moment that our Ss agree with stated cultural ideals with regard to the respective items.) In this case, S's arrangement of items along the "like me" continuum may indicate chiefly his general level of self-regard. The items may sample widely or narrowly the total possible range of levels of self-regard, and the total population of characteristics about which self-regard may vary. Accordingly, S's sort may be influenced to a greater or lesser degree by his general level of self-regard.

The introduction of forced sorting restricts to some extent the range of individual differences in general self-regard which can be obtained from the self-sort alone (Mowrer, 1953b, p. 335; Cronbach, 1953, p. 379; Cronbach & Gleser, 1953). Jones's (1956) work shows us that Ss who are not required to produce a quasi-normal distribution make more nearly U-shaped distributions. This demonstrates empirically that forced sortings prevent Ss from getting as extreme self-regard scores as they would if allowed to express the phenomenal self freely. In any case, a single score based on S's sort could not tell us anything about "patterning" over and above the general degree to which desirable items tend to be "like me" and undesirable items tend to be "unlike me."

A second possibility for item choice would be to pick items which are homogeneous with respect to evaluative tone. (Again for the sake of simplicity let us assume for the moment that our Ss agree with the cultural ideal, according to which these items are highly similar to one another in desirability.) In this case it would be impossible to get a self-ideal correlation at all, unless ridiculously fine and hence unreliable sorting along the ideal dimension were demanded of S. This is true because we have chosen the items on the basis of their homogeneity with respect to the ideal. Nor could a meaningful single score be obtained from the self-sort alone, since we are assuming that widely different areas of self are represented in the items. If the factorial content of the items is known, one could get a series of scores representing S's standing on the various factors. Whether factors obtained by E's treatment of the data represent subregions of the phenomenal self would still remain to be demonstrated, however. Certainly no single score could represent something as complex as the "patterning" of the items.

So far as Q sorts which have actually been used are concerned, no attempt has been made to hold either personal or cultural ideal values constant across items. Therefore the "scores" obtained are probably most adequately described in terms of variations in self-regard. This would be true of either "adjustment" scores or self-ideal *r*s, considered as scores. The burden of proof is on the investigator to demonstrate that "patterning" (as contrasted to self-regard) is systematically revealed by scores based on these *Q* sorts which contain items varying in desirability.

OBSCURING EFFECTS OF DISCREPANCY SCORES AND GLOBAL IN-DICES. Let us look more closely at the kinds of individual differences in pattern which are obscured in the self-ideal *r* obtainable from the *Q*-sort instruments now in use. In making this examination we cannot, of course, assume that *S*'s personal ideal for an item coincides with a cultural ideal for that item. Thus the self-ideal correlation as such gives no information as to (a) the patterning of individual items along the self-sort dimension; (b) the patterning of individual items along the ideal-sort dimension; (c) the patterning of individual item discrepancies between self and ideal placements. A very large number of unique arrangements could yield similar or identical self-ideal correlation coefficients.

The importance of this point is emphasized by considering a few examples in which discrepancies having probably different psychological meaning carry the same weight in determining the size of the self-ideal coefficient.

Example 1. Consider the following two discrepancies: (a) Item X is reported to be "somewhat like me" but "somewhat unlike my ideal." (b) Item X is reported to be "quite like me," but only "somewhat like my ideal." Surely these two discrepancies do not warrant comparable psychological inferences though they may be of equal scale magnitude, and each involves a "self" pile number higher than the "ideal" pile number.

Example 2. Dymond has shown that twenty-six of the one hundred Butler and Haigh items are judged by clinical psychologists to be irrelevant to adjustment. We do know that self-concept theory assumes that low self-ideal correlations are indicative of and/or lead to experienced discomfort and maladjustment. Suppose that we work from these two premises when computing an index of "discomfort" or "experienced maladjustment." Is it logical to assign equal weight to each of the following discrepancies? (a) A self-minus-ideal discrepancy on an item relevant to adjustment. (b) A self-minus-ideal discrepancy on an item irrelevant to adjustment.

Example 3. Imagine two subjects: (a) One places a certain item in a "wish it were much like me" pile and in a "not actually like me" pile.

(b) The other places the same item in the "wish it were not like me" pile and in an "actually much like me" pile. These two types of discrepancies are possibly quite different in psychological meaning, even though the scale magnitude of the discrepancies could be the same.

We must conclude that the self-ideal correlation coefficient buries in a global index some individual differences we ought to be identifying for study. In addition, we agree with Cronbach and Gleser's (1953, p. 459) statement that "combining many traits into any sort of composite index, whether it be a D measure, a Q-correlation or a discriminant function, or any of the other methods presently used, involves assumptions regarding scales of measurement which cannot usually be defended."

Aside from the above questions concerning the adequacy of the self-ideal correlation as an index of "organization" within the self concept, we have also the problem of the meaning of any given size of discrepancy between self and ideal for any item. That is, the objective observer infers that whatever discrepancy exists between the pile number of the item as sorted under "self" and "ideal" instructions represents S's conscious intention to express that particular experienced relationship between what he is like and what he would ideally wish to be like. However, we must realize that this discrepancy score was derived by the *experimenter*, and that the S may or may not have been consciously aware of a discrepancy involving that item. This is true because, with one hundred items to arrange, S may easily forget the exact scale placement of an item under one set of instructions. Thus, despite his intentions to indicate a discrepancy of any given size, he may be unable to reveal his feelings accurately. If he were allowed to make his ideal-sort with a duplicate set of cards, while keeping the self-sort before him for reference, we might be safer in inferring that the size of the observed discrepancies reflects his consciously experienced discrepancies more validly. However, if this method were to be used we would perhaps foster both response sets and deliberate falsification, as we shall point out in connection with certain rating scale instruments to be discussed later.

INDEX OF SELF-ESTEEM. Butler and Haigh were more interested in the construct validity of their instrument as an index of phenomenal self-esteem than as an index of over-all organization of the self concept. Therefore it is relevant to examine the instrument's construct validity for measuring self-esteem.

One might first inquire whether any intercorrelations with other instruments which also purport to measure phenomenal self-regard are available. Apparently none of the other instruments described in this book was considered by the authors to be aimed directly at phenomenal self-regard. However, the Willoughby Emotional Maturity Scale, which was filled in by some of Butler and Haigh's Ss, may be interpreted as being a self-concept report with a generally evaluative tone. Unfortunately, no correlations are given in which individual self-ideal rs are paired with individual Emotional Maturity scores. We do find that the therapy groups which showed significant increase in mean self-ideal r also showed significant increase in self-reported Emotional Maturity. By contrast, the thirteen client Ss who waited sixty days for therapy showed no significant increase in either Emotional Maturity scores or self-ideal rs between initial and pretherapy tests. (The no-therapy control Ss did not take the Emotional Maturity Scale) (Rogers, 1954a).

The TATs were rated on 23 scales, among which were "self concept," "ideal self," and "insight into self and others." Although it does not seem to be stated in the book whether these TAT indications were presumed to be phenomenal or nonphenomenal, the present author is assuming the latter interpretation, since it was stated that all scales were derived from a psychoanalytic frame of reference, and a projective device was employed. Therefore this measure of the self concept will be reported in Chapter V under nonphenomenal measures. It will only be noted here that no correlations were reported between TAT self scales and self-ideal rs. The authors seem to imply that no significant ones were found.

A second indicator of the validity of the self-ideal r as an indicator of self-esteem may be found in the group differences obtained by these investigators. Here we find that the mean self-ideal correlation was significantly different between groups which were presumed on other grounds to vary on phenomenal self-regard. That is, the client group applying for therapy showed a mean initial self-ideal correlation of —.01, while the control Ss who volunteered to take part in research on personality showed a mean initial self-ideal correlation of +.58. The experimental and control groups were satisfactorily matched for age, but only moderately satisfactorily matched with respect to sex, occupation, and socioeconomic status. The lack of perfect matching does not seem sufficient to account for the obtained differences in self-ideal congruence on any obvious basis other than that proposed by the experimenters. However, as Mowrer (1953b) has pointed out, such differences in self-ideal r between groups might be due to test-taking attitudes. For example, a candidate for practically free therapy may wish to show he has high standards but is inadequate, in order to demonstrate that he deserves as well as needs help.

Third, the design of the research permits us to view the problem of validity in terms of experimentally induced changes.[4] No change in mean self-ideal correlation was found for the control group from initial to follow-up tests. Similarly, no change was found during the pretherapy wait period for the therapy clients who had to wait sixty days before undertaking therapy. On the other hand, a significant increase in mean self-ideal correlation was found between pretherapy and posttherapy sorts made by the clients. While such results are congruent with the assumption that self-ideal correlations validly index phenomenal self-esteem, we must note that S may be consciously malingering due to his being too polite to admit to the therapist that he has not been helped (Mowrer, 1953b).

Fourth, we may note that a prediction made on the basis of theory and the assumed validity of the index for measuring phenomenal self-esteem was confirmed: The "adjustment score" for the self-sort, derived by Dymond, increased in the therapy group as the mean self-ideal correlation for that group also increased. Both of these scores were derived from the same instrument, however, so that one cannot say that independent measures have been related. That is, it may be that untrained Ss' opinions of what constitutes "adjustment" corresponds at least fairly well with the judgments of the trained clinicians who assigned "adjustment" scores to the items. In that event, an S who felt like disparaging himself would tend to place "well adjusted" items in the "unlike me" side of the distribution, when sorting for self description, and in the "like me" side of the distribution when sorting for ideal description. This could result in low self-ideal correlations, and in poor "adjustment" score on the self-sort alone. The reverse outcome would hold true for Ss wishing not to disparage themselves.

In this connection we note that there is another study which was based on the theory that self-ideal rs from Butler and Haigh's items should

---

[4]See Chapter IV for a critical discussion of the worth of psychotherapy research for testing personality theories.

correlate with "adjustment." Hanlon, Hofstaetter, and O'Connor (1954) used the California Test of Personality to measure the "adjustment" of 78 male high-school juniors. They obtained a highly significant correlation between Ss' self-reported adjustment and their self-ideal rs.

The four sets of results listed above tend to support, although they do not prove, the contention that the self-ideal r validly indexes phenomenal self-esteem. However, these results do not tell us about the respective contributions of the self-sort and the ideal-sort to each of the four sets of validity-relevant findings. Some light is thrown on the problem by Rudikoff's (1954) analysis of data from eight of the client cases who waited sixty days prior to therapy. She found that in every case there was more shift in the self-sorts than in ideal-sorts from pre- to post-therapy. Only one ideal-ideal correlation was as low as the highest self-self correlation. When she obtained Dymond's adjustment score on all sorts, she found no significant difference in the mean adjustment score of ideal sorts across the four testing points: (1) initial (prewait); (2) pre-therapy; (3) posttherapy; (4) follow-up. In contrast to this, the mean adjustment score of the self-sorts was different enough between pre- and posttherapy tests to be significant at better than the .001 level.

We conclude that the ideal-sort contributes relatively little to the changes in self-ideal rs which are a function of therapy, and relatively little to the theory-relevant association between changes in self-ideal r and changes in the Dymond adjustment score over therapy. We infer that ideal-sorts would contribute relatively little to the validity-relevant group differences, and to the correlations between the self-ideal r and the Willoughby Scale. Apparently there must be considerable congruence between the individuals' phenomenal ideal selves and the cultural stereotype of the ideal self for the Butler and Haigh items. Findings of other investigators suggest that low inter-S variance on ideal-self reports is not restricted to this particular instrument. Chase (1957), using Set #13 of Hilden's self-referent items, obtained discrimination only with the self-sorts. See also Section b below, for a discussion of this issue in connection with rating scales and inventories.

A problem of discriminant validity is raised when we ask whether the self-ideal correlation demonstrates dissatisfaction with self or perhaps more general dissatisfaction. This is a thorny issue, because self-concept theorists predict on theoretical grounds that there will be a correlation between satisfaction with self and satisfaction with others, for example. This makes very difficult the task of trying to establish discriminant validity of one measure as an index of phenomenal self-regard and of another as an index of regard for other persons. This problem has not been directly attacked in the Rogers and Dymond book. We note, however, that with eight client Ss, Rudikoff found that the mean self-ideal correlation and mean ordinary person-ideal correlation were both low at pretherapy (−.06 and +.11 respectively), while at follow-up they were both somewhat larger (+.28 and +.25 respectively). This suggests that the two indices seem to be behaving in quite similar fashion (although it is true that the mean self-ideal correlation showed a statistically significant change from pre- to posttherapy, while the ordinary person-ideal correlation did not). (No ordinary person-ideal rs for control [nontherapy] Ss seem to have been reported. Therefore we cannot compare them with their respective self-ideal rs.)

Levy (1956), in an entirely different study using the Butler and Haigh items, showed that low self-ideal correlations were associated with low actual-ideal correlations on one hundred statements of general applicability to Ss' real and ideal home towns. Of course one may say that S's attitude toward the home town is another reflection of his attitude toward himself, since he might be identified with his town. But the findings at least point toward the necessity of establishing the fact that low self-ideal correlations have discriminant validity for reflecting low self-regard rather than generally negative attitudes. We must conclude that this type of discriminant validity remains to be demonstrated.

One final comment is in order concerning a difficulty which actually occurs with Butler and Haigh's forced sorting procedure, although it is not a necessary drawback if items are properly constructed. In bringing up this issue, we are developing a parallel to a point made by Travers (1951) in regard to forced-choice personality inventories. He pointed out that items must be uniformly structured if forced choice is to be a sensible procedure. In the case of Q sorting, if the dimension along which S must sort is "more or less like me," S may reasonably assume that the relative frequency with which he reacts in the specified ways is the dimension along which he is to array the items. If this is so, then the items should be uniformly phrased with respect to the variable of frequency. For example, items like "I put on a false front" or "I feel helpless" have no frequency of occurrence specified within them. Therefore S's job seems clearly to be one of ordering the items according to the frequency with which he would react or feel in these ways. However, confusion arises if *S* tries to apply the frequency dimension to a literal reading of such items as "I usually like people" or "I often kick myself for the things I do." This is so because a degree of frequency is already built into the statement itself. How can *S* say whether he more frequently "usually likes people," "often kicks himself," or "puts on a false front"? It is not possible to know from published information just how many of the sets of *Q*-sort items which have been used by various other authors contain this error in item phrasing. In future construction of sets of items, it would seem wise to keep this issue in mind.

If frequency ratings are to be used, it would also seem pertinent to make the referents comparable for all items by asking *S*, "How often do you do such-and-such a thing when it is the appropriate response?" Otherwise differences in frequency ratings made by *S*s concerning their own responses may reflect, to unknown degrees, differences in frequency of occurrence of appropriate opportunities for manifesting the respective behaviors.

Sets of Q-Sort Items Other than Those Used by Butler and Haigh

In addition to Butler and Haigh's and Hilden's sets of self-referent statements, twenty-one other sets of *Q*-sort items have been used since 1950 in published studies of self-regarding attitudes. Most of these sets have been used in one or two investigations only, and are therefore identified only briefly in Table I. With the exceptions which are indicated in the table, no information as to specific item content, rationale for item choice, reliability, and/or relevant construct validity for indicating the phenomenal self seems to have been published for the instruments in the table.

One thing which seems clear from studying the published articles is that different *Q*-sort sets differ greatly with respect to item length and complexity. They range from single adjectives (e.g., Block & Thomas, 1955) to brief phrases or sentences (e.g., Butler & Haigh, 1954) to sentences with several parts (e.g., Edelson & Jones, 1954) and even to paragraphs (Stotland, Thorley, Thomas, Cohen, & Zander, 1957). If one's purpose is to develop a projective technique, ambiguity and multiplicity of points within each item might be useful. However, if one is aiming to give *S* a chance to express his phenomenal field clearly, item simplicity and clarity would seem to be very important in *Q*-sort sets. Whether this reasoning would be sustained by appropriate empirical tests of the relative construct validity of longer and shorter items remains to be seen.

As indicated above, the general questions concerning reliability and validity which were raised in connection with Butler and Haigh's self-referent statements could pertinently be asked with reference to *each* of the tabled Q-sort sets considered individually. It is obvious that insufficient information is available to answer them.

Conclusions on the Validity of the Self-Ideal Correlation from Q Sorts as an Index of S's Phenomenal Self-Regard

In addition to what we may be able to say about each separate instrument, we may point out the following difficulties which beset the path to a general conclusion concerning the usefulness of self-ideal correlation as a technique for measuring over-all self-regard: (1) Each investigator has used different items and, in many cases, differing instructions, and there is no information as to how the self-ideal correlation "scores" obtained from different sets of items would intercorrelate if obtained from the same Ss. (2) The exact content of the items has rarely been specified, so the reader cannot venture to compare logical or face validities, or attempt comparative "process analyses." (3) Sometimes the items are said to have been selected for their assumed relevance to a specified class of variables. Insofar as the variables with which the investigators intended to work have unknown relations to one another, one cannot venture an armchair synthesis.

The problem of generalization might be easier if we could safely assume, as some authors apparently do, that the size of the self-ideal correlation coefficient is a valid indicator of over-all self-regard regardless of item content. However, this is an unproved assumption. In Chapter IV, we shall try to compare and synthesize the results of hypothesis testing involving Q sorts as a measure of self-regard. There we shall find that some apparently contradictory results leave us in an ambiguous position, with two classes of interpretation open to us: (a) Variations in item content among the particular instruments used to measure self-regard may not warrant equivalent inferences (i.e., that "over-all self-regard" has been measured in each study). (b) The apparent contradictions may be due to other factors such as varying Ss, instructions, etc.

TABLE I

SETS OF SELF-DESCRIPTIVE *Q*-SORT ITEMS

All of the following sets of items seem to have been aimed toward fairly general feelings of self-regard. Those sets which are discussed in detail in the text are simply listed here with the designation "See text for description." All the other sets of items included in this table appear to have been used only once or twice. Information on these latter sets is summarized in the body of the table. Except as indicated below, no information concerning specific item content, rationale for choice of items, reliability, and/or relevant construct validity for indexing the phenomenal self seems to be available in published sources concerning these infrequently used *Q*-sort sets.

For three-fourths of *all* sets of *Q*-sort items referred to in this table, *no* reliability information is available in published sources. For 90% of *all* sets referred to in the table, *no* information on construct validity for inferring the phenomenal self is available in published sources (except for confirmation of the author's research hypothesis, which was based on self-concept theory plus the *assumption* that the self-concept measure was valid).

Author	*Instrument*
Block & Thomas (1955)	Eighty adjectives, anonymously sorted for self and ideal; r = index of "satisfaction with self."
Butler & Haigh (1954)	One hundred self-referent items. See text for description.
Caplan (1957)	Fifty self-referent phrases in re aspects of self in school, selected from student autobiographies. Sorted for self and ideal.
Chase (1957)	Hilden's 50 self-referent items, set #13, sorted for self and ideal. (See Hilden in text.)
Chodorkoff (1954a, 1954b, 1956)	One hundred and twenty-five short self-descriptive statements chosen to contain items about which Rorschach and TAT information could be obtained. Face validity: four clinicians cooperated in making it.
Cohen (1959)	See Stotland *et al.* (1957).
Edelson & Jones (1954)	One hundred and seventy-six statements taken from 1000 statements made by one S. E covertly classed S's statements according to explicitness, generality,

Table I—Continued

Author	*Instrument*
Edelson & Jones (1954) cont'd	and 22 conceptual roles *E* inductively derived from reading statements. All statements published. They are extremely long and complex.
Engel (1959)	One hundred items, 50 positive and ·50 negative in tone, according to judges. Items relevant to adolescent concerns as defined by Jersild. Favorability of self-attitude in terms of number of favorable items placed in "like me" side of distribution. Microfilm reference is given.
Fiedler, Warrington, & Blaisdell (1952); Fiedler & Wepman (1951)	Seventy-six statements describing Murray traits. ADI reference is given.
Friedman (1955)	Eighty statements derived from common TAT themes and random protocols. Statements listed in 1957 article. Sorted for self and ideal.
Frisch & Cranston (1956)	Seventy-six statements re self concept, half positive, half negative. No source given, but many items listed in article. Sorted for self and ideal.
Hanlon, Hofstaetter, & O'Connor (1954)	Paper-and-pencil *Q* sort, 100 items, five categories, forced choice.
Hilden (1958)	Twenty sets of 50 items each. See text for description.
Kelman & Parloff (1957)	Self-satisfaction *Q* sort; six drives underlying interaction in group, ten items per drive (drives listed in article). *S* sorts according to: (a) how he actually behaves, (b) how he ideally wishes to behave, in therapy group. Sum of scores for each drive obtained and rank ordered. Correlation of Perceived vs. Ideal was *rho* between six ranked scores. Also had Self-awareness *Q* sort, *rho* for six ranks between *S*'s actual scores and scores obtained from observer's sort ' for *S*. Test-retest *rhos* on three patients all = +1.00. *Rhos* on one month retest for three random patients ranged from +.84 (for Ideal) to +1.00 (for Ideal).
Klausner (1953)	Forced distribution into five categories made on 60 statements about the self. *Ss* were 27 adolescent boys. Factored into "reactive aggression," "adjusted inferiority," and "socially isolated self-aggression."

Table I—Continued

Author	Instrument
Kogan, Quinn, Ax, & Ripley (1957)	Ninety-six items sampling 25 personality variables, latter not listed, but ADI reference given. Each variable represented by three or four items judged independently by at least five out of six clinicians as sampling the named variable. Each sort was reduced to 25 scores by averaging groups of items respectively relevant to the 25 personality variables.
Lepine & Chodorkoff (1955)	One hundred and twenty-five self-descriptive statements. Self-ideal r.
Levy (1956)	One hundred statements of general applicability to "home town." Equal number of positive and negative statements (also used Butler and Haigh's items for self and ideal).
McKenna, Hofstaetter, & O'Connor (1956)	One hundred self-referent statements from Rogers and "apparently used by him." Only five categories, forced sort, self and ideal. (See Butler and Haigh, in text.)
Nahinsky (1958)	One hundred items specially devised to describe characteristics relevant to ideal and typical Naval officers. Seven-category forced sort.
Nunnally (1955)	Sixty statements of one subject, in re self, collected from 12 clinical interviews and projective tests, and from interviews with friends and relatives of S. Sorted for "as I am generally" and "as I would like to be," and for 12 other sets of directions. Factor analysis on one S.
Pearl (1954)	One hundred and eighty statements referring to positive and negative self-evaluations of 90 traits referring to values, self-characteristics, relations to people. Three subtests of 60, separately sorted into 11 categories by Q technique. Traits selected by three clinical psychologists from various sources, or constructed so that the most important aspects of the self-concept as seen by them would be represented.
Perkins (1958a, 1958b)	Fifty self-referent statements selected from a universe of statements derived form responses of fourth- and sixth-grade children reported in a survey by Jersild. The statements, their construction, and the sampling procedure are described in 1958a. Test-retest z on self-sort repeated after 2-7 days $= +.65$ on 251 fourth- and sixth-grade children (1958b).

Table I—Continued

Author	Instrument
Smith (1958)	Unrestricted sort of 29 personality descriptive phrases into five categories. (ADI reference.) Self minus Ideal = Discrepancy. Split-half reliability = +.88. Test-retest data questionable as measure of reliability, since one testing session was under drug conditions. Self minus Ideal = +.82 (test-retest).
Stotland, Thorley, Thomas, Cohen, & Zander (1957)	Modified Q sort, five brief paragraphs describing hypothetical situation where person faces potential frustration of a need. Five representative needs: achievement, autonomy, recognition, affiliation, cognition. Five behavioral alternatives. Sometimes used with "a person would" and "a person ideally would," sometimes with "I would" and "I ideally would" instructions, which are assumed in either case to indicate how S himself feels or would act. Odd-even reliability of previously used 15-paragraph form = +.91. Self-esteem score in terms of coincidences of preferred (or least preferred) and ideal reaction. Correlates with GAMIN in low +.70s according to Cohen (1959).
Taylor (1955)	Two hundred anonymous self-descriptions by adults classified as positive or negative by eight judges reduced to 60 positive and 60 negative statements from item analysis using 26 Ss (no details on criteria for item analysis). Eleven categories for sorting. Repeated self-sorts more or less intensively: scattered = approximately three to ten per month; intensively = approximately one per day or oftener. One hundred and twenty college students, one-week test-retest mean r = +.79. Self- and ideal-sorts (intensive Ss) ranged from +.79 to +.88, first pair correlation and last pair correlation, respectively. Mean positiveness of self concept increased significantly in intensive sorters.
Thompson & Nishimura (1952)	One hundred items representing Cattell's trait clusters (from a number of factor analyses), simplified or elucidated by E where it seemed necessary. Nine-point scale. Sort for: (1) own personality, (2) ideal personality. So much stereotypy in adjectives used that there was no greater mean correlation between pairs of friends' ideals than between ideal sorts of persons chosen at random.

b. RATING SCALES, QUESTIONNAIRES, ADJECTIVE CHECK LISTS

The most frequently used types of instruments for inferring over-all or general self-regard are the questionnaire, rating scale, and adjective check list. In terms of the operations used as a basis for inferring self-regard, several main categories of such instruments may be roughly distinguished: (1) those which purport to tap self-acceptance directly, i.e., by asking S how he feels about his standing on the stated characteristics; (2) those which use this direct approach and also derive a discrepancy score between separately obtained self- and ideal-ratings, answers, or checks; (3) those which utilize mainly a self-minus-ideal discrepancy score (written hereafter as [Self—Ideal] to distinguish it from self-ideal correlation); (4) those which rely on S's reports of actual self only, with the ideal end of the scale being assumed by E, or the favorability of the terms being defined in terms of external judges' opinions of desirability.

As with Q sorts, most of these instruments have been employed in only one or a few studies, and the information on their reliability and relevant construct validity is quite incomplete. We shall begin our survey by describing briefly those on which the greatest amount of information is available, and shall make some critical comments on each as seems appropriate. These descriptions will be presented in the order of the categories (1), (2), (3), and (4) listed immediately above. Tests of general self-regard about which little has been published will be described briefly in Table II.

There are a few scales which appear to have been aimed at self-evaluation of some specific ability or performance which was pertinent to an experimenter's hypothesis. These scales are separately presented in Table III.

Finally we shall attempt an over-all evaluative summary of this class of instruments as measures of self-regard. In this evaluative section, we shall state some general problems of *reliability theory* which need to be taken into account in the future development of questionnaires, adjective check lists, and rating scales. In addition, some suggestions will be made concerning the applicability of *scaling procedures* to the development of these types of instruments. And finally we shall take an over-all view of the *construct validity* of these measures.

(1) Instruments Purporting to Tap Self-Regard Directly

Berger (1952) has made an omnibus-type questionnaire purporting to measure Self-Acceptance and Acceptance of Others. As a basis for question construction, he used Scheerer's (1949) definition of the self-accepting and other-accepting person. From preliminary scales, he included items on the basis of (1) their significant relation to total scores made by the upper and lower one-fourth of 200 Ss, and (2) their appropriateness to a given element of the definition. He retained four items pertaining to each element of the definition. Matched-half reliability coefficients for various subgroups were +.746 or better. Construct validity was explored in terms of the correlation with free paragraphs written by 20 Ss and judged by four Es on the basis of Scheerer's definitions. For Self-Acceptance r was +.897. As further evidence of construct validity, he confirmed his prediction that stutterers and prisoners would score lower on Self-Acceptance than did college students matched for age and sex.

Phillips (1951) developed another omnibus-type questionnaire by converting Scheerer's (1949) descriptions of the self- and other-accepting person into simple statements. Twenty-five of the statements concern the self, 25 of them concern others. The five-day test-retest correlation was +.84 for the self items. No information on construct or empirical validity is offered by Phillips, but Omwake (1954) found a correlation of +.73 between Berger's and Phillips's Acceptance of Self Scores. Ss were college women. The self items in this questionnaire are all negatively phrased (i.e., to agree would always be to show poor Self-Acceptance). This means that the questionnaire does not control sufficiently for acquiescence response set. That is, an S's score may be determined to an unknown degree by his tendency to agree with items regardless of their content.

Fey (1954, 1955, 1957) has used several slightly differing forms of an Acceptance of Self and Acceptance of Others Questionnaire. The definitions of the terms, and the means of establishing the relevance of the items to the definitions are not given. With third-year medical students, split-half reliability for Acceptance of Self = +.84, with 60 Freshman medical students, +.92. No information on construct validity is given. The numbers of negatively and positively phrased items in this questionnaire are not balanced, providing insufficient control for acquiescence response set.

Berger, Fey, and Phillips have all predicted on theoretical grounds that Acceptance of Self should lead to Acceptance of Others (and therefore Acceptance of Self scores should correlate positively with Acceptance of Others scores within their respective inventories). Generally speaking, these predictions have received some confirmation. For example, Berger obtained correlations ranging from $+.36$ to $+.69$. Fey's correlations were $+.43$ and $+.40$. Phillips found correlations ranging from $+.51$ through $+.74$, while McIntyre (1952) using Phillips's questionnaire, obtained a correlation of $+.46$. (Each correlation reported in the preceding sentences was based on a different group of Ss.)

These results may be interpreted as indirectly supporting the construct validity of the scales for Acceptance of Self. However, the following cautions are in order before the results are assigned an interpretation bearing on either theory *or* instrument validity:

(1) All three questionnaires are omnibus type, and therefore an unknown amount of the correlation may be attributed to the common set induced by similar item format and the taking of the test at a single sitting. Some of Omwake's (1954) results are relevant to this point. She found some correlations across instruments when Acceptance of Self scores from one instrument were correlated with Acceptance of Others scores from another instrument (e.g., Berger Self-Acceptance *vs.* Phillips Acceptance of Others $r = +.25$; Phillips Self-Acceptance *vs.* Berger Acceptance of Others $r = +.34$). These rs are generally lower than those she obtained when Self Acceptance and Other Acceptance scores were obtained from the same instrument, even though there seems to be considerable overlap in format and content across instruments.

(2) The balancing of positively and negatively worded items is either not stated (Berger) or is not adequately accomplished (Fey, Phillips). Therefore the effects of acquiescence or negation response sets are unknown, and possibly quite large.

(3) The discriminant validity of self-acceptance measures (as contrasted to other-acceptance measures) has not been adequately established. Therefore we may be dealing with two alternate indices of general phenomenal dissatisfaction, rather than relating two theoretically separable constructs measured by means of operationally independent defining instruments.

The Berger, Fey, and Phillips questionnaires have not been published.

Maslow (1942b) believes his "Social Personality Inventory for College Women" measures "self-esteem." Its test-retest correlation over a two-week interval with one hundred Ss was $+.90$. Ss were asked to estimate the accuracy of their own scores, a pertinent criterion for exploring the construct validity of an instrument purporting to measure the phenomenal field. Eighty-one per cent of them thought the score fairly accurate or very accurate.

Jourard and his colleagues have used "self-cathexis" questionnaires and "body-cathexis" questionnaires in various studies (Secord & Jourard, 1953; Jourard & Secord, 1955; Jourard & Remy, 1955; Jourard, 1957). Varying forms of the questionnaires have been used in different studies, but in general each item is rated on a five-point scale from strong positive to strong negative feelings. In one study, using a 40-item form of the "self-cathexis" scale, reliability coefficients were $+.92$ and $+.90$ for 56 men and 56 women, respectively. The rationale for item choice and the type of reliability coefficient were unspecified but the traits are listed in the article (Jourard, 1957). Self-cathexis scores correlated with [Self — Ideal] discrepancies obtained from the same items $+.62$ for males and $+.53$ for females.

In another study the "self-cathexis" scale contained 55 items "believed to represent a sampling of the various conceptual aspects of the self" (Secord & Jourard, 1953). The items themselves are published in the article. On the basis of "considerable preliminary work with college students," items were eliminated if they were difficult to understand or difficult to assign a meaningful rating, or gave little inter-S variability, provided they did not leave an important part of the self unrepresented. This form of the self-cathexis questionnaire had a split-half reliability of $+.78$ for males and $+.83$ for females.

The "body-cathexis" scale used in this study contained 46 items (published in the article), which were selected from a larger pool on the same bases as described for the self-cathexis items. Body-cathexis was inferred from the sum of item ratings. A special body-anxiety score was also derived, being the sum for each S of the 11 items most negatively cathected by a group of Ss of the same sex as S. The body-anxiety score had a split-half reliability of $+.72$ and $+.73$ for males and females, respectively.

Some light is thrown on the construct validity of the 55-item Self-Cathexis Scale and the 46-item Body-Cathexis Scale by the fact that they intercorrelate $+.58$ for males and $+.66$ for females (both significant at the .01 level). On the theoretical assumption that "insecurity" should be associated with poor body- and self-cathexis, the Maslow Security-Insecurity Inventory was correlated with the former scales. The obtained rs were: —.37 for body-cathexis; —.52 for self-cathexis; and —.41 for body-anxiety score. Ss were 47 college men and women.

In another study, a much shorter version of the body-cathexis questionnaire was used, containing only twelve items. Ss were asked to state their ideal and perceived body size for certain parts or dimensions. It was found that cathexis, as measured through direct ratings, correlated significantly with ideal-minus-perceived discrepancies for four of the five body aspects which were studied in this manner. No information on the reliability of these scores is given.

Although four studies involving self- and body-cathexis have been reviewed, clear evaluation of the construct validity of these scales for measuring phenomenal self-regard cannot be given for the following reasons: (a) The content and number of items vary from study to study, sometimes in unspecified ways. The intercorrelations among the various forms of self-cathexis scales and among the various forms of body-cathexis scales are not known. Therefore the studies cannot be unequivocally synthesized. (b) The possibilities of response set have not been eliminated, especially in those studies where the format of the body- and self-cathexis questionnaires is the same.

One final comment is in order concerning *all* the instruments which purport to tap self-regard directly. Each yields a global score which is obtained by summing across items. In no case has it been demonstrated, however, that the items within the instrument are comparable to one another with respect to their perceived salience for S's self-regard, or with respect to their psychological metrics.

(2) *Instruments Purporting to Tap Self-Regard Directly and Also by Means of [Self—Ideal] Discrepancy Scores*

Some self-report instruments utilize a [Self—Ideal] discrepancy score as well as a direct Self-Acceptance score to index self-regard. Bills's Index of Adjustment and Values (Bills, Vance, & McLean, 1951), a well-known example of this type of instrument, was designed to measure variables of importance to self-concept theorists. One hundred and twenty-four trait names were selected from Allport's list of 17,953 traits as representative, in the opinion of the test's designer, of items which occur frequently in client-centered interviews. Forty-nine items showing greatest

test-retest stability on pretesting were retained in the final form. Since only nine negative traits were included, the control for acquiescence response set seems inadequate.

In regard to himself, *S* gives three answers to each item: Col. I: How often are you this sort of person? (to be marked on a five-point scale from "most of the time" to "seldom"). Col. II: How do you feel about being this way? (to be marked on a five-point scale from "very much like" to "very much dislike"). Col. III: How much of the time would you like this trait to be characteristic of you? (to be marked on a five-point scale from "seldom" to "most of the time"). The sum of Col. I (with negative traits reversed) = the Self Score. The sum of Col. II is taken as a direct measure of Self-Acceptance. The sum of the discrepancies between Cols. I and III is taken as the [Self—Ideal] discrepancy, from which Self-Satisfaction is inferred. (The *S* also answers these same questions about other people, defined in terms of a relevant peer group.)

Presumably this should mean that unreliability due to *S*'s inability to remember previous column ratings would not enter into discrepancy scores which are computed across columns, nor into correlations computed across columns. In this respect such an instrument would be superior to a *Q*-sorting technique. However, Bills's procedure may enhance the effects of response set upon discrepancy scores or correlations which are based on column comparisons. Just how response set might affect such statistics cannot be known with the data at hand.

Much more information is available on the norms, reliability, and validity of this instrument than on any other measure of the self concept included in this survey.

Split-half reliabilities for 100 college students ranged from +.53 for Self scores (Col. I) to +.87 for [Self—Ideal] Discrepancies (Col. I—Col. III). Six-week test-retest correlations, with varying numbers of *S*s, ranged from +.83 for Self-Acceptance (Col. II) to +.90 for Self (Col. I). Sixteen-week test-retest correlations for varying *N*s ranged from +.52 for [Self—Ideal] Discrepancies (Col. I—Col. III), to +.86 for Self scores (Col. I) (Bills's Manual for IAV, undated).

Some inferences regarding the construct validity of Bills's scores for measuring phenomenal self-regard may be drawn from the following observations.

(1) In Bills's own work with the instrument, testing conditions

and the stressing of the importance of honesty were assumed to induce frank reports.

(2) Intercorrelations among scores purporting to measure the same construct, or aspects thereof, were obtained by various investigators, as follows:

(a) Correlations among the three scores obtained from the Index of Adjustment and Values itself (Bills's Manual for IAV, undated). This instrument yields three possible alternate indices of self-regard: (*i*) Self. (By assuming that S has accepted a cultural stereotype at the good end of each rating scale, one can infer self-regard by the Self score alone, since the subtraction of Self from the constant stereotype value would not modify the score essentially.) (*ii*) Self-Acceptance. (*iii*) [Self — Ideal] discrepancy score. (Bills evidently intended only the Self-Acceptance and [Self — Ideal] discrepancy scores as measures of self-regard. The present author is responsible for including the Self score in this list.) Bills found that the correlation between Self scores and Self-Acceptance scores = +.90. This implies that these two indices do not have discriminant validity for inferring differing aspects of self-regard, but must be measuring essentially the same construct. He reports that the correlation between Self-Acceptance scores and [Self — Ideal] discrepancy scores was only —.67. This suggests that the latter is revealing something somewhat different from the other two scores. Self scores correlated +.83 with [Self — Ideal] scores. This correlation is inflated to an unknown degree by the common factor, Self. (We shall return below to an analysis of the [Self — Ideal] score.)

(b) When Acceptance of Self (IAV) was correlated with Acceptance of Self (Berger), $r = +.49$ (Omwake, 1954).

(c) When Acceptance of Self (IAV) was correlated with Acceptance of Self (Phillips), $r = +.24$ (reported in Bills's undated Manual); and $r = +.55$ (reported by Omwake, 1954).

(d) For 13 Ss, two judges scored 30-minute, open-ended interviews for Self-Acceptance, and the *rho* with IAV Self-Acceptance scores was +.84 (Bills, 1954a).

(e) Significant relationships were found by Cowen (1956a) between "negative self concept" (worst realistic self-report) and

"positive self concept" (best realistic self-report) from Brownfain's Inventory (Brownfain, 1952), and Self-Acceptance and
[Self — Ideal] discrepancy scores on IAV.

(3) By assuming the construct validity of the IAV scores as indices of Self-Acceptance, and by adopting certain theoretical premises,
predictions were made concerning relationships which would be obtained
between IAV scores and other variables. To the extent that the predictions were confirmed, some support is offered to the inference of construct
validity, as well as to the theoretical premises being tested.

In these studies, high Acceptance of Self was significantly associated
with:

(a) Attitude toward performance, estimates of performance, and
    recall of performance in five level-of-aspiration tasks (Bills,
    1953c). (See Chapter IV below for more details.)

(b) Less perceptual accuracy and greater degree of affect on the
    Rorschach (Bills, 1953a).

(c) Lower incidence of five out of six depression signs on the
    Rorschach (when [Self — Ideal] discrepancy was the index of
    self-regard) (Bills, 1954b).

(d) Reporting of a smaller number of psychosomatic symptoms
    (Bills's Manual for IAV, undated).

(e) Fewer reasons stated by Ss, when explaining their own unhap-
    piness, which were coded by judges as indicative of self-blame
    (Bills, Vance, & McLean, 1951).

(f) Having been taught by a "group therapy" method in a class in
    mental hygiene, as contrasted to traditional classroom method.
    (Although Self-Acceptance showed significant differences,
    [Self — Ideal] discrepancies did not.) (Weider, as quoted in
    Bills's Manual for IAV, undated.)

(g) More optimism with respect to future college success; greater
    satisfaction with present period of life; higher K and lower
    profile on MMPI, especially lower D, Pt, Sc, and Si (Renzaglia,
    as quoted in Bills's Manual for IAV, undated.)

(h) Low Taylor Anxiety Scale scores (when Self, Self-Acceptance,
    and/or [Self — Ideal] discrepancy scores are used as measures
    of self-regard) (Cowen, Heilizer, Axelrod, & Alexander,
    1957). (Some question concerning the role of test-taking
    defensiveness is raised by the finding that Ss in this study who

showed high and low Lie scores respectively differed significantly on Self, Self-Acceptance, and [Self—Ideal] discrepancy scores.)

The eight sets of findings just described throw some light on the construct validity of Bills's self-regard indices by comparing groups of Ss who differed in Self-Acceptance scores, or in [Self—Ideal] discrepancy scores. Also pertinent to the validity of the Self-Acceptance and [Self—Ideal] scores are three studies, described immediately below, in which Ss served as their own controls. In these investigations, E observed each S's reactions to two groups of Bills's adjectives: those on which S had indicated his self-regard was high, and those on which S had indicated his self-regard was low.

(i) Roberts (1952) determined, for individual Ss, which words yielded some and no reported [Self—Ideal] discrepancies, and which yielded high and low reported Self-Acceptance. He found significantly longer free-association reaction times to words which showed: (*i*) some [Self—Ideal] discrepancy *or* (*ii*) low Self-Acceptance, as contrasted to words which showed (*i'*) no [Self—Ideal] discrepancy *or* (*ii'*) high Self-Acceptance. In a replication study, Bills (1953b) obtained nonsignificant trends similar to Roberts's findings. In a second part of his study, Bills predicted that changes over time in [Self—Ideal] discrepancies and Self-Acceptance would be associated with corresponding changes in reaction time. His significant results refuted rather than supported his hypothesis, however.

(j) Cowen, Heilizer, and Axelrod (1955) used a paired associate learning technique with nonsense syllables as response words. The stimulus words were Bills's adjectives, which had been identified for the individual S as having high and low [Self—Ideal] discrepancies, respectively. Significantly elevated learning thresholds were associated with words thus identified as conflictual, when other variables (e.g., frequency) were well controlled.

No matter which of the three Bills scores is used, the process of summating across items implies comparability among items with regard to their perceived salience for S's self-regard and their psychological metrics. There is no information to support these assumptions.

Returning to the question of the validity of the two-part [Self—

Ideal] score, we must ask the following questions: (a) How much variance is contributed by each component to variance in the two-part score? (b) Will the [Self—Ideal] score predict theoretically relevant variables better than they can be predicted by *(i)* the Ideal score, as compared to a cultural norm *or (ii)* the Self score as compared to a cultural norm? If the Ideal score or the Self score have superior empirical validity for predicting behavior (as compared to the predictiveness of the [Self—Ideal] score), this of course does not disprove the construct validity of the [Self—Ideal] score for indexing *S*'s phenomenal self-regard. It may imply that behavior is more accurately predicted when one does not rely entirely on phenomenal self-regard as a predictor. (c) Will the two-part [Self—Ideal] score predict theoretically relevant variables better than they can be predicted by the one-part Self-Acceptance score?

In Bills's undated manual we find some information relevant to Question (a). There we see that the correlation between Self scores and [Self—Ideal] scores is $+.83$, which implies that the Ideal scores are stereotyped and contribute little to the two-part score. Inspection of frequency distributions of college *S*s for each of Bills's 49 adjectives reveals that on 39 of these items at least half the *S*s fall at identical, extreme points on the five-point Ideal-rating scales. For 23 out of the 49 adjectives, at least 66% of *S*s fall at identical, extreme Ideal ratings. For 12 of the 49 adjectives, at least 75% of *S*s fall at identical, extreme points on the Ideal-rating scale. In contrast to this, only four of the 49 adjectives show 59% or more of the *S*s falling at an identical point on the five-point Self-rating scale.

Although there seems to be no information directly relevant to Question (b), a finding we have already cited is obliquely pertinent to Question (c): The correlation between [Self—Ideal] scores and Self-Acceptance scores was $-.67$. This implies that these two scores are indexing somewhat different constructs, and would not be interchangeable as predictors of behavior variables which are theoretically relevant to self-regard.

A particular difficulty with the two-part [Self—Ideal] scores arises in the treatment of signs when summating. The assumption is made that it would be unlikely for *S* to rate his Self more favorably (in terms of a cultural norm) than he rates his Ideal Self. Worchel, in connection with this problem on his Self-Activity Inventory to be discussed below, contends that "in any case it is the amount of discrepancy and not the direction that is important in the prediction of maladjustment" (Worchel, 1957, p. 7). The present author questions whether discrepancies in a "reversed" direction warrant the same psychological inference as do discrepancies in the more usual direction. For this reason, the practice of absolute summation seems questionable without further relevant evidence. It is not clear what defensible change could be substituted.

The question of the influence of "faking good" or "Social Desirability" has of course not been resolved for this instrument any more than for others of its type. As pointed out in Section A above, Cowen and Tongas (1959) have demonstrated for Bills's instrument: (1) high positive correlations *across item means* between rated Social Desirability and Self-ratings; (2) high positive correlations *across item means* between rated Social Desirability and Ideal Self ratings; (3) negligible correlations *across item means* between Social Desirability and [Self — Ideal] discrepancies. However, as discussed earlier in detail, their method does not suffice to demonstrate which, if any, individual Self and Ideal ratings are determined by irrelevant and untrue social desirability considerations. Nor does this method warrant their conclusion that [Self — Ideal] discrepancies for individual Ss are free of this influence, and might therefore be used in preference to either Self or Ideal ratings.

(3) *Instruments Utilizing Mainly a [Self — Ideal] Discrepancy Score to Index Self-Regard*

Some instruments measure general self-regard through discrepancy scores rather than by S's direct statements of self-acceptance.

WORCHEL'S SELF-ACTIVITY INVENTORY. Worchel's (1957) 54-item Self-Activity Inventory (SAI) is a self-concept measure which purports to describe ways of coping with hostility, achievement, sexual, and dependency needs, and their frustration. The rationale behind the choice of item content was that these four need areas were apt to be major sources of conflict for men adapting to military life. (The Inventory was developed for the purpose of screening maladjusted military personnel.) No information is given concerning procedures by which the items were determined to have face validity for their respective purported need referents. In successive revisions, items were retained only if there was a spread in the ratings over at least four categories, with at least 10% of the ratings falling in the category which contained the smallest frequency.

Almost all the items seem to be negatively worded (i.e., to attribute the stated characteristics to oneself would be to derogate the self). This fact means that acquiescence or negation response sets have not been adequately controlled for. The response scale, from which intensity of underlying need-structure is inferred, is graduated from 1 (= "never") to 5 (= "very often"). This scale was used for each of the three categories of response the *S* is asked to use. In Column I, *S* completes the sentence "I am a person who . . . ." In Column II, he completes the sentence "I would like to be a person who . . . ." In Column III he completes the sentence "The average person is one who . . . ." Five scores are derived from the Inventory: Sum of Self; Sum of Ideal; Sum of Other; Sum [Self—Ideal], which is the absolute sum of individual item discrepancies across Columns I and II; Sum [Self—Other], which is the algebraic sum of individual item discrepancies across Columns I and III.

When column scores were correlated across *S*s, *r*s were found to range, for student and cadet samples, from +.12 (Ideal *vs.* Other) to +.64 (Self *vs.* Ideal).

The [Self—Ideal] discrepancy is assumed to index "self-ideal congruence," while [Self—Other] discrepancy is assumed to index "self-depreciation." However, it is obvious that, since each discrepancy score contains "Self," the scores cannot be independent of each other or of "Self." When other variables are related to SAI scores, the findings involving the two-part SAI indices are either insignificant or they are essentially the same as those involving the Self scores (which are actually assigned their values in terms of an implied cultural norm). In the studies where the Self score and the [Self—Ideal] score give essentially similar correlations with other variables, the trends involving the [Self—Ideal] score are often weaker than those involving the Self scores. What could this imply? It seems that no demonstrably new construct has been measured by the two-part score. The empirical predictive validity of the Self score may be somewhat superior. However the [Self—Ideal] score is in principle the more consistently phenomenological index. This statement is based on the asumption that *S*s have been honest in stating their phenomenal ideals. We cannot say, however, with the knowledge at hand, that phenomenal self-regard is less related to theoretically relevant variables than is a self-regard measure which may represent some nonphenomenal ideals.

All the comments just made in regard to Bills's [Self—Ideal] scores would of course be applicable to this [Self—Ideal] score as well. That is, the defensibility of absolute summation of discrepancies, and the question of the relative contributions of each component to the total variance and to correlations with other variables remain unresolved here too. Worchel (1957) has presented information suggesting that the Ideal component is more stereotyped than the Self component for this inventory. This means that in this respect too the Self-Activity Inventory resembles Bills's Index of Adjustment and Values. Inter-S variance for total Ideal ratings was significantly smaller than the inter-S variance for total Self ratings for 50 counseling applicants, and for 153 college students. A similar trend which was not quite significant was obtained with 97 air cadets.

The eight-week test-retest reliability coefficients for Self, Ideal, and Other Person are $+.79$, $+.72$, and $+.78$ ($N = 76$ college students).

Worchel (1957) reports three validating studies for the Self-Activity Inventory. All of them bear only indirectly on the construct validity of this instrument as an index of Ss' phenomenal selves, because they test simultaneously the construct validity of the instrument and some theoretical assumptions of the authors.

In one of these studies it was assumed that college men referred by themselves or others to a counseling or psychiatric bureau, other college students, and aviation cadets were respectively low, medium, and high on "adjustment." They were fairly equal on CA and educational and socioeconomic levels. On Self mean and Ideal mean scores, the students and consultation Ss differed significantly from the cadets. The consultation Ss differed at the .06 level from the other students with respect to Self mean scores. (The parallel results for [Self—Ideal] and [Self—Other] discrepancy scores will not be detailed here, as they cannot be considered to be independent tests from those already reported.)

Unfortunately the procedure and instructions used for the three groups were not held constant. The Inventory was administered individually to the consultation Ss, who also received information that results might be useful in evaluating their problems. In addition, these Ss had volunteered or agreed to come in for some sort of psychological counseling. Thus it seems plausible that this group was ready to be more frank and honest than would be the members of the other two groups. The other two groups received a group administration from their college instructors or from the "principal investigator and two colleagues" (of unknown relation to the cadet Ss).

What bearing, if any, the cadet group thought their scores might have on their military assignments and treatment is not known, but it is plausible that they were motivated to put themselves in as good a light as possible. One may also question the comparability of subject factors other than adjustment (e.g., sophistication) when comparing students with military personnel.

As a consequence of all these unknowns, no clear support for the construct validity of the inventory can be drawn from this study.

In the second study, Self and [Self — Ideal] scores correlated significantly with Taylor Manifest Anxiety scores ($N = 63$ undergraduates), and with Sarason Test Anxiety scores ($N = 65$ different undergraduates). ($p = .01$ for both correlations.)

In a third study, it was assumed that failure to complete a task under self-esteem-orienting instructions threatens self-esteem more than does failure to complete a task under task-orienting instructions. It was further assumed that favorable Self, [Self — Ideal], and [Self — Other] scores all measure "ego strength." Ss' recall ratios for completed and uncompleted tasks were measured when the tasks were done under self-esteem-orienting and task-orienting instructions. The investigator predicted that ego-strength would correlate positively with recall of completed tasks under self-esteem-orienting instructions, but would correlate negatively under task-orienting instructions. In fact, however, correlations involving [Self — Ideal] and [Self — Other] scores were negligible under both conditions. The Self score also failed to correlate with recall of completed tasks under task-orienting instructions. Under self-esteem-orienting instructions, however, Self scores correlated as predicted with recall ratios ($r = +.28$, $p = .05$). This finding gives very slight support to the construct validity of the Self score from this inventory as a measure of "ego strength." It also gives very slight support to the construct validity of the Self score as an index of S's phenomenal self-esteem.

Two additional studies reported in some detail elsewhere in this book throw some indirect light on the construct validity of this instrument. One investigation which is described in Chapter IV, Section C-7 compared performance decrements under self-esteem-threatening stress in groups of Ss who differ with respect to [Self — Ideal] discrepancies (Miller & Worchel, 1956). The other, which is described in Chapter IV, Section C-9, compared the Self-Activity Inventory scores of neurotic, schizophrenic, and normal Ss (Hillson & Worchel, 1957). In each case, hypotheses were stated on the bases of theory and the assumed validity of the instrument for measuring phenomenal self-regard. Some but not all of the hypotheses were verified.

THE INTERPERSONAL CHECK LIST. The Interpersonal Check List was developed by LaForge and Suczek (1955) to measure a number of variables defined by the Interpersonal Personality System (Leary, 1957). The check list is used to get (a) a self-description; (b) an ideal-self-description; and (c) a measure of "self-acceptance" in terms of discrepancies between self and ideal self descriptions.

In the Interpersonal Personality System, Leary (1957, pp. 81-82) and his co-workers distinguish five "levels" of personality, which we may briefly identify thus: I = Public Communication (interpersonal impact of the subject on others); II = Conscious Descriptions (subject's view of self and world); III = Preconscious Symbolization (subject's autistic and projective fantasy productions); IV = Unexpressed Unconscious; V = Ego Ideal (subject's view of his ideal self and his standards).

They wished to develop several measures for each level which could be mutually compared and/or combined across levels, as well as within levels. To make such intra- and interlevel comparisons possible it was necessary to score each and every one of their instruments along the same interpersonal behavior dimensions.

As a point of departure in setting up such dimensions of interpersonal behavior, they examined many behavior terms, and inductively established a sixteen-variable classification scheme. They report that this scheme seems to accommodate most of the words in the English language having a social connotation. In diagramming their classification plan, the sixteen variables are ordered around a circle which is divided into four quadrants by the main axes, dominance-submission and hostility-affection. Each quadrant is subdivided into four parts, yielding sixteen subdivisions of the circle. The successive sixteenths of the perimeter of the circle refer to interpersonal behavior characteristics which are considered to be psychologically adjacent to one another along a circular continuum. For example, "Docile-Dependent" is next to "Self-Effacing-Masochistic." Opposite points on the perimeter stand for psychologically opposite interpersonal behavior characteristics. For example, "Self-Effacing-Masochistic" is placed directly across from "Managerial-Autocratic." The radius of the circle indicates the intensity of the characteristic, from normal, moderate, or appropriate (at the center) to extreme (at the periphery).

Level II appears to refer to the "phenomenal self concept," and Level V to the "phenomenal self ideal." We should note, however, that Leary (1957, p. 132) specifically denies that he and his co-workers are measuring "level of consciousness." They prefer instead to say that Levels II and V are "conscious descriptions" of self and ideal self, because measures at these levels reflect how *S* chooses to present himself, rather than how he sees himself. In a personal communication Leary has said that he does consider Level II measures to be like other investigators' measures of the self concept.

The Interpersonal Check List is one of the instruments used to index both Level II (conscious self-description) and Level V (conscious description of the ideal self). In its most recent form the Interpersonal Check List contains 128 items, eight for each of the sixteen variables in the theory's classification scheme. The eight items for any variable include one of least "intensity," three for each of two intermediate "intensity" levels, and one of highest "intensity." Items are serially listed on the sheet which *S* uses, with adjectives from the sixteen categories intermingled within the list. The *S* describes his actual self and then his ideal self by checking as many adjectives as he wishes.

The Interpersonal Check List has undergone successive revisions, involving "several thousands" of *S*s. Clarity of meaning was a consideration in choosing adjectives (or brief phrases) to be included in the successive revisions. In the final form of the Interpersonal Check List, "intensity" values were assigned on the basis of a combination of two criteria: (1) whether psychologists had judged the item to be good, neutral, or bad from the viewpoint of the subject's culture; (2) the frequency with which subjects had checked the item in earlier forms (e.g., the lowest intensity value was given an adjective checked by 90% of persons, the highest intensity value to an item checked by 10% of persons).

In scoring the Interpersonal Check List, items representing successive pairs of the sixteen interpersonal behavior characteristics are grouped together, dividing the circle into octants. Eight raw scores are obtained for each *S*, by finding the total number of words *S* has checked which belong in each octant of the circle. A circular profile can then be plotted, with the radius of each octant determined by the number of words *S* checked belonging in that octant.

Reliability of the Interpersonal Check List. Two-week test-retest correlations are given for 77 obese women. When the data were grouped by octants, the average of the eight test-retest rs was $+.78$. This reliability coefficient may be somewhat inflated, since Ss' sets to check many or few items regardless of content were not controlled.

Theoretically, the farther apart on the circle the interpersonal behavior characteristics are from one another, the lower should be their intercorrelation. This tended to be true empirically when intercharacteristic correlations were computed on several samples. The theory predicts that characteristics opposite to each other on the circle will correlate negatively. Such negative correlations were not found, however. This lack of predicted negative correlations was partly due to contamination from the response set to check many or few items, regardless of their content. It is possible to remove this influence by dividing each of S's scores by his total number of checks. When this is done, negative correlations do appear between variables opposite to one another on the circle.

Construct Validity of the Interpersonal Check List. No data are given which are specifically pertinent to the construct validity of the Interpersonal Check List for inferring S's phenomenal self or phenomenal ideal self. Indeed, such validity was not the aim of the investigators. Since we are interested in this kind of validity for self-concept measures, however, we would find it valuable to know whether the Interpersonal Check List scores for Level II (conscious self-description) correlate with the other measures which these investigators used to index Level II. Also it would be valuable to know whether the Interpersonal Check List scores for Level V (conscious description of ideal self) correlate with the other measures which these investigators used to index Level V. Leary mentions that Level II and Level V were *each* measured by three other indices besides the Interpersonal Check List. Trained personnel rated diagnostic interviews, therapy interviews, and autobiographies according to the sixteen-variable scheme. No correlations between Interpersonal Check List Level II and any of these other three Level II measures are presented, however. Also no correlations between Interpersonal Check List Level V and any of these other measures of Level V are presented.

It seems that Leary may not have intended the alternate indices of Level II to be aimed at the same construct, despite their common level designation. For example, he gives some hypothetical consideration to variations in "depth" of conscious reports which may be obtained from initial therapy interviews and the check list (Leary, 1957, p. 151).

Some data are given showing the percentage of various diagnostic groups which are high on each of the octants (Leary, 1957, Chapters 18-22). These, however, are not directly useful to us in estimating the construct validity of the instrument for inferring the phenomenal self. The general self-regard levels of various groups of patients and normal persons are discussed briefly in Chapter IV, Section C-9 below.

The ideal-self score was shown to be rather stereotyped in the manner which we have found to be true for many other self-regard instruments. In one routine sample of 207 clinic patients, 90% of the patients' ideal-self scores fell in only one of the four quadrants of the circle.

Leary says that "self-acceptance" may be inferred from the discrepancy between Level II (conscious self-description) and Level V (conscious description of ideal self). He states that "this variable plays a most crucial role in arousing motivation for therapy" (1957, p. 205). No data are cited in support of this contention, however. The relative contributions of self and ideal to the two-part score are not discussed. In a personal communication Leary has stated that he has data relating Level II (conscious self-description) to motivation for therapy. These data are to be published in a book.

Finally we note that Level I (interpersonal impact of the subject on others) is in practice usually measured by S's *self-report* score on certain combinations of MMPI items. This use of self-report to index behavior *as seen by others* is stated to be a matter of practical necessity or convenience, rather than being operationally desirable. It is used despite the fact that these self-reports apparently do not always correlate highly with the following external ratings of S's behavior which Leary considers more appropriate operational definitions of Level I: sociometric ratings from check lists by fellow patients or trained observers; and ratings by trained personnel of the patient's minute-by-minute behavior in a social situation. Because the self-report measures of Level I were specifically *not* intended as indices of Ss' phenomenal fields, we shall not deal with them further here.

(4) *Instruments Purporting to Tap Self-Regard by Self-Ratings on Scales with Assumed or Prejudged Favorability Values*

Brownfain (1952) has developed a frequently mentioned two-part index of self-evaluation called "stability of the self concept." On each of 25 items, S rates himself four times, to indicate respectively (1) his most favorable realistic self concept ("positive self concept"); (2) his most unfavorable realistic self concept ("negative self concept"); (3) his "realistic private self concept"; and (4) his most accurate estimate of himself as he believed other people in the group saw him ("social self concept"). The "stability" score is obtained by subtracting S's "positive self concept" from his "negative self concept" on each of the 25 items, and summing across all items without regard to sign.

Split-half reliability for the "stability" scores was $+.93$ for 62 Ss. In choosing the 25 items, "an effort was made to sample as widely as possible the significant attributes of self-regard" (Brownfain, 1952, p. 598).

Brownfain hypothesized that instability of the self concept may be considered to be a correlate of "self-esteem" and is associated with "poor adjustment." He compared two groups of fifteen Ss who had extremely "stable" and "unstable" self concepts respectively. His results were as follows: (1) Stable Ss gave themselves more favorable "realistic private self-concept" ratings on 21 of the 25 items. Five of these differences were significant at $<.05$ level on a one-tailed test. (2) Stable Ss had a significantly narrower range between their "realistic private" and "social self" ratings on the 25 items taken as a whole. (3) Stable Ss had healthier scores on all factors but G in the GAMIN Inventory. (Two of these differences were significant at the .05 level or better.) (4) Stable Ss received a higher mean rating from fraternity peers on nine out of ten variables in a rating scale. (Intelligence ratings favored the unstable Ss, who did in fact have significantly higher grade point averages and were mostly graduate students.) The content of these scales appears to overlap the 25 items of the self-concept inventory to a considerable degree. (Two of these differences were significant at the .05 level.) (5) Stable Ss expected a higher rating from others on nine of the ten variables, the difference in expected adjustment ratings being significant. (6) Stable Ss showed a significantly narrower total range between their highest and lowest estimate of where fraternity brothers would rate them on these ten variables.

As with any two-part index, one wonders how much each component contributes to the predictive power of the composite stability score. It seems plausible to the present author that negative self concept (worst realistic self-rating) might be carrying the major burden, with relatively less inter-S variance occurring among positive self-concept ratings. If this is so, one could predict the findings as well or nearly as well with the negative self-concept ratings alone as with the composite stability score. This is true because the stability score would be obtained, in effect, by subtracting a constant or nearly a constant from negative self-concept ratings. It is impossible to determine this directly since no separate SD values for positive and negative self-concept ratings are given, nor is each component correlated separately with the dependent variables. However, the following information suggests obliquely that the major variance may be contributed by the negative self concept: When mean private self-concept ratings for each item were correlated with mean stability scores, across 25 items, $r = +.19$ (n.s.). However, when mean private self-concept ratings for each item were correlated with the mean gap between private self-concept rating and negative self-concept rating (the latter expressed as a percent of total instability range), $r = +.75$. (This correlation was taken from the unpublished dissertation on which the article was based.) Further light is shed on this question by Cowen's study (1954), using a modification of Brownfain's scales. Cowen compared Ss with extremely high and extremely low negative self-concept ratings. In one pair of samples in which the difference in mean negative self-concept ratings was 56.9, the difference in mean stability was 46.8, but the difference in mean positive self-concept ratings was only 10.1. In a second pair of samples in which the difference in mean negative self-concept ratings was 64.4, the difference in mean stability was 42.1, while the difference in positive self concept was only 22.3. The differences in mean positive self concept, although much smaller than the differences in negative concept or stability, did differ significantly at the .001 level for the second sample ($p = .08$ for the first sample). This suggests that some significant variance may be contributed to the stability score by the positive self concept. At the same time, however, it implies that much more variance is contributed to the stability index by variance in negative self-concept ratings.

In short, we need further exploration of this index before we can conclude that "stability of self concept" and "negative self concept" are different constructs.

Now let us return to the finding that stability is related to the other self-report variables listed in Brownfain's article. We must point out that these correlations do not constitute clear support for the discriminant validity of "stability" as a measure of phenomenal self-regard. Our line of thought is as follows: Let us remember that the "realistic private self concept" and the "social self concept" ratings were made on exactly the same 25 items used to measure "stability." Let us also remember that there seems to be considerable overlap in content among the 25 items, the GAMIN, and the peer rating scales on which S estimated how fraternity brothers would rank him. Let us assume for the moment that our reasoning was correct concerning the major role of the negative self concept in determining the two-part stability index. We conclude that Brownfain's findings concerning "stability" may be parsimoniously accounted for to an unknown but probably large extent in terms of the degree to which S is willing, under varying instructions, to derogate himself consistently on various instruments having identical or similar content.

Further indirect information on the construct validity of the stability score comes from a second article by Cowen (1956a) based on the two samples of subjects mentioned above (Cowen, 1954). Each of the components of the stability score correlated significantly with all three scores from Bills's IAV. On the other hand, the stability score (a discrepancy score) did not correlate significantly with any of the Bills scores, not even with the [Self—Ideal] discrepancy score derived from Bills's instrument. (Scoring of the IAV was slightly modified from Bills's original scoring.) Cowen (1956) also quotes two doctoral dissertations (Hauser, 1953, and LaFon, 1954). In the first, stability did not correlate as highly with various combinations of rigidity, security, and anxiety measures as did Brownfain's private self concept. In the second, negative self concept correlated more clearly with patterns of Rorschach measures of self-regarding attitudes than did stability.

Can one validly infer different aspects of phenomenal self-regard from each of Brownfain's four scores (positive self concept, negative self concept, realistic private self concept, and stability of self concept)? We conclude that such discriminant validity for each of the four indices remains to be demonstrated. It is suggested (Cowen, 1956a, 1956b) that the negative self concept, when elicited in the context of the other ratings, may seem innocuous to S, and lead him to reveal the phenomenal self more undefensively than he does in making the private "actual self" rating. A group of Ss who gave themselves negative self-concept ratings only were compared to a group who gave both positive and negative self-concept ratings (Cowen, 1956a). The former group's mean negative self concept was significantly more favorable, and 59% of the Ss in that group reported afterwards that their negative self-concept ratings would have been more unfavorable had they been asked to report both positive and negative self concepts. It is not clear, however, whether the groups were matched on relevant variables, since they came from two intact, successive psychology classes.

(5) *Other Rating Scales, Questionnaires, and Adjective Check Lists*

For the remaining rating scales, questionnaires, and adjective check lists which purport to measure self-regard there is little or no available information concerning reliability and/or construct validity. Mostly they have been used in only one study. Consequently they will be identified briefly in Tables II and III where the reader can refer to them as he reads in Chapter IV about the studies which involve them.

TABLE II

QUESTIONNAIRES, ADJECTIVE CHECK LISTS, RATING SCALES FOR INDEXING SELF-REGARD

All of the following instruments seem to be aimed toward fairly general feelings of self-regard. Those instruments which are discussed in detail in the text are simply listed here, with the designation "See text for description." All the other instruments included in this table appear to have been used only once or twice. Information on these latter instruments is included in the body of the table. Except as indicated below, no information concerning specific item content, rationale for choice of items, and/or relevant construct validity for indexing the phenomenal self seems to be available in published sources concerning these infrequently used instruments.

For two-thirds of *all* instruments referred to in the table, *no* reliability information is available in published sources. For 80% of *all* instruments referred to in the table, *no* information on construct validity for inferring the phenomenal self is available in published sources (except for confirmation of the author's research hypothesis, which was based on self-concept theory plus the *assumption* that the self-concept measure was valid). Authors who used the MMPI, GAMIN, Guilford-Zimmerman Temperament Survey, or California Test of Personality are not all listed below.

Table II—Continued

Author	Instrument
Alfert (1958)	List of 25 adjectives "constructed from Murray's set of 20 needs and five of the general attributes." These adjectives paired with adjectives opposite in meaning, and S made dichotomized choices. "A similar but less systematic list of 20 opposite traits" was used for one group of Ss in the study. Sample items are given.
Amatora (1957)	Child Personality Scale, 22 traits, each on ten-point scale. Published manual referred to.
Beilin (1957)	Pupil index; and S's Self-rating scale (components not given).
Berger (1952)	Questionnaire for Self Acceptance and Acceptance of Others. See text for description.
Bills (1951-1954)	Index of Adjustment and Values. See text for description.
Brodbeck & Perlmutter (1954)	Twenty-six-item self-dislike questionnaire. Reduced from 78 items to include only those which correlated at least +.40 with total, on pretest with 36 Ss. Tried to exclude measurement of direct anxiety. Items published in article. All items phrased negatively. Test-retest reliability, time and N unspecified, = +.8.
Bronfenbrenner, Harding, & Gallwey (1958)	Six "favorable" and six "unfavorable" adjectives, each rated on six-point scale. Adjectives published.
Brownfain (1952)	Stability of self concept on 25 rating scales. See text for description.
Bugental & Gunning (1955); Bugental & Zelen (1950)	S writes three answers to question "Who Are You?" Answers analyzed into 17 categories within framework of self-concept theory. Categories cover more than self-regard, e.g., name, sex, age, group membership. Exploratory information on frequency of usage of categories is presented.
Calvin & Holtzman (1953)	Ss ranked selves and others on seven traits defined in article: Leadership, Tolerance, Adjustment, Drive, Tactfulness, Gregariousness, Social Understanding.
Child, Frank, & Storm (1956)	Self-rating on 200 items (10 for each of 20 variables), to represent authors' definitions for Murray needs listed in article. Split-half reliabilities on unspecified N ranged from +.39 to +.91 for separate scales, typically around +.7 to +.8.

Table II—Continued

Author	*Instrument*
Coopersmith (1959)	Self-Esteem Inventory. Fifty items concerned with S's perceptions in four areas: peers, parents, school, self. Items selected and reworded from "Rogers and Dymond scale," plus items designed by E. Items divided into two groups by agreement among five psychologists that they indicate high or low self-esteem. S checks item as "like me" or "unlike me." Twice the sum of high self-esteem items marked "like me" and low self-esteem items marked "unlike me" gives Self-Esteem Score. S also checks items as like or unlike his ideal self. Twice the sum of discrepancies from actual self indexes "dissatisfaction with present self picture." Association between two types of score significant at .01 level. Five-week test-retest reliability, 30 fifth-grade $Ss = +.88$. ADI reference given.
Crandall & Bellugi (1954)	One hundred adjectives chosen from Allport and Odbert's list according to these criteria: (a) clear; (b) used in everyday conversation; (c) agreed-upon social desirability values which covered range of social desirability scale; (d) representative of various levels of Thorndike-Lorge word count. S rates for personal desirability, self applicability, ideal self, novel person seen for few minutes. Seven- (or eight-) point scale used.
Diller (1954)	Ten personality trait names given in article were rated on seven-point scales. Traits selected by dormitory residents as most valuable for successful college adjustment. No separate reliability for self-ratings given.
Diggory & Magaziner (1959)	Linear rating scales for five abilities (defined in article) and for general adequacy of functioning. Five reference points along ability scales, in terms of percent of relevant situations in which S expects to succeed in using the ability. Change in ratings measured in mm. of movement along line.
Dittes (1959a, 1959b)	Self-esteem inferred from sum of three indices: (a) 11 self-rating items, six-point scales, norm to be average man S's age. Most items "adapted from Murray." Examples given in article. Spearman-Brown odd-even $r = +.82$. (b) Four questions on sense of adequacy among peers (correlates $+.34$ with [a]). (c) Ratings S received from discussion group members, used on the assumption that high self-esteem Ss would participate actively, be favorably rated by peers (correlated $+.25$ with [a]).

Table II—Continued

Author	*Instrument*
Eastman (1958)	Bills's Self-Acceptance, abbreviated form (see text for Bills's IAV). Self-Acceptance Spearman-Brown reliability = +.89. Correlated significantly with Marital Happiness scores, as predicted from theory (+.37 and +.35).
Ewing (1954)	One hundred trait names rated on five-point scale for typical and ideal self. No rationale given.
Fey (1954, 1955, 1957)	Questionnaires for Acceptance of Self and Acceptance of Others. See text for description.
Fiedler, Dodge, Jones, & Hutchins (1958)	Twenty seven-point adjective scales. Self-esteem inferred in terms of average favorability. Self-satisfaction inferred in terms of [Self — Ideal] discrepancy. Split-half reliability of self-esteem = +.83; self-satisfaction = +.76 (on one of four groups used). Self-esteem correlated with [Self — Ideal] discrepancy from +.36 to +.60 on four different groups.
Flyer, Barron, & Bigbee (1953)	Six bipolar trait scales, four points on each scale. Anxiety, enjoyment of company of others, use of others for own purposes, sensitivity to criticism, trust of people, self-confidence. Ss rated self and social self and others. Reliability given for group perceptions only.
Froehlich (1954)	S rates 17 abilities, interests, personality characteristics on four-point scale.
Gibson, Snyder, & Ray (1955)	Attitude-Toward-Self Scale constructed from MMPI items, selected by agreement of seven out of ten trained judges. Twenty items having highest pointbiserial *r* with total score selected.
Harvey, Kelley, & Shapiro (1957)	S rates on 14 cm. line 15 items pertaining to five social characteristics significant to college students (friendship, sincerity, broadmindedness, considerateness, sense of humor).
Helper (1955, 1958)	Semantic differential scales, 42 pairs of adjectives found by Cattell to be descriptive of ten major factors + four of Osgood's connotative scales. Favorability = Sum "actual self" ratings on 15 items agreed on by judges as desirable. Acceptability = [Actual — Ideal] discrepancies on remaining 31 items. Favorability and Acceptability Spearman-Brown reliabilities range from +.66 to +.83.
Israel (1958)	Ss rank self and others of living group on orderliness, leadership, intelligence, appearance.

Table II—Continued

Author	*Instrument*
Janis (1954); Janis & Field (1959); Janis & Rife (1959)	Self-esteem inferred (1954) from 38 items selected from "standard inventories," classed by author on basis of manifest content into (a) social inadequacy, (b) inhibition of aggression, (c) depression, (d) neurotic anxiety, (e) obsessional symptoms. First three clusters alleged to indicate self-esteem. Janis and Field (1959) published three other apparently different clusters: (a) social inadequacies, (b) social inhibition, (c) test anxiety. Spearman-Brown rs for the latter range from $+.65$ to $+.91$. Janis and Rife (1959) used only the social inadequacy cluster to infer self-esteem.
Janis (1955)	Self-esteem inferred from Socially Oriented Anxiety cluster from Sarason Test Anxiety Questionnaire. (See Sarason and Gordon, 1953.)
Jourard *et al.* (1954-1957)	Self-cathexis and body-cathexis questionnaires. See text for description.
LaForge & Suczek (1955)	Interpersonal Check List. See text for description.
Lawson & Fagan (1957)	Twenty-item adjective list to be checked for self, good, (prison) guard, prisoner. Exact rationale for item choice not given but items are listed.
Lazowick (1955)	Nine bipolar semantic differential scales given in article. Three scales represent each of Osgood's three factors: I. evaluative; II. activity; III. potency.
Lesser & Abelson (1959)	Self-esteem inferred from (1) total number of classmates S did not judge to be superior to him on five favorable but ambiguous characteristics; (2) child's estimate of how many classmates like him and would choose to sit next to him; (3) discrepancy between rank of child on measure (2) and rank of child's actual sociometric status.
Levanway (1955)	Self-ratings on 18 trait words on five-point scale. Self-Acceptance is inferred.
Linton & Graham (1959)	"Check-list personality inventory of 84 items intended to reveal those consciously held feelings about himself that he is willing to state publicly" (p. 86).
Lorr, Katz, & Rubenstein (1958)	Eighteen five-point graphic rating scales. Patient rates actual self and self he would like to be. Discrepancy between self and ideal indicates self-dissatisfaction. Perhaps these scales are essentially the same as the 21 scales used by Rubenstein and Lorr (1956), but no definite information is published on the present 18 scales. (See Rubenstein and Lorr [1956], below.)

Table II—Continued

Author	*Instrument*
Lundy (1955); Lundy (1958); Lundy, Katkovsky, Cromwell, & Shoemaker (1955)	Eighty MMPI statements randomly placed in groups of four. S to choose one from each group to characterize self, one to characterize his ideal. Self-acceptance = number of agreements on items chosen under the two instructions.
McKee & Sherriffs (1959)	Sarbin's Adjective Check List, to be checked by S as to ideal and real self. (See Sarbin below.)
McQuitty (1950)	Personality questionnaire, 180 items, a few illustrative items published.
Manis (1955, 1958)	Twenty-four bipolar adjective scales from Cattell's factor analysis of Allport and Odbert's adjective trait list. Of Cattell's 12 factors, the eight accounting for most variance are represented by three items each. (Said to be similar to Helper's instrument, q.v.)
Martire (1956)	Twenty-six traits modified from Brownfain, forced sort (but *not* Q) from most to least: (1) important to stand high on; (2) like self. Adjectives listed in article. Anchoring definitions given to S. Mean of each S's [Self — Ideal] discrepancies taken on achievement-related traits only (others ignored in study).
Martire & Hornberger (1957)	Same 26 adjectives as in Martire (1956); but Ss rank in order from 1 to 26, according to: (1) importance to them; (2) characteristic of them; (3) acceptability to society.
Maslow (1942)	Social Personality Inventory for College Women. Used to infer self-esteem. See text for description.
Mason (1954)	Chicago Attitude Scale: each subtest has three positive, three negative, and three neutral items; reliability for aged Ss (method unspecified) +.72 to +.95. Vineland Social Maturity Scale: administered "nondirectively," to infer S's self concept of own social competence from S's spontaneous replies. Caldwell Pictures (1953): forced sort of pictures along scale, once according to degree "like me," once according to degree like "ideal person." Self-concept Questionnaire: 26 items from "Fiedler's Q-sort" Statements which three psychologists considered appropriate for measuring attitudes of "self-worth" in the aged. Two- to four-week test-retest reliability, 25 Ss = +.64. At least five out of six psychologists agreed on feeling tone of items. Score = number of positive views S holds.

Table II—Continued

Author	*Instrument*
Matteson (1956)	Self-Evaluation Scale on which S indicates: (1) conceived self; (2) projected self two years hence; (3) reflected self (as others see him). Number and kind of items, steps in scale not reported.
Miyomoto & Dornbusch (1956)	Five-point scale for four traits: intelligence; self-confidence; physical attractiveness; likeableness. Rated for self, perceived response of peer group to self, perceived response of generalized other to self.
Norman (1953)	Two sets of eight-point rating scales. Scale A = 22 "phenotypic" traits, adapted and modified from Cattell. Scale B = nine "genotypic" variables. Traits listed in article, reference cited for definitions.
Northway & Detweiler (1955)	Ten adjectives given in article, selected by Ss as best to describe good qualities of people. S judged self on each item on five-point scale from "extremely" to "not at all."
Nuthmann (1957)	Eighty student judges given definition of acceptance of self. From large pool, item selected if proportion of judges classifying it as relevant to definition departed from chance at .001 level or better. Items not included in final scale unless seven out of eighty students in fresh group gave self-rejecting answers. Number of True and False answers equalized. Final form of scale was 100 acceptance-of-self answers plus 40 buffer items.
Perlmutter (1954)	"Standard list of traits used in several previous experiments because of the variety and clarity of the items" (p. 133). S checked according to whether (1) he would like to; (2) he did actually possess either "large" or "small" amount of each trait. Self-esteem inferred from number of actual positive traits S reports self as having. High self-esteem = zero undesirable traits; low self-esteem = five or more undesirable traits checked.
Phillips (1951)	Questionnaire for Self Acceptance and Acceptance of Others. See text for description.
Rasmussen & Zander (1954)	Sixteen items pertaining to what constitutes a good teacher, decided on basis of "interviews with faculty groups and search of educational literature to discover what teachers tend to talk about" (p. 242). Eight-point scale for each item. Failure (self-esteem) score = sum of differences between "real performance" rating and "ideal teacher" rating.

Table II—Continued

Author	*Instrument*
Reckless, Dinitz, & Murray (1956); Reckless, Dinitz, & Kay (1957)	Unspecified instrument for measuring boy's conception of self, his family and other interpersonal relations (presumably items selected for logical relevance to resistance to delinquency).
Robinson & Freeman (1954)	Self-Regarding Span = number of minutes and seconds spent telling about (1) self in present; (2) self between ages ten to fifteen; (3) ideal self for future. Rapport previously established by S's telling about preferred season. On Self-test, S was prodded, time taken out for irrelevancies and pauses of more than ten seconds. Same tester administered and recorded. No control for response total. Self-Concern = same responses coded for number of items showing interpretations, emotion, detachment. Interjudge reliability = +.86. Inadequate control for response total. Sensibility Questionnaire: 20 questions, four groups or five each in re concern with past, future, other people's feelings, other people's opinions. Oral administration, E' recording. Answers judged later by E. Split-half reliability = +.86.
Roessler & Greenfield (1958)	Fey Questionnaire (see text for description). Also used suicidal attempts to define low self-acceptance, but no correlation between the two measures of self-acceptance were presented.
Rogers (1958)	"Global apperception technique" for measuring self-ideal congruence, which S expresses directly by sliding a four-inch square of red glass (representing self) behind a four-inch square of blue glass (representing ideal). Congruence between self and ideal measured in centimeters of overlap.
Rokeach & Fruchter (1956)	Self-rejection Subscale (embedded among items measuring Dogmatism, Paranoia). Five items, three from Berger (see text), two from MMPI. All worded so that True answer = rejection of self.
Rosen (1956a, 1956b)	MMPI given three times: (1) under standard instructions (for "self"); (2) to describe S's idea of desirable characteristics of person own age and sex; (3) to describe what society thinks is desirable in person of S's age and sex. Self-esteem not inferred directly, but [Self — Ideal] discrepancy (in terms of number of discrepant items) correlated with various MMPI scales. Author asserts he's not after construct validity of MMPI as measure of phenomenal field.

Table II—Continued

Author	*Instrument*
Rubenstein & Lorr (1957)	Multidimensional Scale for Rating Psychiatric Patients, discussed in Lorr and Rubenstein (1956), Lorr, Schaefer, Rubenstein, and Jenkins (1953). Six factors involve dynamics, four factors involve symptoms. The first six (including 25 items) used in this study.
Rubenstein & Lorr (1956)	Two-part, 21-item, five-point graphic rating scale. Part I = actual self; Part II = as would like to be. Discrepancy score between self and ideal. Covers such areas as intelligence, interpersonal relations, personal standards, estimated personality adjustment (developed partly from Brownfain's instrument, discussed in Chapter III above; and partly on the MSRPP mentioned immediately above in Table II). (See also entry under Lorr, Katz, and Rubenstein, 1958, above.)
Sarbin & Jones (1955)	Personality Word Card: 200 adjectives, no information given on basis of choice, items published as examples are all positive in tone. *S* checks words which characterize himself. Number of words checked on Personality Word Card correlated +.53 with Barron's ego-strength scale on MMPI. (See also Sarbin and Rosenberg.)
Sarbin & Rosenberg (1955)	Gough Adjective Check List: 284 words, no published reference or rationale. Index of Self-Acceptance = number favorable adjectives checked/total number of adjectives checked. Index of Self-criticality = number of unfavorable adjectives checked/total number of adjectives checked. Favorability and Unfavorability in terms of upper and lower 25% of words as rated for favorability by 30 judges. Personality Word Card: 200 words, approximately two-thirds from Gough's List. Rationale for deleting and adding not specified. Split-half reliability = +.81.
P. Sears (1941)	Self-appraisal scale: "How I am" and "How I wish I were," rated on five-point scale from nearly best to nearly worst in class. Academic and nonacademic activities listed in article. Self-minus-wish on self-appraisal of academic activities correlates with size of discrepancy score on level of aspiration task (experimental). Children who admit falling short of ideal are, by other criteria, maladjusted.

Table II—Continued

Author	Instrument
Sears (1936)	Four graphic seven-point rating scales, one each for stinginess, obstinacy, disorderliness, bashfulness (traits prejudged by other groups for desirability).
Sharma (1956)	Ss rate selves twice on a 25-trait list on eight-point scale: (1) actual self; (2) like self to be. Discrepancies summed absolutely. Test-retest for control group = +.90, two- to six-week interval.
Sherriffs & McKee (1957)	Sarbin's Adjective Check List (see Sarbin, above).
Smith & Lebo (1956)	Self-concept of Social Maturity measured through modification of Items 9 through 15 of Vineland Scale. Five alternatives per item (sample item published). (See Table IV for nonphenomenal self-concept measures also used by these authors. No correlations among their self-concept measures presented.)
Solley & Stagner (1956)	Twenty of Osgood's Semantic Differential Scales, 12 of which had high factor loadings on "valuation" factor. Seven-point scale, Ss told 4 = average. Sum of the numbers checked on the 12 valuative scales = score. Test-retest, two months = +.87 on Ss used in this study.
Steiner (1957)	Twenty six-step graphic rating scales, identified by polar terms (not given). S rates self according to (1) realistic, (2) optimistic, (3) pessimistic self. S instructed to imagine a team of psychologists has studied him and agreed on his rating, and to mark scales accordingly. A number of composite scores are derived. Intercorrelations among scores given in article. Some are artifactual since each score being correlated contains common element.
Stotland & Zander (1958)	S evaluated his visual motor coordination and 13 abilities, scaled by undergraduates according to decreasing similarity to an experimental task. S also rated self as a "complete person." Evidently an 11-point scale used for each rating. See Table III for specific task rating scale used in this study.
Tamkin (1957)	Scott-Duke Questionnaire = L and K scales from MMPI plus Self-Acceptance scale based on Scheerer's definition of self-accepting person. (Tamkin calls Self-Acceptance score a measure of "ego-strength.") Split-half, according to Scott (unpublished) = +.94. Correlation with Rogers's Q sort = +.77 according to Scott (unpublished). Differentiates among disorders in predicted fashion.

Table II—Continued

Author	*Instrument*
Tarwater (1955)	"The 'I Quest,'" a problems inventory
Torrance (1954a, 1954b)	Kansas State Freshmen evaluated own percentile standing on ACE, Cooperative English, Cooperative Reading Tests before and after taking tests (eight subscores estimated each time).
Wahler (1958)	Forty-four items pertaining to characteristics commonly regarded as important clinical variables, e.g., anxiety, hostility, dependency, suspicion. Nine-point scale, no forced choice.
Webb (1952)	Rating on five variables: personal charm, security, intelligence, Jewish appearance, Jewish acceptance (terms defined in article); 1 to 7 labelled least to most.
Webb (1955)	Seven-point scale of "intelligence" from "least" to "most"; Ss rated self among military peer group. Ss instructed to give as many high as low ratings. Rerating of self after 11 weeks, $r = +.19$.
Worchel (1957)	Self-Activity Inventory. See text for description.
Wylie (1957)	Six-point scales for friendliness, likeability, generosity, intelligence, sense of humor. Each point defined by verbal description. Order of descriptive points from assumed ideal verified by independent judges. Ss rate selves as they think members of military peer group will rate them. Good ends alternated for response set control. (ADI reference for content, procedures, correlations with Self-Inventory.) Self-Inventory: omnibus-type, True-False items, 15 independently judged to pertain to each of five traits mentioned above. Positive and negative item structure equalized for response set control. (ADI reference for content, reliability, internal analysis, correlations with respective self-rating scales.)
Zelen (1954a, 1954b)	Feelings of Personal Worth from California Test of Personality. Biserial correlation with positive feelings about self from W-A-Y (see Bugental *et al.,* above) was $+.73$ on about 50 Ss.
Zimmer (1954)	Twenty-five trait adjectives on seven-point scale. Adjectives chosen on criteria: six to ten per million on Thorndike-Lorge word count, column G; not representing cultural stereotype of desirable or undesirable trait; having personal or dynamic meaning. Actual

Table II—Continued

Author	Instrument
Zimmer (1954)—Cont'd	adjectives given. *S* rates self: (1) as I am; (2) as I would like to be. Free choice. Self-acceptance inferred from discrepancies.
Zimmer (1956)	Rating scales: eight vertical columns numbered 1 to 11 between two sets of adjectives given in article. Factor analysis of traits yielded three factors: I. Ascendance-submission; II. Maturity-immaturity; III. Adjustment-maladjustment (but results of study not obtained in terms of factors).
Zuckerman & Monashkin (1957); Zuckerman, Baer, & Monashkin (1956)	Sixteen subscales covering "clinically relevant dimensions," a list of eight scaled adjectives describes the points on each subscale. *S* chooses word to describe himself: (1) as he is "in general"; (2) as he "would like to be." Absolute sum of discrepancies in scale values for self and ideal = self-acceptance. Correlations with other scales offered.

TABLE III

SPECIFIC EVALUATION INSTRUMENTS

A number of investigators have devised self-evaluative rating scales very specific to their experimental purposes, e.g., *S* rates how well he did on a particular experimental task, or he rates his standing on one or a few obviously evaluative traits. These instruments are too miscellaneous to subclassify, but are simply listed below. Except as indicated, no information on reliability or construct validity as an index of *S*'s phenomenal self is published.

Author	Instrument
Davids, Henry, McArthur, & McNamara (1955)	Six-point scale for "avowal of aggression," from much less than to much more than most people.
Eastman (1958)	Marital Happiness (Wallace). Wallace's reliability, Spearman-Brown = +.90. Eastman reliability not given.
Festinger, Torrey, & Willerman (1954)	*S* evaluates own performance on tests of ability to "predict without adequate information."
Gerard (1958)	After group discussion, *S* ranks self and other as to knowledge, clarity of explanation, and contribution to discussion.

Table III—Continued

Author	Instrument
Gilinsky (1949)	S estimates own performance on vocabulary test after hearing norms but before taking test. Estimates own IQ.
Goldings (1954)	Linear rating scales for "avowal of happiness" in eight areas (family relations, health, intellectual activity, physical exercise, leisure time, sex relations, personal friendships) and one over-all scale.
Green (1948)	Ss rate self and all others on five-point scale of leadership.
Howard & Berkowitz (1958)	S evaluates own performance on simulated air strategy.
Klein (1948)	S estimates own performance on ten-point scale before and after six motor tasks.
Murstein (1956)	S rates self and fraternity brothers on hostility as defined in article (one-month rerank $rho = +.89$ for 15-member sample). No specific reliability on self-rating given.
Rogers & Paul (1959)	Conscious impunitiveness indexed by $M\%$ score on Rosenzweig PF. See Table IV for Rogers and Paul's index of unconscious self-evaluation of aggression.
Rokeach (1945)	Ten-point graphic rating scale for female beauty.
Stotland & Zander (1958)	Eleven-point scale for rating degree of puzzle success, and eleven-point scale for rating degree of puzzle failure. (See Table II for other scales used in this study.)
Stotland, Thorley, Thomas, Cohen, & Zander (1957)	Self-evaluation on puzzle task, six-point graphic rating scales. Details not specified. Not related to self-esteem (see Table I) except under failure conditions of experiment.

(6) *Summary and Conclusions Concerning Validity and Reliability*

Obviously there have been a great many studies in which phenomenal self-regard has been inferred from rating scales, questionnaires, adjective check lists, or combinations of these techniques. Although some of these instruments (e.g., Bills's IAV, Berger's Acceptance of Self) have been explored more or less extensively, most of the indices have been used only once or twice. Sufficient information is not at hand regarding their reliability or their construct validity for inferring phenomenal self-esteem.

RELIABILITY. *Split-Half Coefficients.* As for reliability, when it is reported at all, it is usually of the split-half variety. This type of coefficient, although it does not measure time-associated errors (instability), is of major interest to the test constructor because it reflects internal consistency, "the only aspect of reliability which can be improved by using better items in an objective test" (Cureton, 1958, p. 733).

Arriving at a meaningful interpretation of the split-half coefficient is not easy, however. Such coefficients must be evaluated in the light of the assumptions one makes about the meaning of "reliability," and the degree to which such assumptions are fulfilled in the formation of the two halves. Specialists in the study of reliability theory have not reached complete agreement with respect to assumptions and specifications, as we shall exemplify below by citing some ideas of Cureton and of Cronbach and his co-workers. Despite some apparent disagreement, there is considerable congruence in these current views, however. Thus far, workers in the area of self-concept measurement have not explicitly considered such issues in relation to their own instruments. Future work in the area should yield more clearly interpretable split-half coefficients, if attention is given to these matters.

Cureton (1958) has argued that the reliability coefficient of any half-test be defined as the variance ratio of true scores to total scores. He specifically rejects any definitions of true score which imply sampling from an infinite item universe. Instead he limits himself to a finite population which can be identified in practice with the pool of items which a test author actually uses in constructing half-tests or alternate forms. Operationally, everything which causes correlation between the two half-tests must be defined as included in the true score. Thus variables which the test constructor may consider theoretically irrelevant or spurious will be part of the true score if such errors are systematically associated across the two halves for any reason.

According to Cureton, the correlations between test halves can be taken as indicating the reliability of each half only when the following conditions are fulfilled: (a) The items have been allocated to the two halves so that each half has the same factorial structure. (b) The items have been allocated to the halves so as to yield almost identical distributions of item-discrimination indices for each factorially homogeneous subset. The items of each such factorially homogeneous subset must be item analyzed against that subset's total to obtain these discrimination indices.

(c) The errors of measurement within each half are statistically independent of each other as well as of the true scores. This implies the necessity to avoid response sets, if they are not theoretically an appropriate part of the true scores. As an additional precaution, to prevent correlated errors of measurement, two items which are exceptionally similar in content must *not* be allocated to different halves. (Many test constructors are under the erroneous impression that such items *should* be allocated to different halves.) (d) The items which have been allocated to the half-tests must be so interwoven into the total test as to preserve simultaneity of administration.

Cronbach and his co-workers,[5] on the other hand, prefer to base their interpretation of the split-half coefficient on an assumption of random sampling of items taken from a larger universe. They make no assumption of homogeneity between halves. In their view, the split-half coefficient can reasonably be interpreted as indicating the adequacy with which the sample of items represents a larger universe.

If each half has many items, the random procedure will approximate that obtained from the "stratified sampling" of items advocated by Cureton. For a given set of items, the reliability calculated on the assumption of randomly parallel forms will be a lower bound of the reliability calculated on the assumption that the items were allocated to forms by the stratified procedure. In any event, the coefficient may be said to reflect the degree to which another sample of items would arrange individuals in the same way as the present sample does.

As we have already said, none of the split-half coefficients offered in the researches under review can be evaluated in terms of either of these sets of assumptions and procedures. However, those coefficients based on long lists of adjectives or questions do at least give a general indication of the degree to which the items are behaving in the same way. This information is of some value in interpreting reported associations between such total scores and theoretically relevant variables.

In contrast to this, some investigators test their hypotheses using a single trait scale, rather than a total score based on a large number of traits. Or they may make repeated tests of the hypothesis, using each of a few trait scales for each of the separate tests. That is, these investigators relate a self-rating value obtained from a single trait scale to some theo-

---

[5]Personal communication, January 12, 1960.

retically relevant variable. In these studies no indication of split-half reliability can be given for the self-rating on any given trait scale. Where coefficients of stability are also unavailable (as is true in almost every study), one cannot tell whether unreliability of the trait scale may be an important factor in weakening the obtained associations between the trait scale and a theoretically relevant variable.

Test-Retest Reliability Coefficients. Regardless of which basis is used for constructing and interpreting the split-half coefficients which may be obtained from the long lists of items, all workers agree on a priori grounds that such coefficients will overestimate the total reliability of a test over time, since the total unreliability includes the instability error as well as the inconsistency error. Dudek (1952) has demonstrated empirically that this is the case under specified conditions of test length and difficulty. Gulliksen (1950) has cited several studies appearing before 1950 which also demonstrated empirically that corrected odd-even coefficients overestimate both test-retest and parallel forms correlations. Such overestimation is partly due to the fact that the split-half coefficient is free of errors associated with time. Then, too, the split-half coefficient cannot be lowered by systematic changes which may occur over time on the variable being measured. In some instances the split-half coefficient may be larger than the coefficient of stability because of the spurious effect of response sets which might be particularly influential at any one testing session (Cronbach, 1946, 1950; Jackson & Messick, 1958).

Response sets would play a specially important role in the numerous instruments where all items are worded negatively (or positively); and in rating scales which have not been preceded by instructions or procedures to avoid halo, the exclusive use of a restricted part of the scale range, etc.

The coefficient of stability is the only appropriate estimate when testing an hypothesis which assumes a relationship over time between the self concept and some alleged influence upon the self concept (e.g., in therapy studies). As we have pointed out, the split-half coefficient is not an adequate substitute for direct empirical exploration of the stability of an instrument over time. Cureton has discussed the serious and unsolved theoretical problems associated with research on stability coefficients in ability testing. As a result of his theoretical analysis, he has argued that "no useful information is provided by the correlation between scores on the same form administered to the same group at two different times" (Cureton, 1958, p. 736). This is in line with his contention that error variance should be uncorrelated with true score if the coefficient is to be interpreted as a reliability coefficient for the combination of factors we are attempting to measure. It is unlikely that error variance is uncorrelated when one obtains a coefficient from two repetitions of the same test.

Self-concept theorists have not discussed such considerations as they might be applicable to self-report instruments. So far as empirical work is concerned, relatively few test-retest *r*s are available on the self-concept measures reviewed in this section. Furthermore, the conditions under which the available data were gathered do not permit firm inferences concerning the influences which may have worked for or against stability.

We conclude, then, that stability of self-concept measures remains a major theoretical and empirical problem.

Reliability Indirectly Implied. In the case where no reliability coefficient for the self-concept measure is reported, one may argue that the finding of predicted correlations with other variables must indirectly imply a certain degree of reliability in the self-concept measure. This is defensible when high intervariable *r*s are obtained. However, low intervariable *r*s are the rule in this area. Such low *r*s might be due to the unreliability of the measures correlated; *or* they might be due to a weak true relationship between variables which have been measured reliably. There is no basis for choosing between these interpretations, so no conclusion about reliability can be drawn from low intervariable *r*s.

SCALING. Scaling problems arise in connection with all those instruments on which *S* describes himself by choosing among several degrees of an adjective or descriptive phrase. Examples of such instruments include the semantic differential scales, graphic rating scales, rating scales with descriptive adjectives to demarcate scale ranges, and questionnaires in which *S* says how frequently the item characterizes him.

With reference to a single item in such an instrument, *E*'s problem is to assign numbers to *S*s to reflect magnitudes on a subjective dimension. As a first step *E* defines the dimension verbally for *S*. *E* then, in effect, asks *S* to regard himself as a "stimulus" and to place this "stimulus" on the subjective dimension *E* has described. To follow these directions, *S* has to do two things: (1) develop a conception of what content and situation the item refers to; (2) develop some psychological metric of the dimension on which he is going to place himself.

In the typical instrument, *S* has to decide for himself to what situations the items refer. For example, is he supposed to rate his degree of self-confidence with reference to dating, participation in sports, or getting along on his job? Is he to take into account both the situations where it would be appropriate and inappropriate to feel depressed? Since the instructions typically do not answer these questions for S, he supposedly places his self-rating on the item with reference to an unknown combination of situational referents. It remains to be demonstrated that scales with such ambiguities yield meaningful scores or ones which are optimally reliable and/or valid indices of self concept.

Assuming that problems of situational ambiguities were satisfactorily resolved, we would still need to explore further the meaning of successive scale steps. How can E interpret S's placement of himself in meaningful numerical terms if he knows nothing of S's psychological metric for the dimension used? How can he interpret the difference between the self placements of two Ss if he does not know that they were using the same psychological metric? Similarly, how can E interpret a difference between S's self placement and his ideal-self placement if he does not know about S's psychological metric? To the extent that we can move from ordinal to ratio scales, we can make our laws involving the scale scores more precise.

Although Guilford (1954), Torgerson (1958), Stevens (1957), and Stevens and Galanter (1957) have discussed how psychophysical methods can be used to derive scales for subjective dimensions, none of the instruments covered in the present review has been refined by the application of such techniques.

Most relevant to the type of scales used by self-concept theorists is recent work by Dudek (1959) and by Cliff (1956), who scaled nine common adverbs of degree in combination with certain evaluative adjectives. Dudek used the constant-sum method, while Cliff employed a successive-intervals method. While each technique was aimed toward achieving a ratio scale, Dudek (1959) reports that the two sets of scale values resulting from the different scaling procedures were not linearly related. Stevens and Galanter (1957) have also noted that for certain kinds of dimensions, "category" scales yield scale values that are curvilinearly related to those derived from methods involving ratio estimations more directly.

The important implications for the present discussion seem to be these: (1) It is possible and desirable to refine rating scale instruments and get more precise knowledge about such subjective continua by applying psychophysical methods. There is available in the literature information which would be useful for devising scales with logical rationales and sound empirical bases. (2) Until we determine why different methods lead to somewhat different scales, "a rigorous operational approach in interpreting and using variously derived scales seems indicated" (Dudek, 1959, p. 547).

VALIDITY. When we consider the validity of questionnaires, rating scales, and check lists for inferring phenomenal self-regard, we may repeat many of the observations we made about Q sorts. One can, for most of the instruments, get little or no idea from published information as to what universe of self-conceptualizations is represented by the items. The rationale and procedures for item choice have often not been indicated, and the wording of questions or definitions of trait terms are often not available for the reader to inspect. A very great variety of items and instruments have been used by different investigators, but there is a sparsity of empirical information about how the various alleged measures of self-regard intercorrelate. Although the reader might wish to attempt to compare logical or face validities, or to try to make comparative "process analyses," the lack of explicit published information precludes such attempts for the most part. It would be easy to fall into the semantic fallacy of believing that variables given the same name by different investigators are in fact the same, or that variables given different names are in fact different.

One kind of process analysis we can partially make involves the comparison of various types of scores employed to index self-regard. It was earlier pointed out that the self-ideal correlation obtained from Q sorting was an index computed by E and did not necessarily directly reflect S's perception of the difference between his actual self and ideal self. In some rating scales or questionnaires, S marks self and ideal for each item as he goes along. In other such instruments there are few items so that S can remember his self-rating when later placing his ideal rating for each item. Thus in the case of many questionnaires, adjective check lists, and rating scales, one can feel fairly sure that the discrepancy S reports is not masked by failures of memory, or by lack of opportunity for direct comparisons. On the other hand, the ease of falsification and possible influence of response sets seem greater for the rating-scale and questionnaire techniques than for Q sorts. So we must conclude that no method yet devised seems to solve all possible problems satisfactorily.

As in the case of the Q sort, many items are given equal weight in determining a global score for the type of instrument discussed in this section. This practice involves some questionable assumptions about the comparability of items with respect to their perceived salience for S's self-regard and with respect to their psychological metrics. A special case of this questionable practice (which also has its counterpart in the Q sort) is the common procedure of dealing with [Self — Ideal] discrepancies without regard to sign. That is, E pays no attention to whether S says his actual self is more favorable or less favorable than his stated ideal self (when "favorability" is indexed by E in terms of the cultural norm). Is it really justifiable to sum without regard to sign? Reversals from the usual type of discrepancy may occur only rarely in rating scales, but this fact remains to be established empirically for each instrument. If reversals do occur with any frequency, their possible psychological meaning and their effect upon the predictive power of total [Self — Ideal] scores should be isolated for further study.

Still unresolved are various problems relevant to the construct validity and empirical validity of the [Self — Ideal] score. For example, the question of the relative contribution of Self rating and Ideal rating to variance in the two-part score has not been satisfactorily answered in regard to any of these instruments, any more than it has been in regard to Q-sorting techniques. Similarly, we do not know the relative contribution of each part of the [Self — Ideal] score to the correlations between the dual index and theory-relevant behaviors.

If inter-S Ideal ratings show little variance as compared to inter-S Self ratings on each item, little or nothing will be contributed by the Ideal ratings to inter-S variability in total [Self — Ideal] scores. We have already cited evidence from Bills's and Worchel's data indicating the occurrence of low inter-S variance in Ideal ratings. Other examples can be pointed out. Jourard and Secord (1955) have shown that inter-S SDs of Ideal ratings for sizes of body dimensions are smaller than SDs of Ss' estimates of the actual size of those dimensions. Rapaport (1958) showed that inter-S variability on "ideal self" was smaller than on "real self" for ten out of twelve MMPI scales. Four of these F tests reached the .05 level or better. Rosen (1956a) reported that inter-S variance on MMPI responses under personal-ideal instructions was smaller than under actual-self instructions or social-desirability instructions.

A number of investigators have found weak or insignificant relationships between Bills's IAV Ideal scores and other variables which did relate significantly to Self, Self-Acceptance, or [Self—Ideal] discrepancies. (See, for example, Cowen, Heilizer, Axelrod, & Alexander, 1957, in re Taylor Anxiety Scores and Lie Scores; Cowen, 1956, in re Brownfain's negative self concept.)

Pertinent to this issue we have also noted that correlations between theoretically relevant variables and Self scores (or directly obtained Self-Acceptance scores) are at least as high and usually higher than those obtained from two-part indices from the same instrument (e.g., from [Self—Ideal] or from [Self—Other]). In the case of the Self scores we are, in effect, dealing with another two-part score, i.e., the Self rating is assigned a value in terms of its distance from an assumed cultural norm. What does this imply? S may or may not have accepted the cultural norm as his personal ideal. Therefore we cannot be sure that the Self score is a consistently phenomenal index of self-regard. If an index which may be partly nonphenomenal predicts behaviors better than does a consistently phenomenal index, this is of potential importance to phenomenological theory, which assigns so much weight to the role of the phenomenal self in predicting behavior.

Another common score used as a basis for inferring self-regard is based on the direct rating by S of the degree to which his status on various characteristics is acceptable to him. Some persons have also inferred "self-acceptance" from the [Self—Ideal] discrepancy score. But one could argue that the direct self-acceptance rating has the greater possibility of having construct validity for inferring self-acceptance, since S presumably takes into consideration while making the direct rating not only how far his actual self is discrepant from his ideal self, but how disturbing or acceptable this discrepancy is to him.

Also pertinent to the question of discriminant validity of the various self-regard measures is an examination of available score intercorrelations involving the same and different instruments. The highest of these correlations seem to involve alternate self-regard scores derived from the same instrument (e.g., Self, [Self—Ideal], and Self-Acceptance from the Index of Adjustment and Values). There is no evidence that scores derived from a certain scoring method (e.g., [Self—Ideal] *or* Self-Acceptance *or* Self) correlate more highly across different instruments (within their respective scoring types) than do scores of different types derived from the same instrument. Actually no systematic explorations of this point have been made.

Thus we conclude: (1) Despite the fact that different scoring procedures have been assigned different verbal labels (e.g., self-acceptance, self-esteem, [Self—Ideal] discrepancy), their discriminant validity for inferring different aspects of phenomenal self-regard has not been demonstrated. (2) While the available data are quite limited, there is some evidence that scores derived from different instruments, utilizing varying content, different operations on S's part, and different scoring procedures do tend to be measuring a common variable or variables, to a slight or moderate degree. (3) The construct validity of any one of these instruments for measuring phenomenal self-regard remains to be demonstrated, although Bills presents the most pertinent and convincing evidence on this question.

c. Coding Plans for Interview Materials

A number of investigators have developed schema for coding interviews with respect to expressed attitudes toward the self. In every case the interest of the investigator was in studying psychotherapy from the viewpoint of self-concept theory, but there is no reason why one could not apply the schema to interviews of other kinds, or to written self-descriptions. In practice, each scheme has been used only by the investigator who devised it and perhaps by one or two other persons, so far as the present writer could determine. For each coding plan some information about interjudge reliability is offered, but no satisfactory demonstration of construct validity for indexing the phenomenal self has been made. (The reader will find a general discussion of problems in psychotherapy research and a description of studies involving coded interviews in Chapter IV, Section C-5. Further reference to some of these studies is in Chapter IV, Section C-10, on self-acceptance and acceptance of others.)

Raimy (1948) seems to have been the first psychologist to introduce this method. Everything the S said between two counselor responses was counted as a unit, and six categories were used for classifying units: positive self-attitude, negative self-attitude, ambivalent self-reference, ambiguous self-reference, other or external reference, and informational question. Three out of four judges coded 356 client responses with percentages of agreement ranging from 50.5% for "ambivalent" to 81% for informational question. One judge after six months reclassified 874 responses with percentages of agreement ranging from 47.5 for the ambivalent category to 87.2 for informational question.

Bugental (1949, 1952) extended Raimy's idea to develop a Conceptual Matrix Method which calls for the distribution of thought units into six categories: (1) self-polar (self-descriptive), (2) self-on-self (one aspect of self affects another aspect of self), (3) not-self-on-self, (4) self-on-not-self, (5) not-self-on-not-self, (6) not-self polar (simple description of not-self). A thought unit is "patterned on, but not identical with the independent clause of formal grammar" (Bugental, 1949, p. 28). Following Raimy, the attitudinal tone of each category assignment is given one of four values: (1) positive or approving, (2) negative or disapproving, (3) ambivalent, (4) descriptive or lacking in affective tone. Four raters and the author rated five protocols with "overall reliabilities of six ratings of five samples" being as follows: for unit determination, 87.4%; for categorization, 59.1%; and for evaluation, 75.0%. Preliminary explorations of stability over time and individual differences in patterns between Ss were made, but no general statement is possible.

Another coding scheme which involves dividing statements according to self- and not-self referents is that of Vargas (1954). He was particularly interested in the emerging of new self-descriptions ("self-awareness") during therapy. We may paraphrase his categories of client statements as follows, giving in parentheses the percentages of agreement between two judges. (The percentages of agreement are based on an unspecified number of statements.)

1. non-self-description
2. self-description (96%)
   a. original self-description (first verbalization of this self-description in therapy) (86.7%)
      1) familiar original = well known to client (75.7%)
      2) emergent original = emerging during counseling (84.4%)
      3) undetermined origin (neither [1] nor [2]) (100%)
   b. repeated self-description (75.7%) (if presented in another new instance, as in recurring symptoms, called another instance of previous self-description) (56.6%)

Stock's (1949) system was more complex than the ones just described. She set up ten content categories for classifying client statements according to their self or other referents and according to qualitatively distinguishable feelings about self in relation to others. Each unit (i.e., each client statement appearing between two successive counselor responses) was placed in one of the ten content categories and was also judged for intensity and direction of feeling according to a specified scaling system. To explore reliability, two judges categorized each statement from three interviews. The percentages of exact agreement for each interview ranged from 68.5 to 82.2.

Scheerer's (1949) scheme yielded greater interjudge agreement than that of Raimy, Bugental, or Stock. With the aid of four judges she made extensive definitions of "acceptance of and responsibility for self" and "acceptance of and responsibility for others" and set up five-point scales for each variable. Each unit of client response (delineated by the investigator) was judged on the appropriate five-point scale of intensity. To explore reliability, three judges rated all units in six interviews. At least two out of the three judges agreed 93.8% of the time. On only four out of 178 Self units did any one judge's rating deviate by two scale points from both other judges' ratings.

As we have already noted, Scheerer's definition of self- and other-acceptance has formed the basis for the development of two inventories purporting to measure "self-acceptance" (Berger and Phillips, described in Section B-1). In addition, her definition has been used by Raskin, who selected four of her points for development of a "locus-of-evaluation" scale which he applied to therapy interviews in an effort to determine whether the client felt dependent on himself or on judgments of others for his self-evaluations. Interjudge reliability on 59 items was $+.91$.

Rosenman (1955) attempted to make distinctions which he believes have been erroneously overlooked by previous theorists and researchers, i.e., he wanted to distinguish S's perceptions of his actions from his perceptions of his evaluations. Using the sentence as his basic unit, he coded Ss' statements as to whether (1) an action or an evaluation was involved; (2) the action or evaluation was positive or negative in tone; (3) the action or evaluation involved a self-toward-self, self-toward-others, or others-toward-self relationship. Further details are given in an unpublished dissertation, and below.

Lipkin (1954) used the phrase as his basic unit, rather than following the precedent of the other investigators in choosing longer, more complicated divisions of the interview material as units. He applied his analysis to special postsession interviews obtained during therapy. Two of his nine categories were "current preception of self" and "past perception of self"; and each categorized phrase was classed as positive, negative, confused, or ambivalent with varying degrees of intensity of the first three being rated. By a complicated reliability formula, interjudge agreements were obtained ranging between 81.9% and 100%.

2. Instruments Purporting to Index Aspects of the Phenomenal Self besides Self-Regard

We have devoted considerable space to various indices purporting to measure self-esteem or self-acceptance. Such constructs are not the only ones which self-concept theorists deem important, but other aspects or attributes of the phenomenal self which theorists have stressed have received little or no attention from research workers.

One characteristic of the phenomenal self which has been repeatedly discussed is its configurational properties. It has been emphasized that the phenomenal self is a more or less internally differentiated Gestalt from which inconsistent self percepts seem to be excluded. Some theorists (e.g., Rogers, 1951a) have postulated a drive for maintaining the organization of the self-concept. No criteria for operationally defining "organization," "configuration," "differentiation," and "(in)consistent" seem to be clearly implied by the theoretical statements; but it seems clear that inconsistency is not to be equated with evaluative tone. That is, a self characteristic which is actually more favorable than S's present self-perception may be excluded because it contradicts the present self concept, while one which is unfavorable may be accepted into the self concept if it fits the presently held view of self.

Probably the reason so little empirical work has been done on these characteristics of the phenomenal self is that the theoretical propositions referring to these characteristics are vague and ambiguous. We need a much more thoroughgoing theoretical analysis of what might constitute meaningful subdivisions of the self concept, what is meant by differentiation within the phenomenal self, and what types of self-concept inconsistencies may occur. In the absence of such an analysis, a few investigators have suggested operational meanings for such terms as "organizational properties," "consistency and inconsistency," and "differentiation."

We have already discussed Butler and Haigh's idea that the Q sort is a possible means of studying the organizational properties of the self concept; and we have questioned their notion on a number of grounds discussed earlier in this chapter.

Following Sarbin's (1952) theory of self-development, Mathews, Hardyck, and Sarbin (1953) postulated three successive developmental levels of "self-organization," labelled: S3, Primitive Construed Self; S4, Introjecting-Extrojecting Self; and S5, Social Self. Apparently these terms refer at least partially to phenomenal self-organization since "self is considered a cognitive structure" and the "selves operate as reference-schemata in the person's cognitive, affective, and conative behavior" (Mathews, Hardyck, & Sarbin, 1953, p. 500). As operational definitions of these three levels, specified profile differentiations on the MMPI are used. No detailed rationale for the construct validity of these scoring criteria is offered, and the connection between the different phenomenal self-organizations and the corresponding MMPI profiles seems to the present writer to be complex, obscure, and tenuous. They obtained some but not all of the predicted associations between self-classification and behavior on cognitive tasks involving conflict and/or categorizing behavior. But for various reasons, including no specified matching of Ss on relevant variables, the design of the study seems to be open to many alternate interpretations. Therefore the results offer no clear support for the construct validity of this index of self-organization.

As indicated above, there is no clear delineation of what might be meant by inconsistency, and many meanings of the term could be imagined. For example, one might suppose that discrepancies between self and ideal could exemplify one type of inconsistency; but since these discrepancies have been considered in detail earlier in this chapter, they will not be discussed here. Two other possible dimensions of consistency-inconsistency are: (1) between S's private-self concept and his social-self concept; and (2) between S's private- or social-self concept and others' concepts of him. Since these matters are fully discussed in Chapter VI, they will not be taken up here. Other dimensions of consistency-inconsistency might involve discrepancies between various aspects of the private-self concept or between various aspects of the social-self concept. No studies have concerned themselves with the former; but Rosalind Cartwright's measure outlined below may pertain to the latter. In addition it seems that we should consider the possibility of discrepancies or inconsistencies within the ideal self. McKenna, Hofstaetter, and O'Connor (1956) found the ideal self to be factorially complex, and this result caused them to point out the need for research on the question of within-ideal discrepancies.

Although we may think of numerous possible meanings of consistency, only two investigators have concerned themselves specifically with a construct they labelled "consistency." The first dealt with consistency between social-self concepts; and the second was interested in consistency between experiences (or stimuli) and the self concept.

Rosalind Dymond Cartwright (1957) has attempted to index consistency among social-self concepts by comparing three Q sorts made by S to describe S's idea of how three different persons viewed him. Mean item variance among the three sorts was the measure of consistency. Such a procedure is subject to all the limitations of Q-sorting techniques and comparisons among sorts discussed earlier in this chapter. Nevertheless, if other sources of unreliability can be minimized, it seems plausible that large mean variances may indicate serious disagreements among S's social-self concepts. Of course, the patterning or configurational aspects of such inconsistencies cannot be so simply indexed.

The only other empirical work on the "consistency" variable is that of D. Cartwright (1956), who had in mind a somewhat different idea of consistency. He was interested in Rogers's contention (1951a) that experiences will be ignored or given distorted symbolization if they are inconsistent with the structure of the self. Cartwright substituted the word "stimulus" for "experience" and defined an inconsistent stimulus as "one having a content or meaning that is either unrelated to or descriptive of the opposite of some aspect of the self-structure" (p. 212). It seems that we have within this definition two rather different meanings of "inconsistent." He used three different kinds of stimuli: nonsense syllables, adjectives, and names of possessions. The operational definition of consistency differed from one of these kinds of stimuli to another. (1) Nonsense syllables which S made up himself were said to be more consistent with self than were syllables selected from Glaze's list. (2) An adjective was chosen to summarize each of a group of Q-sort statements which S had sorted to describe himself. If a Q-sort statement had been placed by S in either one of the two most "like me" piles, the adjective summarizing the statement was said to be a stimulus which was consistent with S's self. If a Q-sort statement had been placed by S in either one of the two most "unlike me" piles, the adjective summarizing it was said to be inconsistent with S's self. (3) Names of possessions were said to be consistent with S's self concept if he had sorted them into "most like me to own" piles, and inconsistent if he had sorted them into "most unlike me to own" piles. The construct validity of these stimuli for measuring consistency between experiences (or stimuli) and the self concept has not been demonstrated. The learning experiment involving the stimuli selected by the above operations is discussed in Chapter IV.

Only one study has specifically concerned itself with "differentiation" within the phenomenal self. Jourard and Remy (1957) have defined "differentiation within the phenomenal self" as "the subject's recognition and differential response to the various parts of which the total self is comprised." They have proposed that "one measure of differential behavior is an individual's *variance* in responding to a questionnaire comprised of items which derive from the same conceptual universe" (Jourard & Remy, 1957, p. 62). The construct validity of such a measure for indexing differentiation within the phenomenal self has not been demonstrated, however, for the reason we shall now explain. Since Jourard and Remy's traits are evaluative, the mean of the self-ratings from all the items (traits) is a self-esteem score. The S whose self-ratings vary a great deal from trait to trait must necessarily get a lower mean self-esteem score than does an S who rates himself consistently at the high end of every trait scale. This implies that the self-concept differentiation score (interitem variance) must correlate with the self-esteem score (item mean). Thus we must question the discriminant validity of their index of differentiation within the self concept.

Summary. Although the alleged configurational properties of the self concept have received much theoretical emphasis, little empirical work has been done to define these properties operationally and relate them to theoretically relevant variables. This is probably due in part to the vagueness of the theoretical formulations concerning such constructs as "organization," "configuration," "differentiation," and "consistency."

We have reviewed five measures, each purporting to index a different configurational construct, each using different operations. Information on relevant construct validity is not available for any of these measures. In some cases it seems that constructs other than the Gestalt properties of the self concept could parsimoniously account for individual differences in the scores. For example, level of self-regard is sometimes confounded with the "configurational" influences upon the index. We raised the question earlier in the chapter as to whether configurational properties can ever be represented by a single score.

IV

Studies Purporting to Relate the Phenomenal Self to Other Variables and/or to Test Some Aspect of Self-Concept Theory

A. An Analysis of Problems of Research Design

We shall turn later in this chapter to results of studies purporting to relate self-concept measures to other variables in order to test hypotheses concerning (1) factors which influence the self concept, and (2) the role of the self concept in behavior. First, however, we shall summarize the most common kinds of problems in research design which one finds in these studies.

The worth of such research depends heavily upon the characteristics of the measuring instruments used. As we brought out in detail in Chapter III, many different instruments have been employed, the majority of them only once or twice; and little or no information on reliability and construct validity is available for a great many of these measures. Therefore while reading about the studies reported in this chapter, the reader will wish to refer to Tables I through IV and to appropriate places in Chapter III or V for details on the content, reliability, and validity of these indices. Appropriate table and/or chapter references will be given with each study as it is discussed.

There are of course other problems of research design besides those concerning measurement, and we need to consider them too. We may profitably summarize here some general considerations about design problems.

As we have indicated in Chapter II, we do not believe the testing of phenomenological theories requires a methodologically distinct approach from that which is appropriate to testing more behavioristic theories. Although R-R correlational designs may be easier, and may even seem at first glance to be more appropriate, we concluded in Chapter II that controlled antecedent-consequent studies are as necessary and appropriate in this area as in any other area of psychology.

As will become apparent later in this chapter, many of the propositions of self-concept theory are historical in the genetic sense or are hypotheses concerning cause-effect relationships. To test such propositions, investigators should plan controlled experiments or "naturalistic" controlled observational setups in which consequents are studied as a function of experimentally manipulated or otherwise specifiably variable antecedents. It is also necessary that the antecedents, consequents, and inferred constructs be chosen and defined as closely as possible in terms of their theoretical relevance. Unfortunately such designs are extremely rare.

Some propositions from self theory are not clearly directional, i.e., they do not specify definitely which variable is antecedent and which is consequent. This leaves us two alternatives. We may resort to cross-sectional research designs, in which two contemporaneous variables are measured and correlated. Or we may seek further refinement and clarification of such theoretical propositions before undertaking research on them. Even if one chooses the first alternative, there are more or less controlled and informative variations of the R-R design.

Specifications for controlled research design have been discussed in numerous places. Among the most recent and directly applicable to this area of research are Underwood's (1957) and Campbell's (1957) analyses. The former covers a wide range of research designs, and demonstrates effectively the limitations and difficulties encountered when trying to use subject variables as independent variables. Campbell does not deal with problems of control in R-R studies, but his analytical summary of experimental designs has been developed with special reference to investigations performed in social settings.

There are so many particular ways in which research designs can be inadequately controlled that space does not permit a detailed analysis here. However, one can make the general statement that the designs of the majority of researches in the area of self-concept theory have been uncontrolled in one or more important respects. A concrete evaluation of each study will be made when it is summarized, but we can list the most common classes of difficulties here (in addition to the problems of measurement already discussed in detail in Chapter III).

1. The method used is often so vaguely indicated as to prevent analysis and make replication impossible. This is particularly unfortunate in a relatively new research area where well-known, standardized methods are not available. Since journal space is limited, more use should be made of the facilities of the American Documentation Institute.

2. In some studies there are not enough different control groups to hold constant or account for all the important irrelevant variables. Frequently the inherent characteristics of the control *S*s, their method of choice, and/or their treatment is inappropriate. Of course where control groups are inadequate in any of these ways, it cannot be concluded that the dependent variable is a function of the alleged independent variable. Factors left uncontrolled in one or another study include all those listed as extraneous by Campbell (1957). Frequently no information is given as to matching or randomizing of groups. Thus in many studies one cannot pinpoint just which factors may afford alternate interpretations of the findings.

3. The use of demographic or sociological independent variables which have unknown relevance to psychological variables precludes clear psychological interpretation of obtained associations.

4. In many studies there is a strong possibility of artifactual contamination between independent and dependent variables, due to overlapping instruments, failure to use blind judgments, effects of common response sets, etc. Artifactual contamination is especially likely to occur when two-part scores are used to measure either or both variables.

5. Various types of overgeneralization occur. In their conclusions and discussions, *E*s sometimes do not respect the limitations imposed by their restricted hypotheses, measuring instruments, groups, and procedures. In some studies it appears that psychological generalizations are based on findings of unclear statistical significance. This is due to *E*s' failure to adhere to commonly accepted statistical conventions.

    a. One-tailed tests have been used in situations where theoretical predictions are not unequivocal and where "reverse" trends are interpreted *ad hoc* by *E*.

    b. Separate replicative interpretations of hypotheses are sometimes based on data which are nonindependent (e.g., repeated tests of the same *S*s with correlated instruments).

c. Within any one study which yields many significance tests, five in one hundred such tests may be significant at the .05 level by chance only. Nevertheless, some *E*s have assigned psychological interpretations to such findings.

d. A special problem of this sort involves establishing a "chance" base line when trying to determine *S*'s accuracy in predicting a particular person's behavior, or when trying to determine the degree of similarity between *S*'s self concept and that of a theoretically relevant other person. What degree of correctness or similarity might be expected by "chance"? What degree of correctness might be expected if *S* predicts another unique person's behavior on the basis of his stereotype about others in general, or others in the predictee's age, sex, or social group? To what extent does the similarity between two particular individuals of special interest to *E* exceed the similarity to be expected between any two persons from the respective groups to which these individuals belong? Of course the latter two questions require control groups of predictees, and are not simply questions of statistical interpretation, based on an assumption about "chance" base lines.

6. Most studies have been one-shot affairs with no replication, or even cross-validation of instruments. It is probable that some of the statistically significant findings are actually due to chance and could not be replicated. Perhaps some of the significant findings may depend on particular idiosyncrasies of procedure and instrument which are theoretically irrelevant. And of course null findings obtained from a single study are uninterpretable.

Campbell (1957) has argued against exact replication on the grounds that replication continues the confounding of (a) theoretically relevant aspects of the independent variable and the observational techniques with (b) specific artifacts of unknown influence. On the other hand, he recognizes the fact that only confusion can result from trying to synthesize results obtained from heterogeneous, unreplicated results. He suggests that a "transition experiment" may be useful. In such an experiment, the "theory-independent" aspects of the independent variable and the observational techniques are varied in a multiple design, one segment of which exactly replicates the original experiment (Campbell, 1957, p. 310).

7. Even though cross-sectional R-R studies cannot support cause-effect inferences, they could, if properly controlled and based on enough responses, afford a factor-analytic interpretation. Unfortunately such an ideal situation rarely occurs among the actual studies.

In evaluating the individual studies, we have not pointed out every criticism which could be made. If we have mentioned one or two weaknesses of method which make the results ambiguous, it has seemed redundant to detail other criticisms as well. Also to save space we have not commented systematically on the well-controlled or ingenious aspects of the various investigations.

B. An Introductory Orientation to Empirical Categories of Studies to Be Reviewed

The investigations of the phenomenal self concept, which constitute the rest of this chapter, will be presented in the order outlined below.

(1) Descriptive studies of the development of the self concept.

(2) Studies of the variables which are presumed to influence the development and current characteristics of the self concept (i.e., studies in which the self concept is the consequent).

> parent-child interaction
> social interaction (other than parent-child)
> body characteristics
> counseling and psychotherapy
> lobotomy
> experimentally induced success and failure
> learning

(3) Studies in which the self concept is related to behavior. This category includes studies of behaviors which are presumed to depend on the self concept (i.e., the self concept is the antecedent), and studies in which the direction of influence between the self concept and the other behavior variables is not specified.

> performance in learning tasks
> self-regard and "adjustment"
> self-acceptance and acceptance of others
> self-regard and ethnocentrism or authoritarianism
> self-regard and level-of-aspiration behavior

One qualification of the above scheme should be pointed out. Contrary to the major heading, a few of the researches on topics listed under (2) are based on the assumption that self-concept variables are antecedents rather than consequents. For example, the topic of experimental failure was classified under (2) because most of the studies concerned the influence of failure upon the self concept. However, a *few* of them are based on the hypothesis that reactions to experimental failure will be a function of self-concept variables. It seems better to keep together all investigations bearing on one factor (e.g., experimental failure), even if that means deviating temporarily from the major classification scheme, which is based on directions of assumed cause-effect relationships.

C. SUMMARIES AND CRITICISMS OF STUDIES, GROUPED IN EMPIRICAL CATEGORIES

1. *Development of the Self Concept*

At present there are no longitudinal data on which to base a description of the development of the self concept. In lieu of such data one might think that results from cross-sectional studies of various age groups could be pieced together to attain a tentative developmental picture. This is impossible, however, due to the wide differences in instruments, relevant characteristics of Ss, and testing conditions in the studies under review.

Six quite disparate investigations, which come as close as any to being developmentally oriented, have been selected for mention here.

Ames's report on nursery school children presents a summary of "data in regard to the growing sense of self such as can be derived from verbalizations to self or to others . . . data are objective in that they consist of actual statements and behaviors of [approximately 100-150] subjects. They are however selective. Behaviors and verbalizations considered most pertinent by the observer were recorded and from these records most pertinent data were further selected" (Ames, 1952, p. 194). "From these observations we have built up a developmental picture of the sense of self as it appears to change from age to age" (from one month through 3½ years) (p. 229). The usual procedures for standardizing recording conditions, exploring interobserver reliability, and demonstrating construct validity of behavior categories as indices of "sense of self" were not followed, since the investigator evidently felt they were inappropriate or unfeasible for exploratory work. The study is suggestive, but rather diffuse and inconclusive.

Using fourth- and sixth-grade children as Ss, Perkins (1958b) obtained a significant increase in self-ideal congruence over a six-month period. (See Table I.) He also found that the sixth-grade children showed greater self-ideal congruence than did the fourth-grade Ss. Several interpretations of these findings are possible: (1) They represent developmental changes of some kind in self-ideal congruence. (2) They may reflect the greater reliability in sorting which would come with greater familiarity with the instrument and improved reading skills. (The two-day test-retest reliability of the self-sort was nonsignificantly greater in the sixth-grade group.)

The only study which compares children of widely different ages is that of Havighurst, Robinson, and Dorr (1946). These investigators were interested in the development of the ideal self, as indexed by compositions written to describe "The Person I Would Like to Be Like." Responses fell mainly into four categories: parents or family members, glamorous persons, attractive visible adults, and composite imaginary persons. Because their nine groups of Ss were not selected so as to yield a closely controlled analysis of any one variable such as age, the authors offer the following very tentative description of an age sequence. Although the trend is not rigid, and some steps may be missed, the children's choices tended to move away from the family circle with age. From ages six to eight, parents or some other family member were typical choices. From ages eight to sixteen, children tended to describe glamorous persons, then attractive visible adults, and finally composite, imaginary persons.

The three other studies which are concerned partially with developmental problems are the investigations of adolescents made by Smith and Lebo (1956), Mussen and Jones (1957), and Engel (1959).

The first two of these researches involved hypotheses about the relationship of the self concept to varying degrees of physical maturity. They are described in detail in Section C-4, below, which deals with body characteristics and the self concept.

The third adolescent study explored the test-retest stability of the self concept in 172 Ss over a two-year period (Engel, 1959). One group of boys and girls was tested in the eighth and tenth grades, while the second group was tested in tenth and twelfth grades. The Ss Q sorted items which had been prejudged for positive or negative tone. (See

Table I.) Results are given in terms of r values which correspond to mean self-self correlations. For 23 of the Ss the average self-self correlation over a ten-day period was $+.68$. By comparison, the average self-self r over a two-year period was $+.53$.

There was no significant difference between the older and younger groups with respect to self-self correlations over the two-year period. This confirmed the author's hypothesis which was based on the assumption that "crystallization of the self-concept is achieved earlier in development" (Engel, 1959, p. 212).

Self-sorts were scored according to the prejudged favorability values of the items. Over the two-year period there was an unpredicted increase in mean favorability of the self concept, significant beyond the .05 level in the case of the older group. Ss whose self concepts were unfavorable on the first test showed significantly greater change in self concept over the two-year period than did Ss whose self concepts were favorable at first testing. Since Ss classed as having unfavorable self concepts included only the lowest 20% of the self-concept distribution for the first test, and Ss classed as having favorable self concepts included the upper 80% of that distribution, it seems that statistical regression effects have not been controlled for in this comparison.

2. Parent-Child Interaction and the Self Concept

RATIONALE

All personality theorists who are concerned with constructs involving the self accord great importance to parent-child interaction in the development of the self concept. This notion follows from such general ideas as these: (a) The self concept is a learned constellation of perceptions, cognitions, and values. (b) An important part of this learning comes from observing the reactions one gets from other persons. (c) The parents are the persons who are present earliest and most consistently. For this reason, and because of the child's dependence on them and his affection for them, the parents have a unique opportunity to reinforce selectively the child's learning. Presumably, then, the parent can influence the development of such aspects of the self concept as the following: (a) the generalized level of self-regard (e.g., by being loved and accepted the child comes to love himself, and through acquisition of accepted [reinforced] behaviors he comes to respect his own functioning); (b) the subjective standards of conduct which are associated with his role and individual status (i.e., the development of the ideal self); (c) the realism of his view of his abilities and limitations, and the acceptance of them; (d) the degree of acceptance in the phenomenal self concept of inevitable characteristics (e.g., hostility, jealousy, sex); (e) the adequacy of his means of appraising accurately his effects on others.

Considering the central importance of such notions in self-concept theory, the paucity of available studies on parent-child interaction is amazing. But contemplation of the difficulties inherent in designing and executing such investigations makes it understandable why they are few in number and generally inconclusive.

At the very minimum we need antecedent-consequent studies in which specified theoretically relevant parent variables are related to theoretically relevant child variables. Cross-sectional researches aimed at establishing antecedent-consequent relationships are not sufficient for a number of reasons. They give us no way of inferring that the supposedly crucial parental variable influenced the child's self concept. Furthermore, they throw light on the self-concept variable(s) at only one, possibly atypical, time. The setting up of formal experiments which systematically vary relevant aspects of parental treatment seems to be out of the question for practical and ethical reasons, but at least we could examine thoroughly the possibility for forming appropriate control groups selected from natural settings.

In contrast to the ideal requirements, the available studies are all of the R-R variety. In some of them, two or more responses from the child are compared (e.g., the child's view of self and of parent). In other studies, one or more child responses are compared with one or more parent responses (e.g., the child's self concept is compared to the parent's self concept).

The results from these investigations cannot be directly synthesized since the assumptions, hypotheses, measuring instruments, and procedures varied so widely. As an introduction to a review of the available literature, we shall first summarize some questions to which the studies were directed. We shall then briefly present and evaluate each study, and finally we shall summarize our conclusions based on this overview.

In formulating the introductory list of questions we have taken the liberty of rephrasing some of the hypotheses, as stated by their authors. By the process of rephrasing and categorizing the hypotheses, we hope to clarify the meanings of the questions which the authors have raised, so that the studies may be more accurately compared and contrasted. Partly the rewording involves "translating" specific terms used by certain authors into the terms used throughout this book. For example, "self-cathexis" is written below as self-regard. The word "child" is used below regardless of the age of the Ss at the time the data were gathered. Thus college students are children if the data concern them and their parents.

More importantly, our rewording is intended to bring out the types of observation by which the hypotheses were actually explored, as distinct from the inferences the authors hoped to draw. Such "operational paraphrasing" may make the questions appear cumbersome and confusing. We sympathize with the reader, but we can only say that the translation process has actually clarified and simplified the questions. This is so because the simplicity of some of the original statements was more apparent than real. For example, the following question appears simple: Do children identify more with like-sex than with opposite-sex parents? In one study what the authors mean by this is: When given a choice, do children describe their like-sex parent or their opposite-sex parent? (Porter & Stacey, 1956). In two other studies, this question would mean: Do children see more similarity between their own self concepts and the self concepts they attribute to their like-sex parent than they do between their own self concept and the self concept they attribute to their opposite-sex parent? (Sopchak, 1952; Beier & Ratzeburg, 1953). To another author, this question means: Do children's self concepts resemble their views of their like-sex parent's characteristics more than their views of their opposite-sex parent's characteristics? (Manis, 1958).

When one studies the literature in this area it becomes apparent that one can meaningfully analyze and compare the aims of the authors only when superficially simple questions are more explicitly formulated. As the reader will soon realize, this particular area of research is at best an extremely confusing one.

Finally, we note that, with one or two exceptions, we have included in these questions only those on which the authors thought they had obtained some positive findings. The list of questions would be much longer, were we to include those which were raised but remained unanswered due to unreplicated null findings. We shall reserve until later our judgment as to which of the "positive" findings are clear and non-artifactual.

QUESTIONS ON PARENT-CHILD INTERACTION
AND THE SELF CONCEPT

The first group of these questions centers around relationships between two views which the child reports, one view concerning himself, and the other view concerning his parent's attitudes toward him.

(a) Is high self-regard in a child associated with his feeling that his parents regard him highly? Is low self-regard in a child associated with his feeling that his parents have low regard for him? (Jourard & Remy, 1955)

(b) Is a child's maladjustment, as inferred from his self-reports, associated with his perception that his parents hold him in low regard? (Manis, 1958)

(c) Is a child's maladjustment, as inferred from his self-reports, associated with his perception that his parents differ from one another in their evaluations of him? (Manis, 1958)

(d) Is a child's self-reported tendency to blame himself associated with any particular memories he has as to parental discipline he received? (Henry, 1956)

The second group of questions also centers around relationships between two views that the child holds. One of these views again concerns the child's concept of himself. The other view is the child's perception of what his parents are actually like, *or* the child's perception of the parents' self concepts.

(e) Where is there more similarity: between a child's self concept and the self concept he attributes to his parent, or between a child's self concept and the self concept he attributes to "most other people"? (Sopchak, 1952)

(f) Where is there more similarity: between a child's self concept and the self concept he attributes to his like-sex parent, or between a child's self concept and the self concept he attributes to his opposite-sex parent? (Sopchak, 1952; Beier & Ratzeburg, 1953). A different version of this question is asked by Manis (1958). Where is there more similarity: between a child's self concept and his description of his like-sex parent, or between a child's self concept and his description of his opposite-sex parent?

(g) In the three related questions included under (g), "adjustment," "anxiety," and "degree of self-regard" are all inferred from children's self-reports. Are the self concepts of well-adjusted children similar to their view of their parents' characteristics, while the self concepts of maladjusted children are dissimilar to their view of their parents' characteristics? (Manis, 1958). Are the self concepts of less anxious children similar to their view of their parents' characteristics, while the self concepts of more anxious children are dissimilar to their view of their parents' characteristics? (Lazowick, 1955). Do children with high self-regard think their parents' characteristics are like their own self concepts, while children with low self-regard think their parents' characteristics are dissimilar to their own self concepts? (Jourard, 1957)

(h) If a child regards his parent highly, will his self concept tend to be similar to his perception of his parent's characteristics? If he holds his parent in low regard, will his self concept tend to differ from his perception of his parent's characteristics? (Jourard, 1957)

(i) If a child thinks that his parent's characteristics are close to the child's ideal for that parent, does the child's self concept resemble his view of the parent's characteristics? Conversely, if a child thinks that his parent's characteristics fall short of the child's ideal for that parent, is the child's self concept dissimilar to his view of the parent's characteristics? (Jourard, 1957)

(j) If a child thinks that his parent's characteristics are close to the child's ideal for that parent, does the child regard the parent highly? Conversely, if a child thinks that his parent falls short of the child's ideal for that parent, does the child have low regard for the parent? (Jourard, 1957)

(k) Are children's self concepts similar in certain respects to their views of that parent with whom they "identify" most closely (when "closeness of identification" is inferred from the fact that the child chose to describe that particular parent when given a choice)? (Porter & Stacey, 1956)

(l) When adjustment is inferred from the child's self-report, do better-adjusted children's self concepts resemble their views of the like-sex parent's characteristics, while less well-adjusted children's self concepts resemble their views of their opposite-sex parent's characteristics? (Manis, 1958; Sopchak, 1952)

(m) Does the child perceive the parent as the "Person I Would Like to Be Like" (i.e., as his ideal self)? (Havighurst, Robinson, & Dorr, 1946)

The questions in both of the groups immediately above involve relationships between two or more views held by the child, each inferred from reports made by the child. The following questions concern relationships between some aspect of the child's reported self concept and some report made by the parent, either about himself or the other parent, *or* about his views concerning the child, *or* about his views of the child's self concept.

(n) Does a child's level of self-regard resemble the level of regard which his parents have for him? (Helper, 1958)

(o) How accurate are parents in estimating their children's self concepts? (Langford & Alm, 1954; Tarwater, 1955)

(p) Will a boy's self concept resemble the boy's concept of his father if the boy's mother "rewarded him for modelling himself on the father" (i.e., if the mother's ideal for the boy resembles her concept of her spouse)? (Helper, 1955)

(q) If parents hold similar ideals for their child, will the child's ideal self remain stable over time? (Helper, 1955)

(r) If a child's self concept is dissimilar to his parent's self concept, is the child a more anxious person than the child whose self concept resembles his parent's self concept? (Lazowick, 1955)

(s) Will children's ideal selves resemble their respective parents' stated ideals for them more than they resemble ideals stated by randomly selected parents for their children? (Helper, 1955)

(t) Does a boy's ideal self resemble his father's ideal for him if the boy's mother has "rewarded the boy for modelling himself on the father" (i.e., if the mother's ideal for the boy resembles her concept of her spouse)? (Helper, 1955)

An Overview of the Studies

Question (a) above concerns possible relationships between the level of a child's self-regard and his perception of how well his parents regard him. Jourard and Remy (1955) found significant correlations between college student Ss' Self-cathexis and Body-cathexis scores and Ss' perceptions of how their mothers and fathers cathected their (Ss') selves and bodies. (See Chapter III above for a description of their instruments.) These correlations support a positive answer to Question (a). They cannot, of course, reveal (1) whether Ss' perceptions of their parents' reactions to them are accurate; (2) whether such parental attitudes shaped Ss' self-cathexes; (3) whether the findings may be partially explainable in terms of response set.

Manis (1958) reports findings relevant to a closely related question: Is a child's maladjustment, as inferred from his self-reports, associated with his perception that his parents hold him in low regard? (Question [b]). He selected extreme "adjustment" groups of college students on the basis of certain MMPI scores. His Ss described their "real" and "ideal" selves, and described each of their parents on 24 evaluative bipolar rating scales. (See Table II.) They also indicated how they thought their parents would rate them on these scales.

Manis (1958, p. 484) reports, without giving specific quantitative data, that "The adjusted Ss felt that they were more highly esteemed by their parents than did the maladjusted Ss." As in the Jourard and Remy study, such findings support a positive answer to the question raised. They cannot, however, reveal whether Ss' perceptions of their parents' feelings toward them are accurate or whether such parental attitudes caused Ss' adjustment or maladjustment. The possibility of a simple response-set explanation is ruled out in this study, however, since adjustment and perceived parental esteem were measured on different instruments.

Another part of Manis's findings concerns the relationship between S's self-reported adjustment and his perception that his parents differ from one another in their evaluations of him (Question [c]). He used the D statistic as a measure of similarity between S's estimates of how his mother and his father viewed him. The adjusted Ss showed significantly smaller D (i.e., dissimilarity) scores, so the findings support the answer that maladjustment (as inferred from the MMPI) is associated with perception of differences between the opinions of one's parents. Manis pointed out the possibility of an artifact. Since adjusted Ss felt their parents esteemed them more highly, their smaller D scores might have been a necessary consequence of the fact that they thought both parents had relatively high opinions of them. Re-examination of the data revealed that the larger D scores of the maladjusted Ss were not due to their feeling that one parent regarded them consistently more favorably than the other. Rather they were apparently due to content differences. For example, the maladjusted S thought his mother would rate him high and his father would rate him low on scales a, b, c, while the reverse would hold true on scales d, e, and f.

Is a child's self-reported tendency to blame himself associated with any particular memories he has as to parental discipline he received? (Question [d]). Henry's (1956) study of enlisted military personnel is pertinent here. He asked his Ss questions in regard to a hypothetical conversation in which one person gets "hurt." When Ss' reported tendency not to blame others in such a situation was held constant, there was a significant positive association between S's perception of the mother as family disciplinarian and the tendency for S to blame himself. Perception of the mother as disciplinarian was particularly concentrated in the group of Ss who would blame themselves but thought they should not. The psychological significance of these "sociological" findings is not clear.

We turn now to results which associate the child's self concept with his view of his parents' characteristics *or* his view of his parents' self concepts (Questions [e] through [m]).

Sopchak (1952) compared the similarity between college Ss' self concepts and the self concepts they attributed to parents, and the self concepts they attributed to "most other people." His Ss took the MMPI under four different instructions: "how I (my mother, my father, and 'most people') would answer." The "identification score" for mother, for example, was a count of the items which S answered in the same way under the instructions "how I would respond" and "how my mother would respond." By this method he found no significant difference between S's "identification" with parents and with most other people. This null answer to Question (e) cannot be definitely interpreted, since it has not been replicated.

Sopchak (1952), Beier and Ratzeburg (1953), and Manis (1958) were all interested in studying the degree of similarity between children's self-reports on the one hand and the children's reports about parents on the other (Question [f]). In Sopchak's study there was a trend for male Ss to answer more items the same way for self and for father, while female Ss tended to answer more items the same way for self and for mother. However, this sex difference was not significant. In a study using similar administrative procedure and similar Ss, but a different "identification" score, Beier and Ratzeburg obtained a significant trend toward greater similarity between self answers and answers attributed to the same-sex parent than between self answers and answers attributed to the opposite-sex parent. Their "identification" score for mother, for example, was based solely on the items which S answered the same way under "I" and "mother" instructions, but in a different way under "father" instructions. Thus only about ten MMPI items in all entered into their identification scores.

In contrast to Sopchak and to Beier and Ratzeburg, Manis's Ss described their parents rather than indicating how their parents would describe themselves. He found no evidence, through the D statistic, that Ss' descriptions of themselves resembled their descriptions of like-sex parents more than they resembled their descriptions of opposite-sex parents.

Three authors were concerned with somewhat interrelated variables ("adjustment," "anxiety," and "self-regard") as they relate to the similarity between children's self concepts and children's views of their parents' characteristics (Question [g]). Manis (1958), in the study described above, found that maladjusted Ss (as inferred from the MMPI) showed significantly higher D (i.e., dissimilarity) scores between self-ratings and ratings describing their parents on 24-adjective scales. That is, maladjusted Ss' self-descriptions tended to differ from their descriptions of either parent. There is a possibility of artifact here for the following reason. The D (dissimilarity) score is a two-part score, one component of which is S's self-report. We cannot be sure from these data to what extent the correlation of D (dissimilarity) with the MMPI may be due to the correlation between S's self-reports on the MMPI and on the rating scales. Although Manis says that examination of the data showed a wide variability among the parent descriptions, this does not suffice to rule out completely the artifactual interpretation suggested here.

Lazowick (1955), in a study based on theories regarding identification, studied the relationship of Taylor Manifest Anxiety Scores to actual parent-child similarity, and to similarity between the child's perceptions of himself and his parent. These actual and perceived similarities were measured on a semantic differential instrument representing Osgood's three factors, evaluation, activity, and potency. (See Table II, and Osgood $et\ al.$, 1957.) The Ss were thirty university students representing extreme deciles of anxiety, and their sixty parents. Low (as contrasted to high) manifest anxiety scores were associated with greater similarity perceived by the child between himself and each of the parents. We have the same difficulties of interpretation here as in Manis's results. That is, the perceived similarity measure is a two-part index. Therefore we cannot rule out the possibility that the relationship found may be more simply interpreted as a correlation between two forms of self-report, i.e., on the anxiety scale and on the semantic differential self-concept measure respectively.

Jourard's (1957) study was also pertinent to Question (g), i.e., it was concerned with the relationships between the child's self-regard and the similarity of the child's self concept to his description of his parents' characteristics. His study involved many other points as well, and its procedure will be described here, since it is pertinent to Questions (h), (i), and (j) as well as to Question (g).

Jourard repeated forty items in each of ten questionnaires, and obtained ten response scores from each of his college student Ss: S's perceived similarity to mother or to father (S could not say he was similar to both on any one item); cathexis for mother, for father, and for self; ideal rating for mother, father, and self; and "real self" ratings for mother, father, and self. (See Chapter III for a description of this instrument.) Twenty-eight correlations were computed to obtain answers to Questions (g) through (j). Of these, all were in the predicted direction, and only two fell short of the .05 level of significance. However, their interpretation is open to question, since various possibilities of artifact are present: (1) There is a common term in the variables correlated to answer Question (i). (2) There is a possibility of intra-S response sets toward use of wide or narrow scale ranges throughout all questionnaires. (3) The use of two-part indices precludes clear interpretation when both parts of such a two-part index are varying. And of course no correlational findings can sustain a cause and effect interpretation, even if the possibility of artifacts were not present.

Question (k) asks: Are children's self concepts similar in certain respects to their views of that parent with whom they "identify" most closely (when closeness of identification is inferred from the fact that the child chose to describe that particular parent when given a choice)? This is the question raised by Porter and Stacey (1956). They studied the similarities between college students' perceptions of themselves and their perceptions of their parents on the ten traits of the Guilford-Zimmerman Temperament Survey. Ss chose to describe that parent whom they felt most competent to rate. The authors inferred that this parent was the one with whom S felt most identified, whether or not this chosen parent was the same sex as the child. Such an inference seems dubious to the present writer. On the assumption that 50% coincidence between any two sets of ratings could be expected by chance alone, they concluded that for nine traits, the similarity in children's self-perceptions and their perceptions of their parents significantly exceeded chance expectancy. For

Masculinity, perceived similarity exceeded chance levels only for Ss who rated like-sex parents. Of course a self-concept theorist looking at their data cannot conclude anything about perceived similarities to parents with whom the child identifies, as contrasted to parents with whom he does not identify, since the latter were presumably not included in the study. For that matter, one cannot be sure whether the child's perceived similarity to the parent significantly exceeds his perceived similarity to a hypothetical "average other" person. This restriction is of crucial importance to a theorist who might wish to use such a study to infer something about the influence of parent characteristics on children's self concepts.

We turn now to the two remaining questions concerning relationships between children's views of self and their views of parent characteristics. Sopchak (1952), in the study described earlier, was interested in the relationship between "tendency toward disorder" and "opposite sex parental identification" (Question [1]). In this respect his interests were similar to those of Manis (1958), but his methods were different. Sopchak (1952) scored the Ss' self answers on the MMPI according to nine diagnostic scales, and correlated each diagnostic score with each of S's "identification" scores. Some of these rs were significant. However, such results do not permit firm conclusions because of the possibility of artifact in measuring adjustment and identification on the same instrument. That is, the two-part "identification" score was based partly on S's answers, and the disorder score was based entirely on S's answer. Thus the correlations may have been considerably influenced by a common term.

As mentioned above, Manis (1958) found no tendency among his group as a whole for his Ss' descriptions of like-sex parents to be more similar to Ss' self-descriptions than were their descriptions of opposite-sex parents. However, Manis thought that adjusted Ss (as contrasted to maladjusted Ss) might show such a trend. His results gave no support to this hypothesis, however.

Havighurst, Robinson, and Dorr (1946) were interested in a different question: Does the child perceive the parent as the "Person I Would Like to Be Like" (i.e., my ideal self)? (Question [m]). They reached some tentative, descriptive conclusions concerning the development of the ideal self, as indexed through coded compositions written to describe "The Person I Would Like to Be Like." His nine groups of Ss were not planned as a basis for a controlled analysis of contributing variables. Responses fell mainly into four categories: parents, glamorous adults, attractive and visible young adults, and composite imaginary persons. The age sequence was not rigid, but in general the choice moved outward from the family circle. From ages six to eight the parent or some other family member was the typical choice, while from eight to sixteen there was a trend toward choosing a glamorous person, then a visible adult, and finally a composite, imaginary person (which was alleged to be the most mature response).

We turn now to studies which relate S's self concept to parent responses (Questions [n] through [t] above).

The chief study of this kind is Helper's (1955) investigation, upon which six of the questions referred to immediately above are based. (See Table II.) His Ss were eighth- and ninth-grade pupils and their parents. He derived his hypotheses about development of children's self concepts from the Dollard and Miller and Osgood theories of verbal learning. Although the learning theory and the related self-concept problem concern S-R relationships, Helper's nine hypotheses are all of the R-R variety, where the Rs which are related come partially from different subjects. Because of the R-R approach, the cross-sectional nature of the study, and several measurement assumptions, any results obtained cannot afford a crucial test of the S-R reinforcement approach, nor can they sustain cause and effect inferences, as Helper himself points out. His nine hypotheses all involve at least one variable measured in terms of a dual score (e.g., discrepancy between the parent's ideal for his child and the child's ideal for self). In four of the hypotheses both the dependent and independent variable are measured in terms of a two-part score. In five of the hypotheses both the dependent *and* independent variables overlap entirely or in part with both the dependent and independent variables of one or several other hypotheses. In addition, the hypotheses are tested separately for boys and girls, and then sometimes for all Ss. Thus it is impossible to know how many significant findings could have been expected by chance alone. It is also impossible to assign clear psychological interpretations to trends which may seem to be in excess of chance expectations because of problems associated with interpreting two-part scores, and because of the other possibilities of artifact. The present writer estimates that seven out of 35 trends (i.e., 20% of them) reach the 5% level or better, in the predicted direction. But since, for reasons enumerated above, these trends are based on nonindependent sets of data, it seems possible that nothing has been found which is clearly in excess of chance. The following paragraph summarizes the reported trends which may have exceeded chance expectations.

Where the mother's ideal for the boy resembles her concept of her spouse, it is assumed that the boy has been rewarded by her for modelling himself on his father. Such reward was found empirically to be associated with (1) similarity between boy's ideal for himself and the father's ideal for the boy, and with (2) similarity between boy's self concept and boy's concept of his father. High sociometric status was found to be associated with (1) similarity between boy's self concept and his concept of his father, and with (2) stability of boy's ideal self concept over one week's time. Similarity between two parents' ideals for the child was found to be significantly associated with stability of the child's ideal self concept over one week's time (significant for girls alone and all Ss but not for boys alone) (Questions [t], [p], and [q]).

There was a weak tendency for children's self ideals to resemble their parents' ideals for them more than to resemble the ideals stated by randomly selected parents for their children. As Helper points out, the weakness of this trend may reflect a stereotypy of parents' ideals for their children (although no data as to degree of such stereotypy are presented). This would be consonant with the many other findings reported in this review to the effect that the ideal self tends to be culturally stereotyped (i.e., less empirically variable than self-concept reports [Question (s)]).

In a further treatment of the same data, Helper (1958) obtained some results bearing on Question (n): Does a child's level of self-regard resemble the level of regard which his parents have for him? He derived "Favorability" and "Acceptance" scores from subpools of self-rating items (and analogously from parents' ratings of their children). The Favorability scores were from "actual self" ratings on items with highly stereotyped ideal self ratings. Acceptability scores were based on [Actual Self — Ideal Self] discrepancies on the remaining items. Correlations between parents' evaluations of their children tended to be small but consistently positive. Favorability scores were correlated between father and son, father and daughter, mother and son, mother and daughter, father and all children, and mother and all children. Of these six possibilities, one correlation (father–all children) was significant at the .05 level. Six Acceptance correlations were also computed, using the same combinations of Ss. Of these six, three were significant at the .05 level: father-daughter, father-all children, mother-daughter. The fact that the correlations are not very high might be due to either of two influences: (1) The parents' level of regard for the children may be different from the children's level of self-regard. (2) The parents and children may have similar attitudes toward the children, but they may not have enough information about how all the Ss in the study are using the rating scale. In other words, since parent-child similarity is measured by a correlation across persons, every subject would need to know the rating scale behavior of all subjects in order to achieve a high correlation, even if respective parents' and children's attitudes were similar.

Langford and Alm (1954) and Tarwater (1955) were interested in the accuracy of parents in estimating their children's self concepts (Question [m]).

The first authors explored this question by means of getting parent predictions and child responses on the California Test of Personality. Unfortunately this study provided no way of controlling for the factors of stereotype as contrasted to individual accuracy, nor for the factor of actual similarity between parent and child, as this might lead to naive projection rather than understanding of the child. Therefore we cannot conclude anything about a parent's insight into his child, as the authors had hoped.

In Tarwater's (1955) study of adolescents and their parents, coincidences were tallied between responses made under four administrations of an inventory called "I Quest." The four sets of responses were: (1) the adolescent's answers concerning his own feelings about self; (2) the adolescent's predictions as to how his parents will respond for him; (3) the parents' predictions as to how their adolescent will respond; (4) the parents' answers as to how their adolescent child "really is." The method and data treatment are vaguely indicated, and problems of artifact were evidently not considered, so detailed critical analysis and conclusions cannot be made. (See Table II.)

Finally we come to Question (r), which asks: If a child's self concept is dissimilar to his parent's self concept, is the child a more anxious person than the child whose self concept resembles his parent's self concept? In a study described above, Lazowick (1955) investigated the relationships of Taylor Manifest Anxiety Scores to similarity between parental self-evaluations and child self-evaluations on a semantic differential instrument. Low (as contrasted to high) manifest anxiety scores were associated with greater similarity between parental self concept and child's self concept.

The interpretation of this correlation is unclear, however, because of the fact that parent-child similarity on the semantic differential is indexed by a two-part score, one part of which is the child's self-evaluation. If the child's self-reported manifest anxiety correlates with his self-evaluation on the semantic differential scales, then the correlation between parent-child similarity on the one hand and Taylor scores on the other could be mainly or entirely due to the correlation between S's two self-reports.

Summary and Conclusions

What conclusions can we draw from our examination of the available studies on parent-child interaction and the self concept?

First it is clear that there are no true antecedent-consequent S-R designs. All the studies used the R-R correlational approach, so no cause-effect inferences are warranted.

The correlations obtained fall into three classes:

(1) Two reports made by the child are correlated, one report concerning his self concept, the other concerning his views of his parents' attitudes toward him.

(2) Two reports made by the child are correlated, one report concerning his own self concept, the other concerning the child's description of his parents' characteristics, *or* the child's view of his parents' self concepts.

(3) A report made by the child concerning his self concept is correlated with a report made by his parent concerning himself or the other parent, *or* his views of the child, *or* his views of the child's self concept.

Although such R-R studies are inherently limited, they may provide theoretically pertinent, suggestive information if they are properly planned. Unfortunately many of them have been plagued with unnecessary methodological limitations of the following kinds: contamination of independent and dependent variables; inflation of correlations by response sets; artifacts due to unanalytical use of two-part scores; use of statistical techniques which seem inappropriate to the hypothesis.

There is some evidence, not entirely free of possible artifact, to suggest that children's self concepts are similar to the view of themselves which they attribute to their parents. There is some limited evidence that a child's level of self-regard is associated with the parents' reported level of regard for him. There is some evidence to suggest that children see the

like-sex parent's self concept (as contrasted to the opposite-sex parent's
self concept) as being somewhat more like their own self concept.

There is some evidence that children with self-reported maladjustment see their parents' views of them as differing from each other.

3. *Social Interaction (Other than Parent-Child) and the Self Concept*

Conceivably there are a number of general ways in which social interaction and the self concept might be related. Perhaps the most obvious and
important possibility is that one's self concept is shaped through interaction with others. Theories of this sort have been stated by Mead (1934),
Cooley (1902), and many more recent self theorists. However, propositions of this kind have not been developed explicitly enough to point
clearly toward definitive, empirical tests. Perhaps partly as a result of such
vagueness, this theoretically crucial class of relationships between variables
has been inadequately explored.

The converse type of relationship might also hold, i.e., one's self
concept might influence one's interactions with others. Here too theoretical
formulations are nebulous.

Most of the studies relating self concept and social interaction involve
associations between self-concept measures and role status variables, including sex role status. It is impossible to specify all the predictions which
might be made concerning these variables. In practice, however, the predictions which were actually explored may be divided into two overlapping
classes: (a) correlation of self-concept patterns with stereotyped conceptions which one might expect of anyone in the stated role; and (b)
differential patterns of self-esteem associated with varying roles.

Of course one could also theorize in the reverse direction, that certain
self conceptions might lead one to play certain roles. For example a person who considers himself to be intelligent might seek a leadership role.
This type of theorizing apparently underlies only two studies reviewed
here (Gebel, 1954; Mussen & Porter, 1959).

It seems to the present author that studies of role status involve a
problem of specificity which limits their usefulness to psychological theorizing. That is, roles (including sex roles) are often essentially sociological constructs. It is not easy to articulate these sociological constructs
meaningfully with psychological constructs. Therefore the relevance of
these studies to psychological theorizing is not always clear. The studies

reported below vary considerably with respect to how obvious and plausible such connections between role and psychological variables are made.

Most studies were based on a rationale concerning the influence of role status upon self concept. Despite this cause-effect assumption, all but one of the studies were of R-R design, in which two responses measured at about the same time were correlated.

At least one R-R study has concerned itself not with role, but with the influence of current peer interaction on the self concept (Manis, 1955). It will be discussed in detail following the survey of investigations involving role and sex differences.

Another group of researches centers around the influence of the self concept on social behavior, especially in friendship choice and attraction to the group. Will persons choose friends similar to themselves whom they can understand and respect? If so, under what conditions and with reference to what self characteristics? Or will they choose friends with traits which differ from theirs, characteristics which perhaps complement their own and lead to less conflict, or to vicarious fulfillment of self ideals? This kind of theorizing has been vaguely stated. However, there are a number of studies which give good agreement on certain empirical points.

The final subdivision of this section on social interaction will be concerned with the relationship between self-esteem and persuasibility.

Before going on to review the particular investigations under the general headings just outlined, we should point out that our classification scheme has necessarily been arbitrary. We have placed in other sections findings which might be pertinent to the general area of social interaction and the self concept. The reader is referred to such studies as those concerning self- and other-acceptance (Section C-10 of this chapter), correlations between the private self and the self as others see one (Chapter VI and Section C-9 of this chapter), and correlations between self concept and authoritarianism or ethnocentrism (Section C-11 of this chapter).

a. Sex and Role as Related to Self Concept

Social Status and Leadership as Related to Self Concept

Four investigators have wondered whether socioeconomic status is associated with any particular self-concept characteristics. Perhaps class status affects self-acceptance (Hill, 1957), or feelings of self worth (Mason, 1954a, 1954b). Perhaps a distinctive patterning of self-concept variables is associated with class status (Klausner, 1953). Or perhaps the characteristics of the ideal self are a function of class status (Havighurst & Taba, 1949).

Hill (1957) found no consistent association between scores on the Index of Status Characteristics and scores on Phillips's Questionnaire concerning Self- and Other-Acceptance. No significance tests are given for the results reported, however. He also had an experimental group of pupils study Warner's "What you should know about social class," while a control group did not study this topic. Then the Phillips Questionnaire was repeated, six weeks after initial testing. Neither high- nor low-status experimental *S*s showed any difference from control *S*s on the second administration of the Phillips Questionnaire. (See Chapter III for a description of that instrument.)

In another study of social class, 27 seventeen-year-old white males were categorized by Klausner (1953) according to Warner's Index of Status Characteristics and Marxian social classifications. The boys' *Q* sorts of 60 statements concerning their self concepts were intercorrelated and factor-analyzed. This resulted in three factors, labelled "reactive aggression," "adjusted inferiority," and "socially isolated self aggression." (See Table I.) The small *N* precluded computation of correlation coefficients between the factors and the socioeconomic variables. However, inspection revealed some suggestive trends toward association between "reactive aggression" and lower middle class or proletariat status, and between "socially isolated self aggression" and bourgeois or upper middle class status. *S*s high on "adjusted inferiority" seem less clearly homogeneous on social class.

Mason's (1954a, 1954b) research involved more than socioeconomic class. She hoped to study the self concept, especially feelings of self worth and affective response to life, as a function of the variables age, economic status, and living conditions (institutionalized-independent). She used several self-concept measures (see Tables II and IV), and three groups of *S*s: sixty indigent, institutionalized *S*s above fifty-five years of age, thirty middle-class independent *S*s above age sixty; and thirty young adults of lower socioeconomic status. Unfortunately, uncontrolled variables in this design make it impossible to assign intergroup differences in self concept to any of the variables purportedly under study. For example, the two older groups differed from one another not only with respect to living conditions, but also with respect to socioeconomic class. Or, to take another example, the groups comparable as to living conditions differed not only as to age, but also as to socioeconomic status.

In Havighurst and Taba's work with sixteen-year-olds in a small Midwestern town, Ss' ideal selves were inferred from their written compositions dsecribing "The Person I Would Like to Be Like." A scale was devised for rating the essays on "moral values . . . ranging from selfish and materialistic to altruistic and spiritual" (Havighurst & Taba, 1949, p. 285). Three judges rank-ordered the 78 papers with respect to this scale, and an average rank was assigned to each essay. (The rank-order correlations between pairs of judges were $+.58$, $+.61$, and $+.68$.) Essays were dichotomized at the median, and Ss were divided according to Warner's criteria into two social-class groups: (1) upper and middle classes, and (2) lower classes.

Tetrachoric r between social class status and ranks of the essays on moral values was $+.27$. However, we cannot conclude that class status as such is associated with expressed moral values because the latter also correlated positively with Stanford-Binet IQ and with average school grades ($+.33$ and $+.39$). No partial correlations are given between moral values and social class, with IQ and school achievement constant.

The four studies taken together do not permit us to conclude anything about the relationship between socioeconomic class and the self concept. The statistically insignificant trends of the first two studies are unreplicated. In the third and fourth studies uncontrolled variables prevent conclusions.

Two researchers were concerned with the association between self concept and particular social roles. Prison guards were studied by Lawson and Fagan (1957), and executives and supervisors by Coates and Pellegrini (1957).

Lawson and Fagan (1957) discovered that prison guards felt the public had a perception of them which was decidedly inferior to their own perception of guards. In fact, however, the "public" Ss did not have an unfavorable stereotype of guards, although "public" respondents shared the guards' unfavorable stereotype of prisoners. It is interesting that in this instance the Ss had refused, as it were, to let their supposed role characteristics influence their self conceptions.

Coates and Pellegrini (1957) report that executives and supervisors tended to agree on characteristics of their respective groups. We cannot know to what extent each was subscribing to a stereotype in characterizing himself and the members of the other group, however. The method is vaguely indicated.

The final studies in this section involve a different sort of hypothesis from the others. In these investigations, *S*s' phenomenal or nonphenomenal self-concept characteristics are correlated with the degree to which *S*s assumed the role of leader in a discussion group.

Gebel (1954) was interested to see whether assuming a leadership role is a function of one's phenomenal self concept. In his study, girls were first rated as emerged leaders and nonleaders of an initially leaderless group discussion. Following the group discussion they were given open-ended interviews initiated by two questions: "What was there about the leaderless group discussion that you liked?" and "Who are you?" Recorded interviews were analyzed according to Bugental's Conceptual Matrix Method. (See Chapter III for this method.) Leaders, as compared to nonleaders, expressed more thought units per interview hour. The frequency of positively toned, negatively toned, and descriptive units in each of the conceptual categories was determined, and the ratio of positive to negative units was computed for each category within the leader and within the nonleader groups. By this measure, leaders tended to have more positive attitudes toward themselves and tended to perceive others' affect on them to be more positive. Surprisingly enough they tended to perceive the world with lower positive affect than did nonleaders. However, leaders also perceived themselves and the world less negatively, and perceived their affect on others less negatively than did nonleaders (Gebel, 1954, p. 316).

Gebel reports that he used chi square to test the significance of his obtained differences, but he gives no information concerning how this technique was actually applied. It is not clear that this is an appropriate statistic for his data.

Another problem of interpretation arises from the fact that all the girls were interviewed immediately after the discussion. This procedure leaves us with two possible interpretations: (1) the girls' characteristic phenomenal fields influenced their leadership behavior in the group discussion; *or* (2) the girls' leadership experiences in the group discussion influenced their subsequent reports of their phenomenal fields.

Mussen and Porter's (1959) study concerned the association between the *non*phenomenal self concept and emergent leadership in ten initially leaderless discussion groups, each consisting of six male college students.

(Although their hypothesis does not concern the phenomenal self concept, their investigation is included here to bring out its relation to other studies of social interaction.) Self-confidence and negativity of self concept, among other variables, were inferred from specially devised TAT scales (see Chapter V). After taking the TAT, Ss discussed a topic for twenty minutes and then rated one another on a ten-item questionnaire concerning their behavior and influence in the group. Extreme groups of Ss receiving the highest and lowest leadership ratings were compared on eight TAT scores, including the self-concept indices. TAT scores were dichotomized as closely as possible to the median. Significantly more of the leaders showed high scores on feelings of adequacy (self-confidence), and significantly fewer of the leaders showed high scores on negativity of self concept.

The fact that the TAT was administered before the discussion means that the self-concept measure could not have been affected by the group experience, as might have been the case in Gebel's study. However, a number of other questions of interpretation arise. Although the self characteristics are the supposedly causal variables, the extreme groups were formed on the basis of the leadership ratings. Leaders differed from nonleaders on TAT scores for *n* Affiliation, *n* Achievement, and *n* Aggression, as well as on the self-concept variables. This leaves open the question whether, for example, negativity of self concept would be associated with rated leadership if other variables such as *n* Achievement were held constant. If *n* Achievement, *n* Affiliation, *n* Aggression, self-confidence, and negativity of self concept are all correlated with one another, it remains to be demonstrated that each self-concept variable is independently related to rated leadership.

We may point out another problem of interpretation, the argument for which goes as follows. The TAT score was a simple count of the number of stories which could be scored for that S for the variable in question. Thus the S who writes a long story would have a greater chance to be scored once for each variable, and therefore he would have a greater chance of scoring high on all variables. Rated leadership was found to correlate significantly with E's tally of how frequently S participated in the discussion. To what extent, then, do the TAT scores correlate with rated leadership because of high verbal output in each of the two situations? This possible artifact might account for the results on the self-concept variables and the *n* Affiliation and *n* Achievement variables. An artifactual interpretation is weakened, however, when one considers that negativity of self concept and *n* Aggression were *inversely* related to rated leadership, a fact which could not occur on the basis of verbal output alone.

If one is willing to asume that the TAT self scales validly index *S*'s nonphenomenal self concept, the findings support the proposition that emergent leaders of discussion groups (as contrasted to nonleaders) have more self confidence and less negative self concepts. However, no cause-effect interpretations can be drawn from this study.

Religious Affiliation and the Self Concept

Sarbin and Rosenberg (1955) used a modified Gough Adjective Check List to compare self concepts of religious groups (Protestant-Catholic-No religion). (See Table II.) All *S*s were students, but their degree of comparability on relevant variables is not known. Even if groups had been matched on other variables relevant to self concept, the findings would not be clearly interpretable psychologically, since one cannot confidently articulate religious categories with psychologically relevant variables.

Kuhn and McPartland (1954) report an association between the kind of religious group affiliation and the number of "consensual references" made in response to the question "Who am I?" Consensual references are to groups and classes whose limits and conditions of membership are common knowledge. (See Table II, Bugental *et al.*, for a description of this instrument.) Their results are not meaningful psychologically for several reasons. First, as we have said above, there is no clear relationship between religious affiliation and psychologically relevant variables. In addition, there was no control over response total in obtaining scores, and there was no attempt to match groups of varying religious affiliations with respect to variables relevant to the "Who am I?" responses.

Sarnoff's (1951) study was concerned with a specified aspect of religious affiliation, namely, the attitude which one has toward his religious group. He found that anti-Semitism among Jewish college males correlated with negativity of attitudes expressed toward parents and selves, and with a negation of the respondent's own uniqueness. The latter attitudes were inferred from the Michigan Sentence Completion Test. (It seems that this test may have been aimed toward unconscious attitudes, but since the study is related to the general topic of this section, it is included in this chapter. See Table IV.) Sarnoff theorizes that anti-Semitism in Jews is actually a function of *S*'s negative self-attitudes which stem from parental rejection rather than from religious persecution. Anti-Semitism is interpreted as "identification with the aggressor," a means of vicariously appropriating wished-for power, and simultaneously derogating self and parents. The possbility has not been entirely ruled out that differences in self-attitudes may have been partially a function of differing experiences with religious prejudice.

Sex Differences and the Self Concept

The available studies of sex differences in self concept have been directed mainly toward two questions: To what degree have males and females accepted particular sex role stereotypes as applicable to men (or to women) in general? To what degree have males and females accepted particular sex role stereotypes as applicable to their own actual or ideal self concepts in particular?

One aspect of these questions concerns the favorability of the stereotypes, and the reflection of such values in the self-regard of individual male and female persons. Related to the matter of favorability toward one's sex is the question: To what degree do men and women feel acceptance of "generalized others"?

Closely akin to the matter of sex stereotypes are questions concerning society's expectations of each sex. In what respects, if any, do males and females feel that society's expectations of them differ? What discrepancies, if any, occur between *S*s' perceptions of society's expectations of them and their personal ideals for themselves? If such personal-social conflicts exist, do *S*s see themselves as conforming to their own ideals more than to society's expectations, or vice versa?

Three studies by McKee and Sherriffs have explored questions concerning male and female stereotypes (McKee & Sherriffs, 1957, 1959; Sherriffs & McKee, 1957). When they used a generalized rating scale, they found that both male and female college students reported that males were superior to females. This finding was accentuated when no neutral response step was provided. Two other methods also led to the conclusion that both sexes have less favorable concepts of the female: forced and unforced responses to adjective check lists (see Table II); and coding for favorability some open-ended lists made by Ss to describe males and females. There is some suggestion that this bias is stronger among females.

Lynn (1959) has referred to some studies of an earlier date than those covered in this review which suggest that there is a progressive increase from age eight in the unfavorability of the female stereotype.

Is the female's self concept like the female stereotype? Is it less favorable than the male's self concept?

McKee and Sherriffs (1959) used empirical means for establishing sex stereotypes and found that Women's Real Self (a group measure) was more sex-typed than Men's Real Self. This was true despite the fact that the female stereotype was more undesirable than the male stereotype.

In the review mentioned above, Lynn (1959) reports some results which suggest that the female's acceptance of the unfavorable stereotype as personally applicable increases from age eight.

Other investigators have explored the favorability of the female and male self concepts without regard to the question of stereotypes.

Matteson (1955) computed an Aspiration Index (actual self minus self hoped for two years hence) and a Discrepancy Index (actual self minus self as he thinks others see him) on 419 college Freshmen. He reports finding no sex differences in either of these scores. Women were less optimistic than men in forecasting first-term grades. Inaccuracies among women's forecasts were disproportionately among those predicting B but actually attaining A. Unfortunately no information was given on abilities or backgrounds of these Ss to see whether some variable(s) other than sex might account for the obtained differences. (See Table II.)

Using a modified Gough Adjective Check List, Sarbin and Rosenberg (1955) found that men exceeded women in checking such adjectives as resourceful, mature, logical, adventurous, realistic, deliberate, efficient. Women exceeded men in checking feminine, emotional, affectionate, pleasant, temperamental. Groups were not specified as being matched, however, and the greater response total of the men was not controlled in the statistical analysis. (See Table II.)

Among 251 fourth- and sixth-grade children tested by Perkins (1958b), the girls had significantly greater self-ideal congruence than did the boys. (See Table I.)

Engel's (1959) study, described in Section C-1 above, yields data on the "Positiveness" of the self concepts of adolescent boys and girls. (See Table II for a description of Engel's specially devised instrument.) In two of the comparisons, the boys had more positive self concepts, while in the other two comparisons, the girls had the more positive self concepts. Apparently none of these sex differences was significant.

In Eastman's study of marital happiness, stated self-acceptance of men and women did not differ. (See Table II.)

Turner and Vanderlippe's (1958) findings agree with those of Eastman, insofar as they obtained no sex differences in self-ideal congruence in 175 college student Ss. They used Butler and Haigh's 100 Q-sort items. (See Chapter III for a description of this instrument.)

As we look over the preceding studies, we cannot clearly state that women's self concepts are always more unfavorable than are men's self concepts (especially when S's own standards for favorability are used). Differences in method make it difficult to compare the studies so as to discover why some positive and some negative findings have been obtained. In some of the studies, exploring sex differences was not the main purpose, and it is probable that dependent variable measures were not specifically chosen for their relevance to a study of sex role. It is also possible that males and females were not matched with regard to pertinent factors in some of the investigations which were not primarily aimed at the study of sex differences. The findings seem more definitely to confirm the occurrence of a commonly accepted stereotype of "women in general" which is less favorable than that for "men in general."

Another question we raised earlier was whether men or women are more accepting of others. If self-acceptance is correlated with acceptance of others, and if women are slightly less self-accepting, they might be expected to accept others less. On the other hand, Zuckerman, Baer, and Monashkin (1956) have speculated that our culture expects men to be more competitive and aggressive. They reason that if men are too accepting, they cannot fully maintain this expected role. Two articles offer empirical findings pertinent to this question.

Berger (1955), applying his own scales to college students and to a variety of problem Ss, found that women scored higher than men on Acceptance of Others, at any given Self Acceptance score. (See Chapter III for a description of his instrument.) Zuckerman, Baer, and Monashkin (1956) found that females scored higher than males in acceptance of others, when Buss's sixteen-adjective scales were the measure, and both patient and normal Ss were used. (See Table II.)

A number of investigators have been interested in the possibilities of conflict among actual, personally desired, and apparently socially desirable self concepts.

In Martire and Hornberger's (1957) study, groups of college men and women similar in age, class, and grade points showed high intercorrelation between mean sex group ratings on ideal self ($r = +.93$ on 26 adjectives). There was a fairly high correlation between mean sex group ratings of actual self ($r = +.87$ on 26 adjectives), and a fairly high correlation between mean sex group ratings of what was socially desirable ($r = +.85$ on 26 adjectives). (See Table II.)

Female Ss showed significantly lower rs for mean ideal self versus mean socially desirable self, and for mean actual self versus mean socially desirable self than they did for mean ideal self versus mean actual self. This suggested to the authors that female Ss conceived of themselves as living up to their own ideals, but their personal ideals and conduct were not congruent with what they perceived society desired of them. A similar trend for men was not significant. (See Table II.)

Rosen's Ss took the MMPI three times, to describe their actual self, their personally desired self, and their perception of socially desired characteristics (Rosen, 1956a, 1956b). The Ss, who were college students, manifested conflicts between actual, personally desired, and socially desired self-reports on the Mf scale. Although it is hard to compare this study with that of Martire and Hornberger, it would appear that Rosen's findings may be contradictory to theirs, insofar as sex differences in this type of conflict are concerned. They say:

> . . . males show some elevation in feminine interests, feel that society wants them to show even more of these interests, probably as a function of their adopted role as liberal arts college students, but personally find somewhat greater masculinity of interests desirable. Their conflict is thus essentially a personal-social one. Females, on the other hand, have a quite feminine mean score and both personally and socially find it desirable to have more masculine interests, again probably as a function of their role as college students, for it is well known that college students progressively show more and more interests which in the normal population are associated with the opposite sex. But they personally consider this role expectancy a desirable one, whereas the average male feels he is pulled in a direction opposite to his own standards (Rosen, 1956b, p. 156).

Engel, in her study of the stability of adolescents' self concepts over a two-year period, assumed that "cultural ambiguities concerning sex roles should be more likely to affect girls than boys." On this assumption, "it was hypothesized that the self-concept of boys would be significantly more stable over the two year period than that of girls. This hypothesis was not upheld" (Engel, 1959, p. 213). (See Section C-1 above and Table II for more details on this study.)

Summary and Conclusions on Sex Differences. Although the rationale underlying some of these studies involves cause-effect relationships, all the investigations follow R-R designs, or relate the sex of the subject with the subject's responses. It is difficult to synthesize the results since methods, instruments, and types of Ss varied widely across studies. Some of the investigations were not primarily set up to explore sex differences, so dependent variable measures were probably not chosen to be especially relevant to sex roles, and sex groups may not have been matched on variables relevant to the self-concept measures.

There does seem to be some evidence to support the following generalizations: (1) College Ss hold stereotypes of real and ideal male and female persons. (2) The stereotype concerning the male is more favorable than that concerning the female. (3) This attitude of unfavorability may be applied by female Ss to themselves as individuals. Generally speaking, the latter tendency seems weaker or less clearly substantiated than is the trend toward females' endorsement of the unfavorable stereotype of "women in general." (4) Women indicate more acceptance of others than do men, even when level of self-acceptance is constant. (5) In one study, there seems to be considerable congruence (a) between mean personal ideals stated by a men's sample and mean personal ideals stated by a women's sample; and (b) between mean reports on social desirability given by a men's sample and mean reports on social desirability given by a women's sample; and (c) between mean actual self ratings given by a men's sample and mean actual self ratings given by a women's sample.

There may be some sex differences with regard to discrepancies which Ss perceive between actual self, personal ideal for self, and social expectations. Resolution of possibly contradictory results in this area awaits further research.

Experimental Role Enactment and the Self Concept

Sarbin and Jones (1955) believe that in role-taking one becomes "organismically involved," and that this organismic involvement should lead to shifts in self concept. In line with this notion they hypothesized that playing the daughter role in an experimental role-taking situation would alter the self concept of the actress in inverse proportion to the judged validity of the actress's role enactment. The measure of self constancy was the number of self-descriptive adjectives checked before but not after (or after but not before) the role-playing session. The hypothesis was supported by a perfect negative correlation, obtained with six Ss, between self constancy and judged validity of role enactment.

A number of features of the design seem to render the findings equivocal, however, even if we are willing to assume the validity of the adjective check list as a reflection of the phenomenal self. For example, we do not know whether Ss were initially matched on the number of adjectives checked for self. It seems plausible that possibilities for change might be artifactually associated with the number of items originally checked. We do not know to what extent judgments of validity of role enactment might have been a function of the quantity of the actress's verbal output during role-playing. (See the correlation of judged validity with As-If Test, mentioned below.) Neither do we know whether self changes were mostly additions or deletions. If they were additions, the results may be an artifact of correlated verbal response totals. There is also another possibility which we can explain as follows: If we judge from the sample adjectives published in the article, all the adjectives used for self-descriptions were favorably toned. It seems plausible to the present writer that Ss who realized they had done well in role enactment might tend, immediately after role-playing, to check a larger number of favorable self-descriptive adjectives. Thus the change could be due to a situationally induced increment in general esteem level rather than to the influence of the role characteristics upon the pattern of self-characteristics.

The authors also hypothesized that the "change in self-description will show the effects of interaction with the *specific other* in the experimental role-enactment situation" (Sarbin & Jones, 1955, p. 238). This was tested in the following way. They employed a measure of "role-taking aptitude" which consisted of the total *number* of relevant words given in answer to an "As-If" test, which asked S how her life would have been different under two hypothetical circumstances. (This measure correlated perfectly with judged validity of role enactment, which incidentally implies that the latter was a function of S's response total while role-playing.) As a measure of specificity of self-concept change they counted among the self-descriptive adjectives which S checked after but not before role-playing all those adjectives S had previously used to describe father and daughter roles. This word count score correlated significantly with the As-If score. The authors interpret this correlation as indicating the specific influence of father-daughter roles upon self-concept shifts. Again it seems that this psychological interpretation is not the most plausible or parsimonious one, particularly since the artifactual explanation of correlation between response totals has not been ruled out.

In short it seems doubtful to the present writer whether this experiment has demonstrated that role enactment influences the self concept. (See Table II for comments on the instrument used.)

b. Peer Interaction and the Self Concept

Manis (1955) proposed a number of hypotheses concerning peer interaction and the self concept. Hypothesis 1 stated that there will be an increase in agreement over time between an individual's self concept and his friends' perceptions of him. Hypothesis 2 stated that the increase in agreement over time between an individual's self concept and his friends' perceptions of him will exceed the increase in agreement over time between that individual's self concept and his nonfriends' perceptions of him.

He measured agreement by applying the D statistic to a twenty-four-adjective check list. (See Table II.) Friendship was measured sociometrically. He found that Ss and their respective friends agreed better about Ss' attributes after six weeks of interaction than they had initially. The interpretation of these findings is not clear, because two dual indices were compared (first and second self ratings, and first and second friend ratings). One cannot know how much of the change in agreement over time is contributed by any of the four components.

As we said above, Manis postulated that improvement in agreement between S and a friend would exceed improvement in agreement between S and a nonfriend. (Apparently he did not use the same S for the friend and nonfriend comparisons.) When we write this hypothesis in "equation" form, we see that one four-part score is being compared with another four-part score. Due to this complexity, one cannot know how to interpret "positive" (or any kind of) findings. To take one example, suppose that the initial self-ratings were not rigidly matched across pairs of *S*s in the friend and nonfriend comparison groups. In this case, confirmation of the hypothesis might simply mean that *S*s with a certain initial self-rating tend to change self-ratings more in six weeks than do *S*s with some other initial self-rating. This is true because it is hypothetically possible that friend and nonfriend ratings might contribute no significant variance.

Parallel types of criticisms seem to apply to Manis's other hypotheses. In addition, the hypotheses are stated and statistically tested as independent postulates, even though they overlap considerably. For these reasons one cannot use his reported results as a basis for clear conclusions about peer interaction and the self concept.

c. SELF CONCEPTS AND FRIENDSHIP CHOICE[1]

Although a variety of measuring instruments and types of *S*s have been used, the studies in this area are in good agreement on certain main conclusions:

1. Persons chosen sociometrically or as friends are seen by the chooser to be more similar to himself than are nonchosen or disliked persons. This has been reported by Davitz (1955) in re preferred activities of children; by Fiedler, Warrington, and Blaisdell (1952) in re *Q* sorts made by fraternity brothers; by Lundy (1956, 1958); and Lundy, Katkovsky, Cromwell, and Shoemaker (1955) in re certain MMPI items. The latter investigators found that, for the characteristics they used, the results were the same for like-sex or opposite-sex choices.

2. Persons chosen sociometrically or as friends are seen by the chooser to be more similar to his own ideal self than are nonchosen or disliked persons. This has been reported by Lundy (1956) and by Lundy *et al.* (1955); by Fiedler, Warrington, and Blaisdell (1952); by Northway

---

[1]For a discussion of a related topic, self-regard and sociometrically measured popularity, see Section C-9 of this chapter. Details concerning the measuring instruments used by the authors cited in the present discussion may be found as follows: Fiedler, Warrington, and Blaisdell (1952), Table I; Lundy (1955, 1958) and Lundy *et al.* (1955), Table II; McKenna *et al.* (1956), Chapter III on Butler and Haigh's items; Northway and Detweiler (1955), Table II; Rasmussen and Zander (1954), Table II; Thompson and Nishimura (1952), Table I.

and Detweiler (1955) in re ten characteristics agreed upon by children as important good qualities; by Thompson and Nishimura (1952) in re Q sorts of evaluative items by young adults. This finding is, of course, not statistically independent of the first, insofar as "normal" Ss tend to show considerable self-ideal congruence.

3. Despite the fact that Ss perceive their friends to be more similar to themselves than are nonfriends, actual similarity between self-reports of friends does not seem to be much if any greater than actual similarity between self-reports of randomly paired Ss or between S and a nonchosen or disliked person (Davitz, 1955; Fiedler et al., 1952; Thompson & Nishimura, 1952).

Related to this category of findings is one obtained by Brim and Wood (1956). They counted the number of consensual references among the answers of courtship and marriage pairs who gave twenty responses to the question "Who am I?" (See Table II, Bugental et al., in re this instrument.) The correlation between the number of consensual references used by S to describe self, and the number used to describe the partner's self was significant. However, the correlation between the number of consensual references used by each partner to describe himself was insignificant. The significant correlations might of course be attributable to response set rather than to selectively perceived similarity, since there were no nonfriend control Ss.

4. Persons chosen sociometrically or as friends are perceived by the chooser to be more similar to S's own ideal self than to S's self concept, except in cases of very high self-ideal congruence. (This finding was reported only by McKenna, Hofstaetter, and O'Connor, 1956, in re Q sorts made by female college students.)

5. One set of investigators (Thompson & Nishimura, 1952) report that the average correlation between S's own ideal and S's evaluation of a friend was significantly higher than the correlation between S's own ideal and his own self concept. In other words, S idealized his friend. On the other hand the correlation between S's own ideal and his evaluation of a nonfriend was near zero and significantly lower than the correlation between his own ideal self and self concept. McKenna et al. (1956) used only friends of S, but they did not replicate Thompson and Nishimura's findings concerning friends stated above. Instead they found the mean self-ideal congruence approximately equal to the congruence between S's ideal and his perception of his friend.

So far as these results take us, it would seem plausible that similarity to self, not dissimilarity, is sought in a friend. However, more refined studies might indicate that this holds true only for certain characteristics or classes of characteristics. The studies reviewed here may have all tapped a preponderance of characteristics in which similarity is desired.

The dynamics of this similarity factor in friendship choice is not revealed by these studies, but we can speculate on possibilities. We have seen in Chapter III that there is a good deal of stereotypy in ideals (i.e., there are cultural norms or generally agreed upon Social Desirability values for many personality characteristics). These often seem to center around items which make for smooth social interaction. Such items seem to have been much used in the present studies. It is therefore not surprising that Ss prefer persons whom they see as manifesting these attributes to a considerable degree. On the other hand, S may perceive similarity between himself and a friend because it makes the friend seem more understandable and predictable, or it gratifies narcissistic tendencies, or fulfills other needs. One might even speculate in the reverse direction, saying that friendly interaction in some way leads to selective perception of similarity of characteristics.

The trend toward idealization of the friend suggests such possible interpretations as culturally acceptable modesty, or vicarious satisfaction through identification with the superior person. The data give no firm support to this or other possible inferences.

Perhaps the most interesting fact from the viewpoint of the phenomenal theorist is that the perception of the friend's greater similarity to one's self and to one's ideal self is present despite the lack of objective indication that friends are more similar to self and ideal than are nonfriends. Before we attach too much significance to this, however, we must note that the objective "lack of similarity" may be in part a function of the method. S was asked to describe the friend as he (S) saw him; but the friend described himself presumably from a private frame of reference. This difference in frame of reference may be partially responsible for the failure to find objective similarity.

Two other studies which seem to belong in this area are not readily integrated with those discussed immediately above:

Rasmussen and Zander (1954) found that discrepancies between a teacher's expressed personal ideal and her perception of the group's standards correlated negatively with her reported attraction to the group. This finding is reminiscent of the perceived similarity between self and friend mentioned above, and this study does not, of course, permit cause-effect inferences any more than do those involving friendship choice. (See Table II.)

Turner (1954) was interested in exploring the idea that self and "imputed other" roles would be "reciprocal" in S's reported reactions to an imaginary theft episode in which S was the thief. Coding categories for types of self and other roles were developed through successive re-readings of the same papers that were used as a basis for the reported results. No information is given on reliability, validity, controls for contamination, etc. Combinations of self and imputed other roles which were alleged to be "harmonious" were obtained most frequently. However, many questions about the methods used make the results uninterpretable.

d. SELF-REGARD AND SUSCEPTIBILITY TO PERSUASION

Finally we shall summarize the findings relating self-regard to susceptibility to persuasion.

Janis (1954, 1955), Janis and Field (1959), and Janis and Rife (1959) hypothesized that self-esteem would correlate negatively with persuasibility in young adults. Their rationale was that compliance is a defensive attempt to avoid displeasing anyone. The composite results of the four studies offer somewhat weak and dubious support for their hypothesis, however. This is so because (1) the trends are small and usually insignificant; (2) the studies are impossible to compare and synthesize directly due to variations in methods and types of Ss; and (3) there is some possibility of artifact.

For example, in two of the four studies (Janis, 1954; Janis & Field, 1959), self-esteem was measured by a specially assembled collection of personality questionnaire items which E subdivided by inspection into three clusters. It seems, however, that the same items were *not* used for the respective clusters in these two studies. (See Table II.) In a third study (Janis & Rife, 1959), only one of the Janis and Field clusters was used as the self-esteem measure. In the fourth study (Janis, 1955) a Socially Oriented Anxiety cluster from Sarason's Test Anxiety Questionnaire was the self-esteem index. (See Table II.)

Also, three different measures of persuasibility were used in the four studies.

The Janis (1954) study supports the hypothesis significantly on one-tailed tests for two out of three clusters of the self-esteem index. However, in the Janis and Field (1959) study, only two out of six *r*s reached the .05 level on a one-tailed test. (One *r* was computed for each of three clusters for males and females separately.) In the Janis (1955) study, the chi square for persuasibility versus Socially Oriented Anxiety (self-esteem) reached only the .09 level on a one-tailed test. (A significant relation between a Test Anxiety cluster and persuasibility was interpreted, after being obtained, as supporting the self-esteem–persuasibility hypothesis.) The only highly significant correlation was obtained by Janis and Rife (1959) between one of the Janis and Field self-esteem clusters and a persuasibility test given to hospitalized, emotionally disturbed adolescent males. (Correlations between persuasibility and the other two self-esteem clusters which were used by Janis and Field are not reported for these patients.) It was hypothesized that the patients' larger range of scores on the self-esteem cluster might account for the fact that a highly significant *r* was obtained from this hospitalized group.

Even if all the correlations had come from comparable procedures and had been highly significant by the more stringent two-tailed tests, a problem of interpretation would remain. This problem lies in the possible confounding between persuasibility and initial opinion. That is, if groups classed as high, medium, and low on persuasibility also differed systematically on their initial opinions, one could not tell whether self-esteem was associated with initial opinions, persuasibility, or both. Apparently the correlation of initial opinion with opinion change was not explored in any of these studies. Related to this question, however, Janis reported in his 1954 article that he examined the precommunication opinions of the personality groups. He says (1954, p. 514), "No significant or consistent differences were found which could account for the observed differences in opinion change." A similar control observation was not reported in the other three studies, however.

Abelson and Lesser (1959) proposed that self-esteem in children is negatively associated with persuasibility. Self-esteem was measured in three ways: (1) asking the child to compare himself with the other children in his class on certain favorable but ambiguous characteristics; (2) asking the child which children in his class liked him and would choose to sit next to him; (3) getting the discrepancy between the rank of the second measure and the child's actual sociometric rank. (It is not clear to the present author why the third index should be called a "self-esteem" measure, since it involves more than *S*'s self-report.)

In contrast to the studies mentioned above, persuasibility was not measured here in terms of a before and after change. The specially devised Persuasibility Booklet contained pairs of pictures of unfamiliar objects. It was assumed that *S*s' attitude toward either picture in a pair would be neutral unless influenced by someone else's expressed opinion. By avoiding before and after measures, the authors hoped to avoid the "initial opinion artifact" discussed above.

The teacher or experimenter indicated which picture she liked better in each pair and then she asked *S*s to indicate their choice. Persuasibility was measured in terms of the number of agreements between child and communicator.

Eleven groups of first-grade *S*s were used, and since there were three self-esteem indices, 33 *r*s were obtained between self-esteem and persuasibility scores. Twenty-two of these *r*s were in the predicted direction, but none was significant. When groups were combined into two over-all sex groups, yielding six correlations, one of these *r*s was significant at the .05 level. (It involved the third "self-esteem" measure.)

In a second study by these authors, children were chosen as being high and low on self-esteem on the basis of a combination of the first and second self-esteem measures. As a first step in the procedure, *E* elicited the individual child's preferences on some pairs of pictures, and in one group of *S*s she agreed with the child's preferences, while in another group she disagreed with them. After this step she attempted to influence the children on fourteen pictures by presenting her own opinion before the child expressed his. Children with low self-esteem were significantly more persuasible on the final fourteen pictures than were children with high self-esteem. Results significant at $< .05$ level were obtained in each of two replications. There was a significant interaction effect, since it was only after experimenter agreement in the initial part of the procedure that the *S*s with low self-esteem scores exhibited greater persuasibility on the final fourteen pictures. The authors speculate that the low self-esteem child reacts sensitively to the approval he seeks from others, and is predisposed to be persuasible only if the communicator indicates to him the likely possibility that they will agree with each other.

Thus in one of their experimental designs these investigators have obtained support for the idea that self-esteem (as measured by their first two indices) is negatively related to persuasibility in first-grade children. Why null results were obtained from the first two measures in their first design cannot be ascertained. It may be that the relation between self-esteem and persuasibility is not obtained unless the experimenter has indicated that the reward of agreement with her is a possibility.

Cohen (1959) feels that within interacting pairs of persons, Ss who are high in self-esteem will exert more influence on a common judgment and/or will perceive themselves as attempting to influence the partner more often than will Ss low in self-esteem. However, it cannot be stated confidently that the evidence he cites supports this idea. He reports briefly the results of one unpublished study which could not be obtained by the present writer for detailed analysis. His second set of possibly pertinent findings were obtained from Ss originally paired on bases other than self-esteem levels (Cohen, 1956). Thus even if we assume the validity of his self-esteem measure (see Table I and Chapter III), we have no way of knowing whether other relevant variables were adequately controlled, as the author himself points out.

Janis, Field, Rife, Abelson, and Lesser all assumed that Ss with low self-esteem are persuasible because they have an especially strong need to avoid displeasing others. In an apparently somewhat related rationale, Moeller and Applezweig (1957a) assumed that yielding in a conformity situation would occur most frequently in persons with high motivation for "Social Approval," but low motivation for "Self Approval." (The latter motivation they sometimes call self-realization or consistency with the self picture.) Although this study is based on a nonphenomenal rather than a phenomenal self-concept measure, it will be included here because of its possible relationships to the studies discussed above.

A specially devised Behavior Interpretation Inventory was used to measure motivation. (See Table IV.) In the conformity experiment a majority of the group had been previously instructed to give erroneous judgments of line length. One of the findings was that Ss who were high in motivation for Social Approval but low in motivation for Self Approval yielded more often to the erroneous majority than did Ss high in Self Approval and low in Social Approval motivation. Ss were approximately matched on the other two scores, Escape and Avoidance. The one-tail $p < .05$.

Moeller and Applezweig (1957a) suggest that conformity, like any behavior, may be expected to appear when it has instrumental relevance for satisfying a need. Behind the hypothesis of Janis *et al.* lies the idea that persons with low self-esteem may find that yielding is instrumental to avoiding social disapproval or getting social approval which they need. Thus one might wonder whether persons high on Moeller and Applezweig's Social Approval motive were somehow similar to the other authors' Ss who had low self-esteem. If this were so, the Moeller and Applezweig experiment would fall into a similar conceptual framework with the others. However, Moeller and Applezweig have correlated their Social Approval scales with a number of self-rating inventories, including Sarason's Test Anxiety measure, with essentially null findings (Moeller & Applezweig, 1957b). This leaves a plausible conceptual synthesis unsupported empirically.

Linton and Graham's (1959) study is more complicated than any of the above investigations because they utilized more measures of personality, including some which purported to index both the conscious and unconscious self images of the Ss. Persuasibility was measured on two questions in an opinion-change test. On the basis of this test, Ss were subdivided into three unequal size groups: those who changed toward the opinions expressed in the persuasive communication (positive changers), those who changed away from the persuasive communication (negative changers), and nonchangers. There was no control group to establish what changes would occur without systematic intervening influence, nor to provide a basis for establishing the cutting points between what might be called nonsignificant change (i.e., nonchange) and significant change (i.e., change in either a positive or negative direction). The negative change group was cut much nearer the 0% change point than was the positive change group. This decision was apparently made partly on the basis of a preliminary analysis of the relation between independent and dependent variables. In any event, we cannot know whether the change groups were matched as to their original answers, but this seems unlikely. If they were not matched on original answers, this leaves the possibility that the personality variables might be associated with the position of S's original answers to the opinion items, rather than being associated with S's changeability of opinion.

On the personality measurement side of the study, the authors assumed the validity of certain Machover figure drawing scales for revealing S's unconscious self image. This assumption has been challenged on the basis of extensive literature reviews by Levy (1950) and by Swensen

(1957). Twelve out of the 38 figure drawing comparisons differentiated positive changers from the other two groups at the .05 level or better. But in the light of the unproven validity of the test as well as the questions already raised about the formation of the groups, one wonders how to interpret these statistical findings.

The authors assumed that passivity or assertiveness of Rorschach M reflects S's unconscious self-image. As inferred from this index, the positive changers showed weaker, more passive self concepts while nonchangers and negative changers showed predominantly strong, assertive self concepts. They point out that a frequent interpretation of a high Hd score on the Rorschach is that it indicates low self-esteem. However, their nonchangers showed higher Hd, which was inconsistent with the M scores of these Ss, and contradicted the authors' ideas that nonchangers should have higher rather than lower self-esteem. In the light of these apparent contradictions, they suggested that high Hd does *not* mean low self-esteem in these cases. In their study, high Hd coupled with assertive M (which is found in nonchangers) is interpreted to mean that nonchangers have an essentially strong self concept (M) coupled with an overly critical attitude toward themselves (Hd). The unproven validity of their indices, the *ad hoc* interpretation of Hd, and the earlier questions about the formation of their groups leaves their results uninterpretable, in the view of the present author.

Their third personality measure was a check list personality inventory of 84 items, intended to reveal those "consciously held feelings about himself that he is willing to state publicly." Results on individual items are not given, but the authors conclude that changers feel inadequate and inferior, nonchangers feel adequate, and negative changers feel physically inadequate. Positive changers feel little assertiveness, nonchangers wish for assertion and independence, and negative changers feel rebellious toward authority and convention, and feel hostile. Detailed comment on their findings with the questionnaire is not possible, since information on which to base an analysis is not given. (See Table II.)

Since the results just listed form part of a larger group of correlations, the authors feel that the data from all their measures (including those discussed here) are mutually supporting and form a meaningful pattern. However, there is need for cross-validation, using groups with comparable initial answers before we can feel confident about any generalizations.

Summary. Considering all the studies reviewed in this section, it is obvious that the obtained statistical trends tend to support the idea that self-esteem measures and persuasibility measures may be inversely related. However, before we conclude that a generalized relationship between "self-esteem" and "persuasibility" has been demonstrated, we must remember the following facts about these studies. (1) Every study used a different combination of self-esteem and persuasibility measures. Intercorrelation among self-esteem measures has either not been demonstrated or is zero. No intercorrelations among persuasibility or conformity measures are available. Therefore we need to avoid generalizations based on assigning the same label to several possibly unrelated instruments. In short, one cannot combine the findings from the several studies into a pattern which has a clear meaning. (2) Many insignificant trends were obtained, including insignificant reversals from predicted associations. (3) The possibility of artifact has not been ruled out in all studies. In particular the "initial opinion" artifact has not been adequately controlled for in the opinion change studies.

Although the pattern of results is not strong and clear, it does look encouraging enough to warrant further systematic and controlled exploration of the hypothesis that "self-esteem" and "persuasibility" may be inversely related under certain specifiable conditions. Before we can infer any causal relation between self-esteem and persuasibility, we must design studies of an entirely different kind from the R-R correlational type reviewed in this section.

4. *Body Characteristics and the Self Concept*

Theoretically a person's body characteristics as he perceives them might exert a central influence on the development of his self concept. The details of such a notion have not been specified by personality theorists, with the possible exception of Freud's views on the influence of anatomical sex differences upon self-regard, and Adler's views on the role of constitutional inferiorities in the development of character. It seems safe to say, however, that self-concept theorists agree on the general idea that body characteristics which are lowly valued by S may be expected to undermine his general self-regard, while highly valued body characteristics should enhance self-regard.

Considering the importance of this idea, it is surprising to find that no controlled study explores this proposition directly. A combination of investigations by Jourard and his colleagues may offer some indirect support. They found a positive correlation between size of body parts and Body-Cathexis for those parts in both male and female subjects. They also obtained positive correlations between Body-Cathexis and [Actual—Ideal] discrepancies in size of body parts in females (Jourard & Secord, 1954, 1955). In a separate study, Secord and Jourard (1953) obtained significant correlations between Body-Cathexis and Self-Cathexis. (See Chapter III for details on the Body-Cathexis and Self-Cathexis scales.) The latter findings may be partially a function of response sets. Insofar as they represent a psychologically meaningful association between independently measured variables, they may be combined with the first two results. The total pattern of findings is congruent with the assumption that deviations of body characteristics from S's ideal may lead to lowered self-regard. However, no firm cause-effect inferences can be drawn, since the studies were of the R-R variety.

Presumably the influence of body characteristics might be especially noticeable at adolescence when body changes which are important for social functioning are numerous, rapid, and obvious. Only two studies relevant to this question are at hand. Methodological limitations restrict our conclusions to saying that there may be some connection between physical maturity and a few (but by no means all) the self-concept measures explored. (Although these studies involve at least partly nonphenomenal self-concept measures, they are classified here for the sake of convenience. For a discussion of the so-called "body image," a clearly nonphenomenal construct, see Chapter V.)

Mussen and Jones (1957) found significant differences in "negativity" of self concept between adolescent boys who were "consistently accelerated" and "consistently retarded" in physical development. Negativity of self concept was indicated when S described the heroes of TAT stories in "negative terms." The validity of the measure was assumed rather than proven.

Smith and Lebo (1956) were also interested in changes in self concept associated with the rapid physiological development of puberty. They used pubic hair ratings as an index of boys' physical maturity and related it to phenomenal and nonphenomenal measures of the self concept. (See Tables II and IV and Chapter V.) Pubic hair ratings, but not CA, correlated significantly with Ss' self-reports on a modified Vineland Maturity Scale. Of 52 characteristics of Ss' figure-drawings, four showed significant correlations with pubic hair ratings. However, the influence of the CA variable was evidently not controlled or partialled out. In Ss' projective stories, the hero's heterosexual development and emancipation from the parents was correlated with the CA rather than with pubic hair rating. In sum, only the self-reported Vineland Maturity ratings seem to correlate with physiological development, when CA, with all that it implies psychologically, has been held constant.

5. *Effects of Counseling or Psychotherapy on the Self Concept*

Psychologists who have done psychotherapy research have had one or both of two aims. Sometimes they have sought empirical information on the numerous factors which presumably induce the desired effects on the patients, or they may also have wished to explore the postulates of a personality theory. While research on therapy *qua* therapy is obviously important and interesting, and should be vigorously pursued, it is not this type of research which concerns us here. Rather we wish to evaluate the degree to which therapy studies have succeeded in verifying postulates from self-concept theory.

To evaluate the theoretical relevance of results from therapy research, one needs to know what predictions the theory would make. According to self-concept theorists, if counseling or therapy is judged by external criteria to be "successful," it will bring about various changes in the self concept, such as the following: (a) increased agreement between self-estimates and objective estimates of the self (the self concept becomes more "realistic"); (b) increased congruence between self and ideal self, if this congruence is very low at the outset of therapy; (c) slightly decreased self-ideal congruence if this congruence is unwarrantedly high at the outset of therapy; (d) increased acceptance of one's own limitations as well as assets; (e) increased "realism" in setting the ideal self; (f) increased consistency among various aspects of the self concept, or among various aspects of the ideal self.

Ultimately we wish to present and evaluate the results of available studies to see to what extent these predictions have been verified. Before we can do that, some methodological limitations must be considered, however. These fall into three groups: those stemming from ambiguities in the theory, those inherent in any therapy research, and those avoidable ones which have actually occurred in the studies reviewed. We turn now to the limitations stemming from the theory.

First of all, the predictions cited above are not as straightforward as the list may make them appear. For example, theorists recognize that increases in reported self-ideal congruence or reported self-acceptance may occur among persons who terminate therapy prematurely, or among persons whose therapy would be externally judged as "unsuccessful." Presumably such trends would indicate increasing defensiveness against recognizing unwanted impulses and characteristics. (See, for example, Loevinger and Ossorio, 1959.)

Also it is usually tacitly assumed that the course of change in regard to any of these aspects of the self concept may be nonlinear, or even irregular, perhaps showing temporary reversals at times as ultimately successful therapy progresses. Self-concept theory does not make definite predictions concerning these details, however. This makes it understandable that most studies have bypassed these complications by utilizing either pre- and posttests, crude divisions of the therapy process, or crude global estimates of preponderant trends.

Regardless of the details of the course of therapy, the predicted long-run trend is toward the changes outlined above, and confirmation of such trends would be congruent with self-concept theory. On the other hand, "negative" findings would be uninterpretable, partly because they might result from some of these unclearly predicted within-therapy irregularities.

We have just said that certain long-range trends would be congruent with self-concept theory. However, we do not believe that "positive" trends from the best possible therapy research can provide well-controlled tests of the postulates of self-concept theory, or of any personality theory. The application of a therapy which is based on a certain theory may appear to afford an opportunity for an "experimental" design which can test some propositions of that theory. However, many crucial difficulties impair the usefulness of the situation for the purpose of theory testing. Some of these difficulties might conceivably be handled through an extensive series of studies involving appropriately chosen and manipulated control groups, and careful attention to the establishment of valid operational definitions of constructs.

At the moment, however, the setting up of such researches is hampered by the vagueness of the theories themselves. They do not clearly specify the theoretically relevant factors in therapy, or provide adequate basis for formation of operational definitions and the measurement of the constructs which are presumed to be involved. Also, since the various personality theories overlap so much, in unclearly specified ways, it would be impossible to devise crucial tests of many of the postulates of any particular theory.[2]

But even if all these problems could eventually be taken care of, we must still take into consideration the second of the three groups of methodological limitations, namely, those inherent in any therapy research. For example, there is the question as to whether therapy with disturbed patients constitutes a situation which permits a systematic, theoretically relevant analysis of the basic processes involved in the current self concept and its development. We might vary systematically the characteristics of patients, of therapists, and of therapy types. But we would also need to give and withhold therapy and to isolate and manipulate factors within the therapy process in a manner incompatible with the ethical or practical requirements of clinical practice. In addition, the nature of the highly personal, close therapeutic relationship implies that certain difficulties will stand in the way of a well-controlled experiment which would be appropriate to the testing of a theory. That is, the therapist is unable to act as a rigorous experimenter in the situation. The patient is unable to act as a suitable experimental subject, and the circumstances are not favorable for achieving the necessary controls and accurate descriptions. Also, since therapy patients are already disturbed persons, therapy measures can say relatively little about the theoretically basic processes in the etiology of their disturbances, much less about normal self-concept development and structure.

If therapy studies are to be used to evaluate theory, then, we must first try to circumvent as many of their limitations as possible. The remaining ones which seem to be necessarily inherent in any therapy process must be recognized. In short, all this implies that therapy studies may throw light on self-concept theory, but other research designs are needed for systematic, definitive tests.

We turn now to the third group of methodological limitations, those avoidable ones which were fairly common in the studies reviewed.

1. Most researchers used *no* control groups, or failed to arrange or treat their groups so as to take care of important factors, which could be

---

[2]Edwards and Cronbach (1952) discuss problems of establishing suitable designs for research in psychotherapy, but they are not particularly concerned with using therapy studies as tests of personality theory.

controlled even within the inherent limitations of therapy. Minimum requirements along this line would seem to include the following:

(a) No-therapy control groups should be used to provide baseline information on test-retest reliability of measuring instruments, including "spontaneous" changes to be expected over comparable time periods, and/or effects of repeated testing upon the *S*s' responses to the instruments. These control *S*s should be matched with therapy patients on a number of relevant variables, certainly including type of problem, personality characteristics, and motivation for change through therapy and/or self-effort. It might appear that *S*s could act as their own nontherapy controls, with changes during a pretherapy waiting period being compared to changes during a therapy period. However, this is not sufficient to determine what would happen to the self concept during a no-therapy period if *S*s were not expecting to get therapy. Neither would this design suffice to hold life experiences comparable for therapy and nontherapy periods, nor would it account for the cumulative effects of repeated testing (see Mertens's 1951 study cited below). (b) If conclusions are to be drawn based on the assumption that the constructs of a certain theory are uniquely involved in a specified kind of therapy, we need comparison groups who are given other varieties of therapy allegedly not involving these constructs. (c) Control groups should be set up to study auxiliary factors of which therapy outcomes may be a function, such as patient characteristics, therapist characteristics, time variations, etc.

2. Judgments of "improvement" are frequently open to the possibility of artifact for the following reasons:

(a) The judge, especially if he is the patient's therapist, or if he subscribes to the "school of thought" underlying the therapy, may be biassed. For example, he may expect and/or want to find improvement. (b) If improvement is judged from the study of interview material, the trend in the verbal responses may represent, not improvement in the sense the therapist intended, but one or more of the following: *(i)* "verbal conditioning" through the therapist's selective reinforcement of the patient's responses, rather than changes in the patient's feelings or attitudes (see Krasner, 1958, for a review of the pertinent literature); *(ii)* the patient's desire to please the therapist by producing the sorts of verbal responses he knows the therapist wants to hear; *(iii)* the patient's desire to remain in or escape from therapy, or certain issues taken up in therapy.

3. There are sometimes possibilities for artifactual contamination between the therapist's or other observer's judgments of improvement and *S*'s self-reports (self-concept measures). This is especially likely to be true if both are taken from the interview material, or if self-concept reports contain many of the same type of statements that patients ordinarily make in therapy. Two common practices enhance the possibility of mutual contamination between measures of improvement and measures of self concept: (a) deriving the statement lists for *Q* sorts from interview materials produced by patients; (b) retesting the patients at various points during therapy.

4. Sometimes alternate self-concept measures, or alternate measures of improvement in therapy, are applied to the same subjects. Null hypotheses concerning the relationship between improvement and self-concept changes are tested with the different measures, as if the tests could be considered to be independent of one another. In fact, if the alternate indices are highly correlated, they may constitute repeated measures of the same variable. In such a case *E* should not assume that each of his significance tests provides an independent test of the hypothesis involving the variable in question. What is required here is the demonstration of operational independence of the various measures purporting to index improvement (or the various measures purporting to index different aspects of self-concept change). Of course the fact that two dependent variables are correlated statistically (or two independent variables are correlated statistically) does not necessarily mean that one is repeatedly measuring the same dependent (or independent) variable. The point is that empirical demonstration of the independence of the measuring operations would strengthen the contention that separate tests of the null hypothesis were warranted.

For example, it sometimes happens that parallel results are not obtained from two studies which measure improvement with theoretically relevant criteria of improvement that are operationally quite distinct. This makes plausible our contention that, when parallel results are obtained from several statistical tests within a given study, one should be careful to check the operational independence of the alternate indices for measuring improvement (or the operational independence of alternate indices for measuring self-concept change).

5. The problem of devising satisfactory indices of the various types of self-concept change is mostly unsolved. In particular, the use of com-

plex, dual indices (e.g., self-ideal correlations derived from Q sorts) tells us only about changes in global scores. Without an item analysis, it is impossible to know what changes in component variables and/or configurations among variables are taking place, even when significant global changes occur. Or the global scores may not change significantly, and individual item changes of potential theoretical relevance may be missed. Group trends in global scores may be the net result of a combination of quite different individual S and item changes, so that group trends may not describe any individual accurately. Since the theory is supposed to apply to the individual, this defect is crucial. (See Chapter III for fuller discussion of this and other problems of self-concept measures.) In addition, scaling problems have not been satisfactorily handled, so that one cannot say that any given statistically significant change represents a psychologically significant "j. n. d." Neither can one say that equal numerical changes involving different scale ranges are psychologically comparable.

6. Insufficient attention has been given to the study of therapy "failures" (in research terms, exceptions to predictions or group trends), with the result that the power of the theory to account for such irregularities has not been explored.

a. Counseled Ss Compared to Noncounseled Ss

Only four studies compare counseled with noncounseled Ss. An investigation comparing Ss who did and did not see some mental hygiene films will be reported together with these four, since this seems to be the most relevant classification for this unique study.

Caplan (1957) found significant increases of self-ideal congruence among seventeen problem boys who received group counseling as contrasted to seventeen noncounseled controls roughly matched for IQ, sex, school record, economic status, and initial self-ideal congruence. There were also significant changes in the counseled (but not in the noncounseled) group in the mean number of classes per boy in which poor citizenship grades were received. (See Table I.)

The therapy research extensively reported in Rogers and Dymond (1954) includes two types of control groups, but even these leave some important factors uncontrolled. Butler and Haigh (1954) report that clients who waited sixty days for therapy showed no improvement in self-ideal congruence over the waiting period (mean rs were −.01 and −.01), while from precounseling to follow-up, the mean r went from −.01 to +.31. (See Chapter III for a discussion of Butler and Haigh's Q-sort items.) This type of comparison does not tell us, however, what changes would have occurred in the waiting Ss if they had not expected that they would get therapy eventually. Perhaps they made less effort to solve their own problems in the interim than would Ss not having such expectation of outside help. Or perhaps they wished to indicate just prior to therapy that they were still in need of help, thus giving a low self-ideal pretherapy r despite changes in their self concept. The therapy patients were also compared to nontherapy controls who showed no change in self-ideal congruence over the period from pretherapy to follow-up (+.58 to +.59). As Calvin (1954) has pointed out, however, this comparison does not specifically indicate what would have happened over this long period to noncounseled controls who started out with self-ideal rs as low as the therapy patients. In this respect, Caplan's control subjects were better matched with his experimentals, so that his results are more convincing. (The difference between initial self-ideal congruence of therapy intakes and controls is much greater in Rogers and Dymond's study than in Wahler's, described in Section C-9 below.)

The Q sorts made by Rogers and Dymond's Ss were assigned an "adjustment" score by Dymond (1954a). (See Chapter III for a discussion of this score.) The results concerning the effects of counseling on the adjustment score parallel those reported by Butler and Haigh in terms of self-ideal congruence. However, the fact that the adjustment score and the self-ideal rs were derived from the same instrument and correlated +.8 with each other indicates that these findings are not independent tests of an hypothesis concerning the effects of therapy on the self concept.

In the same research, Rogers (1954a) found no change in Ss' self-reports on a modified Willoughby E-M Scale during the pretherapy waiting period, and no change in the no-therapy control Ss. But there was a significant change toward reports of greater maturity from pretherapy to posttherapy in Ss who received therapy. Thus his data using self-reports from the same Ss as those studied by Butler and Haigh, and by Dymond, gave results paralled to theirs. Interestingly enough, however, E-M ratings of therapy patients made by their friends, and judgments of therapy success made by the counselor did not relate to each other or to S's self-reports on the E-M scale in any simple fashion.[3]

Not only are self-regard and adjustment presumed to increase with therapy, but consistency within the self concept is alleged to become greater as well. Relevant to this idea is Rosalind Dymond Cartwright's report that nine out of ten therapy cases showed more "consistency" among three self-sorts after therapy than among three self-sorts before therapy. Consistency was measured in terms of mean item variance across the three sorts. On each occasion, the three self-sorts were made by S as he thought he was seen by three persons of his own choice. Before therapy, the mean item variance of experimental Ss was significantly larger than that of control Ss. After therapy, the difference was nonsignificant. However, the controls made the three sortings only once, at the outset of the experiment, and the posttherapy sorts of the experimental Ss were compared to these initial sorts of the control Ss.

This experiment deals with an important issue, but unfortunately one cannot draw conclusions from it about the influence of therapy upon self-concept consistency. This is so because the control and therapy Ss were not matched on initial consistency, and the second (posttherapy) sorts of the experimental group were not compared to second sorts made by the control group.

An additional finding was that items showing low consistency across the three sorts were more often "self-relevant" (i.e., they fell in extreme piles). It seems possible, however, that this result may be an artifact of the association between the pile value of the initial placement of an item and the maximum possible size of difference from that placement of the item and any other placement of it.

As we said earlier, counseling is alleged to increase the "realism" of the self concept. To test this contention, Berdie's (1954) experimental Ss received vocational and educational counseling while control Ss who were comparable on academic ability (ACE) and MMPI profiles did not. The counseling was particularly aimed at increasing Ss' accuracy in ap-

---

[3]Cartwright and Roth (1957), impressed with the "fragmentation of criteria" in the Rogers and Dymond book, factor-analyzed ten criterion measures in an attempt to find some order in such data. Their ten measures, obtained from thirty-one clients, included many of those used in the Rogers and Dymond study. Results are presented for three matrices: pretherapy scores (not factorizable); posttherapy scores; and change scores. It is not clear that a "self-concept" factor emerged.

praising their vocational interests, probable college achievement, college aptitude, and personality characteristics. College men, but not women, improved in accuracy of estimate of probable college achievement and of vocational interests (as indicated by the Strong test). No differences were found between experimentals and controls in accuracy of judging aptitude (as measured by the ACE test) or personality characteristics (as measured by MMPI scores).

Perhaps some changes in the self concept will be effected by viewing mental hygiene films. Mertens's (1951) research which explored this idea may be seen as related to the studies of counseling or therapy. Freshman college women responded to several personality inventories, including five scales supposed to measure self-regarding attitudes: Maslow's Self-Esteem Scale, Bernreuter's B2-S and B4-D scales; and Minnesota Personality Scales III and IV. Experimental Ss saw five mental hygiene films which control Ss who were comparable on initial personality test scores did not see. At posttesting, approximately five weeks after pretesting, both experimental and control Ss showed significant gains on four scales. Mertens thought these changes might possibly be a function of getting away from family conflicts and getting settled into college life. The experimental gain exceeded the control gain in four of the five scales, one such difference being significant. However, the control gain on Maslow's Self-Esteem scale nonsignificantly exceeded that of the experimental Ss. Although the trend in the data is not strong, it is congruent with the idea that the films may have had a tendency to affect self-regarding attitudes. The significant gains of the control group underline the necessity for having such a group in therapy studies if one wishes to conclude anything about the effects of therapy on self-concept changes.

b. THERAPY SUCCESS OR DURATION OF THERAPY CORRELATED WITH SELF-CONCEPT CHANGES

In several investigations there were no nontherapy control Ss, but changes in self-report were correlated with judged improvement in psychotherapy or with the duration of the client's therapy. When this design is used, no conclusions can be drawn, of course, concerning the effects of therapy upon changes which occur in either the self-concept or the improvement criterion. Such procedures may permit us to reach some R-R conclusions, however.

Raimy (1948) first introduced the idea and technique of making a quantified content analysis of therapy interviews in terms of changes in self-concept references. (See Chapter III for a discussion of his method.) At the beginning of counseling, clients disapproved of and had ambivalent attitudes toward themselves. As counseling progressed, fluctuations in approval occurred, with mounting ambivalence. At conclusion of counseling, successful cases showed a vast predominance of self-approval while unsuccessful cases showed a predominance of self-disapproval and ambivalent self-references. This study is important because it demonstrated the possibility of developing and using a fairly reliable theory-relevant coding scheme for therapy interviews. However, firm conclusions about the association between judged improvement and self-concept changes cannot be drawn, because (a) the judgment of successful and unsuccessful cases was done partly by the author who later coded the interviews, and it was based partly on Ss' interview statements; (b) no significance tests are given, reportedly because of the small N (14 cases).

Ewing (1954) reports a correlation of $+.38$ between the counselor's estimate of improvement for each of 39 clients and the amount of change in the pattern of self-report on 100 unspecified trait names. (See Table II.) Change in the self figure was found to be toward the counselor figure, toward the ideal figure, and toward the culturally approved figure (the latter having been developed from 100 ideal-sorts). There is no way to be sure from the reported information whether the counselor's ratings of improvement might have been based on a sample of the same class of verbalizations as went into the self-report, thus presenting the possibility of contamination.

In comparing nondirective counseling clients whose therapy was judged successful and unsuccessful, Rosenman (1955) found that the self-perceptions of successful clients manifested greater increases in positive self-evaluation, positive self-directed actions, and positive other-directed actions. A number of possible sources of artifact are pointed out by the author, however, and no firm conclusions can be reached. (See Chapter III for a description of his coding scheme and Section C-10 of this chapter for further discussion of his findings on the association between self- and other-evaluations.)

(Scheerer [1949] was also concerned with correlations between attitudes toward self and others as a function of therapy. Rudikoff [1954] and Gordon and Cartwright [1954] investigated shifts in acceptance of others as a function of therapy. Their studies are discussed in Section C-10 in connection with other findings on the relations between self-acceptance and acceptance of others.)

The investigations we have summarized above were concerned with self-regard. Another aspect of self-concept change which might correlate with improvement in therapy is increasing "self-awareness" (Vargas, 1954). Using a counselor-judgment criterion of therapy success, Vargas obtained a positive correlation between the success of therapy and the following aspects of "self-awareness": (a) an increase in proportions of descriptions of self; (b) a decrease in repetitions of old self-descriptions; (c) an increase in the number of previously undescribed aspects of self. (See Chapter III for a description of his coding scheme.) Since his Ss were ten clients who were used in the Rogers and Dymond (1954) study, other information was available concerning them. Paradoxically, when judgments of therapy success were made by a psychoanalytically oriented TAT analyst, there was a negative correlation between therapy success and the threefold criterion of "self-awareness." The way to resolve this contradiction is not clear. However, it is pertinent to note that the counselor, with his Rogerian theoretical orientation, may have inadvertently based his success judgments on "intuitive statistical evaluations" of the same sort of self-statements as the investigator was coding more formally from the same interviews. If so, a form of contamination of the criterion may account for the positive correlations.

Lipkin's results (1954) appear to be partially contradictory to those of Vargas, although direct comparison is not possible. He correlated improvement in psychotherapy (blindly judged from pre- and posttherapy TAT protocols) with E's rankings of S on a number of response categories coded from interviews which were recorded after each therapy session. (See Chapter III for a description of his coding scheme.) All nine clients were judged to have improved, and eight of them were coded as perceiving themselves more favorably after therapy than before. A significant positive rank correlation (tau) was obtained between the amount of judged improvement in therapy and the amount of positive and/or negative affect associated with current self-perceptions in the entire set of postsession interviews. The ultimately more successful clients were those who had been consciously more emotionally distressed when they entered therapy (as judged from the postinterview recordings). Therefore their greater number of affective self-references throughout therapy (and the associated judged improvement) may plausibly be a function of initial readiness to acknowledge distress.

We do not know the "adjustment" ratings of the initial TAT protocols taken alone, so we cannot know to what extent the protocol judgments prior to therapy would have correlated with coded emotionality of self-reference at the outset. Thus we cannot know whether total judged improvement (a dual index) is a function of its initial component (first TAT) only. If it were, this would imply that judged improvement might be predicted more accurately as a function of both initial measures combined.

In the next research to be described, it was hypothesized that therapy may lower self-regard, at least during the first stages of the therapeutic process. When Wahler (1958) correlated average self-ratings with average social desirability ratings, he obtained +.75 for outpatient, non-psychiatric veterans, +.66 for psychiatric intakes before therapy, and +.37 for psychiatric patients having therapy. (See Table II.) Wahler suggests that the lower correlation for psychiatric patients might represent the influence of therapy upon willingness to acknowledge socially undesirable characteristics. However, the data do not tell us what the correlation for the therapy patients was at the time of *their* intake, so no firm inference concerning the effects of therapy is warranted on the basis of these correlations. Some suggestive evidence that therapy may increase willingness to give unfavorable self-descriptions is afforded by the significant correlation of +.39 between the number of therapy interviews and the unfavorability of the self-description. (This correlation includes only patients who had some therapy.) Returning to the correlations between average social desirability and self-description, it is interesting to note the relatively similar values obtained for nonpsychiatric patient controls and psychiatric intakes. This finding seems different from the finding of the Rogers group that applicants for psychiatric care showed much lower self-ideal congruence than did controls.

Gibson, Snyder, and Ray (1955) factor-analyzed 20 measures of change obtained from 42 clients who had undergone client-centered therapy. Eight of these measures were taken from the therapy interviews, six were Rorschach indices, and six were MMPI scores, including specially devised measures of "Attitude toward Self" and "Attitude toward Others." Several of these may be said to be measures of success in therapy. (See Table II.) Three interpretable factors were obtained. The six measures having high loading on Factor I were all interview measures. "This factor appears to reflect the kinds of changes trained observers note in a client's emotional tone . . . toward greater relief from tension, and toward a more positive or optimistic attitude about himself and his circumstances" (Gibson *et al.*, 1955, pp. 86-87). The primary loadings on Factor II were the Rorschach scoring categories. On Factor III, six out of seven interpreted loadings can be considered to be self-ratings by the client. Five of them were MMPI scores and one was a client judgment of the interviews. "It appears as though this factor is one measuring change from the client's frame of reference." According to the authors, these self-reported changes seem to involve less feeling of depression or anxiety, a probable rise in activity level, feelings of greater independence, and more accepting attitudes toward self and others (Gibson *et al.*, 1955, p. 87).

One may speculate on the psychological meaning of these factors. But as Hobbs points out in his comments on the article, the factors may represent instrument characteristics more than psychologically relevant intraindividual differences.

An example of this kind of ambiguity which is of particular interest to self-concept researchers is found in comparing Factors I and III. An examination of the measures having high loadings on these independent factors raises some problems of methodology in measuring the phenomenal self. That is, Factor III seems most clearly to be a conscious self-concept index. Factor I indicates the therapist's judgment of the amount of change. However, one of the two measures having the greatest loading on Factor I is Raimy's PNAvQ, which has in some studies been taken as a measure of changes in S's phenomenal self concept. Perhaps the independence of Factors I and III implies that E's coding of the client's interviews by the PNAvQ method does not index S's phenomenal self after all. On the other hand, E has in effect also coded S's responses on self-report devices such as the MMPI when he has applied the a priori scoring method. On this reasoning, both the PNAvQ and the MMPI indices involve the imposition of E's code on S's reports. The fact of E's coding, then, does not necessarily differentiate between a measure "from the therapist's viewpoint" and a measure "from the client's viewpoint." Thus one might conclude that the two factors respectively represent common coding variance, rather than that each factor represents a different viewpoint on the client's progress. This would permit one to assume that the phenomenal self has been measured in both factors.

If that is so, the question arises as to why various measures of the phenomenal self are so uncorrelated. Perhaps something has been discovered about the phenomenal self, i.e., that there are uncorrelated aspects of it. Or perhaps the same aspect of the phenomenal self is being tapped, but the lack of correlation is due to methodological differences between the coding processes after all. Although *E* codes both types of measure, the role of *S* is different in the two. That is, as the authors suggest, the therapist's ratings of the client's phenomenal self are made in the light of his knowledge of other clients' changes in self concept and feeling tone, while a different reference scale must necessarily be used by the inexperienced client in describing his own self concept and feelings through a self-report device.

At present there is no way to choose between various possible interpretations of the independence of Factors I and III. The problems raised by these data are certainly worthy of further exploration.

The next investigations to be reviewed are only indirectly relevant to those summarized immediately above, because, in the following studies, improvement in adjustment is not one of the variables correlated with self-concept change. Instead, premature termination of therapy is related to self-reports, and, as the authors point out, remaining and improving in therapy are not synonymous.

Rubenstein and Lorr (1956) found that *S*s who terminated psychotherapy prematurely were more self-satisfied (on specified rating scales) than were remainers. A similar but nonsignificant trend was found by Lorr, Katz, and Rubenstein (1958), using what was apparently a modification of their previously employed rating scales. (See Table II.) In both studies, terminators and remainers differed on other variables than self-satisfaction (e.g., education, socioeconomic status, degree of illness, *F* scores). Therefore no clear interpretation of the role of satisfaction in remaining could be drawn, even if the trends in the second study had also been significant.

c. Changes in Counseled *S*s

The researches reviewed immediately above included no nontherapy control groups, so no conclusions could be drawn concerning the role of therapy in any changes which were observed. However, the investigators correlated two variables, usually judged improvement in therapy versus self-concept changes. This made it possible to reach some R-R conclusions.

By contrast, none of the following designs includes either a control group or a correlation between judged improvement and self-concept changes. No conclusions can be drawn from any of these studies. They will be reviewed, however, so as to bring out the authors' hypotheses and measuring techniques.

Haigh (1949) analyzed verbatim transcripts of ten counseling cases in terms of "defensive behavior." Defensiveness was said to occur if, in *E*'s opinion, (1) threat existed in the form of incongruence between one of *S*'s particular values, concepts, or experiences, and another particular value, concept, or experience; and (2) the individual reacted to this perceived incongruence in such a way as to distort the reality which he perceived. *Awareness* was said to occur if the client seemed to be aware of the defensiveness of his behavior. In line with Haigh's hypothesis, seven out of ten *S*s exhibited a decrease in *defensiveness,* as measured by halves of the therapeutic process. (The decrease, in terms of total frequency of statements, was significant at the .05 level.) Contrary to *E*'s hypothesis, however, frequency of "awareness" also decreased.

Haigh divided his *S*s into those who showed an increase and those who showed a decrease in defensiveness during therapy. Both of these groups showed a decrease of "awareness." However, Haigh felt that his theory was partially confirmed by the fact that the decrease in awareness was proportionally much greater in *S*s who showed an increasing frequency of defensiveness.

Several problems of method prevent one from drawing clear conclusions from this study. Chief among these is the fact that the same person evidently coded for both variables and knew the hypothesis while coding. The two variables appear to the present writer to have considerable "literary" overlap, so that it seems plausible that the coder could not operationally distinguish between them without contamination. The coder's probable knowledge of the interview number might also have colored his judgments. Also there is no nontherapy control group who, let us say, merely spent two hours talking about themselves, these interviews being separated by time periods comparable to the therapy *S*s' first and last interviews. Therefore there is no base line of expected changes without therapy. Are seven out of ten *S*s changing in a given direction more than might have occurred by chance?

Kelman and Parloff (1957) utilized a number of measures of improvement associated with group psychotherapy of fifteen neurotic patients. Of four measures depending wholly or partly on S's report, only one (a symptom disability check list) showed significant change. A specially devised Self-Satisfaction Q sort showed no significant change. The interpretation of these findings is unclear, since there was no control group. In addition, the ratings by trained observers which *did* show significant change were possibly contaminated by the fact that both pre- and post-ratings were made after therapy. (See also Parloff, Kelman, & Frank, 1954.) (See Table I.)

Pearl (1954) attempted to study changes in California Ethnocentrism and Authoritarianism scale scores, and in self-concept factors over therapy. Lack of a control group, and other design and measurement problems, render his findings regarding therapy uninterpretable, unfortunately. (See Table I.)

Raskin (1952) prepared a "locus-of-evaluation" scale, and applied it to the interviews of ten therapy cases to test his hypothesis that Ss should, during therapy, increasingly use their own standards of self-evaluation. (See Chapter III for a description of his coding plan.) The difference in mean score between initial and final interviews was significant. However, since there was no control group with two comparably spaced interviews but no intervening therapy, we cannot know the role of therapy per se in the findings. It is interesting that locus-of-evaluation scores correlated significantly with ratings of the interviews for self-attitudes, self-acceptance, and insight.

Only counseled Ss were studied by Johnson (1953), who asked each client to state before the initial counseling interview which fifth of the population he thought he was in, so far as intelligence, interests, and personality were concerned, and to indicate his degree of confidence in his self-estimates. How these self-rating scales were defined for the client is not stated in the article. After S took the Otis Higher Intelligence Test, Form A, Kuder Vocational Interest Inventory Form BB, and Bernreuter Personality Inventory, his results were presented to him. Percentile scores were used for the intelligence test, profiles for the interest inventory, and personality tests were discussed in the form of "quintiles or less exact categories."

Immediately after counseling, Ss rerated themselves. One month after counseling, data from the first 100 Ss to reply to a request for a third self-rating were examined. Accuracy and certainty of self-knowledge increased significantly on intelligence and interests, and this increase was maintained for one month. It is impossible to interpret these results clearly because no control groups were used, follow-up and initial groups were not the same, and characteristics of the self-rating scales are not given.

Singer and Stefflre (1954) contend that a shift in correlation is not an appropriate index of whether postcounseling self-estimates are more accurate than precounseling self-estimates. They argue that such a shift does not reveal whether Ss' postcounseling self-estimates show smaller or larger discrepancies from test score values than did the precounseling self-estimates. Accordingly these investigators computed means and standard deviations of before- and after-counseling self-estimates of interest in six areas measured by an Occupational Interest Inventory. The standard deviation was supposed to indicate whether Ss' guesses clustered nearer the test score even if the mean self-estimate did not shift toward the test score after counseling. Twenty-four significance tests were made (six means and six standard deviations computed separately for boys and for girls). Five significant trends supporting the hypothesis were found. These findings are uninterpretable because sufficient information is not given to enable one to know how many "significant" findings should be expected by chance in this situation, and no control group was used.

O'Dea and Zeran (1953, p. 243) concluded that their findings with the MMPI "pointed out and supported the claim that the criteria of success of counseling should in part be concerned with the degree and direction of change in the self-concept and its concomitant effects upon behavior." However, they nowhere presented the relevant data or an analysis of them. Since they had no noncounseled control group, there is no suitable base line for evaluating changes in the MMPI and California Test of Personality, even if the data on these tests had been presented.

d. STUDIES OF SINGLE CASES

Most of the investigations reviewed in this book were aimed toward the establishment of general laws, and they involved groups of Ss. In contrast to this, five researchers have applied "inverse factor analysis" to a study of only one person. Since four of these single cases were therapy clients, all these investigations will be included here.

Inverse factor analysis is based on intercorrelations of many tests or observations made on one individual. For example, Q sorts made by S under different kinds of instructions may be intercorrelated and factor analyzed.

There has been considerable controversy over the place of inverse factor analysis in the correlational domain, and over the interpretation of the factors one gets from this procedure. (See, for example, Stephenson, 1953.) An evaluation of the argument is beyond the scope of this book.

In addition, there is some difference of opinion among psychologists as to the values of studying a single case by this method. For one thing, intensive study of one person might appear to be more appropriate to clinical psychology or to existential psychology than it is to nomological psychology, except as the study of the single case gives the nomological psychologist some hypotheses which may be tested through further research. For another thing, it appears that among existential psychologists, there might be some disagreement as to whether inverse factor analysis is an appropriate tool for understanding the "being" of another person.

In any event, five investigations of a single case are summarized here, as examples of this sort of approach. In some instances the trends were congruent with hypotheses derived from self-concept theory. These trends cannot lead to conclusions about the theory, however, because only one case was involved in each study, and no control observations are available.

Nunnally followed one therapy case over a two-year period. Using sixty statements selected for their unique relevance to this person, Nunnally obtained fifteen pretherapy self-assessments in which the $S \, Q$ sorted the statements under fourteen sets of instructions. The instructions "as I am generally" (present self) were used twice. Through centroid factor analysis, three factors were obtained from the pretherapy intercorrelations: Factor I represented the conceived general mode of behavior. Most of the self-assessments had some loading on this factor, and the variance of the "present self" assessments were almost entirely accounted for by this factor. Factor II represented the patient's conception of her ideal self, the self she should be, the way her mother wanted her to be. Factor III was positively loaded for the patient's perceptions of how her friends regarded her, and negatively loaded for her perceptions of how her mother regarded her and how she was when doing her music work. Nineteen self-assessments were made during the posttherapy period, including two under the instructions "as I am generally." Three factors were obtained from the posttherapy matrix. Although it was expected that each pretherapy factor would correlate highly with its posttherapy counterpart, this was borne out only for Factor I. Nunnally interprets this to mean that the client's factors "transcend their content," an idea which is alleged to have wide implications for self-concept theories. What "transcending their content" means is not fully explained, however.

Nunnally stated five hypotheses, three of which will be summarized here. He postulated first that change in one factor over therapy would be accompanied by a change in at least one of the two other factors. However, he found no such configurational change, since the self (representative of Factor I) showed small change and the ideal (representative of Factor II) showed marked change. Supporting his second hypothesis he found a "movement toward increasing congruence among owned self-assessments after therapy" (Nunnally, 1955, p. 90), i.e., the owned self-assessments tended to "converge upon a central vector (approach a general factor)." Thirdly, he hypothesized that improvement during therapy should be accompanied by the client's increased tendency to make her "assessments of herself as seen by others" (attributed self-assessments) incongruous with Factor I ("present self" or "owned self"). The findings were actually opposite to this hypothesis, i.e., after therapy the client held the opinion that everyone else regarded her much as she regarded herself.

Two of the cases in the Rogers and Dymond research were considered individually in terms of inverse factor analysis (Rogers, 1954b, 1954c). Mrs. Oak, who was considered to be a successful case, made self-sorts, ideal-sorts, and ordinary-person-sorts before therapy, on two occasions during therapy, and at the conclusion of therapy. (See Chapter III for the Butler and Haigh Q-sort items.) These twelve sorts were intercorrelated and factor-analyzed. As in Nunnally's analysis, two of Mrs. Oak's factors clearly represented the Self and the Ideal. Mrs. Oak's third factor represented the Ordinary Person. The self-sorts had significant loadings only on the Self factor, the ideal-sorts had significant loadings only on the Ideal factor, and the ordinary-person-sorts had significant loadings only on the Ordinary Person factor, with the following two exceptions: At the beginning of therapy, the ordinary-person-sort had a negative loading on the Self factor. At the end of therapy, the self-sort had an equal loading on the Self factor and on the Ideal factor.

Mr. Bebb, an unsuccessful therapy client, Q sorted the Butler and Haigh items on five different occasions, to express his actual self, his ideal self, and his concept of the ordinary person. At the end of the seventh interview, the counselor sorted the items three times to predict how the client would sort them to express his concept of his actual self, ideal self, and the ordinary person. These eighteen sorts were intercorrelated and factor-analyzed. In this case too a Self factor, an Ordinary Person factor, and an Ideal factor were identified. In addition, a factor called Conventional Self was obtained. Again, only the self-sorts (including the counselor's sort for Mr. Bebb's actual self) had significant loadings on the Self factor. With two exceptions, only the ideal-sorts (including the counselor's sort for Mr. Bebb's ideal self) had significant loadings on the Ideal factor. The self-sort after therapy had a significant loading on the Ideal factor, and the counselor's sort for Mr. Bebb's actual self at the seventh interview had a significant negative loading on the Ideal factor. Only the Ordinary Person sorts (including the counselor's sort for Mr. Bebb's concept of the ordinary person) had significant loadings on the Ordinary Person factor.

Both Mrs. Oak's and Mr. Bebb's posttherapy self-sort loaded significantly on the Ideal factor, and had about equal loadings on the Ideal and Self factors. From this one might think these cases showed similar trends. However, Mr. Bebb's follow-up self-sort did not show a significant loading on the Ideal factor, while Mrs. Oak's follow-up Q sorts were not included in the factor analysis of her data.

Dynamic interpretations are offered for the factor analysis findings in each of these cases. However, a qualitative analysis, based on examination of item content rather than on the statistical summary of the factor analyses, is necessary in order to make plausible dynamic interpretations which differentiate the two cases.

Frisch and Cranston (1956) obtained fourteen Q sorts from one patient, his therapist, and the therapist's supervisor. These sorts concerned the patient's and the therapist's self and ideal self. When the Q sorts were factor analyzed, three factors were extracted, called "social acceptance," "struggle toward personal acceptance," and "hostility." Although they found no change in the patient's self concept in the over-all sense of being more positive or negative, the self concept did show a decrease in the importance of the "social acceptance" factor and an increase in the importance of the "struggle toward personal acceptance" factor. The authors point out that a number of uncontrolled variables in the situation make the results only suggestive.

Edelson and Jones (1954) devised a set of Q-sort statements particularly for their subject, who was not a therapy client. (See Table I and

Chapter III.) Sixteen sorts (six made by S and ten made by observers) were intercorrelated and factor analyzed. Their numerous hypotheses are unusually complicated so the hypotheses and results cannot be summarized in a brief scope.

e. MISCELLANEOUS

Of indirect relevance to the effects of psychotherapy on the self concept is the study of Sarbin and Farberow (1952) on the effects of hypnotic age regression upon "self perceptions" and "role perceptions." Six students aged nineteen to twenty-six were hypnotically regressed to ages three, six, thirteen, and eighteen, the order being varied in an unspecified way to equate practice effects. Self-perceptions (self-organizations) were inferred by E in an unspecified manner from "structural features of the protocols" such as M, FM, FC. That is, Ss' records under age regression were compared to published age norms. Role perceptions were inferred from verbal and vocal characteristics and content of Rorschach responses. No reliability or validity information is given on either measure and no statistical analysis of the data is given. In general the authors feel that the findings are qualitatively congruent with their hypothesis that role perceptions will regress more than self perceptions in hypnotic age regression.

Froehlich (1954) hoped to show what effect, if any, test-taking alone has on self-ratings of abilities and interests, thus providing a basis for studying changes in self-ratings which might be attributed to the counseling process per se. For seventeen attributes there was a marked tendency for both pre- and posttest self-ratings either to agree or to disagree with test scores. Among Ss who did show a shift from agreement to disagreement or vice versa, there was no clear trend toward greater agreement of posttest self-ratings and test scores. However, a number of serious weaknesses in his method preclude the conclusion that no consistent effects on self-ratings are associated with test-taking. (See Table II.)

SUMMARY

We have pointed out several reasons why research on therapy, although of potential practical value in improving clinical practice, does not provide a suitably controlled opportunity to test hypotheses from personality theories. In addition to these inherent limitations of the therapy "experiment" as a test of personality theory, several common but avoidable methodological difficulties were considered.

Altogether, twenty-nine researches were summarized or referred to in this section. Of these, four had only an indirect relevance to the topic of therapy and the self concept. Five dealt with only one case each, by means of inverse factor analysis, so no general conclusions can be drawn from them. Seven had no control groups, again preventing conclusions. Ten others also had no control groups, but they presented correlations between two or more variables within the therapy process, usually between judged improvement and self-concept changes. Of course nothing can be concluded from these studies concerning the role of therapy in causing the reported changes. So far as the correlational data are concerned, a number of these investigations have not ruled out the possibility of artifactual contamination between the variables which were correlated.

In the correlational studies, variations in procedures, Ss, instruments, and hypotheses were great; and not all the results from the roughly comparable studies were statistically significant. Therefore we cannot safely synthesize the results. We may tentatively say that judged improvement in therapy correlates positively with increases in self-regard, but this has not been repeatedly demonstrated in well-controlled studies. We cannot say at present what different kinds of criteria of improvement in therapy may correlate with improved self-regard.

Only four investigations compared counseled and noncounseled Ss. Two of them compared the level of self-regard of Ss who had received personal counseling with those who had not. In one of these two, several indices of self-regard were applied to the subjects. Although both researches yielded statistically significant increments in self-regard, the psychological significance of the amounts of increase is unknown, since validity and scaling problems are as yet unsolved. We cannot say anything about various factors of which this relationship might be a function, such as kind or length of therapy, personal characteristics of therapist or patient, etc., because these have received no systematic exploration.

One worker examined changes in self-concept consistency in counseled Ss. However, the second (posttherapy) self-reports of counseled Ss were compared to the first self-reports of the control Ss, precluding firm inferences.

There is some limited evidence that viewing mental hygiene films may increase the level of self-regard of the viewing group, as compared to a group which did not view the film.

In a control-group design, one person attempted to increase the accuracy of counseled Ss in appraising their vocational interests, probable college achievement, college aptitude, and personality characteristics. Two significantly positive trends were found for male Ss, but none was found for the female Ss.

Considering all the better-controlled studies, the trends in the data are not contradictory to self-concept theory, and may be said to offer some support to it. However, they cannot be said to constitute a crucial demonstration of any of its postulates. This lack of definitive results is partly due to the inherent limitations in any "experimental" design involving therapy.[4]

6. Effects of Lobotomy on the Self Concept

Lobotomy is the only physical therapy whose effects on the self concept have been explored. Unfortunately no clear conclusions can be drawn from either of the available studies, for reasons to be explained.

Robinson and Freeman (1954) postulated that prefrontal lobotomy alters the structure of the self through reducing the capacity for the feelings of self-continuity. Forty-one prefrontal lobotomy patients with "fair" or "good" results were compared to seventeen control Ss who had had similar illnesses but had recovered without operation. The Self-regarding Span is the number of seconds spent talking about present and past real self and future ideal self. Self-concern is a coded score derived from the same interview data. We must note the following methodological difficulties: (1) Both scores were based on the same interview material (and hence do not provide independent tests of the hypothesis). (2) The interviewing was done by the psychologist who knew the hypothesis, who edited the material as she recorded it, and prodded the patients as she went along. (3) Neither score is properly adjusted for response total, so that we cannot know to what extent the patients' "counts" of other responses bearing on nonself topics might also have been impaired. A Sensibility Questionnaire was administered orally, and was recorded and judged later by the same E. All three tests significantly discriminated be-

---

[4]Wrenn (1958) has briefly reviewed selected studies concerned with the self concept in counseling. In general, his evaluation of the studies is more favorable than that of the present author.

tween the groups, and varied significantly with degree of brain damage within the operated group. However, the findings seem to the present author to warrant no clear interpretation, due to the methodological flaws mentioned above.

Algeo and Pullen (1957) also reported that transorbital lobotomy lowers the Self-regarding Span and scores on the Sensibility Questionnaire. Their method is open to the same criticisms as have just been made of Robinson and Freeman's work, and in addition there seems to be some question as to whether their experimental and control Ss were adequately matched at the outset.

Even if results from a well-controlled study showed that lobotomy has some effect upon the self concept per se, this finding would not appear to be very useful in testing self-concept theory. This is so because it is not clear what theoretically relevant causal variable is being manipulated when one performs a lobotomy. We do not mean to imply, of course, that self-concept measures might not be one kind of useful tool for a practically important evaluation of the effects of lobotomy.

7. Effects of Experimentally Induced Success or Failure on the Self Concept

Two general assumptions underlie the studies in which S is made to feel he has failed or is personally inadequate: (1) The level of self-regard is learned through a combination of rewards and punishments for one's actions and self characteristics. The person learns some things about himself through success or failure in manipulating the physical environment, and some things from the reactions of others to him. (2) A person's level of self-regard is of great importance in predicting his behavior. These assumptions imply the possibility of manipulating failure and success variables in the laboratory, and this is one of the few areas in which any truly experimental work has been done.

The experimenter may make the person fail or experience devaluation on any of a wide variety of tasks or traits. In practice these have included specific puzzle tasks, alleged intelligence tests, alleged indicators of S's emotional stability, and evaluation of S's social characteristics and personal acceptability to others. The degree of importance which S assigns to the tasks or traits has evidently differed considerably from study to study. It seems reasonable that experimental effects would vary as a function of the type of induced failure or devaluation, and its importance to S; but these factors have not been systematically explored.

Another variable of probable relevance is the source of the alleged failure or devaluation. In some experiments E has judged S's failure, presumably on the basis of norms, or S has discovered for himself that he cannot accomplish the task. In other experiments, friends, acquaintances, or participants in experimental discussion groups have supposedly judged the subject.

Self-concept theorists make several general assumptions about possible outcomes of failure, success, devaluation, or high valuation. These assumptions do not clearly imply specific predictions, unfortunately. It is expected that S will try to maintain or retrieve a favorable self-attitude. On the other hand, S supposedly strives to maintain his basic self concept, i.e., he will resist information which is discrepant from his long-standing views about himself. This may mean that he rejects highly favorable reports about himself if they are inconsistent with his self picture. Furthermore, a single artificial failure or success in an experimental setting would not necessarily be expected to have much effect in counteracting much previous learning about the self. (Harvey, Kelley, & Shapiro, 1957; Stotland *et al.*, 1957; Doris, 1959). Therefore null results are of possible theoretical interest, but without replication they are uninterpretable. Thus far, no study has been replicated.

If S fails to maintain a favorable self attitude in the face of induced failure or devaluation, he may lower his self-report. Some Es have predicted that he will lower it mainly or entirely on a scale strictly pertinent to the failed task. Others have suggested that he will also lower his self-report on other dimensions which are related to the task, or even lower a very global estimate of self-esteem. Some investigators have evidently assumed that failure on an academic task, for example, will lower self-esteem on an instrument tapping numerous nonacademic personality characteristics. Much remains to be done to develop an explicit rationale for predicting how widely and along what dimensions the lowering of self-regard should be expected to spread. Diggory and Magaziner (1959) and Stotland and Zander (1958) have specifically considered this problem, as we shall see below.

We also need to refine our rationale concerning the type of person who will respond to failure by lowering his self-report. Doris (1959),

Doris and Sarason (1955), and Sharma (1956) have begun to explore this problem.

So far as measuring changes in self-regard is concerned, we are plagued with problems of interpretation. To what extent does S's change represent mainly a shift in the range of the rating scale he tends to use for self and others, rather than representing a revision in his feelings about himself? This question has been raised particularly by Harvey, Kelley, and Shapiro (1957).

Perhaps S will try to preserve self-esteem by defensive behavior. He may devaluate the source of the unfavorable or failure information. He may claim that the task is unimportant, or the group is unappealing to him. He may blame others rather than himself for his failure. He may increase other behaviors which have yielded him self-esteem in the past. All these possibilities have been explored, and others could be hypothesized. The question arises: What type of person will be most likely to use one or another of these defensive maneuvers?

It seems reasonable that the subject's characteristics will play a role in his reactions to failure or devaluation. In particular, Ss who have generally poor self-regard may react to failure or stressful tasks with greater anxiety than do Ss who have generally high self-regard. On the basis of this rationale, some experimenters have predicted that Ss who have generally poor self-esteem will show less accuracy and speed on the task, will give more physiological indicators of anxiety, and will make comments oriented toward self rather than toward the task, when the task induces failure or the threat of failure.

The available experiments in this area are not neatly classifiable according to the various points of rationale just outlined. Each study is based on a somewhat different combination of these assumptions. Therefore we shall describe each separately and then draw together common conclusions in the summary.

a. Experiments in Which S's Personality Characteristics Are Devaluated

In the first experiment to be summarized, Ss were evaluated on five social characteristics, and the predicted outcomes concerned Ss' ways of defending themselves against unfavorable evaluations.

Harvey, Kelley, and Shapiro (1957) (Table II) used a twelve-cell design, in which each S was experimentally exposed to evaluations of himself which were at one of four degrees of unfavorableness, and were attributed either to a stranger or to a close acquaintance. (Four of the twelve cells contained control Ss for the first two degrees of unfavorableness.) Experimental Ss were given an opportunity to (a) devaluate the source; (b) recall the source's evaluations as more favorable than they actually were; and/or (c) deny that the alleged source was responsible for the evaluation. Control Ss rated another S, acquaintance or stranger, twice. They were tested later for their perceptions of discrepancies between the source's alleged evaluations of them and their remembered self-ratings.

The results are complex and contain some puzzling exceptions. The general trend is for the above-mentioned three kinds of "defensive" reactions to the source to be greater the more informed the source and the more negative his evaluations of S. Experimental Ss showed changes in self-evaluation in the unfavorable direction under all conditions which were significantly greater than changes in control Ss' self-ratings. However, there is no evidence that these changes were a function of either of the independent variables, acquaintance with source or degree of unfavorableness of the source's evaluations. The authors think that the changes in self-evaluation, then, probably do not represent real shifts in self concept, but may reflect merely the manner of *expressing* the self-evaluations (i.e., a shift to using a different range of the rating scale from that originally employed).

Dittes's (1959a) experiment was also based on the idea that personal devaluations of S would lead to defensive behavior, i.e., behavior which could restore self-esteem. Twenty groups of Ss were used, with up to six Ss per group. Each group was given several incentives to do well as a group in discussing an assigned topic. At intervals, Ss evaluated each other's worth to the group. E finally gave each S some personal evaluations which were supposedly the ones S had actually received from his fellow group members. In fact these evaluations were bogus ones, arranged by E to fit his experimental plan.

In setting up performance measures, Dittes assumed that obtaining closure in ambiguous tasks raises self-esteem. Therefore he expected the Ss who had received poor evaluations to try to obtain closure quickly and impulsively on three ambiguous tasks which were administered following the receipt of the personal evaluations. Results with two of his closure tasks supported his expectations significantly. Scores for impulsivity of closure on his three closure tasks did not correlate highly with each other, but he combined them into a single index of closure tendencies. Results with this single index supported his hypothesis at $<.002$ level of significance.

On the basis of a combination of self-report measures (see Table II) Dittes inferred Ss' characteristic levels of self-esteem. He found that experimental devaluation was associated with impulsivity of closure only for Ss with characteristically average or low self-esteem. The experimental devaluation seems to have had little effect on the behavior of Ss who had characteristically high self-esteem. He also determined that Ss with a characteristically low desire for clarity (as inferred from a specific self-report instrument) were more likely to show the predicted association between low experimental evaluation and impulsivity of closure.

Another dependent variable measure in Dittes's (1959b) experiment was the S's degree of attraction toward the group, as inferred from three ratings S made in response to questions which were administered at the end of the experimental session. Dittes assumed that Ss with characteristically low self-esteem would have a stronger need to receive a good evaluation from the group than would Ss with characteristically high self-esteem. If so, Ss with low self-esteem should be more rewarded by the group's favorable evaluation and more frustrated by the group's devaluation than would be the case for Ss with high self-esteem. Dittes further assumed that the degree of gratification or frustration S experienced from the group's evaluations of him would be reflected in his expressed attraction to the group.

The results are congruent with these assumptions. Among those Ss whose characteristic level of self-esteem was high, the devaluated Ss and the favorably evaluated Ss differed insignificantly with respect to their expressed attraction to the group ($p > .50$). Among Ss whose characteristic level of self-esteem was average, the devaluated Ss and the favorably evaluated Ss again differed insignificantly with respect to their expressed attraction to the group. The difference was larger than it was in the case of the high-self-esteem Ss, however, and it reached the $<.20$ level of significance. Among Ss whose self-esteem was low, the devaluated Ss expressed significantly *less* attraction to the group than was expressed by high-self-esteem Ss ($p < .002$).

A third experiment in which Ss' personal characteristics were devaluated is that of Levanway (1955) (Table II). Ss were told that their behavior in a memory experiment suggested serious emotional conflict. Their reactions to this threat were measured in terms of the favorability of their responses to self, to defined others, and to pictures of persons. Contrary to the findings of other investigators, Ss reacted more favorably to self, others, and pictures of persons after threat than they did before threat. However, a number of necessary controls are missing from this study, including a control group, so that the results seem uninterpretable. They certainly are not clearly contradictory to the findings of other experimenters.

b. Experiments in Which Ss Were Made to Fail on Experimental Tasks

In a second group of experiments, S was made to fail on an experimental task. Usually the situation was set up so that his failure indicated lack of intellectual or perceptual motor abilities. These experiments were concerned with the effects of failure upon S's evaluation of his performance on the task, and upon his self-evaluations in other areas. Some of these investigations attempted to explore the conditions under which failure would affect self-evaluation. In this connection, both experimental conditions and the characteristics of the Ss have been examined in some of these experiments.

Howard and Berkowitz (1958) studied Ss' performance on a simulated air strategy problem (Table III) which was presented to S as a test of "effective intelligence." The experimenters assumed that S's reactions toward evaluations of his performance would be affected by a need for self-enhancement, and by a need for subjective certainty or accuracy. They utilized an analysis of variance design with two conditions of wanting to succeed at a task (as reported by S), and five conditions of evaluation of S's performance by Os: (1) three Os giving moderately favorable evaluation, one giving high evaluation; (2) three Os giving moderately favorable evaluation, one giving low evaluation; (3) three Os giving moderately favorable evaluation; (4) one O giving high evaluation; (5) one O giving low evaluation. One dependent variable was S's assessment of how accurate Os' evaluations of him were. An O whose evaluations deviated from the consensus of other Os was seen as probably being in error even if his evaluations were highly favorable. The magnitude of this effect depended upon the extent to which the deviate O's evaluations frustrate Ss' desire for a favorable evaluation. When the frustrating O was the only

O, high-aspiration *S*s did not question his accuracy as much as when there were reality grounds for questioning *O*'s accuracy (i.e., when three other *O*s were more favorable). Thus both reality considerations and desire for self-enchancement were operative in *S*s' assessments of *O*s' accuracy. (We should note, however, that *S*'s *expected* performance correlated with his *desired* performance, so one cannot say to what extent the effects are associated with disruptions of wishes, expectations, or both.)

Will failure on a fairly specific visual-motor task lead to generalized self-devaluation as well as to devaluation of one's ability to do the particular task? Will the prestige of the experimenter be a factor in determining *S*'s reactions to such failure? Will *S* react to his failure differently if he fails in private than he would if he is made to fail in public? Stotland and Zander (1958) explored these questions by studying the effects of various conditions upon *S*'s evaluations of (a) his performance on the failed experimental task; (b) his visual-motor-coordination abilities allegedly involved in the experimental task; (c) his other abilities which had been previously judged to be of decreasing similarity to visual-motor-coordination abilities; and (d) himself as a "complete person." At the outset, the experimenters assumed that all persons wish to evaluate themselves as highly as possible, within the limits set by the facts as they see them. In the experiment, each *S* privately worked on an impossible puzzle, described to him as a test of visual-motor coordination. A four-cell design was used. *E* presented himself to half the *S*s as an expert, and to half as a nonexpert. Within each of these groups, half the *S*s were allowed to fail and put the puzzle away without *E*'s observing them, while the other half were observed by *E* at the end of ten minutes and told they had failed. The task was designed so that the exact extent of failure was ambiguous to all *S*s. When the results from the entire group of *S*s were examined, no consistent consequences of any of these four conditions upon any of the types of self-evaluation were observed. The *E*s than suggested that the *S*s who evaluated their puzzle performances relatively highly despite failure could be assuméd to be more highly motivated toward self-enhancement than were the *S*s who evaluated their puzzle performance less highly. Among the former *S*s it was found that observation of their puzzle failure by an expert yielded lower self-evaluations of visual-motor-coordination abilities than those made by *S*s in the other three conditions. A similar trend was found for the abilities most similar to visual-motor coordination. As predicted, no significant differences were found for abilities less similar to the visual-motor coordination. Among Ss who evaluated their puzzle performance more unfavorably (and who were therefore presumably not as highly motivated toward self-enhancement), no differential effect of the experimental conditions upon self-evaluations of abilities was observed.

Festinger, Torrey, and Willerman (1954) were concerned with the influence of artificially induced success and failure scores upon S's evaluation of his performance on a task which allegedly revealed his ability to make decisions on the basis of inadequate information (Table III). Like Stotland and Zander, they thought the conditions under which S received his failure or success information might help to determine S's self-evaluation. Supporting this idea, they found that the stronger the attraction S indicated that he had for an experimentally formed group, the more favorably he evaluated a good score (or the more unfavorably he evaluated a poor score) which he had allegedly earned on the task.

A number of investigators besides Stotland and Zander have been interested in the effects of task failure upon S's self-evaluations along nontask dimensions.

As part of a complex experiment, Stotland, Thorley, Thomas, Cohen, and Zander (1957) studied the effects of experimentally induced success and failure on reported self-esteem. They thought that general self-esteem was too enduring a characteristic to be affected by a single experimental failure on a puzzle task, and their null results were in line with this expectation. Since the validity of their self-esteem measure is unknown (Table I), and null findings are at best ambiguous, no firm interpretations can be made of their finding of no change in reported self-esteem after experimentally induced failure. (Other parts of their experiment will be described below.)

In contrast to Stotland et al., Sharma (1956) evidently assumed widespread effects, since he predicted that failure on tests of "reasoning ability and insight" would effect changes in total self-esteem scores on Brownfain's instrument, which refers mainly to nonintellectual characteristics (Table II). Sharma also wished to discover whether Ss with any particular personality characteristics were more apt to lower their self-esteem scores after failure. He compared self-esteem changes in groups subjected to failure (stress), success (support), and no special treatment intervening between the initial and final report of self-esteem. The two experimental groups changed their self-esteem scores significantly more than the control group, but the pattern of change was not clear and cannot be firmly interpreted. Some failure Ss raised their self-esteem, and some lowered it, while only one success S lowered his self-esteem. Since self-esteem was measured by a dual index (self minus ideal on Brownfain's twenty-five positively toned adjectives), we cannot know to what extent changes in self-esteem reflect changes in either component of this dual index. Sharma hoped to relate changing of self-esteem to personality variables, using the GAMIN Inventory, the TAT, and the Rosenzweig PF. Out of twenty-eight significance tests, four reached the .05 level or better, two involving failure group changes, a different two involving success group changes. (Failure Ss, but not success Ss, who changed self-esteem ratings were significantly lower on Ascendance scores, and higher on TAT guilt and remorse.) Thus only suggestive support is offered to the idea that personality characteristics may be associated with willingness to change self-ratings after failure.

Another experiment involving the effects of one failure upon other aspects of self-regard is that of Diggory and Magaziner (1959). They addressed their experiment to the following general questions: Will failure in regard to one characteristic lower the person's self-estimate about his other characteristics? Will it lower his global self-evaluation? If the effects of failure do spread in this way, is this spread dependent on the characteristic in which the person failed? They hypothesized that high self-evaluation is dependent on one's perception that his capacities are adequate to the achievement of his goals. If a person considers a given capacity particularly important (instrumental) to goal achievement, and if that capacity is devaluated in a failure experiment, the person will tend to lower his self-ratings on other capacities, and even to lower his global self-rating. But if a given capacity is not considered by a person to be instrumental to goal achievement, experimental failure with respect to this capacity will not affect the person's ratings of his other capacities or of his global adequacy.

To test this hypothesis, the experimenters asked male college students to rate themselves on five capacities and on their over-all adequacy of functioning. (See Table II.) Two groups were chosen, one containing Ss who had rated themselves extremely low on one capacity, and one containing Ss who had rated themselves extremely high on one capacity. Ss were informed that they could get into an exclusive, desirable "Career

Liaison" group if tests showed they had all five supposedly equally important capacities to the required extent.

The Ss were given the opportunity to rerate themselves on the five capacities in the light of the particular goal they were about to seek. These ratings were used as the initial (prefailure) ratings.

No check was made as to whether Ss accepted the idea that all five capacities were equally important to achieving the goal of getting into and succeeding in the Career Liaison group. In any event, Diggory and Magaziner assumed that S would consider his highest rated capacity most instrumental to achieving the goal (or his lowest rated capacity least instrumental). They reasoned that S would think, in effect, "If I have any chance of getting in and succeeding, my highest capacity will be what gets me to this goal." A measurement problem arises here in that S's view of the instrumental importance of a capacity is confounded with S's view of his standing on that capacity. We shall point out below the way this confusion affects possible interpretations of their results.

S was tested on the capacity he had rated very high (or very low), and he was told he had failed this test, so tests on the other capacities would not be necessary. S then rerated himself on all five capacities and on his global adequacy of functioning. As predicted, Ss who failed on a capacity on which they had initially rated themselves high lowered their self-ratings on the untested as well as the tested capacities. Those who failed on a capacity on which they had initially rated themselves low did not change as many self-ratings nor change them as much as did the former group. No significant effects on global ratings were found for either group.

The authors believe these results indicate that failure on a capacity which S sees as most instrumental to goal achievement will affect his other self-evaluations, while failure on a noninstrumental capacity will not affect his other self-evaluations. However, another interpretation also seems possible, as we shall now explain.

If S thinks a given capacity is low before failure, his failure on the test of this capacity may simply confirm his belief in the accuracy of his self-judgment (including all his prefailure self-ratings). Therefore he would tend to repeat his initial (prefailure) self-ratings. Failure on a high scoring capacity may, on the other hand, raise a subject's doubts as to his general accuracy in the use of the rating scales. Hence he will tend to change all his ratings. In other words, as we said above, we need an operational definition of S's view of the instrumental importance of a capacity which is independent of his intial self-rating value of that capacity.

The reader may also wonder whether statistical regression effects could account for the findings, as might be the case if the two groups were not initially matched on self-ratings for the four untested capacities. However, this has been taken care of, since the groups were said to be comparable on initial self-ratings of untested capacities.

Perhaps Ss will be unwilling to admit openly that failing on an intelligence test has lowered their general self-regard. If S is not willing to change his self-ratings, perhaps we can see by less obvious measures that his self-esteem has been lowered. In line with this rationale, Diller (1954) found that after "failing" on an "intelligence test," there was no decrease in overt self-ratings, but a tendency toward decrease in "covert" ratings. (S did not know he was judging his own handwriting.) After "success," overt self-ratings (Table II) were enhanced, and there was tendency toward enhancement of covert self-ratings (Table IV). After failure, self-other attitudes were not correlated, while after success, there was a positive correlation of self-ratings with attitudes expressed toward friends at various distances from self.

We raised the question earlier whether Ss with differing personality characteristics may react differently to failure on intellectual tasks. Doris and Sarason (1955) and Doris (1959) have been interested in this general question. In particular they hypothesize that blaming one's self for intellectual failures may be associated with high anxiety over taking intellectual tests. Of course such "test anxiety" may itself be a symptom of low self-regard, due to general past experience, or to upsetting experiences with tests. If so, the hypothesis may be, in effect, that persons with low general self-regard tend to interpret failure as due to their own shortcomings.

In Doris and Sarason's (1955) experiment, college student Ss who were high and low on test anxiety were given an opportunity to blame themselves and/or others for experimentally induced failures. (Test anxiety was measured by Sarason and Gordon's [1953] questionnaire.) Eight intellectual tests were given and S was arbitrarily made to fail four of them. On two subgroups of Ss, two orders of presentation of the tests were used, one being the exact reverse of the other. After each test S was given the opportunity to explain his failures by ranking eight possible reasons, including three self-blame, three other-than-self-blame, and three neutral possibilities. High Anxiety Ss showed a significantly higher self-blame score than did Low Anxiety Ss, when one order of tasks was used but there was no difference in mean self-blame score between High Anxiety and Low Anxiety Ss with task order reversed. The authors speculate that the reversed order was a less threatening sequence, thus accounting for the finding of no difference for this method of presentation. Whatever the explanation, such results imply that methodological variables must be more fully explored in studies relating failure to self-evaluation.

Using children as Ss in a series of studies, Doris (1959) continued the exploration of the effects of failure upon self-blaming tendencies of persons differing in test anxiety. Self-blaming tendencies for arithmetic inadequacies correlated positively with a general Children's Test Anxiety score under several conditions: (1) before failure on an arithmetic task; (2) after failure on an arithmetic task; (3) in the absence of any special arithmetic task. There was no evidence that experimentally induced failure increased the correlation between Test Anxiety and Self-Blame. This lack of effect of experimental failure is, of course, out of line with some of the results obtained by Doris and Sarason (1955) from college student Ss.

Doris recognized that the correlations from the child Ss might be artifactual, due to common response sets in the Test Anxiety and Self-Blame Questionnaires. Such artifactual contaminations could occur even though E varied the form of the Self-Blame questionnaire to control for artifact. An artifactual explanation seems unlikely, however, in view of the fact that Self-Blame scores obtained from a modified TAT also correlated with Test Anxiety scores obtained from a questionnaire.

Interestingly enough, Test Anxiety scores correlated with Other-Blame scores as well as with Self-Blame, when blame scores were obtained from questionnaires. This led Doris (1959, p. 188) to speculate as to whether "the relationship between test anxiety and blame assignment is a specific instance of a higher order relationship between test anxiety and aggressive attitudes in general." However, he obtained no correlation between Test Anxiety and "other-blame" on the modified TAT, and no correlation between Test Anxiety and Rosenzweig PF scores. These results offer no support to the idea that Test Anxiety is associated with generalized aggressive attitudes. But of course null findings from one study cannot offer a clear refutation either.

We have speculated that Ss high and low on Test Anxiety may actually be high and low on general self-regard. If so, the two preceding studies belong in the same general class as the three we shall describe next.

Worchel (1957), Miller and Worchel (1956), and Solley and Stagner (1956) all thought that *S*s who differed in general self-regard level would differ in their reactions to failure or threat of failure. The outcome variables which they studied were primarily performance measures rather than self-blame or changes in *S*'s self-evaluations.

Worchel's (1957) study, described in Chapter III, may be paraphrased to bring out its relevance to our discussion of the effects of failure. He assumed that inability to complete a task would be regarded by *S* as a greater personal failure if *S* was working under self-esteem-orienting instructions than if he was working under task-orienting instructions. *S*'s completion of each task was experimentally regulated, without *S*'s realizing that fact. Under the self-esteem-orienting (greater personal failure) instructions, *S*s whose self-regard was high were predicted to favor the recall of completed tasks, while *S*s with low self-regard were predicted to remember relatively fewer completed tasks. (Self-regard was inferred from the Self-Activity Inventory which is discussed in Chapter III.) Under the task-orienting (lesser personal failure) instructions, *S*s with high self-regard were predicted to remember relatively more incompleted tasks, as compared to the number of incompleted tasks remembered by *S*s with low self-regard. The results showed that [Self — Ideal] and [Self — Other] scores did not correlate with recall ratios when tasks were done under either set of instructions. The Self scores showed no association with recall of completed tasks under task-orienting instructions. Under self-esteem-orienting instructions, however, the Self scores correlated as predicted with recall scores ($r = +.28$, $p = .05$). Since only one r out of six supported the hypotheses (even though Self was a common factor in each group of three correlations), only very weak support is given the assumptions behind the study.

Miller and Worchel (1956) related [Self — Ideal] discrepancies on the Self-Activity Inventory to changes in accuracy of performance on the McKinney Reporting Test, under continued self-esteem-threatening stress. Each *S* first performed at his own rate for eight minutes on the McKinney Test, then worked for sixteen minutes, during which time he was interrupted every thirty seconds and told he was failing to meet a standard. This stress period was divided into two eight-minute sections of supposedly mounting stress. Finally, *S* worked for eight minutes without stress. On the basis of [Self—Ideal] scores, Ss were divided into three groups, showing respectively high, medium, and low discrepancies. In the second of the two successive stress periods, Ss with medium [Self—Ideal] discrepancies showed significantly less performance decrement (as compared to the prestress period) than did Ss with high or low [Self—Ideal] discrepancies. Also, in the poststress period, the Ss with medium discrepancies came closer to their prestress performance level than did either of the other two groups. (See Chapter III for a discussion of the Self-Activity Inventory.)

Solley and Stagner (1956) (Table II) were interested in the influence of self-regard on reactions to varying degrees of failure (called by them "temporal barriers"). In a well controlled 3 x 3 factorial design, the independent variables were: (1) Ss' evaluations of self on Osgood Semantic Differential Scales (1957); (2) the number of insoluble anagrams (0, 3, or 5) presented between two sequences of soluble anagrams; (3) affective quality of anagram words (negative, neutral, positive). The dependent variables were: (1) solution times; (2) the orientation of spontaneous comments toward self or toward task; (3) changes in palmar sweating from first to last soluble anagram. Findings relevant to the present discussion were: (a) Ss with low evaluation of self showed greater increases in solution time after failure than did Ss with high self-evaluation. This linear finding apparently differs from Miller and Worchel's results. (b) In the presence of insoluble anagrams, Ss with low self-evaluation emitted more self-referent comments, while Ss with high self-evaluation emitted more task-referent comments. (c) On negatively toned words, Ss with low self-evaluation showed marked increases in palmar sweating with increasing numbers of insoluble anagrams, whereas high self-evaluating Ss showed a slight decrement in this measure.

Part of the experiment by Stotland et al. (1957) which was mentioned above is pertinent here. They divided Ss according to Cohen's general self-esteem measure (Table I). Two other independent variables were experimental manipulation of the group's expectations of S, and experimentally induced success or failure on a puzzle task. Self-evaluation of task performance (Table III) was correlated with self-esteem among Ss who were made to fail on the task, but not among those allowed to succeed. That is, persons with high self-esteem may have protected themselves better than those with low self-esteem. If S accepted the group's expectations of him, and he failed, high group expectation was associated with low self-evaluation of task performance. However, if he did not accept the group's expectation of him, the level of group expectation was not correlated with S's self-evaluation of task performance in failure. Unfortunately no cause-effect inferences can be drawn from these last findings, since S's stated concern with the group and his evaluation of his own task performance were both elicited from questionnaires administered in a single session *after* success or failure had been induced.

SUMMARY

We have reviewed fifteen experiments which explored various relationships between self-regard and experimentally induced success or failure.[5] In some studies S received devaluative information about his personal characteristics, and in others he was made to succeed or fail on a task which supposedly revealed his intellectual or perceptual-motor abilities.

We have found that this is one of the few areas of self psychology in which any truly experimental work has been done. Synthesis of these experimental results is risky because each study involved a unique combination of assumptions, hypotheses, procedures, and measuring instruments. Therefore the following summarizing statements are offered quite tentatively.

It seems that Ss will, under certain conditions, change their self-evaluations after experimentally induced success or failure. These changes are most likely to involve self-ratings on the experimental task itself, or on the characteristic which has been evaluated, and are least likely to involve reports on global self-regard. The latter seems to be affected little if any by a single experimental failure or evaluation. There is some evidence that changes in self-rating upward after success are more frequent than are changes downward after failure.

Numerous scaling and measurement problems make the changes which do occur difficult to interpret. Findings of no change in global self-regard after a single failure are congruent with self-concept theory, but such null findings cannot be clearly interpreted without experimental replication.

Whether or not changes in self-rating occur, there may be changes in

---

[5] A study by Benjamins (1950) might belong in this section, but published information was too incomplete for an adequate evaluation of it.

"covert" self-evaluation. However, it remains to be demonstrated that the "covert" measures validly indicate covert self-evaluation.

Changes in self-evaluation have not been the only dependent variable studied. It seems that experimental failure may also lead to various defensive behaviors such as devaluing the source of failure information, failing to recall the low evaluations accurately, engaging in behaviors which have brought self-esteem in the past, or blaming others for one's failure. In addition, there may be performance decrements on the task which threatens S with failure, and concomitant anxiety reactions may be seen.

Changes or lack of changes in self-ratings after failure are probably a function of other variables within the experimental procedure or within the subject. There is limited evidence to suggest that the following may be found to be associated with changes in self-evaluation or with self-blame for failure: S's personality characteristics, such as his basic, global level of self-regard; S's test anxiety; the particular characteristics which have been devalued in the experiment; the degree to which S values the source of his failure or success information and feels the source is well informed. It appears that S is influenced by reality considerations as well as by the desire for self-enhancement. Performance decrements and anxiety indicators on the experimental task may be greater in Ss whose basic level of self-regard is low.

8. Learning and the Self Concept

a. INFLUENCE OF LEARNING IN THE DEVELOPMENT OF THE SELF CONCEPT

Actually all of the classes of variables mentioned thus far in this section assume that the self concept is developed and modified through learning. This implies that principles and theories of learning derived through experimental techniques should be relevant. Helper's (1955) study, however, is the only one discussed thus far which attempted to make an explicit connection with the general psychology of learning; and even his study was not directly concerned with the learning process. Apparently only one experiment involves the learning of self-referent statements, and may thus be said to be trying to effect a direct connection between learning theory and the learning of the self concept (Nuthmann, 1957). (See Table II.)

Nuthmann did a carefully controlled conditioning experiment to see whether "acceptance of self" answers to personality test items could be increased through either of two reinforcements: (a) E's saying "good"; or (b) presentation of a light blink. The results indicate that the verbal stimulus "good" was effective, while the light reinforcement was not. The behavior of Ss who were aware of the purpose of the reinforcement did not differ significantly from that of Ss who were not aware. As Nuthmann points out, the design of the experiment still leaves open the question whether Ss were learning to discriminate on the basis of the over-all emotional tone of the item or on the basis of acceptance-of-self content of the item. Even if the latter were true, the relation between these conditioned verbal responses and considered evaluative statements revealing phenomenal self-acceptance remains undemonstrated. It seems to the present writer to be questionable whether the experiment has demonstrated a relevant principle of development of the self concept.

There is one study in which E attempted to influence Ss' concepts of their ideal selves by teaching a specially constructed unit on American historical biography (Lodge, 1956). As a measure of the ideal self, the sixth-grade Ss wrote essays describing "The Person I Would Like to Be Like." Essays were coded for mention of various categories of persons, including parents, glamorous adults, attractive and visible young adults, composite imaginary persons, and heroes read about. No significant increase in "heroes read about" was found when the first essay was compared with a second essay written immediately after the biographical studies, and a third essay written eight weeks later. (No control group was used.) Failure to find systematic changes apparently cannot be laid to unreliability in the coding scheme, if we can generalize from Havighurst, Robinson, and Dorr's (1946) findings of 85-90% interjudge agreement in assigning papers to categories. It is of interest to note in passing that in Lodge's third essay, the qualities mentioned most often were: friendly; happy-cheerful-full of fun; honest-truthful-sincere; kind-considerate; helpful-thoughtful-altruistic.

b. THE INFLUENCE OF THE SELF CONCEPT ON LEARNING

A number of investigators have been concerned with the relationship between S's self concept and his behavior in experimental learning tasks. The assumption is made that the self-concept characteristics are antecedent to the cognitive behavior. Sometimes it is explicitly assumed that this relationship is basically a matter of the influence of motivation upon learning.

The three available studies are impossible to synthesize into a common conclusion. We can only say that there does seem to be some evidence that R-R connections of this kind are worth exploring further.

Cowen, Heilizer, and Axelrod (1955) assumed that adjectives on which S reported large self-minus-ideal discrepancies would arouse conflict in him when they were presented in a learning experiment, and that this conflict would disrupt learning. They paired nonsense syllables with Bills's adjectives which had been identified for each S as having large and small [Self—Ideal] discrepancies. (See Chapter III for a discussion of Bills's Index of Adjustment and Values.) In line with their prediction, Ss had significantly greater difficulty in learning the nonsense syllable responses which were paired with the "conflictual" adjective stimuli. Other variables which might affect the learning of responses to the two classes of adjectives were apparently well controlled.

D. Cartwright (1956) was interested in Rogers's (1951a) idea that experiences will be ignored or given distorted symbolization if they are inconsistent with the structure of the self. With regard to a memory experiment Cartwright predicted: (a) Ss will recall more accurately those stimuli which he has perceived and organized into some relationship to self. (b) Maladjusted Ss will show a greater differential of this kind than will adjusted Ss.

In his study, adjusted Ss were those who had had no therapy, or had had "successful" therapy. Maladjusted Ss were those who were pretherapy or therapy-failure cases.

"Consistent nonsense syllables" (ones which Ss made up) were recalled better than "inconsistent nonsense syllables" (ones which were drawn from Glaze's list). But as the author remarks, there is a lack of control here, because Ss' syllables more nearly resembled words. "Consistent possessions" (ones which S had indicated were like him to own) were recalled better than "inconsistent possessions" (ones which S had indicated were unlike him to own). The Thorndike-Lorge word frequency of the names of possessions correlated to some extent with ease of recall. Although such word frequency was shown not to account for the results entirely, the idiosyncratic frequency of the word in the past experience of the particular S has not been ruled out as a possible explanation of the results concerning possessions.

Adjectives were chosen to summarize statements which S had Q sorted along a "like me" dimension. Adjectives summarizing those statements which S had indicated were most "like me" were called "consistent," while adjectives summarizing the statements S had said were most "unlike me" were called "inconsistent" for that S. Consistent adjectives were remembered better than inconsistent adjectives. The question about the role of idiosyncratic word frequency might be raised here too.

To test Hypothesis (b), twenty pairs of adjusted and maladjusted Ss were matched on digit-span, and an analysis of variance was performed. The data on possessions showed (1) significantly less efficient recall scores of inconsistent possessions by maladjusted Ss; (2) less efficient recall scores of inconsistent adjectives by maladjusted Ss on the first lists of adjectives only. (For a discussion of measures of self-consistency and self-organization, see Chapter III.)

Although differences in method and theory make it impossible to compare definitively Cartwright's study with that of Bieri and Trieschman (1956), the latters' findings do seem to be somewhat out of line with the theory behind Cartwright's study. In the Bieri and Trieschman research, adjectives to be used as responses in paired-associate learning were ones S reported as being characteristic of himself. Stimuli were names of persons S had judged to be most, intermediately, and least similar to himself.

In paired-associate learning, the greatest number of errors was made in attempting to associate self-characteristic adjectives with names of persons intermediately similar to self. The smallest number of errors was made in associating such adjectives with persons most similar to self. However, this number did not differ significantly from the number of errors made to names of persons least similar to self. Factors such as word length and role titles of the stimulus persons were apparently adequately controlled.

9. *Relationships between "Adjustment" and Self-Regard*[6]

It is obvious that many complexities are involved in trying to define "adjustment" and in attempting to specify the relationship of this concept

---

[6]Occasionally some other aspect of self concept has been related to "adjustment," and the author's theoretical premises will be considered at the point where his article is mentioned in this section of the review.

to "mental health." Scott, in his review of research definitions of mental health and mental illness, concludes,

> though adjustment appears a more conceptually adequate criterion of mental health than does exposure to treatment, the necessity for considering different personal frames of reference and the demands of different social structures poses seemingly insurmountable obstacles to the establishment of mutually consistent operational definitions. All such difficulties which lie 'hidden', as it were, under the psychiatric treatment criterion, come to the fore to plague the researcher trying to establish a criterion for adjustment which applies to the treated and nontreated alike (Scott, 1958, p. 32).

Presumably psychiatric diagnosis is a more valid criterion of mental illness than is simple commitment to treatment, since "it is the community rather than the clinician that operates the case-finding process today" (Scott, 1958, p. 33). But psychiatric diagnosis, though having the merit of being in the hands of professionals, shares with the commitment criterion the limitation that it has not been generally applied to the full range of treated and untreated persons.

Despite the difficulties in defining "adjustment," either conceptually or operationally, it is generally conceded theoretically that a low degree of phenomenal self-regard should be indicative of, or an aspect of, or perhaps even a cause of, "maladjustment." Theorists seem less clear concerning the reverse of this proposition. It is felt that high phenomenal self-regard may indicate (a) good adjustment; or (b) denial of problems and of self-rejection which are actually as serious or more serious than those of Ss who consciously admit low self-regard; or (c) unsophisticated conventionality (Loevinger & Ossorio, 1959).

Studies of relationships between self concept and adjustment are numerous, and various criteria of adjustment have been used. These criteria may be organized for discussion purposes under the headings outlined below. We shall return later to a consideration of the degree to which these criteria seem to reflect any common construct. (For other studies pertinent to the relationship of "adjustment" and self-concept characteristics, the reader should refer to Section C-5, above. That section deals with the effects of counseling and psychotherapy on the self concept.)

Criteria of Adjustment

a. degrees of diagnosed pathology
b. behavior ratings and measurements
    1) teacher, authority, or peer ratings of behavior relevant to adjustment
    2) observable behaviors presumably relevant to adjustment
c. projective test scores presumably relevant to adjustment
d. scores on self-report instruments

The four categories are ordered roughly according to the degree to which the criterion of "adjustment" may be said to be independent of S's statement about himself. Thus, under Category d, all results are open to the criticism that two self-reports may correlate artifactually. In particular, Social Desirability and various response sets may affect the criterion, as well as influencing the self-concept measure. In addition, there may be similar item content in both measures, or in some cases, both measures have been taken from the same set of items.

Studies in Category c, since they too involve comparison of two of S's test responses, may also be open to artifactual contamination, especially if the projectives are fairly easily "seen through" by the respondents.

Supposedly, studies in Categories a and b relate measures which are more independent of one another. Of course teachers, peers, and clinicians may base their judgments of S's adjustment partly on his self-reports, as we pointed out in our discussion of the studies relating judged improvement in psychotherapy to self-concept changes. Investigations vary widely in the degree to which this source of contamination is ruled out. In general, however, studies belonging in Categories a and b seem more potentially interpretable in psychological, as opposed to artifactual, terms than are those in Categories c and d.

In the light of this analysis, it is interesting and discouraging to note that we get more clearly positive and consistent results from studies in Category d than from those in any of the other categories. In contrast, the associations found between self-regard and "adjustment" are low, tenuous, even contradictory when the latter is measured in terms of external observations or of ratings made by an observer (Categories a and b). Two studies which employ multiple criteria applied to the same Ss, thus yielding correlations representative of a number of the above categories, reveal the same trend toward weaker or null correlations from

Categories a and b (Fiedler, Dodge, Jones, & Hutchins, 1958; Turner & Vanderlippe, 1958).

The explanation probably lies partly in the looseness and unclarity of the "adjustment" concept, as rated by external judges. The use of the one term "adjustment" implies a single concept, but the various alleged behavioral indices are not necessarily highly interrelated. After we have described the studies themselves, we shall consider other possible reasons why the strength and direction of the trends may vary among the studies which purport to relate self concept and adjustment.

a. SELF CONCEPTS OF Ss WITH VARYING DEGREES OF
DIAGNOSED PATHOLOGY

Most studies of this type have compared normal Ss with schizophrenics or neurotics or both. Some have subdivided the sick group(s) into finer subdivisions of judged pathology. In the first nine investigations summarized below, only one maladjusted group is involved; while in the next nine researches presented, at least three degrees or types of (mal)-adjustment were compared.

Studies with Two Groups Only

In these investigations, an adjusted group was compared with a maladjusted one. There were no criteria for either satisfactory adjustment or maladjustment which were common to all these studies. Maladjusted groups included neurotics (hospitalized and nonhospitalized), alcoholics, schizophrenics (paranoid and nonclassified), and unclassified hospitalized persons.

Neurotic Ss. Sarbin and Rosenberg (1955) found that normal, volunteer student Ss and student Ss who had been diagnosed as neurotic and recommended for therapy showed significant differences in Self-Acceptance and in a Self-Criticality Index derived from Gough's Adjective Check List. (See Table II.) The neurotic Ss were less self-accepting and more self-critical. No matching criteria are reported, however.

As we mentioned in Chapter III, Rogers and Dymond's (1954) client group applying for therapy showed a mean initial self-ideal r of $-.01$, while the control Ss who volunteered to take part in research on personality showed a significantly different mean initial self-ideal r of $+.58$. The experimental and control groups were satisfactorily matched for age, but only moderately satisfactorily matched with respect to sex, occupation, and socioeconomic status. (See Chapter III for an evaluation of Butler and Haigh's Q sort, from which the self-ideal rs were obtained.)[7]

Although Wahler (1958) had four groups, they appear to be classifiable into two degrees of adjustment: (1) university students and medical outpatient veterans (the latter screened to exclude neurological or psychiatric diagnoses or complaints); (2) nonpsychotic outpatient veterans undergoing psychotherapy, and applicants for admission to the same outpatient psychiatric clinic. Exact information is not given on the comparability of the groups with respect to possibly relevant variables, but it is stated that the three veteran groups are more comparable to one another in age, education, socioeconomic level, and military experience than any of these groups is to the university group. All Ss were male.

For each of the four groups, Wahler computed a correlation across items between the group's average self-rating on each item and the independently judged social desirability values for each item. Correlations for the university males and medical outpatients were $+.755$ and $+.753$. Correlations for psychiatric intake applicants and for psychotherapy patients were $+.661$ and $+.373$. The correlation for psychotherapy patients is significantly lower than the other three correlations. Wahler speculates that the higher correlation for intakes than for psychotherapy patients represents the defensiveness of the intakes rather than their better adjustment.

Items were divided into three groups, according to their independently rated social-desirability values, and an average self-rating was computed for each group of items for each group of Ss. Both psychiatric groups tended to rate undesirable and slightly undesirable items at significantly higher ("like me") levels than did the medical patient controls. The best discrimination between medical patient controls and either psychiatric group was obtained with self-ratings in the slightly undesirable category. Ratings in this category correctly identified 78% of intake and medical control patients and 85% of psychiatric patients and medical control patients.

---

[7] In connection with this problem, the reader may find useful the following "normative" data on Butler and Haigh's 100-item Q sort. All the following mean zs were obtained on nonpatient Ss: McKenna, Hofstaetter, and O'Connor (1956) $= +.44$; Koslosky (cited in McKenna *et al.*, 1956) $= +.75$; Hanlon *et al.* (1954) $= +.42$; Turner and Vanderlippe (1956) $= +.63$.

Alcoholic Ss. Wahl (1956) theorized that low self-regard is an important factor in the development of alcoholism. Unlike the previously reported investigations, this one did not use self-report as an index of self-regard. Instead, inferences of low self-regard among alcoholic Ss were drawn from the fact that there was a high incidence of parental rejection, overprotection, separation, or loss; and a high incidence of large families and reported sibling rivalry. The group studied was an unselected intake sequence of alcoholic patients in a state hospital. Methodological difficulties, recognized by the author, make the results only suggestive, however. For example, there was no known base line of the incidence of such factors in normal persons' case histories, even though some general population statistics are available for some of these factors.

Unclassified or Mixed Hospitalized Psychiatric Patients. Kogan, Quinn, Ax, and Ripley (1957) compared Group Mean Assessments of psychiatrically sick and well groups of adult males. Ss made self-descriptive *Q* sorts and clinicians sorted the same items to describe the *S*, as judged from a diagnostic interview and a "stress" interview. All correlations were computed for group mean arrays, not in terms of individual arrays. They found

> considerable agreement between the way the sick and well groups described themselves; high agreement between the self-descriptions and the clinicians' descriptions of the well group; but no relation between the self-description and clinicians' descriptions of the sick group (Kogan *et al.*, 1957, p. 59).

Thus the self-descriptions of the sick group did not reflect sufficiently the seriousness of their maladjustment. No matching criteria are reported.

Tolor (1957) used the Who-Are-You test to explore his idea that optimal adjustment involves two self-concept requirements: *S* should have an understanding of his own unique qualities as an individual, and should understand how he is related to the general social group. (See Table II, under Bugental, for a description of the Who-Are-You test.) *Ss* in Tolor's study were (1) hospitalized, neuropsychiatric patients (including neurotics, psychotics, organics, and patients with character and behavior disorders); and (2) hospitalized "normal" medical control patients. Three of the fourteen categories of answers significantly differentiated neuropsychiatric and medical control patients. Neuropsychiatric patients gave a significantly greater incidence of "own name" responses, which Tolor

(1957, p. 406) says "suggests an unsuccessful striving on their (NPs) part for self-identification by focussing attention on superficial aspects rather than on deeper facets of the personality." Neuropsychiatric patients gave significantly fewer responses coded for "group membership" and for "uniqueness." From this, Tolor concludes (1957, p. 406), "Emotionally disturbed patients appear to have a far less adequate self concept in terms of level of self-differentiation and group identification than do normals." The validity of this test for such inferences is undemonstrated. In addition, we must note that only 15% of the *normals* gave responses coded for "uniqueness" ("self-differentiation"); and there is some question whether groups were adequately matched on relevant variables.

McQuitty (1950) was interested in relating "adequacy of personality" to "personality integration" (or "integration of the self concept") rather than to self-regard. He writes:

> . . . we suggest that the adequate personality is one in whom the self is well integrated, in the sense that his successive subjective descriptions of self are characteristic of similar categories of people, and as a result of this he can readily accept into his organized conscious concept of self all his interpretations of reality, including, of course, perceptions of himself (McQuitty, 1950, p. 472).

To measure "personality integration" he used a "diversity index" obtained by an extremely complex treatment of the answers given by Ss to a personality inventory (Table II). This diversity index involved comparing S's answers on each successive pair of items in the inventory. The individual S with the lowest diversity score (high integration) is one who most frequently responds with answer pairs in the same way that a large proportion of respondents in the standardization group responded to those answer pairs (McQuitty, 1955, p. 309).

As one result to support his contention that diversity scores index "personality integration," McQuitty reports that the diversity scores of hospitalized patients were significantly higher than those of the standardization group of "community persons." (Hospitalization was, then, his index of "adequacy of personality." It is comparable to "maladjustment" as we use that term in this section.)

Secord (1955) objects to McQuitty's interpretation of the diversity score on several grounds, including the following: (a) The group of community persons was used as a standardization group to develop the diversity score *and also* for comparison with the hospitalized group. (b) There may well have been other differences between the groups besides personality integration, e.g., educational level. Secord showed that the high diversity score of the hospitalized group could have been accounted for more simply in terms of the number of items in which their answers failed to conform to the most common answer given by the group of community persons. On 75 items of the GAMIN Inventory, Secord obtained a correlation of —.85 between McQuitty's diversity score and the simpler "conformity" score. It seems highly likely to the present author that Secord's college *S*s must have given predominantly self-favorable answers, so Secord's conformity score may be plausibly considered to be an index of self-regard.

It appears to the present author that McQuitty's diversity score may also be most parsimoniously interpreted as a self-regard index, since his inventory, too, apparently contained evaluative items. If our reasoning is correct, what McQuitty found was a significant difference in stated self-regard between community persons and hospitalized patients. Since we do not know that the groups were matched on other variables relevant to a self-regard score (e.g., educational level), we cannot be sure that his result is an instance of low self-regard being associated with maladjustment per se.

Schizophrenic Ss. Tamkin (1957) found that schizophrenic *S*s had significantly lower Self-Acceptance scores on the Scott-Duke Questionnaire than did nonpatient *S*s, who were matched with the patient *S*s on race, age, education, sex, and geographical residence. There was great overlap in the distribution of the two groups, however. (See Table II.)

On the theory that Q sorting gets at self-ideal congruence quite indirectly, Rogers (1958) devised a unique "global apperception technique." To express perceived self-ideal congruence directly, S slid a four-inch square of translucent red glass (representing "self") behind a four-inch square of translucent blue glass (representing "ideal self"), and E measured the centimeters of overlap. Thirty paranoid schizophrenic patients showed significantly greater mean overlap than did thirty psychiatric aides from the same hospital. It is not specified whether patient and control *S*s were comparable on variables other than age and sex. Differences in the self-regard measures might seem to be the most plausible way to account for the fact that these trends are opposite in direction to those found by other investigators. However, other unknown differences such as patient classifications might be responsible (Table II).

Epstein (1955) compared self-evaluations of schizophrenic and supposedly normal medical patients matched on age, sex, veteran status, institutionalization, and education. Both "conscious" and "unconscious" self-evaluations were obtained, the former through Ss' direct ratings of their attitudes toward their own voices, handwritings, names, and selves. The latter ("unconscious" self-evaluations) were indexed through Ss' ratings of their own disguised handwriting and voice as compared to other samples; and through the speed of recognition of their own names in a tachistoscope. (See Table IV for details on these instruments.) The conscious evaluations were most comparable to the other studies reported in this section. The details on these scales and treatment of data from them are not published, but Epstein reports, in regard to the conscious evaluations: The normals tended to dislike their handwritings, but to a significant degree they rated favorably their attitudes toward voice, name, and self (t test, .01 level). The schizophrenics to a significant degree liked their handwritings, voices, and names, but not themselves ($p = .01$). Their self-ratings tended to fall at one extreme or the other, so that the variance of these ratings was significantly larger than that of the controls (F test, .01 level). However, "schizophrenics do not evaluate themselves significantly differently from normals, so far as central tendency is concerned, on a conscious measure of self-judgment" (Epstein, 1955, p. 69).

On all measures of "unconscious self-evaluation" the schizophrenics obtained more favorable values than did the normal control Ss, though the difference for any separate measure was not significant. In interpreting this we should note that Ss rated the similarity of the various disguised expressive behaviors to their own such behaviors, and this rated similarity was positively associated with favorableness of "unconscious self-evaluation." Therefore, as Epstein points out, it may be that the reactions to disguised stimuli are actually favorable reactions to expressive behaviors which Ss perceived as similar to their own, rather than being "unconscious self-evaluations." One also wonders whether factors other than self-attitudes were adequately controlled in comparing the tachistoscopic recognition thresholds for names. In view of the unresolved measurement problems, we can conclude only that this study offers no support to the idea that generally low self-regard characterizes schizophrenics.

We shall summarize the preceding eight studies below, after describing the investigations which compared at least three degrees or types of (mal)adjustment.

Studies Comparing at Least Three Degrees or Types of (Mal)adjustment

In these investigations, an adjusted group is compared with two or more maladjusted groups. As in the two-group studies described above, no criteria for defining satisfactory adjustment or maladjustment are common to all these researches. The first three studies to be summarized compared adjusted Ss with neurotic and schizophrenic Ss. The next three investigations made comparisons among patient groups as well as between patient and normal groups. The seventh study compared college students who showed varying degrees of adjustment; and the eighth one compared aviation cadets, students, and counseled students. The final work to be described included nine patient groups and one normal group.

Normal Ss and Two or More Patient Groups. Hillson and Worchel (1957) studied groups of normal, neurotic, and schizophrenic Ss who were "fairly well equated" on sex, age, and educational level, and were comparable, to an unspecified degree, with respect to socioeconomic class. To index self-regard, they used the Self-Activity Inventory which we discussed in Chapter III. They found that neurotic Ss rated themselves significantly more unfavorably than did normal or schizophrenic Ss, while the latter two groups made closely similar Self-scores. A [Self—Ideal] discrepancy, corrected in an attempt to partial out the Self-rating, gave the same group findings as did the Self-score. Using a similarly corrected [Self—Other] discrepancy, they found that both the neurotic and schizophrenic patients made larger mean scores than did normals. (This failed to support their predictions that the schizophrenic pattern of projection would lead to the smallest mean for that group.) Contrary to Adler's theory, there was no evidence of the neurotic's ideal for himself being set "fictitiously" high. In fact the mean ideal of the neurotic group was non-significantly lower than that of the normal, while the schizophrenics' ideal mean was significantly lower than normal.

Friedman (1955) found no significant difference in self-ideal correlations of paranoid schizophrenic and normal Ss (although schizophrenic Ss' *r*s were somewhat lower than those of normal Ss). Neurotic Ss gave self-ideal correlations significantly lower than either the schizophrenic or normal groups. (See Table I.) The groups were roughly equated on age and education, and contained only male Ss.

The third study in this group is not concerned with self-regard. Jones (1956) compared self concepts of normal, neurotic, and schizophrenic Ss using Butler and Haigh's Q-sort items. (See Chapter III for Butler and Haigh's instrument.) The mean ages of the groups ran from 24.0 to 29.7 years, and mean educational levels ran from 11.3 to 12.8 years. The dependent variable measure was the degree of departure from normality in the average curves of item distribution, when free rather than the usual forced sorting procedure was followed. Jones found that departure from normality was greater with increasing degrees of maladjustment (the normal-schizophrenic difference being significant at the .05 level). Jones speculates that maladjusted Ss may be less able to tolerate concepts of low predictability, at least in relation to themselves.

Chase (1957) found a tendency for self-ideal and self-"average-other" correlations to be smallest among psychotics, next smallest among neurotics and largest among character disorders. The differences were not significant, however. Adjusted (nonpsychiatric) patients showed significantly higher self-ideal and self-average-other congruence than did any group of psychiatric patients. The differences were really in the self-sort, since the two groups held similar concepts of ideal self and of the average other. (See Table I.) The groups did not differ significantly in mean age, education, or marital status.

Zuckerman, Baer, and Monashkin (1956) inferred differences in adjustment in two ways: by comparing normal Ss with patients, and by rating the patients' case histories for adjustment. Although their groups were not strictly comparable as to age, education, and vocabulary, the authors demonstrated that these variables were not correlated significantly with the dependent variables, acceptance of self and others. Acceptance of self and others was measured in terms of [Self — Ideal] or [Other — Ideal] discrepancies on Buss's sixteen-adjective scales. (See Table II.) They report that patients were less self-accepting than normals, but within the patient group there was no relation between adjustment and self-acceptance. In fact, in female patients the trend was toward a negative relationship. (Patients showed less acceptance of mother, people, and father than did normals, but only the latter two measures related to adjustment within the patient group. Paranoids showed less acceptance of people and father than did depressives.) Contrary to the prediction of Block and Thomas (1955), self-acceptance was positively correlated with improvement in the hospital. (See Table II.)

In another report, apparently involving different Ss, Zuckerman and Monashkin (1957) state that they found no relationship between self-acceptance [Self—Ideal] discrepancies on Buss's scales and case-history ratings of adjustment, even though the interobserver reliability of the latter was +.77.

Three Degrees of Adjustment in Student and/or Military Groups. Like Hillson and Worchel (1957) and Friedman (1955), Chodorkoff (1954) obtained a curvilinear relationship between adjustment and self-ideal congruence. The adequacy of adjustment of his college student Ss was inferred in an unspecified manner from a clinical evaluation of biographical and projective material. Self-ideal correspondence was indexed by a z value obtained from a Q sort. (See Table I.) Ss with poorest rated adjustment had a low mean self-ideal z, those with somewhat better rated adjustment had the lowest self-ideal z, and those rated as best adjusted showed the highest mean self-ideal z. No information is available as to whether Ss differed in any other relevant ways than in clinically rated adjustment.

In Worchel's (1957) study, referred to in Chapter III, it was assumed that low, medium, and high adjustment would respectively characterize the following three groups: (1) college men referred by themselves or others to a counseling or psychiatric bureau; (2) college students; and (3) aviation cadets. On Self mean and Ideal mean scores, students and consultation Ss differed significantly from the cadets. In addition, the consultation Ss differed at the .06 level from students, with repect to Self mean scores. Due to problems of control explained in Chapter III, these results do not offer unequivocal support to an hypothesis of linear correlation between adjustment and self-regard, however. (See Chapter III for a description of the Self-Activity Inventory used in this study.)

Ten Groups of Ss Compared. The data reported by Leary (1957) are by far the most extensive of any which compare self-concept measures with patterns of diagnosed maladjustment. In two respects this study does not fit in with the others we have discussed: (1) The ten groups of Ss cannot all be differentiated from one another along a continuum of maladjustment, i.e., some groups might conceivably be equally maladjusted, though qualitatively different from each other. (2) His Interpersonal Check List does not yield a single self-regard score. Instead, eight different scores can be obtained for each S, and each of these scores can be placed on a continuum of intensity which bears some relation to an evaluative dimension. The eight types of scores, listed in pairs of alleged opposites, are: managerial-autocratic *vs.* self-effacing-masochistic; responsible-hypernormal *vs.* rebellious-distrustful; cooperative-conventional *vs.* aggressive-sadistic; docile-dependent *vs.* competitive-narcissistic. (See Chapter III for a fuller discussion of the Interpersonal Check List.)

There were ten groups of Ss, with Ns ranging from 28 (for psychotics) to 207 (for clinic admission sample). The six psychosomatic groups were referred for research-testing by physicians (i.e., they were not self-referred for psychiatric diagnosis or treatment). These six groups are called: duodenal ulcer, essential hypertension, obesity (all females), overtly neurotic dermatitis, self-inflicted dermatitis (i.e., scratching and self-inflicted skin damage), unanxious dermatitis. The "neurotic" group consisted of patients in outpatient psychotherapy, many of whom were quite anxious to get this treatment. Psychotic Ss were hospitalized patients, about half paranoid and the rest suicidal-depressed. The "clinic admission sample" consisted of all persons who applied to a psychiatric clinic for diagnostic evaluation over a six-month period. Some sought psychotherapy, but most were referred by physicians because of psychosomatic symptoms. The "normal controls" were patients with physical skin lesions, referred by a dermatologist for research-testing.

Leary points out that these groups are not all equated with one another with respect to such important variables as age, sex, educational level, socioeconomic level, personal desire for psychiatric evaluation or therapy, hospitalized status, and testing conditions. The psychotic group and the clinic admission sample were quite heterogeneous, psychologically.

He reduced the eight scores from the Interpersonal Check List to two gross combinations: (1) competitive-narcissistic-managerial-autocratic-responsible-hypernormal; (2) aggressive-sadistic-rebellious-distrustful-self-effacing-masocistic-docile-dependent. He reports chi square comparisons for each group of Ss versus each other group on these combined scores. The detailed findings cannot be presented here, but he summarizes the consciously reported self concepts of the several groups as follows (Leary, 1956, p. 384):

Self Concept	Patient Groups
Very strong and hypernormal	Hypertension, obesity, unanxious dermatitis
Moderately strong and hypernormal	Normals, psychotics, self-inflicted dermatitis
Very strong and aggressive	Ulcer
Very weak	Neurotic
No commitment to any modal security operation	Clinic admission, overtly neurotic dermatitis

The trends here which may be comparable to those obtained by other investigators are: (1) the self-derogation of the "neurotic" group; and (2) the similarity between the normal and psychotic self-reports. We must remember, however, that these neurotics are a biassed sample of all neurotics, i.e., these Ss had accepted psychotherapy, and in many cases they were anxious to have it. This implies that they recognized their inadequacies and/or wished to impress the clinic with their need for help, characteristics which might not be true for all neurotics. As support for this point, we note that the "overtly neurotic dermatitis" group showed no consistent pattern of self concept. Hypertensives and unanxious dermatitis and obesity patients would be considered by some diagnosticians to be neurotic, since no physical cause was found for their disorders. If they are "neurotic," the fact that they did not show the self-derogatory trend supports the idea that not all groups with neurosis or "moderately severe" maladjustment show low self-regard. As Leary points out, the findings with the psychotics are not clearly interpretable either, because paranoid and suicidal-depressed patients were mixed in the sample.

Summary of Studies Relating Degree of Pathology to Level of Self-Regard

We have reviewed nineteen studies in which level of reported self-regard was correlated with degrees of diagnosed pathology. Almost every study used a different instrument for inferring level of self-regard, and employed different criteria for diagnosing or defining degrees of adjustment. In many studies the groups were not known to be comparable on other variables which might affect their reported self-regard; and testing conditions may not have been comparable for all groups. Therefore our summarizing statements are offered quite tentatively.

If we disregard for the moment whether the studies involved two, three, or more groups, and overview all the investigations which compared normals, neurotics, and/or psychotics, some general trends become apparent, despite puzzling contradictions.

1. In nine studies, diagnosed neurotics and/or mixed patient groups showed significantly lower self-regard than did normal, nonpatient (or medical patient) Ss. There is much overlap between groups, however.

2. On the other hand, varying results have been obtained in comparisons between psychotics and normal persons. Two investigators have reported finding lower self-regard scores among psychotic patients than among normal Ss (one of these writers specifying that schizophrenia was the psychosis involved); and one E has obtained a nonsignificant trend for paranoid schizophrenic Ss to have lower self-regard. Three investigators reported no significant difference between psychotics and normal controls. In contrast to the first six investigations, a seventh study reports significantly *higher* self-regard among paranoid schizophrenic than among normal Ss.

Certainly as one goes from normals through neurotics to psychotics a clear linear downward trend in self-regard is *not* found. In fact, two investigators report significantly greater self-regard in psychotic groups than in neurotic groups, while one reports a nonsignificant trend opposite to this.

When we consider only studies involving more than two groups, it seems plausible that the results to be expected may depend on how widely scattered the groups are along this continuum of maladjustment. We may guess that only when they are scattered very widely may curvilinear results be expected. Thus in four studies, a curvilinear relationship was reported between diagnosed severity of maladjustment and self-regard, with neurotics (or persons with maladjustment of medium severity) having the lowest reported self-regard. Ss who were judged to be best adjusted in these studies had the highest self-regard, but their self-regard was not necessarily significantly better than that of the most poorly adjusted Ss. Three of these studies compared normals, neurotics, and psychotics; while the fourth compared university students of varying degrees of maladjustment. (The latter study constitutes a possible exception to the above generalization, since these groups may not have been widely different from one another along a continuum of maladjustment.)

We may also guess that when groups which are compared are not widely different in adjustment, either linear trends or no significant relationship between self-regard and adjustment will be obtained. Thus two studies which explored only differences within patient groups found no consistent relationship between degree of maladjustment and self-regard. In one three-group study in which the worst-adjusted Ss were persons utilizing the university counseling and/or psychiatric services, a linear relationship was obtained.

In any event, when we couple all of the above observations with those of Kogan *et al.* (1957), which show that the Q sorts of "sick" Ss did not sufficiently reflect their judged pathology, we can see that the level of self-regard is far from being a valid indicator of degree of pathology.

How can we explain the fact that there is no linear relationship between severity of maladjustment and degree of self-regard, when a wide range of maladjustment is studied?

On the one hand, this may well be due to the fact that qualitative differences in patterns of maladjustment may be as important or more important than simple "degree of maladjustment." In other words, even when we can agree on the rank order of various groups along a simple maladjustment dimension, we might find that level of self-regard is associated at least partly with the qualitative differences among the adjustment patterns of the groups (as contrasted to the rank order of the groups with respect to severity of maladjustment). Leary's work and earlier validating work with the MMPI offer some support to such an idea.

When we examine the studies we have just reviewed, we find that the three investigations encompassing normal, neurotic, and psychotic Ss all used schizophrenic or paranoid persons. (In one of them only half the psychotics were paranoid, the other half being suicidal depressive.) It might be that different results would have been obtained if other psychotic Ss had been used as the extremely maladjusted group.

As another possible example of this point about qualitative differences, we should note the low self-regard of the neurotic groups in the studies we have summarized. In all these studies, neurotic Ss were persons who had already recognized their inadequacies, as shown by the fact that they had accepted or even sought treatment. But would all varieties of neurotics, including those not ready to seek or accept treatment, show similar low self-regard? Leary's results with the psychosomatic patients suggest a negative answer to this question.

On the other hand, we must again raise these questions: (1) Did all the instruments which were used index "global level of self-regard"? (2) If not, to what extent are differences among studies and failure to obtain linear findings attributable to that fact? (3) Is "global level of self-regard" (as contrasted to self-regard in given areas) to be expected to correlate linearly with "adjustment"?

These questions must remain unanswered until we get more analytical operational definitions of adjustment and self-regard.

Even if we could state generalizations about the correlation between self-regard and diagnosed pathology, such R-R findings could not, of course, sustain cause-effect generalizations.

b(1) TEACHER, AUTHORITY, AND PEER RATINGS OF BEHAVIOR PRESUMABLY RELEVANT TO ADJUSTMENT

Extreme Groups Differing in Total Pattern

Marked academic underachievement is generally considered to be indicative of "maladjustment." In this context, Walsh (1956) compared self concepts of high- and low-achieving boys, matched for superior IQ and certain other relevant variables. On the Driscoll Play Kit, the doll play of the underachievers, when compared to that of adequate achievers, less frequently depicted the boy doll as (1) free to pursue his own interests; (2) free to express his feelings; (3) accepted as a member of the family; (4) adequate in response to environmental stimuli. It was assumed that these findings indicated differences in self concept. (See Chapter V below for a discussion of Walsh's instrument.)

Another generally accepted indicator of maladjustment is marked antisocial or delinquent behavior. Reckless, Dinitz, and Murray (1956) and Reckless, Dinitz, and Kay (1957) studied the self concepts, life history data, and parental backgrounds and attitudes of boys from a high delinquency area who were nominated by their teachers as likely or highly *un*likely to become delinquent. Among the differences in self concept were these: The potential delinquents expected to go to court or jail some day; they did not desire to avoid trouble at all costs; they conceived of themselves as less obedient sons and did not report on their family relationships or parental discipline as favorably as did the other group. The authors interpret their findings as indicating the "insulating" role of the self concept in preventing the "good" boys from becoming delinquents despite their general neighborhood environment. However their results do not warrant this conclusion because (a) there were a number of important objective differences between the groups (e.g., number of broken homes, parents' reported attitudes toward the boys); and (b) in any event we cannot know to what extent the boys' reports (self concepts) reflect rather than cause the differences in behavior which lay behind their teachers' nominations of them. (See Table II.)

Engel (1959) attempted to relate self descriptive Q sorts, or shifts in Q sort over a two-year period to teacher and peer ratings of adolescents' adjustment. Both rating instruments were specially devised, the peer scale consisting of a modified guess-who technique which could be scored later on an adjustment-maladjustment continuum. The only association found was between a negative to positive self-concept shift and movement toward better adjustment as measured by peer ratings. (See Table I.)

Esteem from Others or Sociometric Choice

Theorists have assumed that high self-regard will lead to better ability to get along with others, and that acceptance by others will maintain or enhance self-regard. On the basis of these notions, a number of investigators have correlated self-regard with sociometric indices. As we shall see below, some of the studies have yielded the predicted positive correlations and others have not.

Using 102 fifth- and sixth-grade children as Ss, Coopersmith (1959) obtained a partial r of $+ .29$ ($p < .01$) between self-esteem and sociometric status, when school achievement was held constant. Self-esteem was measured by a specially devised inventory (see Table II), and sociometric status was indexed in terms of the children's choices of persons wanted as friends.

In another study involving sixth-grade children in their classrooms, Zelen (1954a, 1954b) applied the Bonney Sociometric technique and two measures of "self-acceptance" (California Test of Personality Feelings of Personal Worth and the Who-Are-You test, scored for self-acceptance). He obtained small but significant correlations between each measure of self-acceptance and sociometric acceptance by peers. (See Bugental, Table II, for the Who-Are-You test.)

Although the Ss in Perkins's (1958b) research were fourth- and sixth-grade children, his results cannot be directly compared with those of the preceding two investigations, because Perkins correlated changes in children's self-ideal congruence with changes in acceptance by their peers, as measured by a sociometric procedure. He obtained no relationship between these two kinds of changes over a six-month period. (See Table I.)

In a study of male undergraduate and graduate students, Brownfain (1952) found "stability" of self concept to be associated with knowing and being known by more persons in one's fraternity, and with being better liked and more popular in the fraternity. As we have discussed fully in Chapter III, it seems probable that the major contribution to this association is made by the "negative self concept" (the "most unfavorable realistic self concept"), which is one of the two components of the "stability" score. The other component of "stability" is the "most favorable realistic self concept." (See Chapter III for a discussion of Brownfain's instrument.)

Turner and Vanderlippe (1958) report that college Ss with high self-ideal congruence on the Butler and Haigh items (as contrasted to Ss with low self-ideal congruence on this instrument) ranked higher on all eleven components of a sociometric score obtained from dormitory peers who lived near them. Eight of these differences were significant. (See Chapter III for a discussion of Butler and Haigh's instrument.)

On the other hand Fey (1955) found that Acceptance of Self (as measured on his own scale) did not correlate with acceptance by others. However, Ss showing high Acceptance of Self and low Acceptance of Others tended to be rejected by others, i.e., there was a barely significant negative correlation between [AS — AO] and acceptance by others. His Ss were freshman medical students. (See Chapter III for a discussion of Fey's scale.)

A second study giving negative results is that of Fiedler et al. (1958). They found no relationship between self-esteem (as measured on a twenty-item Semantic Differential instrument) and sociometric status. Only one r between self-esteem and mean esteem by others reached the .05 level. Four nonclinical groups were studied (two military and two college groups), giving eight rs altogether for the two dependent variable measures. (See Table II.)

One might speculate that perhaps Coopersmith's, Brownfain's, Turner and Vanderlippe's, and Zelen's subjects knew one another better than did Ss in the Fey and Fiedler studies, thus accounting for the difference in their findings. However, McIntyre's (1952) negative findings suggest that even when Ss do know each other well, and sociometric indices appear valid to knowledgeable observers of the group, one can get null findings when attempting to relate self-esteem to sociometric status. He found no relation between sociometrically measured acceptance of male Ss in a college dormitory and Ss' scores on either self-acceptance or acceptance of others, based on Phillips's questionnaire. (See Chapter III for Phillips's questionnaire.)

Parenthetically it should be noted that some of the studies reviewed in Chapter VI may be relevant here. A number of these studies show rather low or nonsignificant correlations between self-ratings and ratings of self by others on a variety of evaluative trait scales.

It is obvious that variations in subjects, situations, and instruments make it impossible to compare in a conclusive way the studies reviewed above. It seems that there are enough positive findings, not obviously explainable as artifacts, to suggest that there is some relation, under certain conditions, between self-regard and sociometric status. The research problem at hand is to ascertain more systematically the conditions under which such a relationship might be reliably predicted to hold. And of course researches of an entirely different order will have to be devised to explore the cause-and-effect relationships which have been postulated to account for whatever correlations may be found.

b(2) OTHER OBSERVABLE BEHAVIORS PRESUMABLY RELATED TO ADJUSTMENT

Physical Health

A number of theorists have assumed that self-acceptance should be related to physical health, or at least to one's attitude toward physical health. They have reasoned that low self-regard will lead to or involve anxiety and tension; and that anxiety may lead to psychosomatic disturbances, to a greater awareness of aches and pains perhaps by way of hypochondriacal defenses; and to an increase in actual aches and pains by way of the direct effects of increased tensions (Fiedler et al., 1958). It has also been said that low valuation of self may extend to low valuation of the integrity and capacities of the body, because of the intimate connections throughout development between body functions and self concept (Roessler & Greenfield, 1958).

Several researchers have explored the possibility that low self-esteem will be associated with a high incidence of objective signs of poor health or concern about health. Even if positive findings were attained in such undertakings, they could be only suggestive, for obvious reasons, not the least of which is the possibility of artifactual contamination by "social desirability." That is, a significant correlation could represent varying degrees of willingness to admit undesirable symptoms on several occasions.

Of the three papers reporting correlations of this sort, one gives a positive correlation, the second gives essentially no correlation (one out of three such rs reached the .05 level), and the third reports no significant relation with any one of three separate health scores used, or with the composite score.

Roessler and Greenfield (1958) used two measures of self-acceptance: Fey's self-acceptance scale, and the incidence of suicidal attempts. Each of these was associated positively with the number of visits to the university infirmary for minor somatic complaints during the first semester after admission to the university. All Ss who took the Fey scale had had complete medical examinations and medical histories taken initially, and all had been found to be essentially free of symptomatology at the outset. However, it is not clear that the Ss compared were matched on other relevant variables. (See Chapter III for Fey's instrument.)

In the work already referred to by Fiedler *et al.* (1958), the number of health center visits was correlated with self-esteem (indexed on a twenty-item Semantic Differential) for each of two college groups, and one military group. Only one positive r significant at the .05 level was obtained (with one of the college groups). (See Table II.)

When extreme groups high and low on self-ideal congruence (as measured by Butler and Haigh's Q-sort items) were compared by Turner and Vanderlippe (1958), no significant relationship to a composite health score was found (including days in infirmary, calls for medical assistance, poor health items on entrance medical history blank). The nonsignificant trends for the first two items were in the same direction as those reported by Roessler and Greenfield, but the trend was actually in the opposite direction on the third item. (See Chapter III for Butler and Haigh's instrument.)

All things considered, there seems to be no firm support for any variation of the basic rationale, stated above, that low self-regard will be connected with poor physical health. Whether the weakness of the empirical trends comes from limitations in the method or in the underlying assumptions cannot, of course, be ascertained from these studies.[8]

Stuttering

Three investigators have attempted to relate self-concept variables with stuttering, on the general assumption that stuttering may influence the self concept and vice versa. The findings are not conclusive or clearly interpretable psychologically, due to variations in instruments, Ss, adequacies of control, and direction of findings.

Fiedler and Wepman (1951), using a Q technique, found no characteristic differences between the self concepts of ten stutterers and nonstuttering controls. On the other hand, Berger (1952), employing his own inventory, obtained significantly lower Self-acceptance scores from stutterers than from nonstutterers matched for age and sex. In the third study, Zelen, Sheehan, and Bugental (1954) applied the Who-Are-You technique to stutterers and nonstuttering controls. Stutterers gave significantly more responses classifiable under Age, Positive Affect, and Group Membership (including stutterer) categories; and significantly fewer responses classifiable under Uniqueness of Respondent and Sex

---

[8]Some observers have suggested on the basis of case history material that certain kinds of ill health will undermine self-esteem and distort the self concept. The types of illnesses which are alleged to have this effect have in common the fact that they may greatly distort the person's body image and/or interfere with his performance of routine tasks and ordinary social interactions. In addition it has been suggested that such illnesses may be interpreted by the patient as punishment for his own shortcomings, and that the reception of such "punishment" may reinforce the person's feelings of being an unworthy person. See, for example, Bice (1954) in re cerebral palsy; Glud and Blane (1956) and Cath, Glud, and Blane (1957) in re respiratory poliomyelitis; Grayson (1951) in re paraplegia; and S. Berger (1952) in re paraplegia. In a quantitative study of body-concept disturbances of patients with hemiplegia, Shontz (1956) used a specially devised set of questions concerning identification and location of body parts; and a specified way of coding the Draw-a-Person Test. Patients with hemiplegia involving the dominant hemisphere showed significantly more signs of inefficiency and confusion in response to the questions than did patients with hemiplegia involving the nondominant hemisphere; patients with severe, nonhemiplegic chronic illnesses; and normal volunteer Ss. (All groups were matched for CA.) The latter three groups did not differ significantly from one another; and the DAP "signs" did not discriminate effectively among any of the four groups. On the basis of unspecified clinical information, Shontz asserted that there was no relationship between body-concept signs and degree of expressive aphasia or intellectual deterioration. No attempt was made to link body-concept disturbances with self-esteem.

Categories. They interpret the surprising findings concerning Positive Affect as representing either denial of inferiority feelings, or self-esteem associated with having decided to help themselves through therapy. Their interpretations of other findings also seem to be *ad hoc* and somewhat arbitrary. It is not clear that their groups were matched on relevant variables. (See Table I for Fiedler and Wepman's *Q* sort; Chapter III for Berger's Inventory; Bugental, in Table II, for Who-Are-You technique.)

Miscellaneous

Of possible relevance to the relation of self-esteem to "adjustment" is the finding of Maslow and Sakoda (1952) that *S*s who volunteered for Kinsey's interviews concerning sex behavior had higher self-esteem than did those not volunteering. (Self-esteem was measured by the Maslow Social Personality Inventory, described in Chapter III.) The connection between volunteering and "adjustment" is probably debatable, however.

In the study by Fiedler *et al.* (1958), which has already been discussed, no relationship was found between self-esteem and grade point average, counseling bureau visits, or disciplinary ratings, all of which they had thought might plausibly be considered behavioral indices of adjustment.

Similarly, Turner and Vanderlippe (1958) obtained only nonsignificant trends toward higher grade point averages among *S*s with high self-ideal congruence. (*S*s high and low on self-ideal congruence were comparable on the ACE test.)

In contrast to the above findings with young adults, Coopersmith (1959) obtained a partial r of $+.30$ ($p < .01$) between Iowa Achievement Test scores and self-esteem, when sociometric status was held constant. His *S*s were fifth- and sixth-grade children. (See Table II.)

Eighty-seven out of 102 of Coopersmith's *S*s were rated by their teachers on a fourteen-item Self-Esteem Behavior Rating Form, which concerned such things as the child's self-confidence in a new situation, his need for reassurance and encouragement, and his reactions to failure. The present author assumes that this may be considered to be an "adjustment" rating. Coopersmith (1959, p. 90) writes, "Only in a minority of cases was there a marked discrepancy between the SEI (Self Esteem Inventory) and BRF (Behavior Rating Form) scores." His rationale for computing discrepancies and deciding upon criteria for "marked discrepancies" is not entirely clear from his published report, however.

Among 251 fourth- and sixth-grade children tested by Perkins (1958b), there was no relationship over a six-month period between changes in self-ideal congruence and changes in school achievement as measured by the California Achievement Test. (See Table I.) He does not present any correlations between achievement and self-ideal congruence at any one testing time, so his results cannot be directly compared with those of the preceding three investigators.

Nahinsky (1958) assumed that junior officers choosing to make a career in the Navy were better adjusted situationally than were junior officers voluntarily leaving the Navy. *S*s from the two categories *Q* sorted 100 specially devised items to describe self, ideal officer, and typical officer. Correlations between self and ideal officer were significantly larger in the career group, from which the author inferred that a feeling of inadequacy or not measuring up may be a correlate of poor situational adjustment. Because correlations between self and typical officer were also greater in the career group, the author suggests that a feeling of "fitting in" is an important correlate of situational adjustment. The question remains, however, whether phenomenal self-esteem was a variable in this study, since *S* was never asked whether the "ideal officer" or the "typical officer" coincided with his personal ideal (Table I).

Zimmer's study was "undertaken to check the efficacy of self-concept-ideal-self discrepancies as indicators of conflict, and by inference, of maladjustment. It tested the hypothesis that the presence of conflict over a personality trait is associated with a self-concept-ideal-self discrepancy on that trait" (Zimmer, 1954, p. 447). To determine discrepancies he used specially chosen adjectives, described in Table II. He classified adjectives as nonconflictual or conflictual if *S* showed respectively zero *or* two or more specified complex indicators in a word-association test. His null findings failed to confirm his hypothesis. Thus his results do not agree with Roberts's (1952) significant differences and Bills's (1953b) nonsignificant trends from studies of the same general sort which utilized words from Bills's IAV, and reaction time as a measure of conflict. (The latter studies are described in Chapter III above, in connection with a discussion of the construct validity of Bills's IAV.) Differences in self-report instruments and measures of conflict make it impossible to compare Bills's and Roberts's studies directly with Zimmer's. In all three cases, it is not possible to be sure whether pertinent word characteristics were held constant when comparing discrepant with nondiscrepant words (or when comparing conflictual with nonconflictual words).

Halpern (1955, p. 452) suggested the possibility that "in areas where a person is discontent about his own behavior, disorganizing anxiety may be aroused and distortive defenses may be mobilized ... [causing] aberrations in accurate interpersonal perceptions." Such a rationale leads us to include his study in this section on self-regard and adjustment. He found that Ss predicted responses of others on the GAMIN Inventory more accurately for items on which Ss have indicated they are "pleased" with their own self-ratings than for items with which they are "dissatisfied." This finding may be artifactual, however, because (a) Halpern showed that his Ss' ability to predict accurately lay strictly in the items on which S and the predictee are *actually* similar; and (b) it seems likely, in view of studies on the Social Desirability factor, that S and the predictee would *actually* be similar more often on items which any given S considers to be desirable attributes.

c. PROJECTIVES FOR MEASURING ADJUSTMENT

Although there has been considerable concern with the need to measure the nonphenomenal self concept, very few studies have tried to measure "adjustment" by projective techniques (i.e., by nonphenomenal indices), and relate this to phenomenal self-esteem. Possibly this might be a means of exploring the notion that unusually high self-esteem represents denial of maladjustment, but this approach has not been tried.

In the studies reviewed, a variety of projective measures of adjustment and indices of the phenomenal self have been used. Consequently no synthesis of results is possible. However, the findings of the investigations summarized below suggest that further search for relationships in this area may be worthwhile.

Rorschach Indices

Bills (1954b) obtained a significant correlation between [Self — Ideal] discrepancies and Rorschach signs of depression. (See Chapter III.)

LaFon (1954) postulated that self-acceptance should correlate negatively with anxiety, hostility, and criticality toward self and environment, defensive behavior, and indecisiveness, and should correlate positively with internalization of values, realistic perception, emotional stability and maturity, and capacity for social relationships, and the capacities to integrate the self concept and handle the complexity of relationships with others. To measure self-acceptance he used Brownfain's "stability of self concept" and "negative self concept." (See Chapter III for an evaluation of this instrument.) LaFon assumed that certain Rorschach measures revealed respectively the adjustment characteristics itemized above. Two extreme groups of Ss differing in stability of self concept were drawn from a pool of 146 female undergraduates $(N = 60)$. On 28 Rorschach scoring items, 22 t tests were in the predicted direction, three of them reaching the .05 level or better. From the 60 Ss, two extreme groups of 20 each were drawn, differing with respect to "negative self concept." In 20 out of 28 Rorschach comparisons, differences were in the predicted direction, with seven t tests reaching the .05 level or better. Of course not all the tests of significance were independent of one another. However, we may conclude that there is some trend in these data toward a correlation between phenomenal self-esteem and Rorschach scores purporting to measure "adjustment." In addition, judges attempted to rate the total Rorschach protocols blindly with respect to over-all self-acceptance. Although such ratings were generally unreliable, the differences in means of judges' ratings assigned to the extreme groups of Ss reached the .02 level in each of the two comparisons of groups differing in self concept.

TAT Indices

In the therapy study described in Section C-5 above, Dymond (1954b) rated TAT records on a seven-point scale ranging from "severe disturbance, bordering on psychotic, or psychotic" to "well integrated, happy person, socially effective." No direct correlations between self-ideal rs on the Butler and Haigh items and the TAT adjustment ratings are given. However, the Q-adjustment score on the Butler and Haigh items (which correlated +.92 with self-ideal rs obtained from 23 therapy patients) correlated +.63 with TAT adjustment ratings on 35 Ss at pretherapy. This suggests that self-ideal rs would correlate with Dymond's TAT adjustment ratings.

In the same research, Grummon and John (1954) scored TAT records on the basis of psychoanalytically derived scales of "mental health." They found no correlation between self-ideal rs and their TAT scores. (See Chapter III for the Butler and Haigh items.)

Sentence Completion and Word Association

Crandall and Bellugi (1954) obtained a significant correlation between "adjustment" scores derived from Rotter's Incomplete Sentences Blank and favorability of self concept as revealed on a specially devised instrument. (See Table II.) Paralleling the findings of many other workers concerning the lack of discriminating power of the "ideal self," adjustment was unrelated to the ideal self in this study. Interestingly enough, adjustment as discerned through favorability of peer evaluations of S did not correlate significantly with adjustment inferred from the Rotter Test. Thus the problem of lack of correlation between indices purporting to measure "adjustment" is exemplified again.

Secord and Jourard (1953) used a homonym test as a supposedly disguised index of anxiety about pain, disease, or bodily injury. Their hypothesis that this index of adjustment should be negatively related to phenomenal "body cathexis" (measured by a specially devised instrument) was upheld significantly for females, but nonsignificantly for males. (See Chapter III.)

Davids's (1955) study, comparing five measures of "adjustment," may be seen as an example pertinent to the present discussion, although it was not designed as a test of self-concept theory. Davids was interested in comparing indirect and projective measures of "alienation" (maladjustment) with S's direct reports of (a) his own happiness (taken from the Happiness Self-Rating Scale used by Goldings [1954]—see Table III), and (b) his psychological and physiological disturbances (taken from the Psychosomatic Inventory of Seitz and McFarland [1938]). The direct reports might be thought of as indexing S's phenomenal self concept of his own adjustment. The indirect measure was a specially prepared Sentence Completion Test aimed at tapping eight personality dispositions. Five of these were classified as "negative dispositions" and the score based on them was the "alienation" index. (The interjudge reliability of this instrument ran from 80% to 100% for individual records, across the eight categories plus a miscellaneous category.) The projective measure was a specially devised Word Association test, designed to pertain to the same eight categories and to yield an alienation score also. (Interjudge correlation of ranks assigned Ss was +.89 and +.86 on two groups.) In addition, an experienced clinician ranked Ss on "ego strength" (assumed to be highly correlated with adjustment). These ratings were based on two interviews and an autobiography, so to a certain extent they may be another reflection of S's self-reports.

All five of these measures were applied to two different groups of Ss: (1) twenty male college students who were paid volunteers for taking tests in the interests of scientific research; and (2) twenty-three closely similar paid volunteer students who took the tests in the belief that they were being tested for possible placement in an interesting paid job. In the first group, the average *rho* among the various measures (calculated from Kendall's *W*) was +.65, which is highly significant. In the second group the *rho* was +.45, indicating a significant degree of agreement. When the two correlation matrices were examined, it was found that nine out of ten correlations were larger for the first group than for the second group, whose members would have reason to try to put themselves in a good light when giving their direct reports. This substantiates the idea that the validity of phenomenal self-concept measures may be impaired by Ss' view of the purpose of the investigation. Another point of interest is the finding that the three most unhealthy Ss, by their own reports (two in one group and one in the second group), were also judged most maladjusted by all the other techniques. This is congruent with the assumption that marked phenomenal self-derogation is more indicative of maladjustment than is marked phenomenal self-satisfaction indicative of adjustment.

We should also note that Chodorkoff's study (1955), mentioned under Criterion b above, involved projectives as one basis for the adjustment ratings.

d. Self-Report Instruments as Indices of Adjustment

MMPI

Five studies report correlations between self-concept measures and MMPI scales.

Berger (1955) found that self-acceptance in college students, as measured by his Self-Acceptance Scale, correlated negatively with certain clinical scales on the MMPI (*D, Pa, Pt, Sc* for all Ss; *Hs* and *Pd* for women only). Self-acceptance correlated positively with *K*. One significant correlation in the unexpected (i.e., positive) direction was obtained— the *Hy* scale for men. (See Chapter III for the Berger scales.)

Block and Thomas (1955) reported that large self-minus-ideal discrepancies (on an eighty-adjective *Q* sort) were associated with maladjust-

ment on MMPI scales. Significant differences were found on *Hs, D, Pd,
Ps,* and *Sc* scales. Self-ideal congruence correlated positively with their
Ego-Control scale and with Little and Fisher's Denial and Admission scales,
both derived from the MMPI. This led them to suggest that *S*s reporting
high self-ideal congruence might be maladjusted deniers. (See Table I.)

Rosen (1956a, 1956b) obtained statements from college students concerning self-ideal discrepancies on the MMPI items themselves. He found
a correlation of +.87 between *K* and the number of items showing a discrepancy between *S*'s actual and ideal self. One interpretation of this,
parallel to that suggested by Block and Thomas, is that high self-ideal
congruence results from the defense of denial rather than from good adjustment. Rosen also found that self-ideal discrepancies correlated with
profile elevation in *Sc, Si, D,* and *Ps.* The latter finding would, of course,
be simply two ways of viewing the same self-report of symptoms, since
the stated ideal was to be healthy on these items. In any event, the data
do not permit clear conclusions in regard to self-minus-ideal discrepancies
and adjustment, since the same instrument was used for both dependent
and independent variable measures.

Engel (1959) measured adjustment by the *Pd* and *D* scales of the
MMPI, by peer ratings, and by teacher ratings. The MMPI findings will
be considered here. Adolescents whose *Q* sorts (on a specially devised
instrument) were persistently unfavorable to self over a two-year period
had significantly higher *Pd* and *D* scores than *S*s who persisted in a positive self concept. Shifts from positive to negative self concept over the
two-year period were significantly associated with higher scores on *Pd*
and *D*, while shifts from negative to positive self concept were associated
with significantly higher *K* scores. (See Table I.)

In line with all the findings itemized above are the correlations obtained from psychiatric patients by Zuckerman and Monashkin (1957),
between self-minus-ideal discrepancies on Buss's sixteen-adjective scales
and various MMPI scales. Those correlations involving *F, Hs, D, Pa, Pt,
Sc,* and *Si* were significantly negative, while the correlation with *K* was
significantly positive. (See Table II.)

From the above five studies there is clear support for the contention
that reported self-regard and certain clinical scales of the MMPI correlate
negatively, while self-regard and *K* correlate positively. *S*s differing in
sex, age, and educational and psychiatric status were used in these various
investigations, and a different measure of self-regard was employed in each

study. Therefore the trends are not specific to one type of S or self-regard measure.

Engel dealt with D, Pd, and K scales only. With this qualification, the following MMPI scale correlations with self-regard measures were significant in all five studies: K (the only positive rs); D; Pt; Sc; Si. In three of these studies Hs and Pd correlated significantly with self-regard (although these correlations were significant only for the women Ss in one of the three investigations). Pa correlated significantly with self-regard in two studies.

We have already said that significant correlations between two self-reports are generally suspect, since artifactual explanations are so plausible. In answer to this, one might argue that the MMPI scales have already been demonstrated to have some validity as predictors of diagnosed pathology. This being so, the self-regard scores may be said to have been indirectly associated with external behavior observations of adjustment in such studies as those reviewed above.

By similar reasoning, the unanimous finding that self-regard and K are positively correlated may imply that high phenomenal self-regard is associated with denial of maladjustment in some cases, rather than being indicative of good adjustment. The following major problems remain unsolved, then: (1) the role of response sets and overlapping item content in determining the empirical correlations; (2) the means of distinguishing, within the high self-regard group, those Ss who are adjusted from those who are maladjusted deniers.

Measuring Self-Reported Adjustment

Turning now to other instruments used to measure adjustment, we find that Dymond (1954a) reports a significant correlation between self-ideal congruence and an "adjustment" score based on the same Q-sort array. (See Chapter III.) Ss were those involved in a therapy study. These findings were replicated with college students by Turner and Vanderlippe (1958). These results seem to imply mostly that the Ss had about the same idea concerning what would be "ideal" as the clinicians had about what would be "adjusted."

Brownfain (1952) found that Ss showing a small gap between most optimistic and most pessimistic self concepts also had higher self-esteem scores on the same instrument used to measure "stability" of self concept and were freer of nervousness on GAMIN. (See Chapter III for an evaluation of his stability score.)

Fey (1957) formed four groups, high and low on Acceptance of Self and Acceptance of Others, based on scores from his own scales. He compared the four groups on F-scale, Edwards's PPS and Bills's IAV items. He reports items or subscores which significantly "distinguish any of the four basic groups from the remaining three" (Fey, 1957, p. 46). With 104 items or subscores, it appears that there must have been 416 significance tests. Nineteen significant differences are reported, which it seems would be no more than would be expected by chance. In any event, the significant differences do not form a clearly interpretable pattern; and no cross-validation was done. Fey (1954) also reports that neither Self-Acceptance nor Acceptance of Others related significantly to expressed readiness for therapy. However, Ss showing high Self-Acceptance combined with low Acceptance of Others distinguished themselves by their expressed indifference to therapy. This finding raises again the question of the possible role of denial in some high Self-Acceptance scores. (See Chapter III for Fey's instrument.)

Fiedler *et al.* (1958), in their study frequently referred to under the other categories above, found significant correlations between self-esteem and self-satisfaction (alternate scores from the same self-report items), and between each of these self-concept reports and Taylor Anxiety scale scores.

Cowen, Heilizer, Axelrod, and Alexander (1957) found Taylor Anxiety Scale scores to be associated with Self, Self-Acceptance, and [Self — Ideal] discrepancy scores on Bills's IAV. Worchel (1957) reports that Self and [Self — Ideal] scores from the Self-Activity Inventory correlated with Taylor Manifest Anxiety Scores and Sarason Test Anxiety Scores. (See Chapter III.)

Hanlon, Hofstaetter, and O'Connor (1954) found highly significant linear rs between self-ideal congruence (measured on a modified Q sort) and specific areas and items of the California Test of Personality. Ss were male high school juniors.

Eastman (1958) found a correlation between Marital Happiness, measured by a self-report test, and self-acceptance, measured by self-reported self-minus-ideal discrepancies. (See Table II.)

Bills (undated Manual for IAV) reports a significant negative association between Self-Acceptance, as indexed by the IAV and the number of psychosomatic symptoms reported.

Perhaps a teacher's over-all rating of his own teaching proficiency and his statement as to whether he would choose teaching again (if he were to start over) may be classified as self-report indices of "adjustment." On this assumption, we find pertinent to this section Rasmussen and Zander's (1954) findings that such self-reports correlated positively with reported self-minus-ideal discrepancies on sixteen items pertaining to philosophy and performance in teaching. (See Table II.)

The rationale underlying Taylor and Combs's (1952) procedure differs somewhat from that behind the other studies we have just described. In their view "the well-adjusted individual ought to be better able to accept more unflattering (and hence threatening) facts about himself than would be expected of the less well-adjusted individual" (Taylor & Combs, 1952, p. 89). Rural school children were divided into upper and lower halves on adjustment, as measured by the California Test of Personality. All Ss responded to twenty statements informally agreed upon by graduate students and faculty members as damaging to self, yet likely to be true of all children. All statements were phrased negatively and began with "Sometimes . . . ." This provided inadequate control over response set. Among both boys and girls, a significantly larger number of damaging items were checked by the well-adjusted children, apparently supporting the authors' hypothesis. However, the authors feel that the factor of acquiescence might account for their findings. They also point out another fact which renders the results difficult to interpret, namely, that we cannot know whether all these statements would be viewed by child Ss as being self-damaging.

A final possibly relevant study is that of Maslow (1942b), who compared self-reports on sex behavior with self-esteem (as measured through Maslow's [1942a] Social Personality Inventory). Ss were college females. Low self-esteem scores were associtaed with conventional sex attitudes, virginity, and low masturbation. The relevance of such attitudes to "adjustment" are debatable and complex, however (Chapter III).

e. SUMMARY OF STUDIES ON ADJUSTMENT

In the section immediately above, we reported that positive correlations are typically obtained between level of self-regard and degree of self-reported "adjustment." In all such studies, however, the two self-reports may correlate for artifactual reasons such as the common influence of social desirability on the two instruments. For this reason, studies which employ an external criterion of adjustment are preferable. A few researchers have used projective tests to measure adjustment. Although the trends of the individual studies suggest that future research relating projective tests to level of self-regard may be worthwhile, the studies do not permit any general conclusions, due to variations in hypotheses, instruments, methods, and *S*s.

Some of the investigations which use an external criterion of adjustment involve groups which show extreme and rather obviously differentiable total patterns. For example, sick *S*s are compared to well *S*s, potentially delinquent *S*s are compared to *S*s who are unusually resistant to delinquency, marked academic underachievers are compared with successful achievers. In such investigations the predicted associations are most apt to be obtained, although there is much overlap in level of self-regard between groups.

In a second group of studies, finer degrees of discrimination are required within the "sick" group. Here findings are likely to become clouded and contradictory. This may be due in part to the fact that finer discriminations are more difficult to make. Or it may be due to the fact that qualitative as well as quantitative differences in maladjustment patterns among sick groups are important factors in the level of self-regard.

In a third group of studies, degrees of adjustment are inferred through everyday behaviors (e.g., popularity in the group, number of visits to the college infirmary). In these investigations the associations found are most tenuous or insignificant. A number of plausible explanations for these tenuous or null findings may be offered: (a) Perhaps there is no general dimension, "adjustment," along which nonclinical persons may be arrayed. If, however, we assume that there is such a dimension, we can make two alternate suggestions to account for the failure to get consistently positive results in the third group of studies. (b) Perhaps relatively narrow criteria (such as visits to the college infirmary) are not as validly representative of the adjustment dimension as are global pattern criteria (such as academic underachievement). (c) Perhaps discriminations within a restricted range are more difficult than is identification of extremes.

In support of the idea that there is no general "adjustment" dimension in nonclinical populations, we can cite the results of Fiedler *et al.* (1958). They applied seven nonself-report indices of "adjustment" to four quite different nonclinical groups (two college groups, and two military groups). They say (p. 351), "The most important fact that emerges is the general lack of correlation among different indices [of adjustment]—even among those which are reliably measurable and which could be expected to correlate with each other. Thus, our data yield no evidence justifying the assumption that adjustment, in its present state of definition, should be considered a unitary trait in clinically unselected populations."

It may well be that the more fruitful approach in theorizing and research about adjustment and the self concept will be to make more particularized R-R predictions and empirical explorations. This is the recommendation of Fiedler *et al.* Meanwhile, gathering together under the heading of "adjustment" a diverse group of studies (some of which have not been so categorized by their authors) certainly points up the fact that no easy synthesis of results concerning the relation of "adjustment" to self concept is possible. And of course no R-R studies will clarify whether the degree of self-regard is a cause, effect, or correlate of maladjustment.

10. *Acceptance of Self and Acceptance of Others*

Many theorists believe that the level of self-regard correlates positively with the degree of regard a person has for others. Most often this idea is expressed in terms of a relationship between "self-acceptance" and "acceptance of others." The inferred cause-effect relationships are presumed to be quite complex and they have not been completely specified by theorists. Neither have they been empirically explored. In general, the available data are of two kinds: (a) cross-sectional R-R correlations; (b) co-variation in the two responses over time and/or as a function of some common variable such as therapy, or experimentally induced success or failure.

Various instruments have been used for the stated purpose of inferring "self-acceptance" and "acceptance of others." This section of the review also includes data from some studies in which the instruments were not so labeled by the investigators, but from which self- and other-approval may be inferred since *S*s described themselves and others on obviously evaluative traits.

a. CROSS-SECTIONAL R-R CORRELATIONS

Positive cross-sectional R-R correlations have been found by Berger (1952), Fey (1954), Bills (undated manual), Bossom and Maslow

(1957), Crandall and Bellugi (1954), Henry (1956), Omwake (1954), Sarnoff (1955), Wylie (1957), Worchel (1957), and Zuckerman, Baer, and Monashkin (1956). Zimmer (1956) and Zelen (1954a, 1954b) obtained the only negative findings. Most of these researches involved college students or young adults. The "other" to which S was responding was usually a "generalized other" or parents.

The instruments employed by Berger, Bills, Fey, and Worchel are described rather fully in Chapter III. Correlations between self-acceptance scores and acceptance-of-others scores which are obtained from any of these instruments may be inflated through response sets. These response sets could be due to the omnibus arrangements of self-referent and other referent items having similar format, to the use of the same items for self-rating and rating of others, and/or to Ss' tendencies consistently to use scale ranges around a given location and of a given width.

Omwake (1954) gave Berger's, Phillips's, and Bills's instruments to the same Ss, and correlated self-acceptance scores from each instrument against acceptance-of-others scores from each other instrument. In general, such cross-instrument correlations were lower than correlations between the self-acceptance scores and acceptance-of-others scores based on the same instrument. One of the six rs was insignificant. The two lowest rs involved Bills's Index of Adjustment and Values, which differs most in format and content from the other two measures. Thus Omwake's findings support the idea that response sets may inflate the within-instrument correlations between self-acceptance scores and acceptance-of-others scores.

Crandall and Bellugi (1954) found significant correlations between the favorability of Ss' self-ratings and the favorability of Ss' ratings of a novel person who was briefly observed. They used rating scales based on one hundred adjectives. Again, the possible influence of response sets must be considered. (See Table II.)

Zuckerman, Baer, and Monashkin (1956) found significant correlations between self-acceptance and acceptance of mother, father, and "people" (in normal Ss); and significant correlations between self-acceptance and acceptance of father and "people" (in patients). Acceptance of self and others was measured in terms of [Self — Ideal] discrepancies on Buss's sixteen scales so the influence of response set cannot be precluded. (See Table II.)

Wylie (1957) found significant correlations between self-ratings and mean ratings attributed to others on five evaluative trait scales. Response set influences cannot be precluded, however. With self-ratings constant, there was a significant tendency for Ss who thought their self-ratings might be worse than their originally stated values to score higher on a specially devised Rationalization-Projection Inventory. Many of these inventory items, in effect, attributed to others certain faults or responsibilities for Ss' shortcomings. Therefore these findings may be viewed as another instance of the correlation between acceptance of self and acceptance of others. In this case, wide differences in the formats of the instruments, and the lapse of a week between marking the instruments suggest that response sets cannot be responsible for the correlation. (See Table II.)

Henry (1956) obtained a positive correlation between reported tendencies toward blaming one's self and blaming others in a hypothetical situation in which one participant in a conversation gets "hurt."

Bossom and Maslow (1957) found that the twenty-two "most secure" judges rated standard photos as "warm" more often than did the twenty-two "least secure" judges. Security was inferred from the Maslow S-I Test. (Total N was 105.) Opportunities for response set seem to be minimal in this study.

Among Jewish college males those with high anti-Semitism scores tended to have more negative and fewer positive attitudes toward self and parents than did those with low anti-Semitism scores (Sarnoff, 1955). The format of the instruments used to measure the two variables differed sufficiently to preclude effects of simple response sets. (See Section C-3 of this chapter.)

Of possible indirect relevance to this section is a study by Alfert (1958). A number of pairs of bipolar adjectives were used (see Table II), and Ss chose one of each pair to describe self and one of each pair to describe the ideal self. Degree of self-ideal congruence for an S was inferred from the number of coincidences between adjectives chosen to describe self and to describe ideal self. Ss also predicted what adjectives certain strangers would use to describe themselves. It could be determined whether S showed a proportionately greater tendency to ascribe to strangers (1) adjectives for which S himself had displayed self-ideal congruence, or (2) adjectives for which S himself had displayed a discrepancy between self and ideal. Among all Ss, the greater tendency was to ascribe to strangers proportionately more of the items on which S had reported self-ideal congruence. If we assume that high self-ideal congruence within an individual S indicates high self-regard, we might ask whether Ss with high self-regard showed more of this tendency to attribute their own self-ideal-congruent traits to others than did Ss with low self-regard. No such correlation was found. This study seems to have a number of methodological weaknesses associated with the unanalytical use of complicated global measures, and the application of some questionable statistical treatments. Findings must, therefore, be viewed with reservations.

Zelen (1954a, 1954b) obtained the only completely negative results in this area. Self-acceptance was indexed by the California Test of Personality and the Who-Are-You Test (described in Table II). Neither of these measures correlated with acceptance of others (indexed by the Bonney Sociometric technique). The two measures of self-acceptance intercorrelated highly ($+.73$). Obviously response sets due to instrument format have been ruled out in this study. The interpretation of the negative findings is unclear, however, since the instruments differ from those used in the other studies, and the subjects were children rather than college students or young adults.

Zimmer (1956) asked airmen to rate the self, one "harmonious" peer, and one annoying peer on eight evaluative trait scales. For all traits, correlations between self and other were low, mostly insignificant. There was no tendency for the "self-harmonious peer" correlations to be higher or to go in a different direction from the "self-annoying peer" correlations. The source of these puzzling findings is not clear. It is obvious that, even with response set operating, results do not always confirm the hypothesis that acceptance of self correlates with acceptance of others. (See Table II.)

b. COVARIATION OF SELF-ACCEPTANCE AND ACCEPTANCE OF OTHERS AS A FUNCTION OF TIME AND/OR A THIRD VARIABLE

When we inspect studies in which covariation of self-accepting and other-accepting responses is studied as a function of time and/or a third variable, we find more puzzling results.

Scheerer (1949) reported that acceptance of others increased during therapy and was correlated across therapy interviews with acceptance of self, when both these variables were coded from interviews. Stock (1949) showed that average affect for self and for others was correlated across therapy interviews, when both these variables were coded from interviews. (See Chapter III for a description of their coding techniques.)

Rudikoff (1954) reported that Ss' concepts of self and of "ordinary person" were closer to the ideal after therapy than during the pretherapy waiting period, as measured by appropriate *r* values from Butler and Haigh's *Q*-sort items. (See Chapter III for a discussion of these items.)

On the other hand, Rosenman (1955) stated that both theorists and researchers have variously "stressed, ignored, or combined" categories which should have been analyzed separately when considering self-acceptance and other-acceptance. That is, he proposed to conceptualize separately and to measure by different operations *S*'s perceptions of his *evaluations of* and *actions toward* himself and others. He examined early and late interviews from nondirective counseling cases, eleven of whom had been judged successful, twelve of whom had been judged unsuccessful. The coding scheme is described in Chapter III.

Rosenman (1955, p. 278) reached the following conclusions: "The successfully rated clients see themselves as acting more positively toward others while continuing to evaluate them in a predominantly, and even increasingly negative way . . . . Indeed he [the successful client] was revealed to possess an inverse relationship between positive self- and other-evaluation." These results seem to go against self-concept theories and against some findings of positive associations between self- and other-acceptance.

In his comments following Rosenman's paper, Raimy raises the question whether Rosenman's results may be a function of misleading coding categories. For example, if a mother lavishes attention on a deformed child, this would be coded by Rosenman as positive action toward the child coupled with negative (unloving) evaluation of the child. Raimy points out the desirability of distinguishing between evaluation of an attribute of a person, and evaluation of the total person, in making phenomenological analyses. The extent to which Raimy's suggestion provides a plausible interpretation of Rosenman's puzzling findings cannot be determined from the published data.

Gordon and Cartwright's (1954) data also failed to support the idea that self-acceptance and acceptance of others are positively correlated. They obtained no greater change toward acceptance of others among therapy clients than among controls. Acceptance of others was measured by a Self-Other Attitude scale, especially compiled from *E, PEC,* and *F* Scales of the California study of authoritarian personality; and from Jenkins's Inventory related to democratic leadership and methods, and to tolerance of differing opinions. Since these same clients did show increasing acceptance of self and others, when such acceptance was measured by Q-sort correlations, it appears that the Self-Other Attitude Scale is not measuring the same thing as the more direct measures do. Or perhaps the findings with the more direct measures may be at least partly artifactual.

In a group subjected to experimentally induced "success," Diller (1954) found correlations in the $+.70$s between changes in self-ratings and changes in ratings assigned to friends. No such correlations were found in a group subjected to experimental "failure," however. (See Table II and Section C-7 of this chapter.)

Eastman (1958) obtained an interesting sex difference in acceptance of others, though not in self-acceptance. Although self-acceptance of men and women in his sample did not differ, acceptance of "women in general" was less on the part of both men and women than was "acceptance of men." (See Tables II and III.)

c. SUMMARY

We have cited twenty-one studies which related S's level of self-regard with the level of regard S manifests for other persons. Many of these investigations were specifically concerned with "self-acceptance" and "acceptance of others."

On the whole, the evidence supports the hypothesized association between self-acceptance (or high self-regard) and acceptance of others (or high regard for others). Two considerations induce caution in interpreting these results: (a) Possiblities for artifactual contamination are present in many of the studies, most often through common response sets of various kinds. (b) A few puzzling exceptions and contradictions occur in the reported results.

Since all of the designs are of the R-R variety, no cause-effect inferences can be drawn.

11. *Self-Esteem and Authoritarianism and/or Ethnocentrism*

A number of investigators have correlated self-esteem with some measure of ethnocentrism and/or authoritarianism. The relationship of such studies to self-concept theory is not obvious or straightforward. Presumably acceptance of self is associated with acceptance of others, and since persons who score high on F and E scales are showing hostility toward others, they should be found among those less accepting of self. However, two considerations complicate this simple idea: (a) Presumably the ethnocentric person, although rejecting some others (the outgroups), accepts certain others highly (the ingroup). Or the authoritarian person, although rejecting some others (e.g., intellectuals, nonconformists, homosexuals), accepts certain others highly (e.g., parents, patriots). Thus F and E scale scores, or preference for European over American ways, indicate a mixed pattern of acceptance of others, making theoretical predictions unclear. (b) The acceptance-of-self score, on an instrument based on phenomenological report, may be inflated by denial. This mechanism would be closely related to the repression and denial which is presumed to underlie scores on the F and E scales (Loevinger & Ossorio, 1959). On these grounds, self-esteem or self-acceptance should correlate positively with F and E scores.

A number of investigators have obtained findings which suggest that self-esteem is positively associated with authoritarianism and/or ethnocentrism (Brodbeck & Perlmutter, 1954; Pearl, 1954; Perlmutter, 1954; and Rubenstein & Lorr, 1956). Rokeach and Fruchter (1956), on the other hand, obtained low but significant negative correlations. Gordon and Cartwright (1954) found no changes in F and E scale and similar items occurring in Ss who showed increased self-esteem with therapy. A brief review of the most salient features of these studies will show the reasons why their results cannot be synthesized in order to reach psychologically meaningful conclusions.

Brodbeck and Perlmutter (1954) reported that Ss with high dislike-of-self scores (on a specially devised scale) tend to prefer the European over American way of life (i.e., they dislike their own group). Since all items in the instrument were negatively phrased, there is a question of the influence of acquiescence response set upon both scores. Or there may be some common influence of a tendency toward extreme responses. (See Table II.)

Pearl (1954) factor-analyzed pretherapy self-concept Q-sort distributions of twelve neurotic male patients, and correlated the factor scores with pretherapy E- and F-scale scores from the California scales. The self-concept factors were described thus: (A) self-esteem and self-reliance; (B) lack of awareness and anxiety concerning problems of impulse and hostility control; (C) unidentifiable. Both A and B factors correlated significantly with F- and with E-scale scores, that is, high self-esteem and unawareness of own impulses was associated with high F and E scores. The size of the pretherapy self-ideal correlation also correlated significantly with total E-scale scores. Changes in the various scores over therapy were intercorrelated, the only significant finding being an association of E-scale shifts with shifts in Factor B. On the basis of the information given, one cannot ascertain whether the obtained correlations may be in part artifacts of common scale content and/or social desirability response set. (See Table III.)

Perlmutter (1954) found that Ss reporting lower self-esteem showed significantly more desire to travel in a foreign country than did Ss reporting high self-esteem. Since we do not know whether these Ss were comparable on other factors relevant to desire to travel, these findings are uninterpretable. (His main hypothesis was that S would prefer to live for a year in a foreign country whose typical inhabitants were perceived by S as similar to his own self concept. His results tend to support this idea. However, three out of five positive comparisons involve preferences to live in England, so that the question of the role of language similarity [as against perceived personal similarity] cannot be ruled out.) (See Table II.)

As mentioned earlier, Rubenstein and Lorr (1956) found that Ss who prematurely terminated psychotherapy were more self-satisfied, according to self-rating scales, than were remainers. They also scored higher on F-scale items, implying a positive relationship between self-satisfaction and F. These results also suggest the possibility that such positive relationships may be due to a common factor of denial, which is manifested in leaving therapy and in the two instruments. (See Table II.)

Rokeach and Fruchter (1956) found low but significant correlations between "self-rejection" scores, based on five items, and scores based on F-scale and E-scale items respectively. ("Self-rejection" was factorially discriminable from F and E.) Since all the self-rejection items were negatively phrased, there seems to be a possibility that the acquiescence response set was responsible for the correlation. (See Table II.)

Perhaps psychotherapy will increase one's acceptance of and respect for others. To explore this hypothesis, Gordon and Cartwright (1954) constructed a Self-Other Attitude Scale, consisting of the California E, F, and PEC scales, a number of items from Jenkins's Sentiments Inventory, and some specially constructed items. Ss who had received therapy were compared with equivalent no-therapy controls, as described in Rogers and Dymond (1954). Therapy and control Ss were comparable at the outset on the Self-Other Attitude Scale, and no statistically significant differences in attitude change were found, either on the scale as a whole, or on each subscale taken separately.

SUMMARY

It is impossible to decide on theoretical grounds just what direction of correlation would be expected between level of self-regard and ethnocentrism or authoritarianism. In four of the studies reviewed above, high self-regard was associated with higher F- and E-scale scores, or with preference for the ingroup. In one investigation, high self-rejection was associated with high F- and E-scale scores, and a sixth study gave no evidence of association between self-regard and F or E scores. The significant correlations going in either direction may plausibly be explained in terms of denial or in terms of response sets.

It might seem at first glance that most of these studies contradict the finding of positive correlation between self-acceptance and acceptance of others, which we reported in Section C-10 of this chapter. However, for reasons we have discussed above, the present investigations cannot be clearly compared with those reviewed in Section C-10.

12. *Self Concept and Level of Aspiration Behavior (LA)*

A number of psychologists have postulated that behavior in the experimental Level of Aspiration situation is a function of self-regard. Here again we are confronted with an intriguing but very complex situation which does not lend itself to unambiguous predictions. In order to consider what these two sets of responses might have in common, we must examine the possible interpretations of each separately. Since reported self-regard is presumably the more enduring characteristic, and it may be one of the antecedents of Level of Aspiration behavior, we may profitably begin by examining its meaning.

Some investigators have studied the relationship between LA behavior and self-acceptance, when the latter refers to a positive feeling towards oneself, including one's good and bad attributes. Others have used self-ideal congruence to index self-regard. Although self-acceptance and self-ideal congruence undoubtedly overlap, they are also somewhat different from one another, conceptually and operationally. This implies that they probably will not have the same relationship with experimental Level of Aspiration behavior.

Furthermore, we must point out that self-regard, by either type of definition, may refer to certain traits or areas of functioning, or it may refer to a global attitude toward the total self. Sometimes investigators seem to assume that specific self-regard measures are interchangeable indices of global self-regard. Only by making such an assumption would it seem reasonable to try to relate such self-regard measures to narrowly restricted laboratory tasks used in LA experiments.

Actually, if the index used to measure self-regard refers to limited traits only, there might be little relation between self-regard and experimental behavior, since we know that LA tasks may not be assumed to reveal any over-all or global level of aspiration. (See Bills, 1953c.) For example, it does not seem particularly convincing to postulate a connection between a girl's LA behavior on a code deciphering task and her self-regard with respect to her social effectiveness. Too few researchers, however, have taken care to make the content of the self-regard referents plausibly relevant to the LA task.

Assuming a global measure of self-regard, or a self-regard measure whose content is relevant to the LA task, we still need to consider what LA behaviors would make sense in terms of the two kinds of self-regard measures (direct statements of acceptance as contrasted to [Self—Ideal] discrepancies). A plausible hypothesis would be that self-accepting persons will have small, probably positive, goal discrepancy scores on the LA task. The prediction for the self-rejecting person is less clear: (1) Perhaps he would protect his self-regard by negative goal-discrepancy scores which he could easily exceed; or (2) perhaps he would show unusually high positive goal-discrepancy scores. The latter might stem from a desire to demonstrate superior ambition, or a need to punish the unworthy self through failure. Or it might simply be one more reflection of the type of generally unrealistic goal setting which underlies his poor self-regard.

When we look at [Self—Ideal] discrepancies as measures of self-regard, the situation becomes even more complicated. In a sense [Self—Ideal] discrepancies are derived from a statement of aspirations (ideal self) and a statement of perceived attainment (actual self). It is often assumed that a small discrepancy indicates high self-regard. However, it is important to note that one cannot say from the size of the [Self—Ideal] discrepancy itself what combinations of ideal-rating and self-rating went into making it this size. For example, assume two Ss showing small [Self—Ideal] discrepancies. One has placed his self-rating and his ideal-rating close together, within the range of the scale which would be considered to be moderately favorable, according to the cultural stereotype. The other S also has placed his self- and his ideal-ratings close to each other, but both the ideal- and self-ratings are very near to the point on the scale which would be considered most favorable, according to the cultural stereotype.

Is it reasonable to expect the same LA behavior from these two Ss? In the LA experiment, E sets the "actual self" evaluation of S, so far as the experimental task performance is concerned. Let us assume that there is a parallel between S's reported actual self on the self-regard measure and the "actual self" which E assigns to S (i.e., S's allegedly attained LA score). Let us further assume a parallel between S's reported ideal self on the self-regard measure and his aspiration score in the LA experiment. On this assumption we might predict that the first S mentioned above will show small goal discrepancies and the second S will show large, positive goal discrepancy scores even though both have small [Self—Ideal] discrepancies on the self-regard measure. This is only one example of the difficulties we get into when trying to make psychologically meaningful connections between these two types of behavior, since each type of behavior is measured by a dual index, and the components of each index may vary without affecting the respective total scores.

a. [SELF—IDEAL] DISCREPANCIES, SELF-ACCEPTANCE, SELF-ADEQUACY, AND LA BEHAVIOR

Five articles have used [Self—Ideal] discrepancies as a measure of self-regard. Even among these studies there is no easy comparison, since each used a different instrument for obtaining [Self—Ideal] discrepancies, and a different measure for LA. (In fact, one of these studies employs n Achievement rather than LA as the dependent variable, but it is included here since it seems most nearly to belong in this group.)

In the earliest such undertaking, Pauline Sears (1941) found an association between size of positive discrepancy score in an experimental LA task and the size of stated [Self—Ideal] discrepancies of her child Ss on academic tasks. "Realistic" self was artifically held constant across Ss in the experimental LA situation, so the discrepancy scores must be a function of individual differences in stated level of aspiration. However, one cannot tell from the data presented to what extent the larger [Self — Ideal] discrepancies are due to statements of unusually high ideals, low realistic self, or both. (See Table II.)

Martire (1956), using male college students, obtained no relationship between either Realistic or Wishful LA scores on a scrambled words test and [Self — Ideal] discrepancies on five "achievement related traits." The traits were: Intelligence, Initiative, Creativeness, Motivation, General Success. He did find that Ss making high *n* Achievement scores under both neutral and achievement-related testing conditions showed high [Self — Ideal] discrepancies. (See Table II.)

Lepine and Chodorkoff (1955) used two indices of self-regard: a "self-adequacy" score derived from selected *Q*-sort items, and a [Self — Ideal] discrepancy score based on the entire set of items. (See Table I.) No significant correlations were obtained between either of these indices of self-regard and goal-discrepancy scores from a code deciphering task. A new score was derived, subtracting mean goal-discrepancy score under improving performance from mean goal-discrepancy score under poorer performance. This score correlated +.43 with "self-adequacy," but insignificantly with [Self — Ideal] discrepancy. This latter finding is puzzling, since the two goal-discrepancy scores correlated +.93. This makes it difficult to see how a score derived from these two would be uncorrelated enough with either of its components to behave so differently from either component when related to a third variable. (See Table I.)

Using [Self — Ideal] discrepancies from the Self-Activity Inventory, Miller and Worchel (1956) found no relationship between self-regard and *n* Achievement. (*N* Achievement was measured under "neutral" conditions, apparently.) The use of some female Ss who are known not to give results like male Ss, so far as *n* Achievement is concerned, may have some bearing on these results. (See Chapter III for a description of the Self-Activity Inventory.)

Darts, Rotter's Board, marking out letters, substituting letters, and addition were the five LA tasks which Bills (1953c) correlated with Self Acceptance and with [Self — Ideal] discrepancy scores from the Index of Adjustment and Values. Two of the ten correlations were significant: Rotter Board versus Self Acceptance and mark-out versus [Self — Ideal] discrepancies. On two tasks Ss with Self Acceptance scores above the mean (or with [Self — Ideal] scores below the mean) were significantly more variable on LA scores than were the remaining Ss. (See Chapter III for a discussion of Bills's IAV.)

Problems of interpretation of two-part indices are also posed in connection with Steiner's (1957) work, which compared "stability" of the self concept to LA behavior. He used a "stability" measure similar to Brownfain's (i.e., he scored the range between S's most optimistic and pessimistic self-ratings on twenty variables). These scores were compared to similar "optimistic-minus-pessimistic" ranges in the estimates which Ss made of their performances on a Level of Aspiration task (anagrams). Significant associations were not obtained between these two dyadic indices.

Instability of self concept did tend to be associated significantly with S's expectation that his anagram behavior would be quite different next semester than during the experimental period. Ss with unstable self concepts tended on the LA task to set goals which were high relative to their past performance, and to set goals which proved to be overestimates of actually attained scores. Ss whose realistic self-ratings were near their most pessimistic self-ratings tended on the LA task to set their realistic LA goal nearer to their pessimistic than to their optimistic goal, and to set goals close to or lower than their past performance.

It seems clear that some association between self-perception responses and Level of Aspiration behavior has been found in Steiner's study. However, since each of the indices related is a complex one, one cannot be sure what variables are contributing to the findings. As in Brownfain's study (discussed in Chapter III), one wonders whether a simple self-rating value, or the most pessimistic self-rating taken alone, might not predict LA behavior just as well as do the complex range and ratio scores in which the values of the component variables and their modes of combination are unknown. (See Table II.)

b. LIMITED SELF-EVALUATION AND LA BEHAVIOR

In the next investigation to be described, the self-evaluation and LA variables were quite specifically defined in a mutually relevant manner. Strongly positive findings were obtained (Gilinsky, 1949). As a first step, Ss estimated their own IQs. Then they were given a vocabulary test which allegedly measured IQ. In different groups, Ss were told that 18 correct words was the norm for varying occupational and IQ levels ranging from 80 to 170, by steps of ten IQ points. Ss then estimated their performance on the vocabulary test. The mean LA correlated +.67 with the discrepancy between S's perception of his own IQ and the stated IQ of the reference group. This experiment demonstrated that an aspect of the self concept was useful in predicting S's LA behavior. It of course does not permit us to know what cognitive and emotional variables were involved in producing this relationship.

c. NONPHENOMENAL SELF-REGARD AND LA BEHAVIOR

A completely different means of estimating feelings of adequacy and self-acceptance was used by Cohen, namely, the Rorschach (1954). Although his score purports to measure the *non*phenomenal self, his study is included in this chapter on the phenomenal self in order to bring out its connection with the other studies of LA behavior reported here. Feelings of adequacy, inferred on an unspecified basis from the Rorschach, showed a curvilinear relationship with LA (i.e., high and low extremes of goal-setting go with self-rejection). In view of our lack of knowledge about the self indices used, a detailed critique of this study is not possible.

SUMMARY

On the basis of present theory, it is impossible to state clear postulates concerning the relationship between self-regard and (1) Level of Aspiration behavior on an experimental task; (2) *n* Achievement. We question whether one can reasonably assume that any or all aspects of self-regard will correlate with LA behavior on restricted laboratory tasks. It may be more reasonable to assume that general self-regard will correlate with *n* Achievement.

So far as measurement is concerned, LA behavior and self-regard have both frequently been measured by two-part indices. In addition, each of the six studies which related general self-regard to experimental LA behavior or *n* Achievement used a different measure of self-regard and of LA behavior or *n* Achievement. We should not be surprised, then, that our conclusions from these six studies are as follows: (1) One cannot synthesize the results of these investigations. (2) Many of the findings are negative. (3) Those findings which are positive are difficult or impossible to interpret clearly, mostly because of the unanalytical use of dyadic indices.

One investigator used limited self-evaluations which were closely relevant to the LA task. She obtained a strong association between self-evaluations and Level of Aspiration scores.

Another researcher tried to relate nonphenomenal self-regard to LA behavior. Lack of information about his measuring instrument precludes clear interpretation of his findings.

V

Operational Definitions of the Nonphenomenal Self and Its Relationships to Other Variables

A. General Problems of Construct Validity

As we stated at the outset, theorists who accord a prominent role to constructs concerning the self are not consistently or exclusively phenomenological. Typically, however, they are very vague and incomplete as to (1) what kinds of nonphenomenological constructs shall be admitted into their theories; (2) how these constructs shall be articulated into their system of "postulates"; and (3) how these nonphenomenological determinants shall be tied to observables. Nevertheless some effort has been expended by empirical workers in attempts to measure such processes as unconscious aspects of the self concept and other nonphenomenological variables which they believe to be pertinent to self theories. Researchers who do this seem to base their work implicitly and/or explicitly on two lines of reasoning: (1) It is obvious that the phenomenal self, at least as measured by currently used instruments, is far from providing a sufficient basis for accurate predictions of Ss' behaviors. This lack of predictive power may be presumed to stem in part from the fact that instruments which purport to measure the phenomenal field will provide an incomplete inventory of relevant variables, no matter how highly perfected they may eventually become for the purpose of measuring the phenomenal field. (2) Because of theoretical reasons one might expect that important characteristics of S and his relation with his environment would be unavailable to his phenomenal field. Theorists point out that much important learning occurs pre-verbally, and the need to maintain self-esteem will lead to repression and denial.

Some workers, apparently strongly influenced by Freudian views, seem to imply that the "unconscious self concept" will be more potent than the phenomenal self in determining behavior. (See Fisher and Cleveland, 1958a, for example.)

With the measurement of such nonphenomenal determinants we are again presented with the question of construct validity. The specifications presented in Chapter III for establishing such validity could and should be applied here as well. With few exceptions, however, these specifications have been almost entirely ignored by users of nonphenomenal indices, and such measures have remained largely unvalidated.

In particular there is a unique and difficult requirement of discriminant validity for this type of measure which has received little or no recognition: If one is to say that a certain projective response or score represents an *un*conscious attitude toward the self, one must prove not only that S holds this attitude but that he is unaware of it. At the very least one should check to see whether the same attitude might be consciously present, as inferred from a self-report. If the inferences from the self-report and the projective measure differ, one may then have grounds for exploring the more complex assumption that the projective measure is revealing an unconscious self-attitude. Almost universally, however, this measurement problem has been overlooked by workers interested in the measurement of the so-called unconscious self concept.

B. SURVEY OF SPECIFIC MEASURES USED IN THIS AREA AND OF STUDIES RELATING THE NONPHENOMENAL SELF TO OTHER VARIABLES

There are relatively few studies involving the unconscious self concept, and the state of measurement in this field is undeveloped and confused. Therefore we shall not separate the discussion of the instruments from the discussion of the studies about the unconscious self concept.

We shall organize the chapter according to the instruments used, under the following headings: (1) TAT and other picture-judging and story-telling techniques; (2) Rorschach scores (other than Fisher's scores purporting to index body image); (3) various indices which have been used mainly by Fisher and his associates to index body image; (4) miscellaneous indices which have been used only once or twice, and on which reliability and/or validity information is quite incomplete.

1. TAT AND OTHER PICTURE-JUDGING OR STORY-TELLING
TECHNIQUES

The TAT has been used by several workers for the purpose of inferring something about the self concept. The implication seems to be that
it indexes the nonphenomenal rather than the phenomenal self concept.
However, as the six studies described below reveal, there is no satisfactory
proof that any TAT "score," including the attributes which S assigns to
TAT figures, reflects S's unconscious picture of himself.

Friedman (1955) used as a measure of "projected self," a Q sort
made by E on the basis of his global appraisal of S's stories about cards 1,
3BM, 6BM, 7BM, and 14 of the TAT. (See Table I.) Friedman correlated
this sort with S's self-sort of the same statements which was supposed to
index S's phenomenal self. It was assumed that lack of correlation between
phenomenal self and TAT self indicates "a large portion of personal experience out of awareness." Therefore it was predicted that correlations between phenomenal self and projected self would be higher for normals
than for neurotics and paranoid schizophrenics. He found the expected
rank order among the magnitudes of the correlations, but the difference
between correlations for normal and neurotic Ss was small and not significant. (Those of the paranoid schizophrenics were significantly smaller
than each of the other two groups.)

The findings are puzzling, however, because the self-ideal correlations
of neurotics were near zero while the correlations between their phenomenal self and projected self were as high as those of the normals.
This implies, according to the author's interpretation, that the qualities
they projected into the TAT were their own negative ones of which they
were already aware (as indicated through their self-ideal correlations).

Child, Frank, and Storm (1956) could find no consistent or significant pattern of relationships between TAT scores for twenty Murray
variables and the respective self-ratings. They used the group procedure
of McClelland *et al.* to obtain stories for cards 1, 18BM, 7BM, 13B, 6BM,
12M, 14, and 10. In thus failing to find a correspondence between the
TAT and an alleged measure of the phenomenal self, they of course did
not prove that the low correlations were due to the fact that the TAT
was revealing the unconscious self concepts of their Ss (nor did they
make such a claim). (See Table II for Child's rating scales.)

Davids, Henry, McArthur, and McNamara (1955) gave the TAT to twenty male college students and used the stories they gave in response to cards 3, 6, 7, 8, and 13 of the male series. Amount of aggression and direction of aggression were scored blindly. An experienced clinical psychologist who had known the Ss for about eighteen months also rated each S as to amount and direction of aggression. Ss rated themselves on amount of aggression. The investigators obtained no correlation between self-evaluations of aggression and TAT or clinician's ratings of S's aggressiveness.

At first glance this might seem to imply that the TAT was measuring an unconscious self picture of aggression which differed from S's consciously avowed aggressiveness. However, a highly significant relationship was found between the direction of aggression, as rated from TAT, and strength of aggression, as evaluated by self: Ss showing "anger out" on the TAT evaluated themselves high on aggression, while Ss showing "anger in" on the TAT evaluated themselves low on aggression. Since aggression was evidently not clearly defined for Ss on their self-rating scale, it is quite plausible, as the authors point out, that Ss assumed aggression meant outwardly directed hostility. If Ss did so interpret the self-rating scale, the findings offer no reason to suppose that the TAT was necessarily measuring a variable of which Ss were unaware. Had they been specifically instructed to rate themselves on strength of inwardly directed aggression, their self-ratings might have correlated with degree of "anger-in" inferred from the TAT. This possibility was essentially unexplored by the method used.

Kardiner and Ovesy (cited in Karon, 1958) used the TAT to infer self-hatred in their Negro Ss. Rorschachs, psychoanalytic interviews, and TATs agreed in indicating a large amount of self-hatred in the group. It is not clear, however, that the TAT was revealing nonphenomenal self-hatred.

Mussen and Jones (1957) found that "late maturing boys" showed more "negative self concepts" than "early maturing boys." Negative self concept is inferred if the TAT hero is described in negative terms such as imbecile, weakling, or fanatic. No empirical information on relevant construct validity is offered.

Mussen and Porter (1959) employed five TAT cards and three other pictures to index "negativity of self concept." Their study of the self concepts of college male leaders is discussed in Chapter IV, above. Each story was given one point toward the negativity-of-self-concept score if the hero was pictured as a failure, disgusted, ashamed, angry with himself, or was described in unflattering terms. Each story was also given one point toward a feelings-of-adequacy score if the hero was described as self-confident, self-assured, satisfied with the way things are going, capable of solving his own problems. (N Affiliation, *n* Achievement, *n* Aggression were also scored.) No provision was made for the possible influence of total verbal output upon the opportunity to accumulate points on any or all of these scales. Two judges reached 87% agreement on all scales combined, on 120 stories. Construct validity for inferring "basic self concepts" is assumed.

In the study of nondirective therapy reported in Rogers and Dymond (1954), 23 clients took the TAT three times: before therapy, after therapy, and at a follow-up point. Sixteen control Ss took the test at comparable points in time. By means of a specially prepared set of criteria, the TATs were scored on 23 scales including self concept, ideal self, and self and others (Grummon & John, 1954). Each scale was rated by at least five judges, and interjudge agreement was significant at the .01 level. Two judges rerated 23 protocols after six months to one year, and a *rho* for each scale was computed for each judge. An average *rho* of $+.77$ was obtained for the first 18 scales (which included the three self scales). Apparently the TAT self scales were intended to tap the nonphenomenal self concept, since they were devised by a psychoanalytically oriented researcher and they were obtained from a projective test. If correlations had been presented between the TAT self scales and the self-ideal *r*s which were obtained from these Ss, some light would have been thrown on the discriminant validity of the TAT scales as indicators of the *non*phenomenal self. However, no such correlations are reported. On each of the three self scales, from 38% to 57% of the therapy Ss showed no change. Of those who showed any change, the greater number moved toward a "healthier" rating. By a one-tailed sign test two of these comparisons were significant at the .05 level or better. So far as the nontherapy control Ss were concerned, on each of the three self scales only 25% to 31% showed no change. None of the scale comparisons for these Ss showed significantly more control Ss changing toward healthier scores than toward unhealthier scores. No direct comparisons of the experimental and control groups was made on the self scales. The trends in the data are slight, and the construct validity of the TAT scales for inferring the nonphenomenal self is unknown. We conclude that the findings may give some slight support to the assumption that the scales measure the nonphenomenal self, and to the hypothesis that therapy results in changes toward a "healthier" nonphenomenal self. However, this interpretation is by no means unequivocal. (See Chapter IV, Section C-5, for a detailed discussion of the problems of therapy studies as tests of propositions from personality theory, and for a summary of results obtained with the use of measures purporting to index the phenomenal self.)

Alexander (1951) hypothesized that certain "structural characteristics of the self" (devaluation of self, dependency, anxiety, conflict) would prevent teachers from showing affection for children. Stories told by 25 teachers in response to child and child-adult pictures were coded on the four characteristics, and teachers were then classified as to the amount of affection they would show to children. Staff observers rated the actual behavior of each teacher on a three-point scale of affection and warmth. The operations for arriving at both sets of ratings are incompletely specified, and no reliability or validity information is available in the 1951 reference (although some additional facts about the instrument are given in Alexander, 1950). The correspondence between the two sets of data is reported to exceed the .01 level, but the method of determining chance expectancy is not clearly specified and seems possibly inappropriate. Consequently there is doubt whether even R-R conclusions can be reached.

Goldings (1954) found no correlation between twenty Ss' "consciously avowed" (self-rated) happiness and the amount of happiness attributed to photos of persons with ambiguous expressions. (The latter was assumed to indicate "projected happiness.") When six Ss with extreme self-ratings were removed, a correlation of $+.56$ was obtained for the remaining Ss.

Rogers and Walsh (1959) hypothesized that "defensiveness" would influence "unwitting self-evaluation." Defensiveness of female college students was measured by the K scale of the MMPI. In a paired-comparisons tachistoscopic procedure, each S was presented with her own photograph coupled with each of four other photographs which had been judged by Es to be of average attractiveness. S was prevented from recognizing her own picture by superimposing each photograph quickly, at a low illumination level, on a neutral line-drawing of a face. Defensive Ss "unwittingly" evaluated their own photographed facial expressions as significantly less attractive than did nondefensive Ss, when the latter unwittingly evaluated their own photographed expressions. The externally judged attractiveness of the photographs of defensive and undefensive *S*s was equal. The authors suggest that "the defensive group's self-devaluation may have been based upon a feeling of self-dissatisfaction which was denied conscious expression in the interest of maintaining self-esteem" (Rogers & Walsh, 1959, p. 304). However, a number of control problems leave this conclusion in doubt. Chief among these is the fact that *S*s made no conscious evaluation of the attractiveness of the photographs. The authors unwarrantedly assume that a high *K* score indicates a high conscious evaluation of one's own photographed facial expression (as if the kind of symptom denial indicated by *K* necessarily extends to all aspects of the self concept).

Rogers and Paul (1959, p. 461) wished to test the hypothesis that "an extreme degree of conscious impunitiveness has a cognate substratum of unconscious aggressiveness." Conscious impunitiveness was indexed by *M*% scores on the Rosenzweig Picture Frustration Study. "Unwitting" self-evaluation of aggressiveness was indexed by the ratings of photographs for aggressiveness of facial expression, in a procedure exactly parallel to that used by Rogers and Walsh, described immediately above. Rogers and Paul (1959, p. 461) conclude that "the impunitive group's unwitting aggressive self-evaluation may have been based upon the denial of aggressive aspects of the self in the interest of maintaining self-esteem." This conclusion too must be questioned. First of all, it is not known that Rosenzweig's score indexes conscious self-evaluation of aggressiveness. Even if it did, it remains to be demonstrated that *S*s whose conscious self-evaluation of aggression is low on the Rosenzweig would also *consciously* evaluate the aggressiveness of their own facial expressions as being low in aggressiveness (as the authors' hypothesis seems to imply).

Mason (1953), in a study of self-attitudes in aged persons, used the fifteen Caldwell Pictures. *S* told a story to each picture, and the stories were judged for "feeling tone" of the identification figure. In addition, *S* made a forced sort of the pictures themselves, according to the degree to which they were (1) like me, and (2) like an ideal person. No information on reliability or validity is given. In this study, Mason applied a number of other self-concept measures to the same *S*s (see Table II). However, intercorrelations among the measures, which might have thrown some light on convergent and discriminant construct validity, are not presented.

In a somewhat related technique, Smith and Lebo (1956) had pre-

and postpubescent boys complete, in the third person, two stories involving, respectively, heterosexual development and emancipation from parents. Six psychologists reached 87% agreement in assigning the heterosexual stories, and 75% agreement in assigning the emancipation stories to one of five categories along a scale of maturity. Although the *E*s presumed that the stories revealed self-attitudes of their *S*s without *S*s' being "aware of the purpose of the task," no evidence of such construct validity is presented. These *E*s applied to the same *S*s (1) a figure-drawing test which also purported to measure the nonphenomenal self concept (see Table IV); (2) a Vineland Maturity Scale purporting to measure the phenomenal self concept (see Table II). No intercorrelations among the measures are given to throw light on convergent or discriminant validity of the various measures. As indicated in Chapter IV, the authors hypothesized that physiological development (as indexed through pubic hair ratings) would be associated with self-concept differences. None of the nonphenomenal measures was significantly related to pubic hair ratings, however, when CA, with all that it implies psychologically, was held constant. The only positive findings, with CA controlled, involved the Vineland Scale.

Walsh (1956) used the Driscoll Play Kit to have forty *S*s make up ten stories from incomplete stems. Each verbatim story was judged globally on a five-point scale in each of five categories, detailed directions for which are published. Exact scale agreement among three judges across all categories ranged from 68% to 93% on forty randomly selected stories. *S*'s self concept was inferred from the behavior and attitudes he attributed to the boy doll. Twenty bright, academic underachievers showed more "inadequate and crippling" self concepts than did twenty matched, bright, normal achievers. This finding is interpreted in two ways: (1) as support for the validity of the instrument for inferring the self concept; (2) as confirmation of the author's hypothesis in regard to the relationship between self concept and underachievement.

Although this is a projective test, there is no demonstration of its discriminant validity in contrast to what would have been obtained by questioning the boys about their phenomenal self concepts. Also the fact that the *E* who administered the play test scored all the stories raises some question of contamination of findings. It seems possible that she might have remembered the source of some of the stories, even though identifying data had been removed from the protocols before scoring was begun.

Summary of Picture-judging
and/or Story-telling Techniques

Six studies used Ss' stories which were given in response to varying parts of the TAT, and two other studies employed Ss' stories to non-TAT pictures to index some aspect of the unconscious self concept. Each author wished to infer different things about the unconscious self concept, and these varied inferences included: (1) aggression or self-hatred; (2) negativity of self-attitudes, devaluation of self, and feelings of adequacy; (3) over-all self concept and over-all ideal self.

Most or all of the scoring schemes were apparently devised for the particular study in which they were used. Questions concerning the construct validity of any of these scores for indexing the nonphenomenal self concept remain unanswered. Only two researchers correlated their TAT scores with phenomenal self-concept measures, and in each case the results suggest significant congruence between the phenomenal and the supposedly nonphenomenal measures. This raises the question whether TAT scores have discriminant validity for indexing the nonphenomenal self concept.

Since the studies are so disparate with regard to hypotheses, types of Ss, pictures, and scoring schemes, no synthesized conclusions can be drawn.

The other picture-judging and/or story-telling techniques reported in this section are too varied to summarize as a group. Frequently the methods used in these investigations have been uncontrolled in ways which preclude clear conclusions. In only one of these researches was an attempt made to explore discriminant validity by correlating the nonphenomenal measure with a corresponding phenomenal one. In this instance, some congruence between the two measures was suggested, which raises the question whether judging ambiguous photographs indexes the nonphenomenal self concept.

The reader is referred to Table IV, where we have briefly identified some techniques, in addition to those discussed above, which purport to index the nonphenomenal self concept.

TABLE IV

INDICES OF THE NONPHENOMENAL SELF CONCEPT

All of the following measures seem to be aimed toward some aspect of the unconscious self concept. Scores based on picture judgments, story-telling (including TAT stories), Rorschach records, or indices of "body image" are discussed in the text. They are also mentioned in the table, and if further information on these scores is available in the text, that fact is stated in the table.

Except as indicated, no information on rationale, scoring procedures, reliability, or construct validity for inferring the nonphenomenal self concept is available in published sources.

For nine-tenths of *all* scores mentioned in this table, *no* information is available in published sources concerning reliability or construct validity for indexing the nonphenomenal self concept.

Author	*Instrument*
Alexander (1950, 1951)	Stories told to pictures. See text for description.
Beloff & Beloff (1959)	S was presented with three double faces in a stereoscope, each composite photo to be rated on a seven-point scale of attractiveness. Card I = two randomly chosen strangers (warm-up trial); Card II = two strangers whose photos S had previously rated as equal to himself in attractiveness; Card III = S's own picture and a third stranger S had previously rated equal to himself in attractiveness. (S's own photo was *not* shown to him during prerating.) Data from stereoscope test eliminated if S recognized his own photo. Ss tended to rate Card III most attractive. Possibility of S's consciously thinking Card III looked like him was not ruled out, so interpretation of unconscious self-judgment not too clear.
Child, Frank, & Storm (1956)	TAT scored for 20 Murray variables on which Ss rated themselves.
Cohen (1954)	Feelings of adequacy and self-acceptance inferred from Rorschach by unspecified means.
Davids, Henry, McArthur, & McNamara (1955)	S's aggression rated from TAT. See text for description.
Diller (1954)	S's own handwriting in mirror evaluated among three other samples. (1) S writes free personality sketch scored by Js on: (a) number of flattering remarks;

Table IV—Continued

Author	Instrument
Diller (1954)—Cont'd	(b) degree of expansiveness. (2) *S* rates each sample on attractiveness. (3) *S* ranks four samples in order of attractiveness. Supposed to indicate *S's* "covert" self-attitude, not necessarily "unconscious attitude."
Diller & Riklan (1957)	Self-revealing tendencies inferred from Rorschach *M*.
Epstein (1955)	Three measures of unconscious self-attitudes: (1) speed of recognition of own name in tachistoscope (2) own handwriting, mirror, upside down and right side up (3) own voice played forwards and backwards (2) and (3) were each rated by *S* as to: (a) "liking"; (b) similarity to his conception of his own. Data discarded if *S* admits recognition of his own (increasing likelihood of construct validity for measuring *non*phenomenal self). No correlations among these alleged measures of unconscious self-attitudes are given (in support of their common assumed construct validity), nor are they correlated with *S's* conscious evaluations of own handwriting, voice, name, self, and figures drawn by him (in exploration of their discriminant validity as measures of nonphenomenal, as contrasted to phenomenal, self).
Fisher & Cleveland (1958a)	Various indices of body image. See text for description.
Friedman (1955)	*Q* sort made by *E* from *S's* TAT protocol. See text and Table I for description.
Goldings (1954)	*S*s rated satisfaction (happiness) of people in a series of 30 pictures and photographs with ambiguous expression. Purports to tap *S's* "projected happiness." (See Table III for Goldings's measure of phenomenal happiness.)
Grummon & John (1954)	TAT scored for self concept, ideal self, and self-and-others. See text for description.
Haimowitz & Haimowitz (1952)	Attitudes toward self scored from Rorschach, by unspecified method.
Kardiner & Ovesy (in Karon, 1958)	Self-hatred of Negroes inferred from Rorschach and TAT. See text for comment.

Table IV—Continued

Author	*Instrument*
Linton & Graham (1959)	Self-assertive or passive M on Rorschach alleged to indicate self-assertive or passive unconscious self concept. High Hd on Rorschach alleged to indicate self-criticality and preoccupation with self and body. Machover figure drawing scores also used. (See text for description.)
Mason (1953)	Caldwell Pictures sorted and used as basis for story-telling. See text for description. See Table II for Mason's measures of phenomenal self concept.
Moeller & Applezweig (1957a, 1957b)	Behavior Interpretation Inventory. Forced choice inventory to measure motivations for Escape, Avoidance, Social Approval, and Self Approval. Latter also called Self-realization or "consistency with the self picture." Forty-nine stems describe behavior modes from Murray. Each of four possible stem completions represents one of the four motives. Stems and completions were written by test constructors on rational basis. Split-half and test-retest coefficients for each motive score on several samples are given in manual (1957b). Applezweig (personal communication) says profile of scores is intended to reflect the unconscious self-image. Zero correlations were obtained between BII scores and self ratings of each of the four motives.
Mussen & Jones (1957)	Negative self concept inferred from TAT stories. See text for description.
Mussen & Porter (1959)	Feelings of adequacy and negativity of self concept inferred from five TAT cards and three other cards. See text for description.
Newstrand (1958)	Eavesdropping Question: (1) what would S most like, and (2) what would most disturb S to hear about self, if eavesdropping. "Best and worst self image" alleged to bound self concept fairly accurately.
Rogers & Paul (1959)	S judged own photograph for aggressiveness, unaware it was hers. See text for description.
Rogers & Walsh (1959)	S judged own photograph for attractiveness, unaware it was hers. See text for description.
Sarbin & Farberow (1952)	"Organization of self concept" inferred from "structural features of Rorschach protocols."
Sarnoff (1951)	Michigan Sentence Completion Test. Fifty sentences from a 100-item "unpublished test developed at the University of Michigan for use in the Veterans Ad-

Table IV—Continued

Author	Instrument
Sarnoff (1951)—Cont'd	ministration Research on Selection of Clinical Psychologists" (1951, p. 206). Percentages of interrater agreement in scoring ranged from 91 to 100.
Secord (1953); Secord & Jourard (1953)	Homonyms Test, from which inferred Body Anxiety. Seventy-five words have, as one meaning, referents of pain, disease, injury, or other body content. Five seconds per word, S writes free association. Split-half reliability males +.63; females +.66. Interscorer agreement, $r = +.99$.
Smith & Lebo (1956)	Scored human figures drawn by Ss on 52 items, "determined by survey of procedures reported in literature." Assumed validity, because Levy had concluded (1950) figure drawings may represent projections of self concept. Story completion to infer heterosexuality and emancipation from parents. See text for description. See Table II for their phenomenal self-concept measures.
Walsh (1956)	Driscoll Play Kit used as basis for finishing incomplete stories. See text for description.

2. Rorschach Scores (Other than Fisher's Scores Purporting to Index "Body Image")

The ways in which the Rorschach has been used to infer unconscious self-attitudes have been very vaguely specified by most authors who employed this instrument, and the pattern of results from the studies in which it has been used is not conclusive. The Barrier score which has been more explicitly defined by Fisher will be discussed in detail in Section 3 below. The remaining studies are briefly sketched in the following paragraphs.

Diller and Riklan (1957) assumed that high M on the Rorschach represented self-revealing tendencies. Apparently on the premise that what one would usually reveal or conceal are negative aspects of the self concept, they predicted that number of M would correlate with number of negative self statements on the Robinson-Freeman Self-Continuity Test. (See Table II.) Although their hypothesis was supported, it seems to the present author that the possibilities of artifact were not adequately controlled. That is, since number of M correlated with total number of self statements on the Robinson-Freeman test, no clear interpretation of the relation between number of M and negativity of conscious self concept seems possible. The authors have considered the problem of total R on each instrument, but their means of ruling it out as the explanation of their correlation seems to the present author to be inadequate.

Cohen (1954) inferred feelings of adequacy and self-acceptance from the Rorschach by unspecified means, and related it to level of aspiration. His results are described in Section C-12 of Chapter IV.

Haimowitz and Haimowitz (1952) scored the Rorschach for attitudes towards self, among other variables. The exact method of scoring is not given, and the interjudge reliability for this particular score is not stated. Congruent with the assumptions of self-concept theory, therapy Ss showed an increase in the positiveness of their attitudes toward self. The increase was not quite significant, however. Control Ss who did not receive therapy did not differ significantly from therapy Ss on initial ratings of attitudes toward self. When the control Ss were retested after time periods comparable to the test-retest periods for therapy Ss, they showed slight and insignificant increases in positiveness of attitude toward self. (See Chapter IV, Section C-5 for a detailed discussion of the problems of therapy studies as tests of propositions from personality theory, and for a summary of results obtained with the use of measures purporting to index the phenomenal self.)

Sarbin and Farberow (1952) inferred the "organization of self perceptions" from "structural features of the [Rorschach] protocols," e.g., M, FM, FC. It is not clear whether phenomenal or nonphenomenal self is allegedly measured, but the study referred to is summarized in Chapter IV, Section C-5, which is concerned with psychotherapy and the self concept.

3. Various Indices of "Body Image"

Fisher and Cleveland (1958a) have considered "body image" to be an important, largely nonphenomenal aspect of the self concept. They point out that the current use of the term is loose and generalized, with very few specific connotations. It refers roughly to "the body as a psychological experience, and focuses on the individual's feelings and attitudes toward his own body" (p. x). The word "image" they consider misleading since they, and most workers who use the term, regard the body image as being largely nonphenomenal.

In reviewing commonly used figure drawing techniques as a measure of "body image," they conclude: "Although the figure drawing may be a potentially valuable method for studying body image . . . It is still mainly used in a vague, impressionistic manner and there has been limited success in differentiating which aspects of the drawing are linked with body image, which with drawing skill, and which are due to the manner in which the drawing is obtained" (Fisher & Cleveland, 1958a, p. 35).[1] Brown and Goitein (1943) assume that skill in drawing plays no part in their test in which S, while blindfolded, draws the outline of himself from the back, the side, and in a lying-down position. They assume that the drawing portrays not merely the physical experience of a man's bodily integration, but an "inner intuition of self integration." However, no pertinent validity data are presented.

a. ANISEIKONIC LENSES

Several observers have studied the influence of aniseikonic lenses upon verbal reports of body image, and upon subsequent draw-a-person tests presumed to reflect body image. The rationale offered is that the use of lenses creates "an unstable and moderately unstructured perceptual field into which it is relatively easy for one to project unconscious feelings about his body," and that "individuals most resist the perception of novelty or distortion in those body areas about which they have the greatest anxiety or conflict." This rationale is attributed by Fisher (1958, p. 293) to Wittreich and Grace. Wittreich and Grace found certain group differences in the effects created by the lenses (e.g., normals differed from neurotics, boys from girls, younger Ss from older Ss). However, the type of studies undertaken and the pattern of results as cited in Fisher and Cleveland (1958a) do not appear to form a pertinent, adequate basis for clarifying the construct validity of the technique.

---

[1] Levy (1950, pp. 257-258), in a review of studies of figure drawing as a projective test, concluded even more broadly that "the technique of analyzing drawings is without experimental validation, rarely yields unequivocal information . . . ." In a more recent review, Swensen (1957) states on page 435 that "there have been few studies that would appear to bear at all upon the question of whether or not human figure drawings do, in fact, represent the drawer's perception of himself" and he concludes (on page 437), "The results suggest that for many, or perhaps most, Ss, the figure drawn does not represent the S's own body . . . the most outstanding conclusion that can be drawn is that definitive research on the basic meaning or significance of human figure drawing is lacking."

Fisher used aniseikonic lenses to have Ss view left and right hands at arm's length, in order to judge comparative size between members of each pair of homologous fingers. Following the general rationale of Wittreich and Grace, Fisher assumed that persons with a "well crystal-lized body image distinction between right and left body sizes would tend to perceive differences in finger sizes consistently in a given direction. On the other hand, the person with poorly articulated right-left body image distinctions was expected to be relatively conflicted and anxious about the size judgments and therefore either unable to experience differences at all or able to experience only inconsistent differences." "A continuum of bigness and smallness was selected because it seemed to embrace roughly a number of left-right polarities about which there has been speculation in the literature (e.g., strong versus weak, masculine versus feminine)" (Fisher, 1958, p. 293).

No specific validation data bearing on the construct validity of this technique are given, however. We may apply here Cronbach and Meehl's (1955) suggestion that some light may be thrown on the construct validity of a measure by the degree of success in obtaining correlations which are predicted on the basis of the assumed validity of the measuring technique and certain theoretical premises. Some such predicted correlations of definiteness of right-left GSR gradients were obtained. Not all the predicted relations were found, however. For example, results with left-handed Ss were negative.

b. Distorted Pictures

Another index of "body image distortion" used by Fisher and Abercrombie (1958) involved tachistoscopic presentation of pictures of normal persons and distorted persons (e.g., with arm missing). Scores were derived in terms of the number of errors S made in seeing distortions which were there, and in reading distortions into normal pictures. Here it was assumed that tachistoscopic distortion scores reflected S's over-all poorly integrated schema of his own body. The latter, it was also inferred, would include poor left-right differentiation in body schema. Therefore tachistoscope scores should index confusions in left-right differentiation, too. However, the only information bearing on the construct validity of this technique is the fact that some of the correlations with definiteness of left-right GSR gradients, predicted from the assumed validity of the technique and certain theoretical premises, were obtained.

Not all the predicted correlations were obtained, however. For example, no consistent correlations were found between predominance of left or right location in tachistoscopic distortion errors and the GSR gradient. And, again, no correlations were found for left-handed *S*s. (Because of previously obtained negative results, mentioned above, no specific predictions had been made in this study for left-handed *S*s, however.)

Since the tachistoscopic distortion technique and the size judgments of hands with aniseikonic lenses both purport to reveal the same construct, it would be desirable to know the correlation between these two measures. Such data have not been published, however. Both of these indices purport to reveal *un*conscious left-right body-image distortion. Therefore a pertinent discriminant validity study would involve comparison of both scores with *S*s' reports of their *conscious* perceptions concerning the relative size, strength, perfection of shape, and degree of motor control of the homologous body parts, especially as these conscious reports seem realistic in the light of objective measurements.

c. RORSCHACH BARRIER SCORES

By far the most widely studied body image index is Fisher and Cleveland's Barrier score on the Rorschach. At the outset of their work they assumed that this score has validity for inferring the degree to which people "experience their body boundaries as definite and firm versus indefinite and vague" (Fisher & Cleveland, 1958, p. 56). The sort of boundaries which the individual attributes to his body was expected to "tell a good deal about his overall life-building operations" (p. 56).

This score is based on content involving distinctive surfaces, enclosed openings, or containerlike properties. It is assignable to Rorschach protocols with a high degree of interjudge reliability, but no test-retest reliabilities are given. Since total *R* correlated $+.41$ to $+.66$ with Barrier scores, *R* must be controlled. This can be done either by asking *S* to give a fixed number of responses, or by reducing the records to a set number of responses, or by showing that groups to be compared in a study do not differ in *R*. Even with *R* controlled, the number of *W* is significantly greater among High Barrier *S*s, and the *F*+% is significantly smaller among High Barrier *S*s. Before *R* is controlled, shading total is significantly higher among High Barrier *S*s. The relevance of these facts to the psychological interpretation of the Barrier score is not clear. The Barrier score is not significantly related to intelligence (Wonderlic, MAT, Wechsler).

Their original hunch that Barrier scores validly indicated the firmness of Ss' body image boundaries came from inspection of the Rorschach protocols of arthritic patients who showed muscle stiffness. They reasoned that both muscle stiffness and Rorschach boundaries were defense against feelings with catastrophic implications.

In an attempt to validate the body image basis of the Barrier score, they made and tested a number of predictions. Among various groups of normal Ss, the following predictions were confirmed at the .02 level or better. High Barrier scores will be associated with (1) checking of many exterior body symptoms; (2) a small number of sentence completions with body vulnerability connotations; (3) fewer body associations to Secord's (1953) homonyms. The following predictions were *not* confirmed. High Barrier scores will be associated with (1) a higher number of skin to body interior sensations checked in a three-minute period; (2) higher number of muscle to interior sensations checked in a three-minute period. In addition, no relation of Barrier scores to Sheldon's body types was found.

Among abnormal or physically ill Ss the following predictions were confirmed at the .02 level or better. High Barrier scores will be associated with (1) small number of body disintegration themes in Projection Movement Sequences; (2) an "inside stump" phantom limb phenomenon (as contrasted to "outside stump" phantom limb phenomenon among low Barrier scorers). As predicted, Barrier scores of polio patients were not a function of degree of physical impairment. High Barrier scores were found more often among patients who were rated as better adjusted to their illnesses.

In one study of physiological reactivity under stress, high Barrier scores were found to be associated with (1) lower interior reactivity, as indicated by pulse rate, stroke volume, and cardiac output; (2) higher exterior reactivity as indicated by total peripheral resistance. Since not all these statistical tests can be independent of one another, it is difficult to interpret their significance levels. All the trends were in the predicted direction, however.

In another stress study, high Barrier scorers showed (1) greater increment in their physiological reactivity of exterior body layers (EMG significant at .01, GSR at .10-.05); and (2) significantly smaller increment in reactivity of interior body layers under stress (heart rate, stroke volume, cardiac output all at .01 level).

As we stated earlier, Fisher and Cleveland proposed a theory about the role of the perceived firmness of the body image boundary in the location of psychosomatic symptoms. They obtained a number of differences between high and low Barrier scorers which were congruent with this theory and with the assumption that Barrier scores were valid indicators of the firmness of body image boundaries. These findings, which throw some light on the construct validity of the Barrier scores, will be summarized immediately below.

The authors hypothesized that a firm body image boundary would lead to a location of psychosomatic symptoms in exterior sites. As predicted, they found high Barrier scores among arthritis, dermatitis, and conversion symptom patients, as contrasted to low Barrier scores among colitis and stomach disturbance patients. One might reason that the high and low Barrier scores were determined by pain or disturbance at the body site, rather than being indicators of the body image characteristics which somehow lead to the location of the psychosomatic symptoms. However, the authors infer that pain or disturbance at a particular body site did not determine the size of the Barrier scores, because (1) significantly more arthritis patients had high Barrier scores than did patients suffering back pain from injuries; (2) significantly more neurodermatitis patients had high Barrier scores than did patients suffering skin damage from chemical injury. As the authors point out, however, these control observations are not as convincing as they might be, because the duration of symptoms was longer in both of the psychosomatic groups than it was in the injury groups.

In some studies of cancer patients, the authors extended their assumptions concerning the role of firmness of body image boundaries in producing disease. It was predicted that high Barrier scores would be found among patients with cancer at exterior body sites, while low Barrier scores would be found among patients with cancer at interior body sites. This prediction was confirmed at the .001 level. Again we may raise the question whether the Barrier scores were determined by the focusing of the patient's attention on the respective body sites, due to sensations which are associated with cancer and its treatment at those sites. No control observations which rule out such an interpetation are reported.

As we said at the outset, Fisher and Cleveland believe that the body image is largely unconscious, and that their Barrier score indexes certain aspects of this unconscious body image. In line with this belief, they predicted that only a chance relationship would be found between Barrier scores and Bills's Acceptance of Self scores and Discrepancy scores, which purport to measure the conscious self concept. This prediction was confirmed. (See Chapter III for a discussion of Bills's instrument.)

The null relationship between the self-report test and their body image score appears to them to support the discriminant validity of their index. However, these findings do not seem to the present author to be particularly pertinent to the construct validity of the Barrier score for measuring unconscious firmness of body image boundaries. This is true because the Bills instrument does not contain items which give the S an opportunity to report on his conscious body image boundaries. The chance relationship between Barrier scores and Bills scores may be due to this lack of congruence between the dimensions which the two measures purport to tap at the unconscious and conscious levels, respectively. These null findings may be more relevant to establishing the discriminant validity of the Barrier score as an index of some of the more complex constructs involving unconscious processes which will be described later.

As we have just implied, to establish the discriminant validity of the Barrier scores as indices of *unconscious* body image boundaries, we need studies in which Ss' Barrier scores are compared with their conscious descriptions of body boundaries as such. No such investigations have been reported. Two previously mentioned studies come closest to the sort of validity test which would be useful. One of these studies supports the discriminant validity of the Barrier scores, because, in this investigation, no association was found between Barrier scores and the ratio of reported skin or muscle sensations to interior body sensations. However, the second study does not obtain null findings, i.e., a significant positive association was obtained between Barrier scores and the ratio of reported exterior symptoms to interior symptoms, as checked by S in three minutes. These positive findings fail to support the discriminant validity of the Barrier scores as an index of unconscious body image boundaries.

Fisher and Cleveland infer that, if Barrier scores measure *unconscious* body image boundaries, these scores should correlate with other indices which are alleged to tap unconscious body image boundaries. In accordance with this they found that, among males, high Barrier scorers drew more elaborate facades for houses. (Corresponding results with females were not significant.) In another study, high Barrier scores were associated with dreams which were rated blindly by four clinical psychologists to be "more firmly bounded."

It may be concluded that there is some correlation between size of Barrier score and location of physical reactions at the exterior or interior regions of the body, when these physical reactions are indexed by any one of the following observations: (1) S's report of symptoms he experiences; (2) S's possession of externally observable symptoms; (3) S's physiological reactivity as measured objectively. Sufficient information is not at hand to conclude that the Barrier score validly indexes the construct "unconsciously perceived degree of firmness and definiteness of body boundary." However, the findings make such an interpretation plausible.

Even if we assume the construct validity of the Barrier score for indexing unconsciously perceived firmness of body image boundaries, the design and scope of the studies which have been executed thus far do not permit us to choose between the following alternate interpretations, suggested by Fisher and Cleveland: (1) The degree of firmness of body image boundaries which one unconsciously perceives leads to differences in location of symptoms and reactivities. (2) Physical changes precede and cause the differences in body image boundaries and Barrier scores. Fisher and Cleveland lean to the first interpretation.

The findings cited thus far are pertinent to the validation of the Barrier score as an index of body image boundaries with "body" left in. However, as their book progresses, these authors offer wide-ranging speculations, with accompanying studies which have some bearing on these speculations. They conclude their book with quite a different assertion as to the probable type of construct indexed by their Barrier score. Thus: (Fisher & Cleveland, 1958, p. 367) ". . . we have almost taken the 'body' out of 'body image,' by postulating that the body-image boundary does not really mirror the actual properties of the body surface, but that it is rather a representation of attitudes and expectancy systems which have been projected onto the body periphery . . . . [Although] some of our best predictive studies (e.g., psychosomatic and physiological) grew out of our assumption that the Barrier score could be conceptualized as indicating the degree to which the individual assigned certain attributes to his body . . . we regard the Barrier score as having little to do with the actual physical appearance of the individual's body [but] . . . as a measure of important properties associated with the body as a social object . . . this position of the body, intermediate between 'outside' and 'inside' . . . makes it a unique projection screen for patterns of attitudes . . . we have concluded that the body image is formed of these projected attitudes."

Space does not permit us to review in detail the extremely wide range of speculations made by the authors concerning these other proposed construct meanings of the Barrier score. One of the chief characteristics allegedly associated with high Barrier scores is "self-steering" behavior. This association is supposed to be a function of the high Barrier Ss' inferred greater clarity and firmness about their "identity." Self-steering behavior is allegedly manifested by (1) high level of goal setting, (2) high need for task completion, (3) low suggestibility, (4) ability to express anger outwardly when frustrated, (5) degree of orientation toward self-expressiveness, (6) ability to tolerate stress, (7) ability to maintain a realistic orientation in unrestricted perceptual situations. To support these predictions, findings are cited (based on various groups of Ss) relating high Barrier scores to the following behaviors: (1) high aspiration; (2) high n Achievement; (3) low inactivity in the TAT; (4) overachievement in college students; (5) instructors' ratings of Ss' pursuit of independent goals in class; (6) higher recall of incompleted tasks; (7) low suggestibility (i.e., low acceptance of inappropriate blots) in Ink-blot suggestion test; (8) low suggestibility as measured by Postural Sway Test; (9) more anger-out reactions; (10) more self-gratifying answers to the question as to how S would spend his time, had he but one month to live; (11) less deterioration of behavior under stress as shown in (a) less error time on SAM Pseudoscope, (b) fewer errors on regular mirror drawing; (c) realistic lowering of level of aspiration to suit failure in hand-steadiness test; (d) less decrement in digit symbol; (e) better rated adjustment to polio.

These findings are not without puzzling contradictions and exceptions, however, such as the following: (1) curvilinear relations between n Achievement and Barrier scores among clinical psychology students; (2) no association between instructors' ratings of S's life goals and Barrier scores; (3) greater suggestibility (as measured by autokinetic phenomenon) among high Barrier scorers; (4) more difficulty in expressing anger outwardly among arthritics and breast cancer patients who also were high Barrier scorers; (5) no relations between Barrier scores and perceptual stability as tested by Witkin's rod and frame test; (6) lower rated officer potential among high Barrier scorers; (7) in one study greater digit span decrement under stress among high Barrier scorers.

Fisher and Cleveland present plausible *ad hoc* interpretations for these findings which fail to support their originally formulated hypotheses. However, it must be concluded that several factors make it impossible to know much about the construct validity of the Barrier score as an index of their very much widened and complicated body image constructs. For one thing, the constructs have not been defined clearly and consistently. Therefore one cannot confidently and clearly relate the pattern of reported findings to the constructs. For another thing, the studies which are cited are mostly ones which were originally designed and executed for another purpose by other investigators. As a consequence of this fact, the studies differ among themselves in conditions of Rorschach administration and in the means which must be used for controlling R total. This means that in the different studies there may be various unidentified, irrelevant effects upon the Barrier score.

Since the groups used from study to study were quite different, one cannot clearly interpret the contradictions which occur when an effect is found within one study, but not within another (e.g., when high Barrier is found to be associated with "anger out" in Funkenstein and King's *S*s, but with failure to be able to express anger outwardly in arthritics). In addition, it is often impossible to know whether the groups compared within any one study were adequately equated with respect to variables which would probably be relevant to Fisher and Cleveland's constructs. Even if the groups formed by the original investigator for his own purposes were appropriately equated for those purposes, they may not have been comparable with respect to variables relevant to Fisher and Cleveland's scores. And, finally, the correlation of W with high Barrier, even when R total is controlled, may raise some ambiguities about the psychological interpretation of results involving the Barrier score.[2]

SUMMARY OF THE DISCUSSION OF BODY IMAGE

Body image is a term with no clear literary or operational definition.

---

[2]Fisher and Cleveland's theories and findings are summarized in their book (1958a). Some of the studies and speculations are presented in more detail in journal articles. In addition to references to these authors cited in the text of this book, see: Cleveland and Fisher (1954), (1956), (1957); Fisher (1959); Fisher and Cleveland (1955), (1956a), (1956b), (1956c), (1957), and (1958b); Ware, Fisher, and Cleveland (1957).

Two senses in which the term has been used are: (1) *S*'s perceptions of his physical characteristics and his feelings and attitudes toward his physical characteristics; (2) *S*'s general "attitudes which are associated with the body as a social object" (but which have "little to do with the actual physical appearance of the individual's body") (Fisher & Cleveland, 1958a, p. 367). The body image, in either of these senses, is assumed to be largely or entirely unconscious.

Fisher and his associates have introduced a number of measures which purport to tap various aspects of the body image. These include *Ss*' reports while using aniseikonic lenses, *Ss*' reports about distorted pictures which are tachistoscopically presented, and specially devised Rorschach scores. The rationale behind each technique and the implications which are drawn from the findings are complex. The first two techniques remain unvalidated.

Among the Rorschach indices, Fisher and Cleveland emphasize the Barrier score, based on content. In addition to other constructs, unconsciously perceived firmness of body image boundaries is allegedly revealed by the Barrier score. With some exceptions, the reported studies are congruent with, but do not demonstrate the construct validity of, the Barrier score for this purpose. In particular, no studies of discriminant validity are presented, i.e., comparisons between Barrier scores and conscious reports of the perceived firmness of body image boundaries.

Fisher and Cleveland also wish to use the Barrier score to infer some more general attitudes, as in the second sense of the term "body image" which we mentioned above. Here their definitions and rationale are not entirely clear and are very complex. To test their ideas they have frequently used the data of other investigators, rescored for their own purposes. We have questioned whether such a practice permits one adequately to control relevant variables. In any event, the pattern of findings is somewhat confusing and contradictory, so that the construct validity of their score for inferring the more complex "body image" attitudes remains to be demonstrated.

C. Summary Comments on Studies Involving the Unconscious Self Concept

Since constructs concerning the phenomenal self appear to be insufficient bases for predicting behavior, a number of psychologists have felt that constructs concerning the nonphenomenal self may be worth postulating. However, the investigations which purport to relate the nonphenomenal self concept to theoretically relevant variables have not yielded a clear pattern of results, for a number of reasons: (1) Theoretical formulations which have introduced nonphenomenal-self constructs have thus far been very vague and inadequate. (2) Problems of establishing construct validity of indices purporting to reveal the unconscious self concept have not been clearly recognized or coped with, and consequently no measure in use has been demonstrated to be adequate for this purpose. (3) The research designs in many of these studies have not been adequately controlled. (4) There have been wide differences from study to study in hypotheses, types of *S*s, instruments, and procedures which have been employed.

There are enough provocative findings from some of the separate studies to suggest that this line of theory and research might be worth pursuing more systematically.

VI

Studies Concerned with the "Insightfulness" of the Self Concept

A. INTRODUCTION

Next to researches involving self-regard, the most numerous studies relevant to self-concept theory are those which concern "insight." This term has been used in the psychological literature with a number of literary and operational meanings, and most or all of the latter have involved evaluative traits. Thus this chapter is, in a sense, an extension or elaboration of Chapter IV.

We shall not attempt a comparative review of the literary meanings of "insight" to various theorists, nor of the alternative roles it is assumed to play in their theories. When we consider only the lines of thought which underlie the empirical studies performed to date, we see them falling mainly into two groups: In the classical Freudian and neo-Freudian view, lack of insight is alleged to be accompanied by defensiveness and/or maladjustment, when the latter is defined in terms of S's experience and/or an observer's diagnosis. So far as phenomenal theorists are concerned, it sometimes seems that they too espouse this view. On the other hand, they occasionally seem to be saying that the S will not become anxious (and hence defensive) unless and until he becomes at least dimly aware of the disparity between his phenomenal self and the views others hold of him (Rogers, 1951b, p. 321). Of course such a disparity may render S more potentially vulnerable, in the sense of increasing the likelihood that a discomfort-producing discrepancy will come to his attention. But until that eventuality does occur (i.e., until at least a dim awareness of the inappropriateness or incompleteness of the self concept develops), lack of insight presumably would not lead to anxiety or defensiveness. (It may, of course, lead to maladjusted or inappropriate behavior, as judged by an external observer.)

Many workers have indicated that there is a great deal of surplus meaning to their concept of "insight" beyond that which their operational definitions cover. We shall take it for granted, then, that in this sense, all the operational definitions to be discussed need to be improved. Our comments concern methodological problems of a more restricted nature.

B. Varieties of Operational Definitions

1. *Discrepancy Scores*

Most, but not all, operational definitions of insight which have been used involve a discrepancy between S's self-report and the report of an O concerning S. The reader will recognize that such definitions lead into all the problems associated with a two-part index, parallel to the difficulties discussed in connection with the [Self—Ideal] discrepancy scores. Much of the present analysis will be taken up with such problems.

In order to subclassify and analyze this kind of operational definition, we must first note the following possibilities on the part of S and O.

So far as S *is concerned:*

a. He may tell how he privately sees himself with respect to characteristics which can be measured relatively objectively, e.g., "intelligence," or with respect to feelings and behaviors less objectively measurable. This type of report includes S's social-self concept to an unknown degree, the extent of such inclusion depending partly on E's instructions. Examples are Brownfain's "private self" (1952), probably Calvin and Holtzman's "self concept" (1953), and probably Sears's self-ratings (1936).

b. He may report his "social-self concept," i.e., regardless of how he personally evaluates himself, he tells how he thinks particular or generalized others see him. More specifically, S may try to guess how other(s) will rate him, or may try to guess the score he will make on O's test.

These two sets of instructions do not result in identical self-ratings, as shown by several investigators who obtained self-reports from the same Ss under the two sets of instructions (Brownfain, 1952; Flyer, Barron, & Bigbee, 1953; Goldings, 1954; Israel, 1958; and Miyamoto & Dornbusch,

1956). Therefore, it is important to specify clearly the instructions under which *S* makes his self-reports, if we are to evaluate results appropriately.

Even under ideal conditions, either of these reports, taken at face value, can include only *S*'s phenomenal self concept.

So far as O *is concerned:* The report concerning *S* made by "another informed person," which Hilgard (1949) has called the "inferred self," has several possible variants.

First, as regards *the source of* O's *information,* we may identify:

  a. informal interaction (e.g., Brownfain, 1952; Calvin & Holtzman, 1953; Flyer, Barron, & Bigbee, 1953; Green, 1948; Israel, 1958; Murstein, 1956; Norman, 1953; Rokeach, 1945; and Sears, 1936).

  b. special observational procedures such as standardized observational techniques or the application of tests and diagnostic tools (e.g., Arsenian, 1942; Brandt, 1958; Klein, 1948; Torrance, 1954).

In the latter case, but not the former, the informed person is usually more or less an expert by training.

Secondly we note that *what* O *is trying to infer about* S may also vary, thus:

  a. O may report on the impression *S* makes on him personally, as to overt behavior and/or covert inferred characteristics such as feelings or abilities, e.g., "I like *S*," "*S* seems to me to be intelligent."

  b. O may try to report on the impression *S* makes on a more or less specified group of others, perhaps including O, in regard to overt and/or covert characteristics, e.g., "*S* is well liked by the boys in this fraternity," "*S* maintains rapport with patients to whom he gives therapy."

  c. O may try to report his inferences concerning *S*'s self concept, including those aspects of which *S* is conscious and those of which he is not.

It seems likely that reports of Os made under these varying frames of reference will be far from identical, but we have no systematic information as to how they differ. In any event, it is not possible clearly to classify the available studies as to which of these *S* and *O* reports have been used. Therefore it is not entirely certain just how many of the possible combinations of *S* and *O* reports have been attempted thus far. And because of ambiguity in the operational definitions of *S* and *O* reports, one cannot clearly interpret and synthesize the results of studies on "insight."

If in spite of these difficulties we consider possible combinations of

Ss' and *Os'* reports which have actually been used, we find the following seem to be most *common types of scores:*

a. *S* reports his personal view of himself; and this is compared to *O*'s report on *S*'s actual characteristics. *O*'s report is based on informal peer interaction and includes in unknown amounts *O*'s idea of the group's impression of *S*, and *O*'s own impression of *S* (e.g., Bandura, 1956; Brownfain's Insight I, 1952; Calvin & Holtzman, 1953; Flyer, Barron, & Bigbee, 1953; Murstein, 1956; and Sears, 1936).

b. *S* reports on himself as he thinks specified *Os* will view him (social-self concept), and this is compared to *O*'s actual statements about *S*. Each *O*'s statements are based on informal peer interaction and they include unknown amounts of *O*'s own impression of *S* and *O*'s idea of the group's impression of *S*. (Bronfenbrenner *et al.,* 1958; Brownfain's Insight II, 1952; Flyer, *et al.,* 1953; and Wylie, 1957).

c. *S* reports on what he expects to make or do on a standard test and this is compared to his actual score or standing (Brandt, 1958; Klein, 1948; and Torrance, 1954).

d. *S* reports on himself without knowledge that *O* will be reporting on him also. *S*'s reports are then compared to *O*'s. The latter have usually been based on projective tests or hidden observations, but sometimes on more objective test scores (e.g., Beilin, 1957; Child, Frank, & Storm, 1956; Friedman, 1955; and Kelman & Parloff, 1957).

It is apparent that studies covering this array of possibilities could not lend themselves to easy synthesis, even if each design was well enough controlled within itself.

2. *Insightfulness of* S *Directly Inferred by an Observer*

A second general type of insight measurement has employed direct inferences of this characteristic itself by *O*. That is, *O* rates *S* as to how insightful *S* is concerning specified or general characteristics. Such a procedure requires *O* to infer both what *S* thinks about himself *and* whether those thoughts are accurate in terms of *O*'s other impressions or sources of information about *S*. Two assumptions are made: (1) *O*'s ideas about *S*'s self-picture and actual characteristics are more accurate than *S*'s; (2) *O* can intuitively synthesize his impressions of *S*'s self concept and *S*'s actual characteristics with optimum weighting assigned to the variables involved (Reed & Cuadra, 1957; Weingarten, 1949).

3. *Insightfulness of* S *Inferred from a Specially Devised Self-Insight Test*

Gross (1948, p. 223) based his Self-Insight Scale on the following nonoperational definition of insight: "Self-insight is the acceptance and admission of both the presence and absence of personality traits within oneself when this acceptance runs counter to a system of emotionally toned ideas or when the admission of the presence or absence of these traits clashes with one's feelings of self-esteem." Sixty-four psychologists judged a large group of items, and items were retained in the final form of the scale only if they fell in one of the following two combinations: (1) judged to be true of most persons in our society, but "disesteemed"; (2) judged to be false of most persons in our society, but "esteemed." This procedure of item selection necessarily implies that "insight" is equivalent to derogating one's self whether or not such a derogation is objectively warranted. Such a definition seems theoretically inappropriate and the operations do not permit the establishment of discriminant validity of the instrument as a measure of insight per se. Two of the four validating studies for which formal statistics are reported consist, in effect, of correlations between the Self-Insight scale and some other self-report on which S has the opportunity to admit undesirable characteristics. In a third study there was no relation between the Self-Insight scale and professors' ratings of the self-insight of social work students, even though the ratings were based largely on socially undesirable characteristics. A low but significant *rho* with Chapin's Social Insight scale was obtained. We must conclude that this scale is not a satisfactory measure of "self-insight."

C. CONSTRUCT VALIDITY OF [SELF—OTHER] DISCREPANCY MEASURES OF INSIGHT

The most commonly used insight measurements involve combinations of two classes of variables (S's reports and O's reports). It is evident that the problem of construct validity of such insight measurements is even more complicated and confused than was the question of construct validity of some of the measures of self-regard which we discussed earlier.

1. S's Self-Reports

To understand insight measures, we need first of all to know something about the construct validity of S's reports. Many of the problems here are the same as those already detailed in Chapter III. In addition, some other difficulties crop up. Since S's reports may be óbtained under varying instructional sets, we need empirical information and process analyses to establish what S is doing under the varying sets, and to what extent the same or different constructs are being tapped.

A priori theoretical considerations make plausible the idea that, even with the clearest instructions, there can be no sharp separation on S's part between his private-self concept and his social-self concept. On the other hand, as mentioned above, the work of a number of investigators shows that there are significant differences in self-concept reports obtained under private-self and social-self instructions. This matter should be systematically explored further. In any event, when instructions to S are loose, we certainly cannot know to what extent S is trying to give private-self or social-self reports. Therefore we cannot determine the degree to which idiosyncratic interpretations of the instructions influence individual Ss' insight scores, and the consequent findings.

Let us suppose for the moment that instructions to S tell him definitely to report his social-self concept, and that he is willing and able to express his social-self concept within the limitations of the technique E is using. Even under these conditions S's task in an insight study is more complicated than it is in some of the simpler self-regard studies. This is true because S, if he is to receive a nonartifactual insight score, must have some knowledge of the characteristics of the instrument itself. That is, he must know something about the general way O's test scores distribute themselves (in the case of objective tests); or he must know something about the general rating behavior of Os (in the case of rating scales). This is, of course, a version of the problem of stereotype and individual accuracy, discussed by Cronbach (1955), Gage and Cronbach (1955), and by Bronfenbrenner, Harding, and Gallwey (1958). It has been surmounted to a certain extent in some insight studies by having S rank himself in a specified group. This procedure rules out (1) the effect of intra-S differences in knowledge of the characteristics of test score distributions; and (2) the possibilities that Os will vary from Ss in elevation of all their ratings, as can happen with the use of rating scales (e.g., Bandura [1956]; Brownfain's Insight I [1952]).

Another special complication of S's report of social-self in an insight study is due to the fact that he may be trying to estimate any one or an unknown combination of the following factors: (a) each single O's opinion; (b) how the Os' opinions will average out, if several are to be taken; (c) the degree to which each O will speak for himself or will vacillate between that and an expression of his (O's) idea of how "generalized others" view S. Although instructions could presumably be written which would tell S what to aim for, this would not serve to control Os' individual or collective behavior to fit in with S's expectations.

The study of Bronfenbrenner et al. (1958) is concerned with some of the complications mentioned in the above paragraph. They distinguish conceptually between (a) S's accuracy in predicting the *average* opinion which a specified group of Others hold about him and (b) S's accuracy in discriminating differences among the individual Others' opinions of him.

Their research interest was in the ability of S to discriminate individual differences among five specified Os' ratings of him. The authors wished to develop a measure of S's "ability to estimate correctly the *relative position* of ratings made by a series of others on a particular item" (Bronfenbrenner et al., 1958, p. 48).

As their measure they used the correlation between S's estimates and Others' ratings of S "within items." That is, for each item, the estimate which S made of an individual O's rating of him was expressed as a deviation from the mean of the estimates S made of all the Os' ratings of him on that item. The rating an individual O made about S on the given item was expressed as a deviation from the mean of the ratings which that O had given on that item to the five Ss whom he rated. The five sets of within-item deviations constitute five sets of paired observations. Since there were twelve items, and five sets of paired observations for each item, a correlation coefficient could be computed for each S, based on sixty paired observations. (See Table II for a listing of their items.)

By this means the authors hoped to rule out the problem of differences in elevation (mean level) between S's estimates and Os' ratings; and to rule out interitem differences in elevation. Thus they hoped to get a "pure" measure of S's sensitivity to individual differences among Os' opinions of him

We question whether their procedure is appropriate to their purpose. Let us examine some of the unresolved ambiguities in this measure. For simplicity's sake we shall examine first the possibilities which could occur if the correlation for a given S were based on the five estimates he made for a *single* item.

The size of this within-item correlation between S's estimates and Os' ratings will depend on the dispersion in both the estimates and the ratings. Thus a perfect correlation can be obtained only if the following conditions hold true: The Os differ with respect to where they rate S on the item; and S estimates accurately the rank order of the ratings Os give him on the item. A zero correlation, on the other hand, could be obtained in various ways, among which are the following nodal possibilities: (1) Os all agree with one another in rating S (e.g., each O places S at his [the O's] mean). With no dispersion among Os' ratings, zero r must occur, regardless of what estimates S makes. Under these circumstances S may correctly perceive that Os' views of him are alike, but he would attain a zero correlation nevertheless. (2) S estimates that all Os will give him the same rating. With no dispersion among S's estimates, zero correlation must be obtained, regardless of what Os' ratings of S are like. Again S may be correct, if Os' ratings of him show no dispersion, but he would attain a zero r nevertheless. (3) S's estimates and Os' ratings have equal dispersion, but S is incorrect in estimating the rank order of Os' ratings. In this case a zero correlation would always indicate poor perception on S's part of individual differences actually present among Os' ratings.

Even if both S's estimates and Os' ratings show some dispersion on the item, and the rank order of S's estimates shows a stated, fair degree of accuracy, widely varying values of r may be obtained. The value of r in such a case will depend on the variance in S's estimates and on the variance *within* each O's ratings of all the Ss he rates. For example, if S's estimates cover a narrow range and he misestimates two O ratings, the correlation could be high and positive if each O he misestimates has a narrow dispersion among his ratings of all Ss. However, if each O he misestimates has a wide dispersion among his ratings of all Ss, the correlation will be near zero.

Thus far we have analyzed the possibilities for correlations which might be obtained using the five pairs of observations on a single item. Actually each S's score in the Bronfenbrenner study amounted to an average within-item correlation, across twelve items. It seems unlikely that zero dispersion would occur among five Os judging a given S on every one of the twelve items. Nevertheless the logic of our analysis applies, since there may well be systematic differences from S to S in the range of inter-O differences they are asked to estimate, considering all twelve items. That is, S's score is determined not only by his ability to judge individual differences in Os' judgments of him but also by the difficulty of the discrimination task with which he is presented.

Perhaps because of the measurement problems just described, Bronfenbrenner *et al.* obtained zero reliability coefficients when they correlated first-person sensitivity scores (within-item rs) based on six of the items against first-person sensitivity scores (within-item rs) based on the other six items.

In sum, under the conditions of this study, the within-item correlation is not a measure of S's sensitivity to individual differences in Os' opinions of him. The S about whom Os disagree will automatically have the greatest chance of getting a high correlation between his estimates and Os' ratings of him. Conversely, an S about whom Os agree will never be able to get a high correlation between his estimates and Os' ratings of him, even though he may be completely accurate in perceiving the degree of individual differences among Os (i.e., that there are no individual differences among Os in his case). If we were making a visual perception test to discover individual differences in Ss' abilities to discriminate brightness differences, we would consider it necessary to present all Ss with equally fine discriminations to be made. If we did not do this, we would not feel that individual differences in Ss' scores would tell us anything about individual differences in Ss' abilities to discriminate brightness differences. The same logic applies to the present study. Since Ss were undoubtedly required to make unequally difficult discriminations among Os' opinions of them, one cannot use these scores to index individual differences in Ss' abilities to differentiate among Os' opinions of them.

Discriminant Validity of Discrepancy Scores

A second source of serious troubles involves the discriminant construct validity of the two-part insight score. Let us assume for the moment that the Self and Other components of this two-part insight score have a high degree of validity as indices of S's and O's concepts concerning S. We must still demonstrate that individual differences in "insight" reflect something more than individual differences in self-reported self-regard. For example, suppose that the defensiveness of insightful Ss is compared to the defensiveness of noninsightful Ss, when insight is measured in terms of a discrepancy between S's and Os' reports about S. Suppose further that Ss' self-ratings are not equated between insightful and noninsightful groups. This would mean that differences in insight are confounded with differences in self-regard. If correlations between "insight" and defensiveness are obtained in studies having this confounding, the correlations might be parsimoniously interpreted as meaning that defensiveness is associated with level of self-regard rather than with level of insight.

2. O's Reports on S

Then there are many problems of construct validity of O's reports. O's statements of his own personal impressions of S are subject to the same pitfalls which we discussed in connection with S's self-reports on self-regard measures. (See Chapter III.) But when O presumes to say not only what he thinks of S, but to report what others think of S, the situation of course becomes more complicated. This is so because O's opinions of others' opinions of S may be biassed through insufficient knowledge, motivational distortions, etc. When O relies on tests, especially projectives, he is making many assumptions concerning the validity of these tests for inferring anything about S's actual characteristics, and/or inferring anything about S's self concept, conscious or unconscious. Some of these assumptions are poorly supported or completely unsupported.

When we try to combine S and O variables to make an insight score, we run into further pitfalls. One of these concerns the question whether lack of insight represents S's failure to try to utilize a dimension corresponding to the one used by O; and/or S's having a different view of himself on the same dimension as that used by O. For instance, in Sears's (1936) and in Calvin and Holtzman's (1953) studies, S was most probably rating himself in the private frame of reference. Therefore, if his rating did not correspond to the pooled Os' ratings, we cannot know whether (a) S could have predicted the pooled Os' ratings, but he was not trying to do so; *or* (b) S was trying to predict the pooled Os' ratings, but he was unable to do so. If the latter alternative is correct, we are then faced in some studies with the question: Is S's failure due to lack of insight concerning his social-self characteristics, or is it due to the various methodological difficulties we have just mentioned?

D. Errors of Method in Relating Insight to a Dependent Variable

In addition to the problem of confounding of self concept and insight, we must note several other frequently repeated methodological errors.

The most common error involves artifactual contamination between the independent and dependent variables, in the following manner. In one way or another, all investigators have used some measure of "adjustment" as their dependent variable, and many have used self-reports of S as their index of adjustment.[1] Now we know from many studies reported earlier in this book that evaluative self-reports tend to intercorrelate positively. We have also said immediately above that self-reports have not usually been held constant across groups which differed in insight. These facts imply that positive findings from such studies may simply be artifacts of the well-known tendency for two evaluative self-reports to correlate positively.

Another version of the same kind of artifact may be seen in studies where insight has been related to "projection," and projection has been measured partly through Ss' ratings of others. We know from a number of studies presented earlier in this book that Ss' evaluative self-ratings tend to correlate positively with the evaluative ratings which those Ss assign to others. If the groups that differ in insight also differ in self-rating, the relationship between insight and projection may simply be an artifact of the tendency for Ss' ratings of self and of others to correlate positively.

Occasionally other sources of contamination between dependent and independent variables crop up, as when the same instrument, or items from the same instrument, are involved in some way in both the independent variable and the dependent variable.

And finally, it seems to the present writer that some investigators have assigned psychological significance to findings which might have occurred by chance alone.

When we turn to an analysis of the studies in which insight is rated directly by O, we find that insight as an independent variable has apparently been confounded with other variables here, too. In Weingarten's

---

[1] See Chapter IV, Section C-9 for a discussion of problems in the measurement of adjustment.

study (1949) groups which differed in rated insight also differed in rated tension. When the data are examined with tension held constant, no consistent relation between insight and the dependent variables is present. In Reed and Cuadra's (1957) study, Os were supposed to ignore Ss' unpleasant qualities in rating Ss' insight. If O was not successful in following this direction, however, the correlation between insight and the dependent variable might amount to a correlation between two O judgments of Ss' unpleasant characteristics.

E. SUMMARY OF STUDIES RELATING INSIGHT TO A DEPENDENT VARIABLE

Since there has been so much methodological difficulty with studies of insight over a period of more than twenty years, the studies will be rather fully summarized below. In this way it is hoped that the various ways in which common problems recur will become apparent.

For purposes of discussion, the studies will be ordered according to the type of dependent variables which have been related to insight. This classification is only a rough one set up for convenience. It will be seen that all these dependent variables may plausibly be considered to be some variant of personal "adjustment" measures of S.

1. adjustment (or personality variables associated with adjustment) as inferred from:
   a. S's self-reports
   b. an external observer's diagnosis
   c. a score based on a combination of a and b
   d. S's having undergone psychotherapy
2. defensive behavior, inferred from S's responses on a nonprojective instrument or a projective technique
3. competence as a therapist
4. success in a vocation

1.a. *Adjustment Inferred from S's Self-Report*

One of the studies relating insight to a self-report measure of adjustment is that of Calvin and Holtzman (1953), who used a number of measures of insight, and the MMPI as their index of adjustment. The insight measures consisted of variously derived discrepancies between each fraternity S's self-ranking and the pooled group ranking of S on seven traits.[2] $[G-S]_c$ was "that part of the original discrepancy between self and group judgment for a particular trait and individual which remains after the spurious relationship between G and $[G-S]$ has been eliminated" by means of a correction based on the regression of $[G-S]$ on G. A positive or negative $[G-S]_c$ was considered to indicate, respectively, greater self-enhancement or greater self-depreciation than that of "the average individual with a comparable G score" (Calvin & Holtzman, 1953, p. 41).

Four basic scores were studied:

1. Algebraic Sum $[G-S]_c$ over all seven traits (a general measure of self-enhancing tendencies)
2. $[G-S]_c$ for the trait Adjustment only (a measure of self-enhancement for this trait)
3. Absolute Sum $[G-S]_c$ over all seven traits (a general measure of insight)
4. $[G-S]_c$ for the trait Adjustment only, considered without regard to sign (a measure of insight for that trait)

The first measure was found to have an estimated split-half reliability of $+.56$, but it did not correlate significantly with any MMPI scale.

The second measure (self-enhancing tendencies for the Adjustment trait only) correlated inversely with nine MMPI scales, the rs for D, Pt, and Sc scales reaching the .01 level or better $(N = $ all 79 $Ss)$. It will be noted that self-rating must have correlated positively with self-enhancing tendencies if G was ruled out.

The estimated split-half reliability of the third measure was only $+.19$, so its relation to the MMPI was not pursued.

Using the fourth measure pertaining to Adjustment only, two extreme groups of 24 High and 14 Low Insight Ss were selected. Since the sign of the discrepancy was not taken into account, both self-enhancers and self-depreciators could be included in the Low Insight group, and it is not reported what proportion of each was in the group. It was found that High Insight Ss consistently obtained more favorable T scores on the MMPI scales than did Low Insight Ss, with the differences for Hs, Pd and Mf reaching the .05 level or better. The conclusion was drawn that

---

[2]For more information on this instrument, see Table II. Four different fraternities were used, but the data were pooled by a method described in the article.

these results were "substantiating the claim which is frequently made that lack of insight is a sign of maladjustment" (Calvin & Holtzman, 1953, p. 43). In interpreting these results we need to note the likely possibility that self-rankings of the High and Low Insight groups were not held constant.[3] Although we can only speculate, it seems plausible that the average self-ranking value of the High Insight group might have been more favorable than that of the Low Insight group. For example, if the factor of stereotype accuracy is taken into account, it seems likely that Ss giving themselves moderately good self-rankings would stand the best chance of getting a low $[G-S]$, and hence a low $[G-S]_c$. If so, the mean self-ranking of the High Insight group might be moderately favorable. Also, from a purely statistical point of view, it seems plausible that there might be greater opportunity to obtain an extremely deviant $[G-S]_c$ by ranking oneself extremely low than by ranking oneself extremely high. Thus there would be more self-depreciators than self-enhancers in the Low Insight group. If this reasoning is correct, then the High Insight group would have a more favorable absolute self-ranking than the Low Insight group. Thus the findings with the MMPI could plausibly be interpreted as another instance of the correlation between two evaluative self-reports. In the absence of definite knowledge that self-ranking was equated between insight groups, we cannot feel sure that the results are attributable to the association of maladjustment with lack of insight per se.

Another study purporting to associate insight with experienced maladjustment as inferred from a self-report measure is that of Smith (1958). He defined insight in terms of summed discrepancies between S's self-ratings on 29 traits (made in the placebo condition of a drug experiment) and the corresponding ratings of S by two psychologists who had interviewed and tested S for 20 hours. (See Table II.) (The psychologists' ratings were used only if they agreed closely and each psychologist had confidence in his ratings, so an average of 18.5 traits per S actually entered into the insight score.) Insight thus measured correlated negatively at the .01 level with S's self-minus-ideal and self-minus-social discrepancies, obtained from the same 29-trait rating instrument. Unfortunately the factor of self-rating was not held constant when studying the relation of insight to experienced maladjustment. Even more important, the self-ratings

---

[3]In a personal communication dated May 30, 1959, Dr. Holtzman stated that, while he did not have the original data at hand, he believed there was some possibility that high and low Insight groups differed appreciably in self-rankings.

entered into both the independent and dependent variable scores. This means that the results are probably artifactual, and that they offer no clear support to the idea that insight and experienced maladjustment are inversely related.

Reed and Cuadra (1957) hypothesized that lack of social sensitivity would correlate with scores on Gough's Delinquency Scale (De), since the latter was based on the idea that a psychopath is unable to see himself as seen by others. Their measure of lack of social sensitivity is included in this chapter dealing with insight, because the index seems to be essentially comparable to the "insight" measures of other authors. When Reed and Cuadra compared the high and low De scorers among their female student nurse Ss, they found that the high De scorers (1) predicted less accurately which adjectives their peers would check as decriptive of them; and (2) indicated their expectancies of peer descriptions in terms of more unfavorable adjectives.[4] Despite these expectations, there were no differences in the adjectives actually used by the group to describe high and low De scorers. Since unfavorability of self-reports was not held constant across groups which varied in insight, we may say that these results indicate a tendency toward derogatory self-reports across two instruments, instead of a correlation between Delinquency scores and lack of insight.

These authors also defined insight in terms of nominations of the five most and five least insightful Ss, obtained from these same peers some months after the initial study. Insight was defined for nominators as follows: "An insightful person has the ability to recognize and understand the motives underlying her behavior and is aware of the effects of her behavior on other persons. She is alert to what other people think of her as a person. (In making judgments do not be influenced by intelligence, likeability, etc., which are not necessarily related to insight. An unpleasant person for example could still be an insightful person)" (Reed & Cuadra, 1957, p. 388).

Nominations were converted to T scores, and Ss in extreme quarters of the De distribution showed a difference in these T scores at the .02 level of significance. If the nominators were successful in avoiding the influence of likeability or unpleasantnes of Ss on their nominations, these findings offer support to the hypothesis that insight and maladjustment (as defined by self-reports) are inversely related.

---

[4] Apparently the Gough Adjective Check List was used. For this instrument see Table II, Sarbin et al.

Finally, Brownfain (1952) found that "stability of the self-concept" (his presumed index of maladjustment) did not relate significantly to either of the following indices: (1) Insight I (Group's mean rank of S minus S's most accurate estimate of group's mean rank summed absolutely over items); (2) Insight II (Group's mean rank of S minus S's private self summed absolutely over items). These measures of insight were among the dependent variables in this study, rather than being independent variables. Thus insightful and noninsightful groups equated for self-rating were not formed for comparisons of stability of self concept. For this and other reasons, we cannot make a clear interpretation of these null findings regarding the relationships of insight to stability. (For an evaluation of the stability score, see Chapter III.)

1.b. *Adjustment Inferred from an External Observer's Report*

Some studies attempt to relate insight to adjustment when the latter is indicated by an external observer's report on S.

When adjustment is measured by judgments of therapists or other persons not involved in the original insight ratings, the danger of contamination is smaller than in those studies where two of S's responses are correlated. Nevertheless, the need for holding self-rating experimentally constant across groups is still present, and for the same basic reason, i.e., so that the results cannot be interpreted as a correlation between self-rating and observer-rating of S, rather than as a relation between insight and observer ratings.

One of the earliest of these studies is that of Green (1948), who related insight into one's leadership ability with adjustment as rated by one's teachers.

In this investigation, twenty-three male students rated themselves and each other on a five-point scale of leadership ability (Table III). Rank orders were inferred by E from the rating data. Out of nine Ss nominated by their teachers as neurotic, five showed more overestimation of self than was shown by any non-neurotic S. The remaining four neurotic Ss fell at the upper end of the normal Ss' range of self-overestimation. The present writer has determined that the means of the self-ratings of the neurotic and non-neurotic Ss seem to be quite similar (3.0 as contrasted to 2.9). There appears to be very little variability in self-rating within either group. This implies an association between being considered neurotic by one's teachers and being rated low on leadership ability by one's peers. It also tends to support the contention that insight and adjustment are inversely correlated, when self-rating is held approximately constant. The author reported no tests of statistical significance, however.

Holt's (1951) study is another one in which insight is related to an external observer's report about S. Holt attempted to find some personological correlates of insight, using as Ss ten male college student volunteers who were intensively studied at the Harvard Psychological Clinic. A ten-member Diagnostic Council assigned pooled ratings to each S, using a six-point scale for each of 148 personality variables. Insight was defined as the sum of the squared discrepancies between S's self-ratings and the Council's pooled ratings for S on each of 35 "overt needs." (The 35 overt needs were among the 148 characteristics, providing an opportunity for contamination between independent and dependent variables in 35 of the correlations.) Insight scores thus derived correlated +.70 with Dr. Murray's ranking of Ss in order of their "insight into overt aspects of one's personality." When Insight scores were correlated with the 148 rated variables of personality, six of the *rhos* reached significance levels of .05. Although the author suggests interpretations of these correlations in terms of the psychological significance of insight, it seems to the present writer that they do not require any such interpretations, for two reasons: (a) Six out of 148 correlations significant at the .05 level might be expected to occur by chance alone (even if 35 of them were not possibly inflated by an artifactual common factor). (b) The factor of self-regard was not held constant when comparing Ss who differed in insight. Holt also discusses at length a correlation between Insight scores and rated Projection, which was unexpectedly positive. However, this correlation falls considerably short of the .05 level so that it, too, does not seem to demand psychological interpretation.

In an earlier section, we indicated that acceptance by one's peers might be considered to be an external criterion of "adjustment." On that assumption, some results reported by Brandt (1958) are pertinent here. Each sixth- and eleventh-grade S estimated whether each of his classmates would stand higher or lower than he on three academic and three physical tasks. "Students who were most frequently chosen on the 'friendship' and 'friendly to everybody' items of the social reputation test . . . exhibited more overrating in relation to underrating than did students who were least frequently chosen on the 'friendship' item and/or most frequently selected on the 'not friendly to everybody' item . . . ($p < .001$)" (Brandt, 1958, p. 83). Before we can conclude, however, that overrating per se is the crucial variable in this correlation, we need to know whether the self-rankings of the "accepted" students were comparable to the self-rankings of the "nonaccepted" students on all tasks.

In Arsenian's (1942) study, 125 male college Freshmen estimated their quarter standing on various entrance tests, as compared to all Freshmen entering college at that time. Fifteen students estimated their quarter standing accurately on all the tests. Thirteen students over- or underestimated their standing by one quarter on five or six tests. Arsenian compared these two groups with respect to a number of variables, including those test scores on the basis of which Ss had been classified as accurate or inaccurate in their self-estimates. Case history comparisons were also made. Arsenian (1942, p. 302) concludes, "Students who grossly over- or underestimate their abilities, knowledges, and adjustment are as a group somewhat less intelligent and less well-adjusted." His methods do not warrant such a conclusion, however, because (1) none of the obtained differences was reported as being statistically significant; (2) there was contamination between the dependent and independent variables; (3) accurate Ss were not matched with inaccurate Ss with respect to self-estimates (so "lack of insight" is confounded with level of self-regard).

In the next study to be mentioned (Daphne Bugental & Lehner, 1958), an unusual and questionable measure of accuracy of self-perception was related to external observers' reports concerning S's popularity and leadership attributes. To measure accuracy of self-perception, Ss took the Guilford-Zimmerman Temperament Survey and then rated themselves directly on the factors that the test presumes to measure. T scores for the test scores (based on the 48 Ss in all groups in the experiment) were subtracted from T scores for the direct self-ratings (also based on all 48 Ss in the experiment). This procedure seems dubious from a number of standpoints: (a) It assumes that S is implicitly defining the factors in a manner relevant to the test, when he is using the rating scale. (b) It also assumes that S knows something about the distributions of self-ratings and test scores of all the other persons in the experiment and is using these persons as a reference group when making his self-ratings. (c) Self-rating was evidently not held constant when variations in accuracy of self-perception were being explored. Their hypothesis was that persons voted "well liked" by members of a small discussion group would show greater accuracy of self-perception than would persons voted "leaders" of the group. Their obtained null findings are uninterpretable for various reasons, including those mentioned above.

1.c. *Adjustment Inferred from a Combination of S's Self-Reports and an External Observer's Diagnosis*

Norman's (1953) study is a complex one in which the dependent variables are made up of a combination of *S*'s self-reports and external observers' reports. Norman related four types of insight to several other variables. An outline of his design reveals that his results are inconclusive because one or both of the problems of artifact encountered so often in studies of insight affect each of his findings. That is, self-rating has not been held constant across *S*s who differ in insight; and in some of his correlations there is a common contaminating factor between the independent and dependent variables.

His *S*s were 72 of the students used in Kelley and Fiske's study of prediction of success in the field of clinical psychology. All scores except the sociometric index were based on 31 traits which are listed in Norman's article. (See Table II.) Each *S* rated himself and was rated by three peers, and four insight scores were derived: Insight I = sum of absolute differences between peers' ratings of *S* and *S*'s self-ratings. Insight I Overestimation = algebraic sum of differences between peers' ratings of *S* and *S*'s self-ratings. Insight II = absolute sum of differences between the assessment staff's rating of *S* and *S*'s self-ratings. Insight II Overestimation = algebraic sum of differences between the assessment staff's rating of *S* and *S*'s self-ratings.

Considering only that part of Norman's report which bears on insight as an independent variable, we find that he relates it to the following dependent variables: (a) two measures of Self-Other Identity which were, respectively, the absolute and algebraic sum of differences between self-rating and ratings *S* assigned to others; (b) two measures of Reality of Perception which were, respectively, the absolute and algebraic sum of differences between ratings *S* assigned to peers and the ratings assigned to those peers by the remaining peers (other than *S*); (c) Net Acceptance. The latter was derived from a fifteen-item sociometric questionnaire, and consisted of the sum of nominations *S* received in answer to positively toned questions minus the sum of nominations he received in answer to the negatively toned questions.

As stated above, in none of the comparisons was the factor of self-rating held constant when correlating insight with a dependent variable. Therefore, on this ground alone, none of the results would be clearly attributable to relations between insight per se and another variable. In addition, when any one of the insight measures is related to either one of the Self-Other Identity measures, the common factor of the self-rating in each measure would artifactually contaminate the findings. The Net Acceptance score seems relatively distinguishable operationally from the insight measures. However, four of the twenty-four Ss whose responses determined a given S's Net Acceptance score were the same as those used in obtaining the insight scores. Since each instrument consists of a broad variety of evaluative statements, a correlation with Net Acceptance might, to an unknown degree, be a manifestation of the consistency with which the peer group negatively evaluates S.

Tarwater's (1953) design is similar to Norman's in that the dependent variable (understanding of others) is derived from a response of S combined with a response of an Other. Tarwater tentatively equated "self-understanding" with a good Emotional Adjustment Score (or a good Total Adjustment Score) on the Bell Adjustment Inventory. The Emotional, but not the Total, score correlated significantly with success in predicting one's spouse's responses to the inventory. Since the original assumption that such a score measures "self-understanding" is not logical or convincing, and since artifactual problems common to this type of design have evidently not been considered, one cannot conclude from this study that understanding of others is a by-product of understanding the self.

1.d. *Adjustment Inferred from S's Having Undergone Psychotherapy*

If one assumes that therapy should result in improved adjustment, and that adjustment and insight are correlated, one may postulate that improvements in insight should follow therapy. Kelman and Parloff (1957) studied changes in "self-awareness" associated with group therapy. To index self-awareness they used (1) correlations between S's self-sort and a sort made about S by a trained observer who had seen S in and out of the therapy group, but had not participated in the therapy (see Table I), and (2) accuracy of S's prediction of sociometric ratings he would receive from other patients on three variables (respect, regard as leader, desire as friend). Neither measure of self-awareness showed significant changes over therapy, although certain other measures did show significant change (which suggested that the self-awareness measures might have been expected to show change). The findings from this study cannot be clearly interpreted, however, because (1) insufficient information is available concerning the instruments; (2) two of three significant changes which were found may have been artifactual because the "before" and "after" ratings were both obtained after therapy; and (3) no control group was used.

2. *Adjustment Inferred from Defensive Behavior*

Another group of studies relates insight to adjustment when the latter is measured in terms of defensive behavior, usually "projection." Projection is most commonly defined operationally as attribution of traits to others. In one study S was said to "project" only if he consistently attributed more of an unfavorable trait to others than the group as a whole attributed to these same others (Wylie, 1957). In another study, however, the ratings Ss assigned to others were simply compared across insightful and noninsightful groups, without an attempt to see if S's ratings of others deviated from the pooled value for those others (Sears, 1936). As we have already pointed out, we know from many studies that there is a positive correlation between the ratings Ss give themselves and the ratings they give to others. Therefore, in forming insightful and noninsightful groups, one should be careful to hold the self-rating part of the insight measure constant across groups. Otherwise the relationship between the independent and dependent variables may parsimoniously be attributed to a correlation between self-ratings and ratings assigned by the self to others, rather than being due to an association between "insight" and "projection."

Sears did not hold self-ratings constant when making his comparisons between insightful and noninsightful groups. However, it is possible, using his published data, to compare groups in which self-rating is apparently at least approximately equated between groups, while insight varies. Thus Groups A and D both rate themselves favorably, but A lacks insight. Groups B and C both rate themselves unfavorably, but C lacks insight. In A *vs.* D comparisons, results for only two out of four traits show the noninsightful Group A members assigning more unfavorable ratings to others than do the insightful Group D members. In B *vs.* C comparisons also, results for only two out of four traits show noninsightful Group C members assigning more unfavorable ratings to others than do insightful Group B members. Thus when self-rating is held approximately constant, Sears's data do *not* support the contention that "projection" is associated with lack of insight.

His puzzling, partly positive findings appear to have been artifactual in the following way: To test his hypothesis, Sears held group rating constant and varied insight by varying self rating. When noninsightful Group A (self-rating good, rating from group bad) was compared to insightful Group B (self-rating bad, rating from group bad), he found Group A members rating others more unfavorably than did Group B members. This was artifactual because, in order to get into Group A in the first place, S had to place himself in the top half of the distribution (thus assigning poorer ratings than his own to at least half of the Ss he rated). Also, in order to get into Group B, S had to rate himself in the bottom half of the distribution (thus assigning better ratings than his own to at least half of the Ss he rated). When Sears compared noninsightful Group C (self-rating bad, rating from group good) with insightful Group D (self-rating good, rating from group good), he naturally obtained the puzzling finding that the *insightful* group attributed more *un*favorable ratings to others. These findings are artifactual for the reasons just outlined. (See Table II.)

Rokeach (1945) studied the relation of "insight" and "projection," utilizing college women's self- and group-ratings of beauty, made on a ten-point graphic rating scale (see Table III). Recognizing some of the difficulties with Sears's method, he attempted to devise a more refined insight score. First he determined how much S's self-rating (B_{sr}) deviated from the average of the ratings S gave to her peers (B_{ar}). This difference was subtracted from the deviation between the average beauty rating S received from the group (B_s) and the grand mean for all Ss (which was 6.07). "Projection" was measured in terms of the average rating S assigned *to* others (B_{ar}). Thus it can be seen that B_{ar} entered into S's classification on the independent variable (insight), *and* into her projection score (the dependent variable).

Rokeach formed two main groups, according to the group ratings Ss received: Beautiful and Homely. Within each of these, using the method described above, he formed four subgroups: those who slightly, and those who markedly over- and underestimated themselves. Although he obtained no statistically significant findings, he did obtain some regular trends within the Beautiful group. Even if these trends had been significant, they would apparently have been artifactual, if the following reasoning is correct:

Considering first the Beautiful group, we may infer that group ratings were held approximately constant across the four subgroups, while "insight" most probably was varied mainly in terms of varying Ss' self-ratings. That is, in the following formula, which expresses the design of the experiment, (B_s) was apparently approximately constant across all Beautiful subgroups which varied in insight, and of course 6.07 was always constant across such subgroups.

"Insight"	was related to	"Projection"
$(B_s - 6.07) - (B_{sr} - B_{ar})$	was related to	B_{ar}

The major burden of the relationship would then reduce to

$(B_{sr} - B_{ar})$	related to	B_{ar}

Whatever findings one might obtain would be most parsimoniously interpreted in one or both of the following ways: (1) covariation of the two scores due to the common variable, B_{ar}; or (2) covariation between B_{sr} and B_{ar}. It would not be parsimonious to attribute variations in "projection" to variability in "insight" until it could be shown that neither of the above two possibilities would account for the findings.

An exactly parallel argument could be made for the case of the four subgroups within the Homely group.

When Wylie (1957) matched self-ratings very closely across experimental groups, and varied insight by varying group ratings, she could find no consistent evidence that defensiveness was associated with "lack of insight." Defensiveness was measured in two ways: (1) consistent underestimation of others on a rating scale; (2) by a specially devised Rationalization-Projection Inventory pertaining to the traits being rated. The Rationalization-Projection Inventory had fairly good split-half reliability, and both it and underestimation of others did relate to absolute self-rating values and to certainty about self-ratings in a manner predicted by phenomenal theory. This implies that the null results with the insight variable were probably not due simply to errors of measurement. (See Table II.)

Torrance (1954a, 1954b) studied the relationship of rationalization to accuracy of estimate of one's performance on academic tests. Before and after taking the ACE Psychological Examination, the Cooperative English Test, and the Cooperative Reading Achievement Test, 1,215 Freshmen who were just entering college estimated their standing, in relation to their classmates, on each of eight subscores. On both occasions they also listed factors which might have adversely affected their performance but not the performance of their fellow students. All such factors were assumed to be rationalizations (a somewhat questionable assumption, it seems to the present author). Only the rationalizations offered at posttest were considered in analyzing the data. A discrepancy was considered only if it was at least one quarter (25 centile points), and such discrepancies were summed across eight subscores. Torrance established two classes of over- and underevaluators; and a class of accurate evaluators.

It was found that women who rationalized fell more often, at pretest, in the extreme overevaluating group than did women in general (significant at the .02 level). A similar trend in posttest evaluation was insignificant. At posttest, however, rationalizing women fell less frequently in the accurate class of self-evaluators than did women in general. Similar trends for the men were insignificant.

Unfortunately these results and others reported for the particular categories of rationalization cannot be interpreted unequivocally, because the actual scores of the accurate Ss and overestimating Ss were not held constant. For statistical reasons, it seems that the actual scores of overestimators must have been lower than those of the accurate Ss or of the group in general. For example, 95% of Ss placed their scholastic ability in the upper half at pretest; so accurate Ss must have made fairly good scores. If this is so, the findings may be attributable to an association between limited ability and the tendency to rationalize rather than to a relationship between lack of insight into one's ability and the tendency to rationalize.

Murstein's study (1956) enables us to compare the degree of "projection of hostility" shown by Ss who differ in insight but have approximately the same self concepts (self-ranking scores on hostility). (See Table III.) He measured projection in two ways: (1) by means of a Rorschach hostility score based on content; (2) in terms of the favorability of S's rating of an examiner's interview behavior under two conditions: (a) the examiner gave S a favorable report on S's Rorschach, saying, among other things, that it indicated that S was warm and friendly;

(b) the examiner gave S an unfavorable report on S's Rorschach, saying, among other things, that it indicated that S was cold and hostile.

Four extreme groups of 20 Ss each were used, these being drawn from a pool of 536 Ss from 25 living groups who had ranked one another within their respective living groups with respect to friendliness (hostility). The numbers in parentheses in the following table are the approximate standard deviation values of the self-ranking scores from the mean of the normalized, pooled self-rankings.[5]

Group Number	Group Ranking of S	Self-ranking of S	Insightful?
1	Friendly	Friendly ($+4.2$)	Yes
2	Friendly	Hostile (-6.1)	No
3	Hostile	Hostile (-4.6)	Yes
4	Hostile	Friendly ($+2.6$)	No

By looking at Groups 1 and 4 we can compare Ss who vary in insight but whose self-rankings are nearly equal at a "friendly" point. Murstein found that Group 4 (noninsightful) showed a nonsignificant trend toward higher Rorschach hostility scores. It may be noted, however, that Group 4 has a somewhat less friendly self-ranking as well as being uninsightful, so the trend, if significant, could be associated with either self-ranking value or degree of insight.

By looking at Groups 2 and 3 we can compare Ss who vary in insight but whose self-rankings are nearly equal at a "hostile" point. Group 3 (insightful) showed significantly more hostile Rorschach scores. This cannot be attributed to their having more hostile self-ranking, however, because it is the Group 2 Ss who have a somewhat more hostile self-ranking. One could say that Ss who are noninsightful about their own *friendliness* were projecting more *friendliness*. In any case, as the author points out, classical projection theory would have to be modified in order to conceptualize these findings.

When each of the four groups was divided into halves, which were matched on Group and Self rank, and one half received a "hostile" interpretation of their Rorschach record while the other received a "friendly" interpretation, the following findings were obtained: (1) No main effect was found between either self-ranking or group ranking and derogation

---

[5]These figures were obtained from the unpublished dissertation on which the published article was based.

of the examiner's interview behavior. (2) Regardless of group- or self-rankings, there was significantly greater derogation of the examiner when he was hostile in interpreting S's Rorschach record. (3) A significant interaction effect occurred, thus: greatest derogation of the examiner was found among those who considered themselves friendly (whether or not insightful) and received a hostile interpretation of their Rorschachs.

The results seem to offer no support to the idea that lack of insight per se is associated with projection of hostility, when self-rankings of hostility are held approximately constant and projection is measured either by a Rorschach score or by the S's devaluation of a threatening person. The self-ranking, regardless of its insightfulness, was significantly associated with devaluation of a threatening person.

Chodorkoff (1954a) measured insight in terms of the correlation between a Q sort made by S to describe himself and a Q sort made jointly by several observers to describe S as seen through his TAT, Rorschach, word association test, and biographical inventory. (See Table I.) He stated three hypotheses which we may paraphrase as follows: (1) Insight is negatively correlated with perceptual defense. (2) Insight is negatively correlated with adjustment ratings. (3) Adjustment ratings and perceptual defense are negatively correlated.

To measure perceptual defense, he compared means and sigmas of visual recognition thresholds for ten "threatening" and ten "neutral" words. The threatening and neutral words had previously been chosen for each S in terms of his reaction times to fifty threatening and fifty neutral words used in the word association test. To measure adjustment he used two criteria: (a) number of checks on the Munroe check list based on Rorschach protocols; (b) rated adjustment on eleven subscales based on Maslow and Mittelman's text.

Although all of his hypotheses were supported, a number of uncontrolled features of the design make it seem likely that the results are artifactual and do not warrant the psychological interpretation given them. Both of the adjustment indices were derived from the sources also used as a basis for the judges' Q-sort opinions which were used to measure "insight." This could lead to contamination between the independent variable, insight, and the dependent variable, adjustment, in the test of the second hypothesis. (The author himself pointed out this weakness.) In addition, we do not know whether the level of self-regard was held constant across groups which differed in insight. Therefore we cannot know to what extent the adustment measures (or the perceptual defense measures) may be a function of variations in self-regard rather than of variations in insight. This throws doubt on the interpretation of the findings pertinent to Hypotheses 1 and 2.

It is interesting to note that in the group as a whole there was no difference in visual recognition threshold for threatening and neutral words. There was, however, a highly significant inter-S correlation between perceptual defense and rated adjustment. This supported Hypothesis 3. However, perceptual defense was measured with words drawn from the word association test, which in its turn was used as one of the bases for rating adjustment. Therefore, there is a source of contamination between these two variables which may account artifactually for the correlation supporting Hypothesis 3.

Finally, the correlation between perceptual defense and insight, which allegedly supports Hypothesis 1, may possibly be a function of the common basis (word association test) involved in both the insight measure and perceptual defense measure.

Weingarten specifically eschews a "classical projection" interpretation of her dependent variable measure. However, her study seems most nearly to fall into this category, so it will be discussed here.

Although most investigators have used a discrepancy score as a measure of insight, Weingarten (1949) had Ss' insightfulness rated directly from anonymous autobiographies. She says (p. 378), "A person's capacity to understand the dynamics of his behavior patterns and emotional reactions and the extent to which he represses, falsely emphasizes or misunderstands his own motivations can be estimated from the psychological congruence of the various aspects of the total picture he presents. Such ratings of insight . . . " were made on a seven-point scale. In addition, Ss' autobiographies were rated for self, family, and social tensions. In the belief that they were cooperating in a research project on scoring techniques, Ss later "scored" the answers supposedly given by someone to an Intuition Questionnaire. Ss' degrees of self, family, and social tension, as judged from their autobiographies, were correlated respectively with the degrees of self, family, and social tensions which Ss attributed to the alleged respondent on the Intuition Questionnaire. All rs were low positive, and two of them reached the .05 level.

Of chief relevance to our discussion of insight is Weingarten's statement that insightful Ss were less apt to be influenced by their own emotional problems in making clinical evaluations of others than were the noninsightful *S*s. However, the present author notes that when *S*s' own rated tension is held constant, by comparing high and low insight groups having the same tension level, four of the six possible comparisons go against Weingarten's hypothesis. It seems, then, that Weingarten's conclusions must have been based on comparisons which were contaminated by the tension variable.

3. *Adjustment Inferred from Psychotherapeutic Competence*

The next two studies are based on the assumption that insight into self should be positively related to psychotherapeutic competence.

Kates and Jordan (1955) related insight to the degree of psychotherapeutic promise shown by clinical psychology students.[6] To do this, they obtained from fourteen such students (1) a fifty-word free self-description; (2) fifty-word free descriptions of each other *S*. These were pooled by the authors into a composite "social stimulus self" description for each *S*. They were also coded for mentions of specific classes of traits. (3) Rankings of therapeutic promise of each other *S*, which were pooled for each *S*. Ten judges blindly matched the self-descriptions and the social-stimulus-self-descriptions, with accuracy significant at the .01 level. This showed that some degree of insight occurred in the self-descriptions of the *S*s.

Contrary to what many theorists might predict, however, the authors found an inverse relationship (—.62) between rated psychotherapeutic promise and insight (frequency with which the *S*s' self-descriptions and social-stimulus-self-descriptions could be accurately matched). To interpret this finding we must note that rated psychotherapeutic promise correlated positively with a number of favorable social-stimulus-self traits (likeability, maturity, empathy), and negatively with an unfavorable social-stimulus trait (lack of self-confidence). Thus it appears that at least part of the negative relation between insight and psychotherapeutic promise is attributable to the fact that *S*s manifesting obvious behavioral inadequacies tended to mention these in their self-descriptions, thus making their self-descriptions more unique and easier to match with social-stimu-

---

[6]The label "insight" has been attached by the present author to Kates and Jordan's discrepancy measure.

lus-self-descriptions. In other words level of self-regard was not constant among Ss varying in insight.

The interpretation of the findings for the more adequate Ss seems not to be so clear. There are at least two alternatives: (1) Ss with adequate characteristics are not so uniquely distinguishable from one another. If this is so, accuracy of matching self-descriptions and social-stimulus-self-descriptions is not a valid indicator of degree of insight. (2) As Kates and Jordan suggest, mature Ss will not be greatly preoccupied with their obvious adequacies, but will tend to be concerned with and mention their less obvious and less mature characteristics. The published findings do not enable us to choose between these alternatives. In any case, no simple relationship seems to hold between insight, as measured here, and psychotherapeutic promise.

Bandura (1956) hypothesized that insight into one's anxiety concerning one's sex, hostility, and dependency needs would be associated with psychotherapeutic competence as rated by supervisors. Forty-two psychotherapists in four settings ranked themselves and varying numbers of peers as to degree of anxiety concerning each of the three needs. Insight was defined in a "one-sided" way, thus: (1) An insightful S was one whose self rank on anxiety equalled or exceeded the pooled rank he received from the group. (2) An uninsightful S was one whose self rank on anxiety was lower than the pooled rank he received from the group. For all three needs, significant associations were found between pooled group rankings of Ss' anxiety levels, and Ss' rated psychotherapeutic competence. Ss' self-rankings for anxiety did *not* significantly relate to therapeutic competence, however. It is not surprising, then, that when group rankings are partialled out, *r*s between insight and therapeutic competence are insignificant, since one would be essentially retesting the association of self-rankings and competence. In view of the association of group rankings with competence, it seems possible that, with self-ranking held constant by matching two groups at a low (nonanxious) self rank, insight and competence would be found to be related in the manner predicted by the hypothesis.

4. *Adjustment Inferred from Vocational Success*

In the final study to be summarized, vocational "adjustment" is the dependent variable.

Klein (1948) asked aviation cadets to give pre- and postperformance estimates of their achievement on six psychomotor tasks (Table III). He gave instructions intended to ego-involve Ss in making accurate estimates. When standard scores on the psychomotor tasks were held constant by means of partial biserial rs, there was a very slight trend for cadets who overestimated their task performance to fail in flying training more often than would be expected for that standard score. The reverse trend occurred for those who underestimated their performance. All twelve partial biserial correlations were negative, and it appears to the present author that about two of them reached the .05 level of significance. If we assume a statistically significant finding, the data are still insufficient to clarify the dynamic underlying trends, as the author points out. For one thing, it seems to the present writer that the method of gathering Ss' estimates, and of determining over- or underestimation, does not permit one to know whether Ss' inaccuracies are of the stereotype or individual variety. That is, on the ten-point descriptive self-rating scale which Ss used, a self-overestimation may indicate optimism about oneself, the group, or both. This is so because S evidently did not indicate whether he thought the group average performance would fall in the middle of the scale, nor did he express his own performance in relation to such a perceived norm for his group.

F. Conclusions Concerning the Relationship of Insight to Adjustment

We have noted that insight is usually measured in terms of a discrepancy between O's and S's reports about S, and that such insight scores have been related to various measures of "adjustment," including defensive behaviors. It has been amply demonstrated by studies cited in Chapter III that phenomenal self-regard (self-ratings) correlates with many of these measures of adjustment. Therefore, any study which does not hold self-ratings constant when attempting to measure insight leads to ambiguous, probably artifactual, findings. Most studies have been uncontrolled in this and other respects.

Specifically, in nineteen of the studies which we have just discussed, insightful Ss are compared to noninsightful Ss, when insight is measured in terms of a discrepancy between Self and Other reports about S. In at least sixteen of these studies, the self-ratings of the insightful groups are different from the self-ratings of the noninsightful groups. Thus, differences in insight are confounded with differences in self-regard in these sixteen studies. In fifteen of the sixteen studies where such confounding occurs, "insight" is reported to be related to "adjustment." In one of the fifteen investigations, self-regard was shown to be uncorrelated with the dependent variable. We might parsimoniously interpret the remaining fourteen by saying that the dependent variable was a function of self-regard, since self-regard was not held constant across groups differing in insight. On the other hand, there are three studies in which the authors held self-regard constant across groups which differed in insight, or they presented their data in such a way that the present writer could make comparisons across groups which had comparable levels of self-regard. Of these three studies, only one gave a possibly significant association between insight and a dependent variable. In short, there is no clear evidence that insight is significantly associated with adjustment or defensive behaviors. However, even the three relatively well controlled studies do not cover a wide enough range of behavior characteristics and do not use sufficiently precise instruments, to warrant our acceptance of the null hypothesis at this time.

It is clear that research on insight has not gotten us very far, due to methodological errors. What implications can now be drawn concerning the possibilities of ever doing fruitful research on the role of insight in behavior?[7] Certainly many of the more gross sources of artifact can be avoided if a properly detailed and explicit analysis is made of the procedures used to define independent and dependent variables. But can positive suggestions be made for a systematic development of such studies? And is even such a positive program inherently limited in the light it can throw on the dynamic postulates of personality theorists concerning insight?

It seems to the present writer that researchers need first to study separately the self components of the two-part insight measure. That is, they should establish more organized and complete knowledge of the construct validity of their self-measures as indices of phenomenal self-regard. They should also establish the empirical relationships of the self-concept measures to theoretically relevant dependent variables. It will no doubt be found that self-concept measures do not suffice to make as reliable pre-

---

[7]One could also consider the role of antecedent factors in the development of insight, but since the researches analyzed have not been primarily concerned with that, it will not be gone into here.

dictions of behavior as one would like to make, and they will need to be supplemented by "objective measures."

Among these objective measures may be O's opinions of S, based on a variety of sources. With valid self-concept measures held constant, one can see whether objective measures, including O's reports, increase the accuracy of prediction of various dependent behavior variables. That is, one could see whether multiple rs which include objective measures of S's characteristics are higher than those obtained between self-concept measures and dependent behavior variables alone.

Insight studies may be viewed as only a special case of this type of multiple r exploration. That is, one could compute a multiple r by adding any number of objective measures to the correlation between self-concept and behavior. However, only one sort of objective measure would be pertinent to studies of insight. This objective measure must purport to index the same dimension(s) as S's report.

Let us suppose we have an objective measure which indexes the same dimension as S's report. Let us suppose further that its addition to the correlation increases the accuracy of our prediction of S's behavior. Under suitable conditions, the difference between S's and O's reports may then be said to index S's insightfulness, and S's behavior may be said to be a function of "insight." (The suitable conditions must include a satisfactory handling of scaling problems.)

Even if these proposed studies warrant the conclusion that S's behavior is a function of "insight," they still would not warrant the dynamic interpretation which investigators interested in insight studies wish to assign. That is, further converging operations would be necessary before one could say that the predictive discrepancy between S's self-report and the objective index involves repression or active avoidance of perception on S's part.

G. Descriptive Facts about the Occurrence of Insight

In addition to the central issues about the relation of insight to adjustment, the studies under review here permit us to answer partially some descriptive questions about the occurrence of insight itself, and the variables of which it may be a function.

1. *In general, how closely do S's self-reports coincide with reports of others, and with objective data?*

Such correlation coefficients are generally low, although they may reach satisfactory significance levels. For example, on 22 characteristics from her Child Personality Scale, Amatora (1956) found rs ranging from +.10 to +.67. Fourteen of 22 rs were significant at the .01 level for 200 boys; 17 out of 22 rs were significant at the .01 level for 200 girls (Table II).

Webb (1952) found correlations ranging from +.22 for "security" to +.60 for intelligence between self-ratings and mean group ratings on five traits, made by fraternity Ss (Table II).

Goldings (1954) found generally positive *rhos* between twenty Ss' "avowed happiness" scores and independent judgments of Ss' happiness made by five judges. Only two of the five *rhos* were significant, however (Table III).

Powell (1948) found little relation between Bernreuter scores (assumed to index self-perceived adjustment) and adjustment scores based on dormitory counselors' ratings of Ss, or on peers' descriptions of S on a "Guess Who" test. However, since Ss were using a different instrument than were their raters, these negative findings cannot reveal Ss' degree of insightfulness into self.

In Beilin's (1957) investigation also, self-perceived adjustment and externally judged adjustment were apparently measured on different instruments. (Beilin was not aiming to measure "insight," but his research may be viewed as relevant to the present discussion.) In contrast to Powell's null findings, Beilin obtained significant correlations between externally judged adjustment and self-reports of adjustment obtained from an unspecified number of boys who were between the ages of nine and eighteen at the beginning of the study. A composite Pupil Index of "personal" and "social" adjustment was computed by averaging standard scores from inventory, sentence completion, rating scale, and nominating-type instruments by which pupils described themselves. The Teacher Index was another composite "personal" and "social" adjustment score, based on a nomination form, a Thurstone-type rating scale of responsible behaviors, and a scale of psychoneurotic items. The Pupil Index of self-perceived adjustment correlated +.47 ($p =.01$) with the Teacher Index of the pupils' adjustment.

Four years later, Ss' current self-ratings pertinent to "individual adjustment," and Ss' self-reports on a "morale scale" of Rundquist and Sletto, were correlated with three external criteria of adjustment: a com-

munity reputation criterion of how well Ss were "getting along," an interviewer's "global estimate" of the interviewee's "adjustment," and the
interviewer's rating of the interviewee's "adjustment." (The two interviewer criteria of Ss' adjustment were essentially similar, correlating
+.91. The interviewers' ratings correlated only +.31 [$p = .01$] with
the community reputation score, however.) The Ss' self-ratings did not
correlate significantly with the community reputation scores, but they
correlated +.51 with the interviewer's rating of adjustment, and +.49
with the interviewer's global estimate of adjustment. The correlations between Ss' self-reports on the morale scale and the three external criteria
of adjustment were all significant at the .05 level or better. We must
remember, however, that the interviewers' measures were based on Ss'
interview behavior, including his reports about himself given in the interview. Therefore correlations between the interviewers' ratings of adjustment and Ss' self-reported adjustment may be inflated because they are
based partly on two self-reports made by S.

Miyomoto and Dornbusch (1956) report an apparently significant
relation between Ss' self-ratings and others' ratings of S on four traits:
intelligence, self-confidence, physical attractiveness, likeableness. They also
found, however, that self-ratings tended to be closer to S's perception of
how others would rate him than to others' actual ratings of him. Ss were
college students, in fraternities and sororities. No significance tests are
given (Table II).

Rubenstein and Lorr (1957) found higher self-peer correlations than
did the investigators just mentioned, but stereotypy may partially account
for this. In their study, each of 67 psychotherapists from three disciplines
rated himself and was rated by two psychotherapist peers who were well
acquainted with him. (Sometimes a rater described more than one col-
league, and sometimes the rated S acted as rater for another S.) Twenty-
five items were used in their data analysis. These items covered six out
of ten factors previously isolated from their Multidimensional Scale for
Rating Psychiatric Patients (Table II). For each person, across 25 items,
self-ratings were correlated against the average of two peer ratings. Fifty-
five out of 67 correlations ranged from +.53 to +.87 ($\sigma = .204$ if
$r = 0$). Therapist ratings tended to be more homogeneous than patient
ratings had been shown earlier to be, which would tend to hold down
the present correlations. Conversely stereotypy could inflate such correlations. A sample of 15 intercorrelations of therapists' self-ratings ranged

from $+.25$ to $+.68$, with an average z of $+.48$, showing that stereotypy of self-ratings must have entered into the relatively high self-peer correlations.

In a report on Steier's unpublished work with four groups of fifth- and eighth-grade children, Russell (1953) gives self-peer correlations ranging from $+.22$ through $+.49$ on social adjustment and from $+.45$ through $+.55$ on self adjustment. Self-teacher correlations ran from $+.28$ through $+.65$, considering both kinds of adjustment. The rating scales were adapted from the California Test of Personality. Self-standard-test correlations on academic achievement ran from $+.35$ through $+.54$, while self-teacher correlations on academic achievement ran from $+.36$ through $+.61$.

Using Naval Aviation Cadets, Webb (1955) obtained a correlation of $+.43$ between self-ratings on intelligence and the group's ratings of Ss' intelligence; and a correlation of $+.21$ between self-ratings on intelligence and Otis scores. The eleven-week test-retest self-ratings were very un-reliable ($r = +.19$). Thus, unreliability may have lowered the above correlations. Just why the self-ratings were so unreliable cannot be defi-nitely determined from the published information on procedures and data. Webb suggests that it is associated with the "shortness" or "single item" characteristic of the self-rating; and in a later article (1956) he proposes a procedure for obtaining more reliable self-ratings.

With the exception of one investigation, none of the studies mentioned thus far required S to guess where others would rate him. That this might be a factor in lowering the obtained correlations is suggested by the find-ings of Flyer, Barron, and Bigbee (1953). They obtained self-ratings from air officer candidates on six traits, in answer to two questions: "How do you see yourself?" and "How do others see you?" On all six traits, ratings which Ss received from their living-group members correlated higher with their self-ratings in answer to the question "How do others see you?" One wonders if the correlations would have been even higher had S been in-structed to guess how these particular others (i.e., the members of his current living-group) would rate him. (See Table II.)

On the other hand, Wylie's (1957) findings seem not to be in line with such a speculation. Her basic airman Ss were specifically instructed to guess how their living-group members would rate them, yet she obtained only one significant r (for Intelligence) out of five traits (Table II).

Differences between the two studies in traits, scales, and Ss make direct comparisons impossible, however.

Torrance (1954, p. 212), using eight subscores from academic aptitude and achievement tests, reports "little relationship between self-estimate and achieved standings among 1215 entering college Freshmen." The correlations ranged from +.11 to +.35 for pretest evaluations; and from +.22 to +.41 for posttest evaluations.[8]

In Arsenian's (1942) study, 125 male college Freshmen estimated their quarter standing on various entrance tests as compared to all Freshmen entering college at that time. Estimates made before testing yielded corrected contingency coefficients with actually obtained quarter placements ranging from +.30 for the ACE Psychological Examination to +.57 for the Cooperative English Vocabulary.

Israel, using female student nurses in Stockholm, discovered that "the number of Ss who were more accurate than chance in their self-evaluations and in their subjective estimates of their evaluation by the group is so small for all four abilities that the null hypothesis has to be accepted" (Israel, 1958, p. 37). However, considering trends for the group as a whole, those who evaluated themselves high and/or made high subjective estimates of the group's ranking of themselves received higher ranking from the group on Intelligence and Leadership. Differences were nonsignificant for Orderliness and Appearance (Table II).

Interpretations of low correlation coefficients are ambiguous, because we cannot know to what extent S's inaccuracies are of the stereotype or of the individual variety. That is, in order to get high correlations across Ss between Ss' self-ratings and the ratings Ss receive from others, each S must be able to estimate two sorts of things: (1) the elevation and dispersion among Os' ratings of all Ss; (2) the particular rating he will receive from the Os. Consequently no firm conclusions can be drawn from the available data as to the extent of idiosyncratic inaccuracy in self-ratings among persons in general, or among persons from any specified population.

2. *Is there any systematic tendency for Ss to overestimate or underestimate when rating or ranking themselves? Is the degree and/or direction of inaccuracy a function of characteristics of the Ss?*

---

[8]These coefficients were obtained from the unpublished dissertation upon which the published article is based.

It seems that the tendency is to overestimate one's standing on socially desirable characteristics.

Green (1948) found that 20 out of 23 young male students and 16 out of 23 young female students overestimated their standing on leadership ability, as rated by their respective peer groups. The ranges of over- and underestimation differed considerably between sex groups, but statistical significance tests were not reported; nor were they warranted in view of differences between the groups other than sex. (See Table III.)

Brandt (1958) asked each sixth-grade S to tell whether each other child in his classroom would fall above or below him on arithmetic, vocabulary, and spelling tests; and on three physical tasks. The boys were more accurate than the girls when over-all accuracy scores were considered. When all those "wrong" ratings which *were* made were analyzed, errors in the overrating direction were 52% more prevalent than underrating errors. Differences were significant for each task and each group, taken separately. This tendency was significantly greater among boys: "Over ratings were approximately twice as prevalent as under-ratings among boys, but only 25% more prevalent among girls" (Brandt, 1958, p. 82).

In Froehlich and Moser's study (1954), ninth-grade pupils drew their own percentile rank profiles on eight subtests of the Differential Aptitude Test, and approximately fifteen months later redrew the profiles from memory. Correlations between remembered and obtained percentiles ranged from +.41 to +.57. On seven subtests the median of remembered percentiles exceeded the median of obtained percentiles. No significance tests were given, however. Although both high- and low-standing pupils tended to remember their percentiles as less extreme than they had actually obtained, the net effect in the group was toward remembering one's standing more favorably than it was. On seven subtests, the proportion of students in the upper 30% who remembered their percentiles as being in the upper 30% exceeded the proportion of students in the lower 30% who remembered their percentiles as being in the lower 30%. No significance tests were given for this comparison, either.

In the study of Kansas State Freshmen, mentioned above, overestimation was evidently quite marked. For example, 95% of all Ss placed themselves in the upper half in academic ability, and among those who actually achieved the bottom quarter, 62% estimated that they would stand in the top fourth. Torrance (1954a, p. 212) reports that "women underevaluate themselves more frequently." However, no exact data are given to support this statement.

Wylie (1957), in the study referred to above, found significantly more overestimation than underestimation of self on four out of five traits. (These particular findings are not published in the article referred to.)

In Goldings's study (1954), two different groups of Ss were asked to rate their own happiness, as compared to that of their friends and associates, on linear rating scales. In both groups the numerical average of self-ratings for happiness was significantly higher (happier) than the numerical value of the "average referent" point of the scale. On the assumption that the groups tested were not in fact above the average of their friends and associates, these results may possibly be interpreted as another example of self-overestimation of a socially desired characteristic. (See Table III.)

In Arsenian's (1942) study, mentioned above, 266 self-estimated quarter-standings deviated one quarter or more from actually attained quarter-standings. Sixty-two percent of these were overestimates, 38% were underestimates. No significance tests are given for this difference, however.

Russell (1953) summarizes briefly several early or unpublished studies in which children were found to overestimate their standing on a variety of achievement and personality characteristics. In four of these, girls overestimated their standing more than did boys, or rated themselves higher than did the boys.

The only study not in agreement with those listed above is that of Israel (1958). He found that female student nurses in Stockholm tended to underevaluate themselves significantly on leadership, orderliness, intelligence, and appearance when rank-ordering themselves among the peers in their living-group. (See Table III.)

It seems safe to conclude that self-overestimating trends are more frequent. Studies published since 1948 seem to indicate a somewhat greater tendency toward overestimation among male Ss, while the trend in Russell's report of earlier or unpublished studies was toward overestimation among females more than among males. In any event, since the sex groups studied are not known to be comparable with respect to possibly relevant variables, one cannot draw any firm conclusion about sex differences at this time.

One might presume that other subject variables are associated with accuracy of self-rating or self-ranking. For example, is overestimation more common among Ss who are in fact low on a trait? Purely in terms of rating scale or ranking possibilities, this would be statistically probable; and, for example, Calvin and Holtzman (1953) found that mean group rankings correlated with [Group—Self] discrepancies. However, before we assign psychodynamic significance to such trends, we need further evidence, based on studies in which statistical opportunities for overestimating (or underestimating) the self are held constant between actually "good" and "bad" Ss. (Calvin and Holtzman did not in fact attempt to assign psychological significance to this correlation.)

Similarly, although one might imagine that accuracy of estimation in a number of self-characteristics is a function of S's intelligence, we would have to guard against artifacts in research purporting to find this. Let us suppose that there is a correlation among various traits actually possessed by persons, e.g., leadership, intelligence, and poise; and that there is a general tendency for Ss to rate themselves favorably on a number of traits. Those who are in fact intelligent will then stand a greater chance of being accurate on all three ratings, even if they were made under a nondiscriminatory self-favorable response set. On the other hand, actually unintelligent Ss would be inaccurate on all traits while operating under the same nondiscriminatory favorable response set.

The data from one experiment suggest that ego-involvement of S may be a factor in self-overestimation, but certain methodological difficulties do not permit a firm conclusion (Gerard, 1958). In this study, Ss who presumably felt involved in a discussion because their performance allegedly would affect their course grade tended to rank their own knowledge, skill in explanation, and amount of contribution more favorably than did Ss who discussed the same topics without having received such ego-involving instructions. The ego-involved Ss tended to rank themselves higher on the three variables than did uninvolved Ss, but no significance ratios are given for this comparison. Involved Ss ranked themselves higher than others ranked them, and overestimated the rank others would give them, whereas uninvolved Ss did not show these effects. However, there are certain difficulties of interpretation associated with E's having assigned different roles to different group members. Also, the use of a score comparing self- and other-ranks necessarily exaggerates the trend in an artifactual manner, since the two parts of this dual index are necessarily tied together. For these reasons, no firm conclusions seem to be warranted by these data. The studies summarized in Section E of this chapter are also pertinent to this question.

3. *Is accuracy of self-estimate a function of the variables being estimated?*

The answer appears to be "Yes," although we cannot be sure why this is so. Those traits on which *S* would have most objective evidence, on a basis permitting him to compare himself uniformly to others, are usually among the most accurately estimated (e.g., characteristics such as intelligence and leadership). The studies of Amatora (1956), Green (1948), Israel (1958), Wylie (1957), and Webb (1952) support this idea.

It is plausible that a combination of lack of comparable standards of objective evidence and intensity of desire to be considered high on socially or personally desirable traits may enter into poor accuracy of self-evaluation with reference to such characteristics as likeability, good sportsmanship, and thoughtfulness of others. We must not forget that interobserver reliability among the group raters will also be poorer for such characteristics as these, probably for the same reasons as *S*'s self-rating is inaccurate. The methods and findings to date do not permit firm conclusions. This is partly because we do not know the extent of rating variability from trait to trait, and such variability can affect the size of a correlation coefficient without necessarily reflecting variations in *Ss*' absolute accuracy of self-rating. It would seem worthwhile to pursue further the relationships between characteristics of the traits being rated and the accuracy of self-evaluation, with populations of *Ss* constant and methodology properly arranged to permit psychologically meaningful comparisons.

4. *Is there any intra-*S* consistency in the tendency to lack insight regarding a number of characteristics?*

Sears (1936) reported that he found little such consistency. Webb (1952), on the other hand, showed that the probability was significantly greater than chance that a given *S* would overestimate himself on several characteristics. Calvin and Holtzman found a split-half correlation of only +.35 between self-enhancing scores on two groups of three traits each, even when the choice of traits put into each half was "based upon a cluster analysis of the trait intercorrelations and represents an attempt to make the two sets of scores as comparable as possible" (Calvin & Holtzman, 1953, p. 42). A similar split-half correlation between scores indicating "lack of insight" without regard to the direction of discrepancy was only +.19.

In his study mentioned above, Brandt (1958) assigned an accuracy score to each *S*'s self-estimate on arithmetic, vocabulary, spelling, and three physical tasks. By a complicated system, accuracy scores were corrected for "ease of judgment," i.e., for whether the child's actual performance was near the extremes, hence easy for him to sense. Brandt reports that between-individual variations in accuracy of self-estimate was significantly greater than within-individual variation. (In this part of the data analysis, both the sixth- and eleventh-grade Ss were used.) Brandt (1958, p. 77) writes, "Almost every conceivable pattern of accuracy of self-estimate prevailed. Although there was a tendency for students to differ in a general sense with respect to accuracy of self-estimate, there was also a tendency among the majority of students (inconsistent group) for some area of the self-concept to be more sharply differentiated than other areas."

On the whole, available data permit no firm conclusion as to the generality of Ss' overestimating tendencies across traits, although it seems likely that at least weak trends toward such generality are present. It seems plausible that further research might establish the following generalizations: (1) There is considerable but not complete independence in S's tendencies to overestimate or underestimate himself from trait to trait, with the influence of stereotype accuracy upon his estimate ruled out. (2) The degree of such intertrait independence is a function of the degree to which the traits overlap with respect to (a) content or meaning as perceived by S, and (b) subjective importance to S's self-regard.

5. *Summary of descriptive facts about insight*

The typical but not unanimous finding is that Ss' self-ratings show low but significant correlations with the ratings which Ss receive from others. This seems to hold true for a wide variety of traits and persons. Probably the correlations for some traits are higher than for other traits. Before definitive, clearly interpretable statements can be made about the degree of correspondence between self-ratings and ratings received from others, further research is necessary in which certain methodological difficulties are eliminated. For example, the influence of stereotype accuracy should be ruled out, the instructions to Ss should make clear the frame of reference he is to use in making his self-ratings, and intertrait differences in variability among self-ratings should be taken into account.

There is considerable evidence that self-overestimation is more common than is self-underestimation. This holds true for a wide variety of traits and persons. Here too further research is needed before more definitive detailed statements can be made concerning the conditions of which overestimation is a function. For example, the roles of subject variables and of the objectivity and salience of traits remain to be explored in controlled research designs.

There is some limited evidence to suggest that there are consistent individual differences in the tendency toward overestimation, underestimation, or accurate estimation across a variety of traits. Detailed information on this matter remains to be established, however.

VII

Conclusions and Implications

The psychological literature of the last two decades shows a marked resurgence of interest in personality theories concerning the self, and a great increase in the number of researches which have been inspired by these theories, or have tested hypotheses pertinent to them. Now that we have reviewed in detail the recent empirical literature, the time has come to attempt an over-all evaluation of the current state of affairs in this area, in terms of its broader implications.

We have noted that the empirical researches on constructs concerning the self cannot be classified according to theoretically relevant categories because the theories are vague, incomplete, and overlapping; and because no one theory has received extensive, empirical exploration.

On the whole, we have found that there are enough positive trends to be tantalizing. On the other hand, there is a good deal of ambiguity in the results, considerable apparent contradiction among the findings of various studies, and a tendency for different methods to produce different results. In short, the total accumulation of substantive findings is disappointing, especially in proportion to the great amount of effort which obviously has been expended.

How can we explain this state of affairs? What are its implications? Let us consider these questions now in the light of our earlier appraisal of theoretical and methodological problems.

Part of the explanation lies in the scientific shortcomings of all those personality theories which emphasize constructs concerning the self. The first question is whether such constructs, as presently formulated, are adequate analytical and predictive categories. Let us examine the scientific utility of these constructs.

We may begin by asking why some persons have felt the need to postulate such inferred variables referring to the self. It is obvious that on a nonscientific level, self-referent cognitions and feelings have subjective validity. But of course this is no necessary justification for putting constructs concerning the self into a theory which purports to be scientific. To some, however, these constructs have seemed to be necessary to give a complete, scientific account of human behavior.

What sorts of observations are theorists trying to account for by introducing constructs referring to the self? For one thing, psychologists of a number of schools of thought have noted that antecedent conditions, defined in terms of interexperimenter agreement, are not sufficient to predict either group trends or individual differences in human behavior. They have suggested that one could increase the accuracy of predictions of behavior if one found out what the subject perceives, knows, or feels about the "objective" situation, including his own characteristics. We have discussed this issue and its research implications in Chapter II.

Personality theorists have also pointed out that general behavior theorists, for purposes of their own, have thus far delimited their theories in such a way that they are unable to account for some of the behaviors one can observe in the clinic, in school, and in other "everyday life" situations. For example, general behavior theories in the area of motivation have been mostly concerned with organic drives and physically painful aversive stimuli. To theorists interested in the self, these do not seem to be adequate motivational constructs to account for all the kinds of behavior they wish to explain. In fact, the general experimenal psychologist himself has recognized this limitation, as evidenced, for example, by the recent emphasis upon "ego-involvement" as an independent variable, or as a variable which must be controlled in experiments on basic learning and perceptual processes.

In addition, many personality theorists have felt that the organizational or configurational properties of human functioning are not subsumed by the constructs of most present-day general behavior theories. It was partly to account for the apparent interrelatedness of observed behavior sequences that gestalt characteristics were attributed to the phenomenal and nonphenomenal self, and the centrality of self-regarding attitudes was postulated.

While constructs concerning the self may seem to be needed for the above reasons, the way they have been used poses a dilemma. That is, these constructs have been stretched to cover so many inferred cognitive and motivational processes that their utility for analytic and predictive purposes has been greatly diminished.

What are the implications of this dilemma? One possibility is that theories which depend heavily on overgeneralized self-referent constructs should be abandoned as potentially fruitful scientific tools. Certainly if the construct system cannot be more precisely reformulated, this alternative seems the correct one.

But perhaps the constructs and hypotheses can be improved. For example, it appears that more molecular inferred variables may have greater research utility. That is, such characteristics as self-actualization, self-differentiation, and self-consistency have not led to enlightening research. By contrast, constructs such as self-acceptance or self-esteem, especially when referring to specified attributes, have yielded more manageable and fruitful research procedures.

An additional alternative to abandoning self theories may be to improve their predictiveness by the addition of more variables. The question is whether, in introducing and emphasizing constructs of certain kinds, some personality theorists have also restricted their conceptual systems to such an extent that they have limited the predictiveness of the theories. In other words, they may be simply failing to take into account the role of some important determinants of behavior. A possible example of this kind of restrictiveness is the emphasis of self-concept theory upon the subject's conscious processes.

For instance, certain psychologists have thought that self-concept research yields weak or equivocal results because the theory does not systematically include the unconscious self concept, or other unconscious cognitive and dynamic processes. With reference to the unconscious self concept, for example, some theorists believe that one should be able to predict behavior more accurately from a knowledge of S's unconscious self concept than one can from a knowledge of his conscious self concept. And of course it follows that unconscious self-concept measures, if added to conscious self-concept measures, should improve the predictiveness of the latter.

Quite possibly the omission of valid unconscious-self-concept measures could be one of the reasons why we have had such limited success in predicting important behaviors. However, there is as yet no proof that one can predict behavior as well, let alone better, with unconscious-self-concept measures than with conscious-self-concept measures. The state of validation of unconscious-self-concept measures is even more parlous than is the state of validation of conscious-self-concept measures. Therefore the burden of proof is presently on the person favoring the addition of the unconscious self concept to the variables from which we try to predict behavior. Although it seems quite plausible that phenomenological theories could become more predictive by the addition of constructs concerning the nonphenomenal self, our point here is that this has not been demonstrated with the indices we now have.

A similar argument applies to any of the currently available indices of other unconscious processes, such as the unconscious motivations postulated by Freudian theorists. Although valid measures are not at hand to test unequivocally the value of adding such constructs to phenomenal theory, these nonphenomenal constructs may someday prove to be of equal or greater predictive value than phenomenal constructs.

One must remember, too, that we cannot say how much the obtained associations between conscious self-concept measures and behavior would be strengthened if the conscious self-concept measures themselves could be made more reliable and valid.

There is another important limitation of self-concept theory which also stems from the theory's emphasis on the subject's conscious processes. In stressing the importance of S's view, objectively measurable variables have been slighted. It has been suggested that predictions of behavior could be made more accurate by the inclusion of objectively specifiable antecedent factors, including facts about S's previous experiences, S's objective characteristics, and objectively defined current stimuli. In this connection, it might prove profitable to effect more connections with the general experimental psychology of learning, motivation, and perception. There are many pertinent facts, already established through experiment, to which theorists stressing the self have not referred. And some of the constructs of these theorists, e.g., in regard to learning, might also have utility in making predictions of interest to personality theorists who emphasize the self.

Again it remains to be demonstrated whether behavior can be predicted more efficiently by objective measures than by indices of the phenomenal self, or whether adding objective measures to self-concept measures improves the predictions one could make from either type of measure alone.

Not all theories which emphasize self-referent constructs are phenomenological. But in the case of self-concept theory, the objection may be raised that the addition of objective measures and measures of unconscious processes is inconsistent with the phenomenal premises of the theory. However, this cannot be taken too seriously since, for one thing, self-concept theory is already internally inconsistent, as we have pointed out in Chapter II. For another thing, empirical improvements in predictiveness should be the test of the worth of any suggestion about broadening self-concept theory.

We have just mentioned the internal inconsistency in self-concept theory. In fact, internal inconsistency apparently characterizes all personality theories which emphasize constructs concerning the self, although the vagueness of their statements often makes it impossible to identify inconsistencies with certainty. On this score alone none of these theories, as presently formulated, can be called wholly scientific. Probably these inconsistencies are partly responsible for the poor state of research findings in this area.

Not only are delimited constructs and internal consistency among postulates necessary, but "lower-order" hypotheses are required as well, if personality theories which stress the self are to become scientifically useful. Some psychologists have argued that general behavior theorists have been too molecular, and that they have failed to attack really significant aspects of human development and functioning. Even if one were to accept this allegation, it does not follow that stating vague, overarching, unverifiable generalizations will remedy the situation. As Morison (1960) reminds us, it may be satisfying to psychologists' needs to have a comprehensive theory, but it is probably more scientifically productive in the long run to begin one's work with limited but testable hypotheses.

If, as was suggested above, self theorists were to seek connections with general behavior theories, the "tough-minded" approach could be helpful in making the needed reformulations in hypotheses involving the self.[1]

Thus far we have tried to explain the state of the research findings in terms of shortcomings in the theories which emphasize constructs concerning the self. Now let us examine some changes in research procedures which, if carried out, might lead to more definitive outcomes.

Corresponding to the need for more limited theoretical constructs

---

[1]We have not, of course, attempted an exhaustive appraisal of self theories in the light of criteria for a good scientific theory, nor have we attempted a detailed comparison of the scientific usefulness of various personality and general behavior theories. Such an undertaking is beyond the scope of this book.

is a requirement for more limited and well-analyzed measuring instruments. The instruments which have been applied thus far have tried to cover too much too soon, in a fashion parallel to the premature overinclusiveness of the theoretical constructs. Microanalysis of newly devised indices is badly needed. That is, one must undertake a slow accumulation of information in regard to reliability and construct validity at the item level, if any clear meaning can be attached to one's measures. It is particularly important to avoid the use of complex two-part indices until the component parts have been thoroughly explored. The experimental conditions leading to optimum validity must be ascertained and this information systematically applied to researches which use self-concept measures. And of course scaling procedures should be systematically applied to the instruments so that one can get some idea of the psychological meaning of statistically significant changes or group differences.

Corresponding to the need for more lower-order hypotheses is a requirement for more systematic, analytical designs. For example, analysis of variance designs are called for, because some of the apparent contradictions may be due to interaction of variables which are as yet unexplored in a systematic way by any presently available studies. Also, more use of the "transition experiment" described by Campbell (1957) would be highly desirable.

The wide use of R-R designs, in which two responses are correlated, is one of the main reasons why the substantive results in this field are generally inconclusive. Such R-R designs can, of course, never lead to cause-effect inferences. They may throw some light on theoretical questions, but often they have not been well enough controlled to do even that. Although it might seem that some kind of R-R design is uniquely demanded by self-concept theory, we have shown in Chapter II that this is not the case.

And, finally, there have been a great many avoidable methodological difficulties at the design level. This is certainly a difficult area to work in, and it is understandable that artifacts cannot always be ruled out by those who pioneer. However, there are pertinent methodological precautions which have been worked out in other areas of psychology, and they can and should be applied to this one.

In short: It is true that personality theories which stress the self have addressed themselves to important, unanswered questions concerning human behavior. However, the empirical evidence supporting the theories is limited, in proportion to the effort expended. This seems to be due in part to each of the following four factors: (1) the lack of proper scientific characteristics of the theories themselves; (2) the inevitable difficulties encountered in formulating relevant, well-controlled research in a new area; (3) the understandable fact that individual researches in a new area are not part of a planned research program, and therefore cannot be easily synthesized; (4) avoidable methodological flaws.

When we examine the history of scientific thought we find that prescientific speculations seem to be a necessary way of beginning to understand any phenomenon one is trying to explain. From some of these kinds of prescientific efforts, hypotheses of a scientific sort have come, when proper steps were taken. Those who have presented personality theories which stress self-referent constructs have performed a useful pioneering function, and their work may well point to a scientific metamorphosis with regard to the psychology of personality.

However, as time has passed and a considerable body of research has accumulated, it seems that a crisis situation is at hand with regard to personality theories and research which emphasize the self. For one thing, the usefulness of these theories is called into question by the state of the empirical evidence, because the latter is partly a a function of ambiguities in the theories.

If personality theories stressing self-referent constructs are going to be counted among scientifically useful theories, the time has come for them to move in the directions we have outlined above. If the theoretical difficulties cannot be overcome, both the theoretical and empirical efforts might just as well be abandoned, so far as their probable contribution to scientific psychology is concerned.

On the other hand, these theories are concerned with important issues. Therefore, a serious attempt to develop lower-order hypotheses which begin to deal wtih these issues in a more restricted, manageable way might well be worthwhile.

It appears that limitations and flaws in research design have been at least as important as the theoretical shortcomings in determining the poor state of the available evidence. These can undoubtedly be overcome if the basic problems of hypothesis formation are clarified, and careful attention is given to methodological requirements.

If theorists and researchers who are interested in self-referent constructs decide to face the crisis and do what is necessary to put their work on a more solid footing, the process will be arduous and time-consuming. In this respect these workers are in the same position as any other psychologist, or any other scientist for that matter. That is, the required procedures are not peculiar to these theories. Morison (1960) has represented very well our final thoughts on this matter: Although interpreting the facts thoughtfully and going beyond them are the most important things, gradualness, drudgery, and patience are the price of attaining those significant increments in factual knowledge from which valid psychological laws may be formed.

Bibliography

(See page 349 for supplementary listing.)

Adler, A. *The practice and theory of individual psychology.* New York: Harcourt Brace, 1924.

Alexander, T. The prediction of teacher-pupil interaction with a projective test. *J. clin. Psychol.,* 1950, 6, 273-276.

Alexander, T. Certain characteristics of the self as related to affection. *Child Develpm.,* 1951, 22, 285-290.

Alfert, E. Two components of assumed similarity. *J. abnorm. soc. Psychol.,* 1958, 56, 135-138.

Algeo, Nancy B., & Pullen, M. S. Personality changes following transorbital lobotomy. *J. clin. Psychol.,* 1957, 13, 308-309.

Amatora, Sister Mary. Validity in self-evaluation. *Educ. psychol. Measmt,* 1956, 16, 119-126.

Ames, Louise B. The sense of self of nursery school children as manifested by their verbal behavior. *J. genet. Psychol.,* 1952, 81, 193-232.

Angyal, A. *Foundations for a science of personality.* New York: Commonwealth Fund, 1941.

Arnold, F. C., & Walter, V. A. The relationship between a self- and other-reference sentence completion test. *J. counsel. Psychol.,* 1957, 4, 65-70.

Arsenian, S. Own estimate and objective measurement. *J. educ. Psychol.,* 1942, 33, 291-302.

Bandura, A. Psychotherapist's anxiety level, self-insight, and psychotherapeutic competence. *J. abnorm. soc. Psychol.,* 1956, 52, 333-337.

Beier, E. G., & Ratzeburg, F. The parental identifications of male and female college students. *J. abnorm. soc. Psychol.,* 1953, 48, 569-572.

Beilin, H. The prediction of adjustment over a four year interval. *J. clin. Psychol.,* 1957, 13, 270-274.

Beloff, Halla, & Beloff, J. Unconscious self-evaluation using a stereoscope. *J. abnorm. soc. Psychol.,* 1959, 59, 275-278.

Benjamins, J. Changes in performance in relation to influences upon self-conceptualization. *J. abnorm. soc. Psychol.,* 1950, 45, 473-480.

Berdie, R. F. Changes in self-ratings as a method of evaluating counseling. *J. counsel. Psychol.,* 1954, 1, 49-54.

Berger, E. M. The relation between expressed acceptance of self and expressed acceptance of others. *J. abnorm. soc. Psychol.,* 1952, 47, 778-782.

Berger, E. M. Relationship among acceptance of self, acceptance of others, and MMPI scores. *J. counsel. Psychol.,* 1955, 2, 279-284.

Berger, S. Paraplegia. In J. F. Garret (Ed.), *Psychological aspects of physical disability.* Department of Health, Education and Welfare. Washington: U. S. Govt. Printing Office, 1952. Pp. 46-59.

325

Bice, H. V. Some factors that contribute to the concept of self in the child with cerebral palsy. *Ment. Hyg.,* 1954, 38, 120-131.

Bieri, J., & Trieschman, A. Learning as a function of perceived similarity to self. *J. Pers.,* 1956, 25, 213-223.

Bills, R. E. Rorschach characteristics of persons scoring high and low in acceptance of self. *J. consult. Psychol.,* 1953, 17, 36-38. (a)

Bills, R. E. A validation of changes in scores on the Index of Adjustment and Values as measures of changes in emotionality. *J. consult. Psychol.,* 1953, 17, 135-138. (b)

Bills, R. E. A comparison of scores on the Index of Adjustment and Values with behavior in level-of-aspiration tasks. *J. consult. Psychol.,* 1953, 17, 206-212. (c)

Bills, R. E. Acceptance of self as measured by interviews and the Index of Adjustment and Values. *J. consult. Psychol.,* 1954, 18, 22. (a)

Bills, R. E. Self-concepts and Rorschach signs of depression. *J. consult. Psychol.,* 1954, 18, 135-137. (b)

Bills, R. E. Index of Adjustment and Values. Manual. Alabama Polytechnic Institute, Auburn. Mimeographed. Undated.

Bills, R. E., Vance, E. L., & McLean, O. S. An Index of Adjustment and Values. *J. consult. Psychol.,* 1951, 15, 257-261.

Block, J., & Thomas, H. Is satisfaction with self a measure of adjustment? *J. abnorm. soc. Psychol.,* 1955, 51, 254-259.

Bossom, J., & Maslow, A. H. Security of judges as a factor in impressions of warmth in others. *J. abnorm. soc. Psychol.,* 1957, 55, 147-148.

Brandt, R. M. The accuracy of self estimate: a measure of self-concept reality. *Genet. psychol. Monogr.,* 1958, 58, 55-99.

Brim, O. G., Jr., & Wood, Nancy. Self and other conceptions in courtship and marriage pairs. *Marriage fam. Living,* 1956, 18, 243-248.

Brodbeck, A. J., & Perlmutter, H. V. Self dislike as a determinant of marked ingroup-outgroup preferences. *J. Psychol.,* 1954, 38, 271-280.

Bronfenbrenner, U., Harding, J., & Gallwey, Mary. The measurement of skill in social perception. In D. C. McClelland, A. L. Baldwin, U. Bronfenbrenner, & F. L. Strodtbeck, *Talent and society.* New York: Van Nostrand, 1958. Pp. 29-111.

Brown, E. A., & Goitein, P. L. The significance of body image for personality assay. *J. nerv. ment. Dis.,* 1943, 97, 401-408.

Brownfain, J. J. Stability of the self-concept as a dimension of personality. *J. abnorm. soc. Psychol.,* 1952, 47, 597-606.

Brunswik, E. *Perception and the representative design of psychological experiments.* Berkeley: Univer. of California Press, 1956.

Bugental, Daphne E., & Lehner, G. F. J. Accuracy of self perception as related to two leadership roles. *J. abnorm. soc. Psychol.,* 1958, 56, 396-398.

Bugental, J. F. T. An investigation of the relationship of the conceptual matrix to the self-concept. In *Abstr. Doctoral Dissertation,* Ohio State Univer. Press, 1949, 57, 27-32.

Bugental, J. F. T. A method of assessing self and not-self attitudes during the therapeutic series. *J. consult. Psychol.*, 1952, 16, 435-439.

Bugental, J. F. T., & Gunning, Evelyn C. Investigations into self-concepts: II. Stability of reported self-identifications. *J. clin. Psychol.*, 1955, 11, 41-46.

Bugental, J. F. T., & Zelen, S. L. Investigations into the self-concept. I. The W-A-Y Technique. *J. Pers.*, 1950, 18, 483-498.

Butler, J. M., & Haigh, G. V. Changes in the relation between self-concepts and ideal concepts consequent upon client-centered counseling. In C. R. Rogers and Rosalind F. Dymond (Eds.), *Psychotherapy and personality change*. Chicago: Univer. of Chicago Press, 1954. Pp. 55-75.

Caldwell, Bettye McD. *Picture Series*. Washington Univer. School of Medicine, St. Louis, 1953.

Calkins, M. W. The self in scientific psychology. *Amer. J. Psychol.*, 1915, 26, 495-524.

Calvin, A. D. Some misuses of the experimental method in evaluating the effect of client-centered counseling. *J. counsel. Psychol.*, 1954, 1, 249-251.

Calvin, A. D., & Holtzman, W. H. Adjustment and the discrepancy between self concept and inferred self. *J. consult. Psychol.*, 1953, 17, 39-44.

Campbell, D. T. Factors relevant to the validity of experiments in social settings. *Psychol. Bull.*, 1957, 54, 297-312.

Campbell, D. T., & Fiske, D. W. Convergent and discriminant validation by the multitrait-multimethod matrix. *Psychol. Bull.*, 1959, 56, 81-105.

Caplan, S. W. The effect of group counseling in junior high school boys' concepts of themselves in school. *J. counsel. Psychol.*, 1957, 4, 124-128.

Cartwright, D. S. Self consistency as a factor affecting immediate recall. *J. abnorm. soc. Psychol.*, 1956, 52, 212-218.

Cartwright, D. S., & Roth, I. Success and satisfaction in psychotherapy. *J. clin. Psychol.*, 1957, 13, 20-26.

Cartwright, Rosalind D. Effects of psychotherapy on self-consistency. *J. counsel. Psychol.*, 1957, 4, 15-22.

Cath, S. H., Glud, E., & Blane, H. T. The role of the body-image in psychotherapy with the physically handicapped. *Psychoanal. Rev.*, 1957, 44, 34-40.

Chase, P. H. Self concepts in adjusted and maladjutsed hospital patients. *J. consult. Psychol.*, 1957, 21, 495-497.

Chein, I. The awareness of self and the structure of the ego. *Psychol. Rev.*, 1944, 51, 304-314.

Child, I. L., Frank, Kitty F., & Storm, T. Self-ratings and TAT: their relations to each other and to childhood background. *J. Pers.*, 1956, 25, 96-114.

Chodorkoff, B. Self-perception, perceptual defense and adjustment. *J. abnorm. soc. Psychol.*, 1954, 49, 508-512. (a)

Chodorkoff, B. Adjustment and the discrepancy between the perceived and ideal self. *J. clin. Psychol.*, 1954, 10, 266-268. (b)

Chodorkoff, B. Anxiety, threat, and defensive reactions. *J. gen. Psychol.*, 1956, 54, 191-196.

Cleveland, S. E., & Fisher, S. Behavior and unconscious fantasies of patients with rheumatoid arthritis. *Psychosom. Med.*, 1954, 16, 327-333.

Cleveland, S. E., & Fisher, S. Psychological factors in the neurodermatoses. *Psychosom. Med.,* 1956, 18, 209-220.

Cleveland, S. E., & Fisher, S. Body image and small group behavior. *Hum. Relat.,* 1957, 10, 223-233.

Cliff, N. The relation of adverb-adjective combinations to their components. Multilith technical report. Project Designation NR 150-088, October, 1956, Princeton University.

Coates, C. H., & Pellegrini, R. J. Executives and supervisors: contrasting self-conceptions and conceptions of each other. *Amer. sociol. Rev.,* 1957, 22, 217-220.

Cohen, A. R. Experimental effects of ego defense preference on interpersonal relations. *J. abnorm. soc. Psychol.,* 1956, 52, 19-27.

Cohen, A. R. Some implications of self-esteem for social influence. In C. I. Hovland & I. L. Janis (Eds.), *Personality and persuasibility.* New Haven: Yale Univer. Press, 1959. Pp. 102-120.

Cohen, L. D. Level of aspiration behavior and feelings of adequacy and self-acceptance. *J. abnorm. soc. Psychol.,* 1954, 49, 84-86.

Combs, A. W., & Soper, D. W. The self, its derivative terms, and research. *J. indiv. Psychol.,* 1957, 13, 134-145.

Cooley, C. H. *Human nature and the social order.* New York: Scribner's, 1902.

Coopersmith, S. A method for determining types of self-esteem. *J. abnorm. soc. Psychol.,* 1959, 59, 87-94.

Cowen, E. L. The "negative self concept" as a personality measure. *J. consult. Psychol.,* 1954, 18, 138-142.

Cowen, E. L. An investigation of the relationship between two measures of self-regarding attitudes. *J. clin. Psychol.,* 1956, 12, 156-160. (a)

Cowen, E. L. Administrative set and sex difference as factors in the negative self-concept score. *Canadian J. Psychol.,* 1956, 10, 51-56. (b)

Cowen, E. L., Heilizer, F., & Axelrod, H. S. Self-concept conflict indicators and learning. *J. abnorm. soc. Psychol.,* 1955, 51, 242-245.

Cowen, E. L., Heilizer, F., Axelrod, H. S., & Alexander, S. The correlates of manifest anxiety in perceptual reactivity, rigidity, and self concept. *J. consult. Psychol.,* 1957, 21, 405-411.

Cowen, E. L., & Tongas, P. N. The social desirability of trait descriptive terms: applications to a self-concept inventory. *J. consult. Psychol.,* 1959, 23, 361-365.

Crandall, V. J., & Bellugi, Ursula. Some relationships of interpersonal and intrapersonal conceptualizations to personal-social adjustment. *J. Pers.,* 1954, 23, 224-232.

Cronbach, L. J. Response sets and test validity. *Educ. psychol. Measmt,* 1946, 6, 475-494.

Cronbach, L. J. Further evidence on response sets and test design. *Educ. psychol. Measmt,* 1950, 10, 3-31.

Cronbach, L. J. Correlations between persons as a research tool. In O. H. Mowrer (Ed.), *Psychotherapy, theory and research.* New York: Ronald Press, 1953. Pp. 376-388.

Cronbach, L. J. Processes affecting scores on "understanding of others" and "assumed similarity." *Psychol. Bull.*, 1955, 52, 177-193.

Cronbach, L. J. Proposals leading to analytic treatment of social perception scores. In R. Taguiri & L. Petrullo (Eds.), *Person perception and interpersonal behavior.* Palo Alto: Stanford Univer. Press, 1958. Pp. 353-379.

Cronbach, L. J., & Gleser, Goldine C. Assessing similarity between profiles. *Psychol. Bull.*, 1953, 50, 456-473.

Cronbach, L. J., & Meehl, P. E. Construct validity in psychological tests. *Psychol. Bull.*, 1955, 52, 281-302.

Cureton, E. E. The definition and estimation of test reliability. *Educ. psychol. Measmt*, 1958, 4, 715-738.

Davids, A. Comparison of three methods of personality assessment: direct, indirect, and projective. *J. Pers.*, 1955, 23, 423-440.

Davids, A., Henry, A. F., McArthur, C. C., & McNamara, L. F. Projection, self-evaluation, and clinical evaluation of aggression. *J. consult. Psychol.*, 1955, 19, 437-440.

Davitz, J. R. Social perception and sociometric choice of children. *J. abnorm. soc. Psychol.*, 1955, 50, 173-176.

DeSoto, C. B., Kuethe, J. L., & Bosley, J. J. A redefinition of Social Desirability. *J. abnorm. soc. Psychol.*, 1959, 58, 273-275.

Diggory, J. C., & Magaziner, D. E. Self-evaluation as a function of instrumentally relevant capacities. *Bull. de l'Ass. int. de Psychol. appl.*, 1959, 8, 2-19.

Diller, L. Conscious and unconscious self-attitudes after success and failure. *J. Pers.*, 1954, 23, 1-12.

Diller, L., & Riklan, M. Rorschach correlates in Parkinson's Disease: M, motor inhibition, perceived cause of illness, and self-attitudes. *Psychosom. Med.*, 1957, 19, 120-126.

Dittes, J. E. Effect of changes in self-esteem upon impulsiveness and deliberation in making judgments. *J. abnorm. soc. Psychol.*, 1959, 58, 348-356. (a)

Dittes, J. E. Attractiveness of group as a function of self-esteem and acceptance by group. *J. abnorm. soc. Psychol.*, 1959, 59, 77-82. (b)

Doris, J. Test anxiety and blame assignment in grade school children. *J. abnorm. soc. Psychol.*, 1959, 58, 181-190.

Doris, J., & Sarason, S. Test anxiety and blame assignment in a failure situation. *J. abnorm. soc. Psychol.*, 1955, 50, 335-338.

Dudek, F. J. Concerning "reliability" of tests. *Educ. psychol. Measmt*, 1952, 12, 293-299.

Dudek, F. J. A comparison of scale values for adverbs determined by the constant-sum method and a successive intervals procedure. *Educ. psychol. Measmt*, 1959, 19, 539-548.

Dymond, Rosalind F. Adjustment changes over therapy from self-sorts. In C. R. Rogers & Rosalind F. Dymond (Eds.), *Psychotherapy and personality change.* Chicago: Univer. of Chicago Press, 1954. Pp. 76-84. (a)

Dymond, Rosalind F. Adjustment changes over therapy from Thematic Apperception Test Ratings. In C. R. Rogers & Rosalind F. Dymond (Eds.), *Psycho-

therapy and personality change. Chicago: Univer. of Chicago Press, 1954. Pp. 109-120. (b)

Eastman, D. Self acceptance and marital happiness. *J. consult. Psychol.*, 1958, 22, 95-99.

Edelson, M., & Jones, A. E. Operational explorations of the conceptual self system and of the interaction between frames of reference. *Genet. Psychol. Monogr.*, 1954, 50, 43-139.

Edwards, A. L. *The social desirability variable in personality assessment and research.* New York: Holt, 1957.

Edwards, A. L., & Cronbach, L. J. Experimental design for research in psychotherapy. *J. clin. Psychol.*, 1952, 8, 51-59.

Engel, Mary. The stability of the self-concept in adolescence. *J. abnorm. soc. Psychol.*, 1959, 58, 211-215.

English, H. B., & English, Ava C. *A comprehensive dictionary of psychological and psychoanalytical terms.* New York: Longmans, Green, 1958.

Epstein, S. Unconscious self-evaluation in a normal and a schizophrenic group. *J. abnorm. soc. Psychol.*, 1955, 50, 65-70.

Eriksen, C. W. Subception: fact or artifact? *Psychol. Rev.*, 1956, 63, 74-80.

Ewing, T. N. Changes in attitudes during counseling. *J. consult. Psychol.*, 1954, 1, 232-239.

Festinger, L., Torrey, Jane, & Willerman, B. Self-evaluation as a function of attraction to the group. *Hum. Relat.*, 1954, 7, 161-174.

Fey, W. F. Acceptance of self and others, and its relation to therapy readiness. *J. clin. Psychol.*, 1954, 10, 269-271.

Fey, W. F. Acceptance by others and its relation to acceptance of self and others. *J. abnorm. soc. Psychol.*, 1955, 50, 274-276.

Fey, W. F. Correlates of certain subjective attitudes towards self and others. *J. clin. Psychol.*, 1957, 13, 44-49.

Fiedler, F. E., Dodge, Joan S., Jones, R. E., & Hutchins, E. B. Interrelations among measures of personality adjustment in nonclinical populations. *J. abnorm. soc. Psychol.*, 1958, 56, 345-351.

Fiedler, F. E., Warrington, W. G., & Blaisdell, F. J. Unconscious attitudes as correlates of sociometric choice in a social group. *J. abnorm. soc. Psychol.*, 1952, 47, 790-791.

Fiedler, F. E., & Wepman, J. M. An exploratory investigation of the self-concept of stutterers. *J. speech hearing Disorders*, 1951, 16, 110-114.

Fisher, S. Body image and asymmetry of body reactivity. *J. abnorm. soc. Psychol.*, 1958, 57, 292-298.

Fisher, S. Prediction of body exterior *vs.* body interior reactivity from a body image schema. *J. Pers.*, 1959, 27, 56-62.

Fisher, S., & Abercrombie, J. The relationship of body image distortions to body reactivity gradients. *J. Pers.*, 1958, 26, 320-329.

Fisher, S., & Cleveland, S. E. The role of body image in psychosomatic symptom choice. *Psychol. Monogr.*, 1955, 69, No. 17.

Fisher, S., & Cleveland, S. E. Relationship of body image boundaries to memory for completed and incompleted tasks. *J. Psychol.*, 1956, 42, 35-41. (a)

Fisher, S., & Cleveland, S. E. Body image boundaries and style of life. *J. abnorm. soc. Psychol.*, 1956, 52, 373-379. (b)

Fisher, S., & Cleveland, S. E. Relationship of body image to site of cancer. *Psychosom. Med.*, 1956, 18, 304-309. (c)

Fisher, S., & Cleveland, S. E. An approach to physiological reactivity in terms of a body image schema. *Psychol. Rev.*, 1957, 64, 26-37.

Fisher, S., & Cleveland, S. E. *Body image and personality.* Princeton, N.J.: D. Van Nostrand, 1958. (a)

Fisher, S., & Cleveland, S. E. Body image boundaries and sexual behavior. *J. Psychol.*, 1958, 45, 207-211. (b)

Flyer, E. S., Barron, E., & Bigbee, L. Discrepancies between self-descriptions and group ratings as measures of lack of insight. *U.S.A.F. Hum. Resour. Res. Cent. Res. Bull.*, 1953, No. 53-33.

Freud, S. *The ego and the id.* London: Hogarth Press, 1950.

Friedman, I. Phenomenal, ideal and projected conceptions of self. *J. abnorm. soc. Psychol.*, 1955, 51, 611-615.

Friedman, I. Objectifying the subjective—a methodological approach to the TAT. *J. proj. Tech.*, 1957, 21, 243-247.

Frisch, P., & Cranston, R. *Q*-technique applied to a patient and the therapist in a child guidance setting. *J. clin. Psychol.*, 1956, 12, 178-182.

Froehlich, C. P. Does test taking change self-ratings? *Calif. J. educ. Res.*, 1954, 5, 166-169.

Froehlich, C. P., & Moser, W. E. Do counselees remember test scores? *J. counsel. Psychol.*, 1954, 1, 149-152.

Fromm, E. Selfishness and self-love. *Psychiatry*, 1939, 2, 507-523.

Gage, N. L., & Cronbach, L. J. Conceptual and methodological problems in interpersonal perception. *Psychol. Rev.*, 1955, 62, 411-422.

Garner, W. R., Hake, H. W., & Eriksen, C. W. Operationism and the concept of perception. *Psychol. Rev.*, 1956, 63, 149-159.

Gebel, A. S. Self-perception and leaderless group discussion status. *J. soc. Psychol.*, 1954, 40, 309-318.

Gerard, H. B. Some effects of involvement upon evaluation. *J. abnorm. soc. Psychol.*, 1958, 57, 118-120.

Gibson, R. L., Snyder, W. U., & Ray, W. S. A factor analysis of measures of change following client-centered therapy. *J. counsel. Psychol.*, 1955, 2, 83-90.

Gilinsky, Alberta S. Relative self-estimate and the level of aspiration. *J. exp. Psychol.*, 1949, 39, 256-259.

Goldings, H. J. On the avowal and projection of happiness. *J. Pers.*, 1954, 23, 30-47.

Gordon, T., & Cartwright, D. The effect of psychotherapy upon certain attitudes toward others. In C. R. Rogers & Rosalind F. Dymond (Eds.), *Psychotherapy and personality change.* Chicago: Univer. of Chicago Press, 1954. Pp. 167-195.

Grayson, M. Concept of "acceptance" in physical rehabilitation. *J. Amer. med. Ass.*, 1951, 145, 893-896.

Green, G. H. Insight and group adjustment. *J. abnorm. soc. Psychol.*, 1948, **43**, 49-61.

Gross, L. The construction and partial standardization of a scale for measuring self-insight. *J. soc. Psychol.*, 1948, 28, 219-236.

Grummon, D. L. Personality changes as a function of time in persons motivated for therapy. In C. R. Rogers & Rosalind F. Dymond (Eds.), *Psychotherapy and personality change.* Chicago: Univer. of Chicago Press, 1954. Pp. 238-255.

Grummon, D. L., & John, Eve S. Changes over client-centered therapy evaluated in psychoanalytically based Thematic Apperception Test Scales. In C. R. Rogers & Rosalind F. Dymond (Eds.), *Psychotherapy and personality change.* Chicago: Univer. of Chicago Press, 1954.

Guilford, J. P. *Psychometric methods.* (2nd ed.) New York: McGraw-Hill, 1954.

Gulliksen, H. *Theory of mental tests.* New York: Wiley, 1950.

Haigh, G. V. Defensive behavior in client-centered therapy. *J. consult. Psychol.*, 1949, 13, 181-189.

Haimowitz, Natalie R., & Haimowitz, M. L. Personality changes in client-centered therapy. In W. W. Wolff & J. A. Precker (Eds.), *Success in psychotherapy.* New York: Grune & Stratton, 1952. Pp. 63-93.

Hall, C. W., & Lindzey, G. *Theories of personality.* New York: Wiley, 1957.

Halpern, H. M. Empathy, similarity and self-satisfaction. *J. consult. Psychol.*, 1955, 19, 449-452.

Hanlon, T. E., Hofstaetter, P., & O'Connor, J. Congruence of self and ideal self in relation to personality adjustment. *J. consult. Psychol.*, 1954, 18, 215-218.

Harvey, O. J., Kelley, H. H., & Shapiro, M. M. Reactions to unfavorable evaluations of the self made by other persons. *J. Pers.*, 1957, 25, 398-411.

Havighurst, R. J., Robinson, M. Z., & Dorr, M. The development of the ideal self in childhood and adolescence. *J. educ. Res.*, 1946, 40, 241-257.

Havighurst, R. J., & Taba, Hilda. *Adolescent character and personality.* New York: Wiley, 1949.

Heider, F. On Lewin's methods and theory. *J. soc. Issues*, 1959, Suppl. Series No. 13.

Helper, M. M. Learning theory and the self concept. *J. abnorm. soc. Psychol.*, 1955, 51, 184-194.

Helper, M. M. Parental evaluations of children and children's self-evaluations. *J. abnorm. soc. Psychol.*, 1958, 56, 190-194.

Henry, A. F. Family role structure and self blame. *Soc. Forces*, 1956, 35, 35-38.

Hilden, A. H. Q-sort correlation: stability and random choice of statements. *J. consult. Psychol.*, 1958, 22, 45-50.

Hilgard, E. R. Human motives and the concept of the self. *Amer. Psychologist*, 1949, 4, 374-382.

Hill, T. J. Attitudes toward self: an experimental study. *J. educ. Sociol.*, 1957, 30, 395-397.

Hillson, J. S., & Worchel, P. Self concept and defensive behavior in the maladjusted. *J. consult. Psychol.*, 1957, 21, 83-88.

Holt, R. R. The accuracy of self-evaluation: its measurement and some of its personological correlates. *J. consult. Psychol.*, 1951, 15, 95-101.

Horney, Karen. *The neurotic personality of our times.* New York: W. W. Norton, 1937.

Howard, R. C., & Berkowitz, L. Reactions to the evaluators of one's performance. *J. Pers.*, 1958, 26, 494-507.

Humphreys, L. G. Note on the multitrait-multimethod matrix. *Psychol. Bull.*, 1960, 57, 86-88.

Israel, J. Self-evaluation in groups. *Acta Sociologica*, 1958, 3, 29-47.

Jackson, D. N., & Messick, S. Content and style in personality assessment. *Psychol. Bull.*, 1958, 55, 243-252.

James, W. *Principles of psychology.* New York: Holt, 1890. 2 vols.

Janis, I. L. Personality correlates of susceptibility to persuasion. *J. Pers.* 1954, 22, 504-518.

Janis, I. L. Anxiety indices related to susceptibility to persuasion. *J. abnorm. soc. Psychol.*, 1955, 51, 663-667.

Janis, I. L., & Field, P. B. Sex differences and personality factors related to persuasibility. In C. I. Hovland & I. L. Janis (Eds.), *Personality and persuasibility.* New Haven: Yale Univer. Press, 1959. Pp. 55-68.

Janis, I. L., & Rife, D. Persuasibility and emotional disorder. In C. I. Hovland & I. L. Janis (Eds.), *Personality and persuasibility.* New Haven: Yale Univer. Press, 1959. Pp. 121-137.

Jessor, R. Phenomenological personality theories and the data language of psychology. *Psychol. Rev.*, 1956, 63, 173-180.

Johnson, D. G. Effect of vocational counseling on self-knowledge. *Educ. psychol. Measmt*, 1953, 13, 330-338.

Jones, A. Distribution of traits in current Q-sort methodology. *J. abnorm. soc. Psychol.*, 1956, 53, 90-95.

Jourard, S. M. Identification, parent-cathexis, and self-esteem. *J. consult. Psychol.*, 1957, 21, 375-380.

Jourard, S. M. A study of self-disclosure. *Scientific American*, 1958, 198, 77-82.

Jourard, S. M., & Lasakow, P. Some factors in self-disclosure. *J. abnorm. soc. Psychol.*, 1958, 56, 91-98.

Jourard, S. M., & Remy, R. M. Perceived parental attitudes, the self, and security. *J. consult. Psychol.*, 1955, 19, 364-366.

Jourard, S. M., & Remy, R. M. Individual variance scores: an index of the degree of differentiation of the self and the body image. *J. clin. Psychol.*, 1957, 13, 62-63.

Jourard, S. M., & Secord, P. F. Body size and body-cathexis. *J. consult. Psychol.*, 1954, 18, 184.

Jourard, S. M., & Secord, P. F. Body-cathexis and the ideal female figure. *J. abnorm. soc. Psychol.*, 1955, 50, 243-246.

Karon, P. B. *The Negro personality.* New York: Springer, 1958.

Kates, S. L., & Jordan, R. M. The social stimulus self and the self image related to personality and psychotherapy. *J. soc. Psychol.*, 1955, 42, 137-146.

Kelman, H. C., & Parloff, M. B. Interrelations among three criteria of improvement in group therapy: comfort, effectiveness, and self-awareness. *J. abnorm. soc. Psychol.*, 1957, 54, 281-288.

Kenny, D. T. The influence of social desirability on discrepancy measures between real self and ideal self. *J. consult. Psychol.*, 1956, 20, 315-318.

Klausner, S. Z. Social class and self concept. *J. soc. Psychol.*, 1953, 38, 201-205.

Klein, G. S. Self-appraisal of test performance as a vocational selection device. *Educ. psychol. Measmt*, 1948, 8, 69-84.

Kogan, W. S., Quinn, R., Ax, A. F., & Ripley, H. S. Some methodological problems in the quantification of clinical assessment by Q array. *J. consult. Psychol.*, 1957, 21, 57-62.

Krasner, L. Studies of the conditioning of verbal behavior. *Psychol. Bull.*, 1958, 55, 148-170.

Kuhn, M. H., & McPartland, T. S. An empirical investigation of self-attitudes. *Amer. sociol. Rev.*, 1954, 19, 68-76.

LaFon, F. E. Behavior on the Rorschach Test and a measure of self-acceptance. *Psychol. Monogr.*, 1954, 68 (10) No. 381.

LaForge, R., & Suczek, R. The interpersonal dimension of personality: III. An interpersonal check list. *J. Pers.*, 1955, 24, 94-112.

Langford, Louise M., & Alm, O. W. A comparison of parent judgment and child feelings concerning the self-adjustment and social adjustment of twelve-year-old children. *J. genet. Psychol.*, 1954, 85, 39-46.

Lawson, E. D., & Fagan, E. R. Stereotypes of prison guards. *J. correct. Psychol.*, 1957, 2, 13-22.

Lazowick, L. M. On the nature of identification. *J. abnorm. soc. Psychol.*, 1955, 51, 175-183.

Leary, T. *Interpersonal diagnosis of personality.* New York: Ronald, 1957.

Lecky, P. *Self-consistency, a theory of personality.* New York: Island Press, 1945.

Lepine, L. T., & Chodorkoff, B. Goal setting behavior, expressed feelings of adequacy and the correspondence between the perceived and ideal self. *J. clin. Psychol.*, 1955, 11, 395-397.

Lesser, G. S., & Abelson, R. P. Personality correlates of persuasibility in children. In C. I. Hovland & I. L. Janis (Eds.), *Personality and persuasibility.* New Haven: Yale Univer. Press, 1959. Pp. 187-221.

Levanway, R. W. The effect of stress on expressed attitudes toward self and others. *J. abnorm. soc. Psychol.*, 1955, 50, 225-226.

Levonian, E., Comrey, A., Levy, W., & Procter, D. A statistical evaluation of Edwards Personal Preference Schedule. *J. appl. Psychol.*, 1959, 43, 355-359.

Levy, L. H. The meaning and generality of perceived actual-ideal discrepancies. *J. consult. Psychol.*, 1956, 20, 396-398.

Levy, S. Figure drawing as a projective test. In L. E. Abt & L. Bellak (Eds.), *Projective psychology.* New York: Knopf, 1950.

Linton, Harriet, & Graham, Elaine. Personality correlates of persuasibility. In C. I. Hovland & I. L. Janis (Eds.), *Personality and persuasibility.* New Haven: Yale Univer. Press, 1959. Pp. 69-101.

Lipkin, S. Clients' feelings and attitudes in relation to the outcome of client-centered therapy. *Psychol. Monogr.*, 1954, 68, 1-30.

Lodge, Helen C. The influence of the study of biography on the moral ideology of the adolescent at the eighth grade level. *J. educ. Res.*, 1956, 50, 241-255.

Loevinger, Jane, & Ossorio, A. Evaluation of therapy by self-report: a paradox. *J. abnorm. soc. Psychol.*. 1959, 58, 392-394.

Lorr, M., Katz, M. M., & Rubenstein, E. A. The prediction of length of stay in psychotherapy. *J. consult. Psychol.*, 1958, 22, 321-327.

Lorr, M., & Rubenstein, E. A. Personality patterns of neurotic adults in psychotherapy. *J. consult. Psychol.*, 1956, 20, 257-263.

Lorr, M., Schaefer, E., Rubenstein, E. A., & Jenkins, R. L. An analysis of an outpatient rating scale. *J. clin. Psychol.*, 1953, 9, 296-299.

Lundy, R. M. Self perceptions and descriptions of opposite sex sociometric choices. *Sociometry*, 1956, 19, 272-277.

Lundy, R. M. Self perceptions regarding masculinity-femininity and descriptions of same and opposite sex sociometric choices. *Sociometry*, 1958, 21, 238-246.

Lundy, R. M., Katkovsky, W., Cromwell, R. I., & Shoemaker, D. J. Self acceptability and descriptions of sociometric choices. *J. abnorm. soc. Psychol.*, 1955, 51, 260-262.

Lynd, Helen M. *On shame and the sense of identity.* New York: Harcourt Brace, 1958.

Lynn, D. B. A note on sex differences in the development of masculine and feminine identification. *Psychol. Rev.*, 1959, 66, 126-136.

McClelland, D. C. *Personality.* New York: William Sloane, 1951.

McFarland, R. A., & Seitz, C. P. A psychosomatic inventory. *J. appl. Psychol.*, 1938, 22, 327-339.

McIntyre, C. J. Acceptance by others and its relation to acceptance of self and others. *J. abnorm. soc. Psychol.*, 1952, 47, 624-626.

McKee, J. P., & Sherriffs, A. C. The differential evaluation of males and females. *J. Pers.*, 1957, 25, 356-371.

McKee, J. P., & Sherriffs, A. C. Men's and women's beliefs, ideals, and self-concepts. *Amer. J. Sociol.*, 1959, 64, 356-363.

McKenna, Helen V., Hofstaetter, P. R., & O'Connor, J. P. The concepts of the ideal self and of the friend. *J. Pers.*, 1956, 24, 262-271.

McQuitty, L. L. A measure of personality integration in relation to the concept of self. *J. Pers.*, 1950, 18, 461-482.

Manis, M. Social interaction, and the self concept. *J. abnorm. soc. Psychol.*, 1955, 51, 362-370.

Manis, M. Personal adjustment, assumed similarity to parents, and inferred parental evaluations of the self. *J. consult. Psychol.*, 1958, 22, 481-485.

Martire, J. G. Relationships between the self-concept and differences in the strength and generality of achievement motivation. *J. Pers.*, 1956, 24, 364-375.

Martire, J. G., & Hornberger, R. H. Self congruence, by sex and between the sexes, in a "normal" population. *J. clin. Psychol.*, 1957, 13, 288-291.

Maslow, A. H. *Manual for Social Personality Inventory for College Women.* Palo Alto: Stanford Univer. Press, 1942. (a)

Maslow, A. H. Self esteem (dominance feeling) and sexuality in women. *J. soc. Psychol.,* 1942, 16, 259-294. (b)

Maslow, A. H. *Motivation and personality.* New York: Harper, 1954.

Maslow, A. H., & Sakoda, J. M. Volunteer error in the Kinsey Report. *J. abnorm. soc. Psychol.,* 1952, 47, 259-262.

Mason, Evelyn P. Some factors in self-judgments. *J. clin. Psychol.,* 1954, 10, 336-340. (a)

Mason, Evelyn P. Some correlates of self judgment of the aged. *J. Gerontol.,* 1954, 9, 324-337. (b)

Mathews, R., Hardyck, C., & Sarbin, T. R. Self-organization as a factor in the performance of selected cognitive tasks. *J. abnorm. soc. Psychol.,* 1953, 48, 500-502.

Matteson, R. W. Self-estimate of college freshmen. *Personnel Guid. J.,* 1956, 34, 280-284.

May, R. I. The origins and significance of the existential movement in psychology. II. Contributions of existential psychotherapy. In R. May, E. Angel, & H. F. Ellenberger, *Existence: a new dimension in psychiatry and psychology.* New York: Basic Books, 1958. Pp. 3-91.

Mead, G. H. *Mind, self and society.* Chicago: Univer. of Chicago Press, 1934.

Mertens, Marjorie S. The effects of mental hygiene films on self-regarding attitudes. U.S.N. Spec. Dev. Cent., Tech. Rpt. SDC 269-7-22, 1951.

Miller, K. S., & Worchel, P. The effects of need-achievement and self-ideal discrepancy on performance under stress. *J. Pers.,* 1956, 25, 176-190.

Miyamoto, S. F., & Dornbusch, S. M. A test of interactionist hypotheses of self-conception. *Amer. J. Sociol.,* 1956, 61, 399-403.

Moeller, G., & Applezweig, M. H. A motivational factor in conformity. *J. abnorm. soc. Psychol.,* 1957, 55, 114-120. (a)

Moeller, G., & Applezweig, M. H. Manual for the Behavior Interpretation Inventory Form 59R. *Tech. Rpt. #2,* Project NR 172-228, Connecticut College, New London, 1957. (b)

Morison, R. S. "Gradualness, gradualness, gradualness." *Amer. Psychologist,* 1960, 15, 187-197.

Mowrer, O. H. (Ed.). *Psychotherapy: theory and research.* New York: Ronald Press, 1953. (a)

Mowrer, O. H. "Q Technique"—description, history and critique. In O. H. Mowrer (Ed.), *Psychotherapy: theory and research.* New York: Ronald Press, 1953. Pp. 316-375. (b)

Murphy, G. *Personality: a biosocial approach to origins and structure.* New York: Harper, 1947.

Murstein, B. I. The projection of hostility on the Rorschach and as a result of ego threat. *J. proj. Tech.,* 1956, 20, 418-428.

Mussen, P. H., & Jones, Mary Cover. Self-conceptions, motivations, and interpersonal attitudes of late- and early-maturing boys. *Child Develpm.,* 1957, 28, 243-256.

Mussen, P. H., & Porter, L. W. Personal motivations and self-conceptions associated with effectiveness and ineffectiveness in emergent groups. *J. abnorm. soc. Psychol.*, 1959, 59, 23-27.

Nahinsky, I. D. The relationship between the self concept and the ideal-self concept as a measure of adjustment. *J. clin. Psychol.*, 1958, 14, 360-364.

Newstrand, Marjorie B. The eavesdropping question: a new projective technique to aid in determining self-image. *J. proj. Tech.*, 1958, 22, 312-319.

Norman, R. D. The interrelationships among acceptance-rejection, self-other identity, insight into self, and realistic perception of others. *J. soc. Psychol.*, 1953, 37, 205-235.

Northway, Mary L., & Detweiler, Joyce. Children's perception of friends and non-friends. *Sociometry*, 1956, 18, 527-531.

Nunnally, J. C. An investigation of some propositions of self-conception. The case of Miss Sun. *J. abnorm. soc. Psychol.*, 1955, 50, 87-92.

Nuthmann, Anne. Conditioning of a response class on a personality test. *J. abnorm. soc. Psychol.*, 1957, 54, 19-23.

O'Dea, J. D., & Zeran, F. R. Evaluating effect of counseling. *Personnel Guid. J.*, 1953, 31, 241-244.

Omwake, Katherine. The relation between acceptance of self and acceptance of others shown by three personality inventories. *J. consult. Psychol.*, 1954, 18, 443-446.

Osgood, C. E., Suci, G. J., & Tannenbaum, P. H. *The measurement of meaning.* Urbana: Univer. of Illinois Press, 1957.

Parloff, M. B., Kelman, H. C., & Frank, J. D. Comfort, effectiveness and self-awareness as criteria of improvement in psychotherapy. *Amer. J. Psychiat.*, 1954, III, 343-352.

Pearl, D. Ethnocentrism and the self-concept. *J. soc. Psychol.*, 1954, 40, 138-147.

Perkins, H. V. Teachers' and peers' perceptions of children's self-concepts. *Child Develpm.*, 1958, 29, 203-220. (a)

Perkins, H. V. Factors influencing change in children's self-concepts. *Child Develpm.*, 1958, 29, 221-230. (b)

Perlmutter, H. V. Relations between the self-image, the image of the foreigner, and the desire to live abroad. *J. Psychol.*, 1954, 38, 131-137.

Phillips, E. L. Attitudes toward self and others: a brief questionnaire report. *J. consult. Psychol.*, 1951, 15, 79-81.

Porter, L. G., & Stacey, C. L. A study of the relationship between self-ratings and parent-ratings for a group of college students. *J. clin. Psychol.*, 1956, 12, 243-248.

Powell, Margaret G. Comparisons of self-ratings, peer-ratings and expert's ratings of personality adjustment. *Educ. psychol. Measmt*, 1948, 8, 225-234.

Raimy, V. C. Self-reference in counseling interviews. *J. consult. Psychol.*, 1948, 12, 153-163.

Rapaport, G. M. "Ideal self" instructions, MMPI profile changes and the prediction of clinical improvement. *J. consult. Psychol.*, 1958, 22, 459-463.

Raskin, N. J. An objective study of the locus-of-evaluation factor in psychotherapy. In W. W. Wolff & J. A. Precker (Eds.), *Success in psychotherapy.* New York: Grune & Stratton, 1952. Pp. 143-162.

Rasmussen, G., & Zander, A. Group membership and self-evaluation. *Hum. Relat.*, 1954, 7, 239-251.

Reckless, W. C., Dinitz, S., & Kay, Barbara. The self component in potential delinquency and potential non-delinquency. *Amer. sociol. Rev.*, 1957, 22, 566-570.

Reckless, W. C., Dinitz, S., & Murray, Ellen. Self-concept as an insulator against delinquency. *Amer. sociol. Rev.*, 1956, 21, 744-746.

Reed, C. F., & Cuadra, C. A. The role-taking hypothesis in delinquency. *J. consult. Psychol.*, 1957, 21, 386-390.

Roberts, G. E. A study of the validity of the Index of Adjustment and Values. *J. consult. Psychol.*, 1952, 16, 302-304.

Robinson, Mary Frances, & Freeman, W. *Psycho-surgery and the self.* New York: Grune & Stratton, 1954.

Roessler, R., & Greenfield, N. Personality determinants of medical clinical consultation. *J. nerv. ment. Dis.*, 1958, 127, 142-144.

Rogers, A. H. The self concept in paranoid schizophrenia. *J. clin. Psychol.*, 1958, 14, 365-366.

Rogers, A. H., & Paul, C. Impunitiveness and unwitting self-evaluation. *J. proj. Tech.*, 1959, 23, 459-461.

Rogers, A. H., & Walsh, T. M. Defensiveness and unwitting self-evaluation. *J. clin. Psychol.*, 1959, 15, 302-304.

Rogers, C. R. *Client-centered therapy.* Boston: Houghton Mifflin, 1951. (a)

Rogers, C. R. Perceptual reorganization in client-centered therapy. In R. R. Blake & G. V. Ramsey (Eds.), *Perception: an approach to personality.* New York: Ronald Press, 1951. Pp. 307-327. (b)

Rogers, C. R. Changes in the maturity of behavior as related to therapy. In C. R. Rogers & Rosalind F. Dymond (Eds.), *Psychotherapy and personality change.* Chicago: Univer. of Chicago Press, 1954. Pp. 215-237. (a)

Rogers, C. R. The case of Mrs. Oak: a research analysis. In C. R. Rogers & Rosalind F. Dymond (Eds.), *Psychotherapy and personality change.* Chicago: Univer. of Chicago Press, 1954. Pp. 259-348. (b)

Rogers, C. R. The case of Mr. Bebb: the analysis of a failure case. In C. R. Rogers & Rosalind F. Dymond (Eds.), *Psychotherapy and personality change.* Chicago: Univer. of Chicago Press, 1954. Pp. 349-409. (c)

Rogers, C. R., & Dymond, Rosalind F. (Eds.). *Psychotherapy and personality change.* Chicago: Univer. of Chicago Press, 1954.

Rokeach, M. Studies in beauty: II. Some determiners of the perception of beauty in women. *J. soc. Psychol.*, 1945, 22, 155-169.

Rokeach, M., & Fruchter, B. A factorial study of dogmatism and related concepts. *J. abnorm. soc. Psychol.*, 1956, 53, 356-360.

Rosen, E. Self-appraisal and perceived desirability of MMPI personality traits. *J. counsel. Psychol.*, 1956, 3, 44-51. (a)

Rosen, E. Self-appraisal, personal desirability and perceived social desirability of personality traits. *J. abnorm. soc. Psychol.*, 1956, 52, 151-158. (b)

Rosenman, S. Changes in the representation of self, other, and interrelationship in client-centered therapy. *J. counsel. Psychol.*, 1955, 2, 271-278.

Rotter, J. B., & Rafferty, J. *Manual, The Rotter Incomplete Sentences, College Form.* New York: Psychol. Corp., 1950.

Rubenstein, E. A., & Lorr, M. A comparison of terminators and remainers in out-patient psychotherapy. *J. clin. Psychol.*, 1956, 12, 345-349.

Rubenstein, E. A., & Lorr, M. Self and peer personality ratings of psychotherapists. *J. clin. Psychol.*, 1957, 13, 295-298.

Rudikoff, Esselyn C. A comparative study of the changes in the concept of the self, the ordinary person and the ideal in eight cases. In C. R. Rogers & Rosalind F. Dymond (Eds.), *Psychotherapy and personality change.* Chicago: Univer. of Chicago Press, 1954. Pp. 85-98.

Russell, D. H. What does research say about self-evaluation? *J. educ. Res.*, 1953, 46, 561-571.

Sarason, S. B., & Gordon, E. M. The test anxiety questionnaire scoring norms. *J. abnorm. soc. Psychol.*, 1953, 48, 447-448.

Sarbin, T. R. A preface to a psychological analysis of the self. *Psychol. Rev.*, 1952, 59, 11-22.

Sarbin, T. R., & Farberow, N. L. Contributions to role-taking theory: a clinical study of self and role. *J. abnorm. soc. Psychol.*, 1952, 47, 117-125.

Sarbin, T. R., & Jones, D. S. An experimental analysis of role behavior. *J. abnorm. soc. Psychol.*, 1955, 51, 236-241.

Sarbin, T. R., & Rosenberg, B. G. Contributions to role-taking theory: IV. A method for obtaining a qualitative estimate of the self. *J. soc. Psychol.*, 1955, 42, 71-81.

Sarnoff, I. Identification with the aggressor: some personality correlates of anti-Semitism among Jews. *J. Pers.*, 1951, 20, 199-218.

Scheerer, E. T. An analysis of the relationship between acceptance of and respect for self and acceptance of and respect for others in ten counseling cases. *J. consult. Psychol.*, 1949, 13, 169-175.

Scott, W. A. Research definitions of mental health and mental illness. *Psychol. Bull.*, 1958, 55, 29-45.

Sears, Pauline. Level of aspiration in relation to some variables of personality: clinical studies. *J. soc. Psychol.*, 1941, 14, 311-336.

Sears, R. R. Experimental studies in projection: I. Attribution of traits. *J. soc. Psychol.*, 1936, 7, 151-163.

Secord, P. F. Objectification of word-association procedures by the use of homo-nyms: a measure of body-cathexis. *J. Pers.*, 1953, 21, 479-495.

Secord, P. F. "Personality integration" in response to self-inventories. *J. Pers.*, 1955, 23, 308-316.

Secord, P. F., & Jourard, S. M. The appraisal of body-cathexis: body-cathexis and the self. *J. consult. Psychol.*, 1953, 17, 343-347.

Sharma, S. L. Some personality correlates of changes in self-esteem under condi-tions of stress and support. *J. Educ. & Psychol. Baroda*, 1956, 14, 154-165.

Sherriffs, A. C., & McKee, J. P. Qualitative aspects of beliefs about men and women. *J. Pers.*, 1957, 25, 251-264.

Shontz, F. C. Body-concept disturbances of patients with hemiplegia. *J. clin. Psychol.*, 1956, 12, 293-295.

Singer, S. L., & Stefflre, B. Analysis of the self-estimate in the evaluation of counseling. *J. counsel. Psychol.*, 1954, 4, 252-255.

Smith, G. M. Six measures of self-concept discrepancy and instability: their interrelations, reliability and relations to other personality measures. *J. consult. Psychol.*, 1958, 22, 101-113.

Smith, M. B. The phenomenological approach in personality theory: some critical remarks. *J. abnorm. soc. Psychol.*, 1950, 45, 516-522.

Smith, W. D., & Lebo, D. Some changing aspects of the self-concept of pubescent males. *J. genet. Psychol.*, 1956, 88, 61-75.

Snygg, D., & Combs, A. W. *Individual behavior: a new frame of reference for psychology.* New York: Harper, 1949.

Snygg, D., & Combs, A. W. The phenomenological approach and the problem of "unconscious" behavior: a reply to Dr. Smith. *J. abnorm. soc. Psychol.*, 1950, 45, 523-528.

Solley, C. M., & Stagner, R. Effects of magnitude of temporal barriers, type of goal and perception of self. *J. exp. Psychol.*, 1956, 51, 62-70.

Sopchak, A. P. Parental 'identification' and 'tendency toward disorders' as measured by the Minnesota Multiphasic Personality Inventory. *J. abnorm. soc. Psychol.*, 1952, 47, 159-165.

Spence, K. W. The nature of theory construction in contemporary psychology. *Psychol. Rev.*, 1944, 51, 47-68.

Steiner, I. D. Self-perception and goal-setting behavior. *J. Pers.*, 1957, 25, 344-355.

Stephenson, W. Correlating persons instead of tests. *Charact. & Pers.*, 1935, 4, 17-24.

Stephenson, W. Some observations on Q-technique. *Psychol. Bull.*, 1952, 6, 483-498.

Stephenson, W. *The study of behavior.* Chicago: Univer. of Chicago Press, 1953.

Stevens, S. S. On the psychophysical law. *Psychol. Rev.*, 1957, 64, 153-181.

Stevens, S. S., & Galanter, E. H. Ratio scales and category scales for a dozen perceptual continua. *J. exp. Psychol.*, 1957, 54, 377-411.

Stock, Dorothy. An investigation into the intercorrelations between the self-concept and feelings directed toward other persons and groups. *J. consult. Psychol.*, 1949, 13, 176-180.

Stotland, E., Thorley, S., Thomas, E., Cohen, A. R., & Zander, A. The effects of group expectations and self-esteem upon self-evaluation. *J. abnorm. soc. Psychol.*, 1957, 54, 55-63.

Stotland, E., & Zander, A. Effects of public and private failure on self-evaluation. *J. abnorm. soc. Psychol.*, 1958, 56, 223-229.

Sullivan, H. S. *Conceptions of modern psychiatry.* Washington: William Alanson White Foundation, 1947.

Swensen, C. H., Jr. Empirical evaluations of human figure drawings. *Psychol. Bull.*, 1957, 54, 431-466.

Symonds, P. M. *The ego and the self.* New York: Appleton, 1951.

Tamkin, A. S. Selective recall in schizophrenia and its relation to ego strength. *J. abnorm. soc. Psychol.*, 1957, 55, 345-349.

Tarwater, J. W. Self-understanding and the ability to predict another's response. *Marriage fam. Living*, 1953, 15, 126-128.

Tarwater, J. W. The adolescent's question: "Who understands who I am?" *Understanding the Child*, 1955, 24, 11-14.

Taylor, C., & Combs, A. W. Self-acceptance and adjustment. *J. consult. Psychol.*, 1952, 16, 89-91.

Taylor, D. M. Changes in the self concept without psychotherapy. *J. consult. Psychol.*, 1955, 19, 205-209.

Thompson, W. R., & Nishimura, Rhoda. Some determinants of friendship. *J. Pers.*, 1952, 20, 305-314.

Tolor, A. Self-perceptions of neuropsychiatric patients on the W-A-Y test. *J. clin. Psychol.*, 1957, 13, 403-406.

Torgerson, W. S. *Theory and methods of scaling.* New York: Wiley, 1958.

Torrance, E. P. Rationalizations about test performance as a function of self-concepts. *J. soc. Psychol.*, 1954, 39, 211-217. (a)

Torrance, E. P. Some practical uses of a knowledge of self-concepts in counseling and guidance. *Educ. psychol. Measmt*, 1954, 14, 120-127. (b)

Travers, R. M. W. A critical review of the validity and rationale of the forced choice technique. *Psychol. Bull.*, 1951, 48, 62-70.

Turner, R. Self and other in moral judgment. *Amer. soc. Rev.*, 1954, 19, 249-259.

Turner, R. H., & Vanderlippe, R. H. Self-ideal congruence as an index of adjustment. *J. abnorm. soc. Psychol.*, 1958, 57, 202-206.

Underwood, B. J. *Psychological research.* New York: Appleton-Century-Crofts, 1957.

Vargas, M. J. Changes in self-awareness during client-centered therapy. In C. R. Rogers & Rosalind F. Dymond (Eds.), *Psychotherapy and personality change.* Chicago: Univer. of Chicago Press, 1954. Pp. 145-166.

Verplanck, W. S. Burrhus F. Skinner. In W. K. Estes, S. Koch, K. MacCorquodale, P. E. Meehl, C. G. Mueller, W. N. Schoenfeld, & W. S. Verplanck, *Modern learning theory: a critical analysis of five examples.* New York: Appleton-Century-Crofts, 1954.

Wahl, C. W. Some antecedent factors in the family histories of 109 alcoholics. *Quart. J. Stud. Alcohol*, 1956, 17, 643-654.

Wahler, H. J. Social desirability and self ratings of intakes, patients in treatment, and controls. *J. consult. Psychol.*, 1958, 22, 357-363.

Walsh, Anne M. Self concepts of bright boys with learning difficulties. *N. Y. Bur. of Pub. Teachers College, Columbia Univer.* 1956, XIII.

Ware, K. E., Fisher, S., & Cleveland, S. Body-image boundaries and adjustment to poliomyelitis. *J. abnorm. soc. Psychol.*, 1957, 55, 88-93.

Webb, W. B. Self-evaluation compared with group evaluations. *J. consult. Psychol.*, 1952, 16, 305-307.

Webb, W. B. Self-evaluations, group evaluations and objective measures. *J. consult. Psychol.*, 1955, 19, 210-212.

Webb, W. B. A procedure for obtaining self-ratings and group ratings. *J. consult. Psychol.*, 1956, 20, 233-236.

Wiener, M., Blumberg, A., Segman, Sarah, & Cooper, A. Judgment of adjustment by psychologists, psychiatric social workers, and college students, and its relationship to Social Desirability. *J. abnorm. soc. Psychol.*, 1959, 59, 315-321.

Weingarten, Erica M. A study of selective perception in clinical judgment. *J. Pers.*, 1949, 17, 369-406.

Worchel, P. Adaptability screening of flying personnel, development of a self-concept inventory for predicting maladjustment. School of Aviation Medicine, U.S.A.F., Report No. 56-62, 1957.

Wrenn, C. G. The self-concept in counseling. *J. counsel. Psychol.*, 1958, 5, 104-109.

Wylie, Ruth C. Some relationships between defensiveness and self-concept discrepancies. *J. Pers.*, 1957, 25, 600-616.

Young, H. H., Holtzman, W. H., & Bryant, N. D. Effects of item context and order on personality ratings. *Educ. psychol. Measmt*, 1954, 14, 499-517.

Zelen, S. L. Acceptance and acceptability. An examination of social reciprocity. *J. consult. Psychol.*, 1954, 18, 316. (a)

Zelen, S. L. The relationship of peer acceptance, acceptance of others, and self acceptance. *Proc. Iowa Acad. Sci.*, 1954, 61, 446-449. (b)

Zelen, S. L., Sheehan, J. G., & Bugental, J. F. T. Self-perception in stuttering. *J. clin. Psychol.*, 1954, 10, 70-72.

Zimmer, H. Self-acceptance and its relation to conflict. *J. consult. Psychol.*, 1954, 18, 447-449.

Zimmer, H. Motivational factors in dyadic interaction. *J. Pers.*, 1956, 24, 251-261.

Zuckerman, M., Baer, M., & Monashkin, I. Acceptance of self, parents and people in patients and normals. *J. clin. Psychol.*, 1956, 12, 327-332.

Zuckerman, M., & Monashkin, I. Self-acceptance and psychopathology. *J. consult. Psychol.*, 1957, 21, 145-148.

Unpublished Dissertations and Dissertation Abstracts

Aaronson, L. Self-distortion and distortion of others. *Dissertation Abstr.*, 1957, 17, 1590-1591.

Adelson, D. Attitudes toward first names: an investigation of the relation between self-acceptance, self-identity and group and individual attitudes toward first names. *Dissertation Abstr.*, 1957, 17, 1831.

Aidman, T. An objective study of the changing relationship between the present self and the ideal self picture as expressed by the client in non-directive psychotherapy. Unpublished doctoral dissertation, Univer. of Chicago, 1951.

Alden, Priscilla J. An exploratory study of self-rated empathy. *Dissertation Abstr.*, 1954, 14, 707-708.

Allison, Sarah G. Parent and peer group friend attitudes as they relate to the self-concept of the juvenile delinquent. *Dissertation Abstr.*, 1957, 17, 3086.

Aronfreed, J. M. Moral standards and defenses against guilt. *Dissertation Abstr.*, 1957, 17, 172-173.

Aronson, Carolyn E. The relation between self-concept and reaction to stress. *Dissertation Abstr.*, 1955, 15, 2285-2286.

Asch, M. J. Negative response bias and personality adjustment. *Dissertation Abstr.*, 1957, 17, 1704.

Balester, R. J. The self-concept and juvenile delinquency. *Dissertation Abstr.*, 1956, 16, 1169-1170.

Barron, F. X. Psychotherapy, as a special case of personal interaction: prediction of its outcome. Unpublished doctoral dissertation, Univer. of California, 1950.

Barry, J. R. An investigation of the relationship between adjustment level and characteristics of verbal reactions toward self and world. Unpublished doctoral dissertation, Ohio State Univer., 1949.

Beardslee, Betty A. The learning of two mechanisms of defense. *Dissertation Abstr.*, 1957, 17, 173-174.

Berger, S. The role of sexual impotence in the concept of self in male paraplegics. *Dissertation Abstr.*, 1952, 12, 533.

Block, J. An experimental investigation of the construct of ego-control. Unpublished doctoral dissertation, Stanford Univer., 1950.

Block, Jeanne. An experimental study of a topological representation of ego-structure. Unpublished doctoral dissertation, Stanford Univer., 1951.

Blodgett, Harriet E. An experimental approach to the measurement of self evaluation among adolescent girls. *Dissertation Abstr.*, 1953, 13, 871-872.

Bourestom, N. C., Jr. The interrelationships between two personality inventories and other behavioral measures. *Dissertation Abstr.*, 1956, 16, 2208.

Bowdlear, C. Dynamics of idiopathic epilepsy as studied in one case. Unpublished doctoral dissertation, Western Reserve Univer., 1955.

Bower, E. M. The application of Q methodology in investigating changes in self and ideal-self as a result of a mental health workshop. *Dissertation Abstr.*, 1954, 14, 1616-1617.

Boxer, M. A study of the relationship between self-awareness and social sensitivity. *Dissertation Abstr.*, 1952, 12, 719-720.

Branson, B. D. An investigation of manifest anxiety and the role of discrimination in self-ideal discrepancy and complex tasks. *Dissertation Abstr.*, 1957, 17, 2063.

Brodney, F. E. The construction and validation of the U.S. Naval School officer candidate, self-description blank. *Dissertation Abstr.*, 1957, 17, 1606.

Brophy, A. L. Self, role, and satisfaction. *Dissertation Abstr.*, 1957, 17, 1616.

Bruce, P. A study of the self-concept in sixth grade children. *Dissertation Abstr.*, 1957, 17, 2915.

Bugental, J. F. T. An investigation of the relationship of the conceptual matrix to the self-concept. *Abstracts of Doctoral Dissertations* No. 57, Ohio State Univer. Press, 1949.

Burch, I. A. The self-inflation hypothesis: a study in construct validation. *Dissertation Abstr.*, 1957, 17, 395-396.

Burgess, T. C. A study of certain relationships between self concept, vocational interests, and occupational stereotypes. *Dissertation Abstr.*, 1955, 15, 373-374.

Butler, J. M. Self evaluations of personality by adolescents. Unpublished doctoral dissertation, Univer. of Minnesota, 1949.

Calogeras, R. C. Some relationships between fantasy and self-report behavior. *Dissertation Abstr.*, 1957, 17, 1591-1592.

Candee, B. L., Jr. The recall of trait adjectives associated with conflicting ratings. *Dissertation Abstr.*, 1955, 15, 761-762.

Chase, P. Concepts of self and concepts of others in adjusted and maladjusted hospital patients. Unpublished doctoral dissertation, Univer. of Colorado, 1956.

Chertok, E. The social process of self-conception. *Dissertation Abstr.*, 1955, 15, 2330.

Christensen, G. M. The relationhsip between visual discrimination and certain personality variables. *Dissertation Abstr.*, 1957, 17, 901.

Clancy, D. D. The relationship of positive response bias or acquiescense to psychopathology. *Dissertation Abstr.*, 1957, 17, 2055.

Cohen, A. R. The effects of individual self-esteem and situational structure on threat-oriented reactions to power. *Dissertation Abstr.*, 1954, 14, 727-728.

Cohen, H. M. The relationship of the prison program to changes in attitudes and self-concepts of inmates: an evaluation of self-concept, acceptance of self, ideal self, and predisposition toward crime and delinquency in prison inmates. *Dissertation Abstr.*, 1958, 18, 653-654.

Costa, L. D. Test anxiety, self-acceptance, and task performance in an induced failure situation. *Dissertation Abstr.*, 1957, 17, 1593.

Couch, C. J. A study of the relationships between self-views and role-taking accuracy. *Dissertation Abstr.*, 1957, 17, 687.

Davidson, K. S. Accuracy of self-appraisal and clinicians' interpretations of Rorschach protocols. *Dissertation Abstr.*, 1954, 14, 1098-1099.

Dawkins, P. B. H. The construct validity of a self-rating scale. *Dissertation Abstr.*, 1957, 17, 2678.

DeLisle, Frances. A study of the relationship of the self-concept to adjustment in a selected group of college women. Unpublished doctoral dissertation, Michigan State College, 1953.

Dellen, J. E. An investigation into the relation between desire for change in social institutions and desire for change in self. *Dissertation Abstr.*, 1954, 14, 199-200.

Doleys, E. J., Jr. The effect of failure on verbal learning as a function of self-acceptance. *Dissertation Abstr.*, 1957, 17, 3096.

Dolinko, P. Set and conceptual defense. *Dissertation Abstr.*, 1957, 17, 1388.

Dunn, M. B. Global evaluation of children's drawings of "person" and "self." *Dissertation Abstr.*, 1955, 16, 1254-1255.

Fabian, W. A. An investigation of the relationship between measures of insight and measures of projection and distortion in ratings. *Dissertation Abstr.*, 1954, 14, 711.

Faust, V. A study of the relationship between self-concept discrepancies and personal adjustment. *Dissertation Abstr.*, 1955, 15, 2468-2469.

Fishman, S. Self-concept and adjustment to leg prosthesis. Unpublished doctoral dissertation, Columbia Univer., 1949.

Fitts, W. H. The role of the self-concept in social perception. *Dissertation Abstr.,* 1955, 15, 463.

Fogelson, H. The clinician's accuracy of self-insight in relation to his evaluation of a projective test. Unpublished doctoral dissertation, Univer. of California, 1952.

Force, D. G. A comparison of physically handicapped children and normal children in the same elementary school classes with reference to social status and self-perceived status. *Dissertation Abstr.,* 1954, 14, 1046.

Fordyce, W. E. Applications of a scale of dependency to concepts of self, ideal-self, mother and father. *Dissertation Abstr.,* 1953, 13, 591.

Fox, Margaret. A quantitative study of changes in verbal behavior occurring in counseling. Unpublished doctoral dissertation, Univer. of Chicago, 1951.

Gaines, G. R. A Q-technique study of characteristics of the hypothetical "ideal" college graduate. *Dissertation Abstr.,* 1957, 17, 397.

Goldberg, Miriam L. Leadership and self-attitudes. *Dissertation Abstr.,* 1955, 15, 1457-1458.

Goldfarb, A. An experimental study of performance under stress in relation to intellectual control and expressed self-acceptance. *Dissertation Abstr.,* 1954, 14, 1457.

Goodman, H. Self-insight, empathy, and perceptual distortion: a study of the relationships between measures of self-insight, empathy, and perceptual distortion as obtained from ratings made by individuals on themselves and others in their group. *Dissertation Abstr.,* 1953, 13, 120.

Goodrich, E. G. The generality of self constructs. *Dissertation Abstr.,* 1955, 15, 1114.

Green, Leah A. A study of creativity and the self-attitudes and sociability of high school students. *Dissertation Abstr.,* 1957, 17, 1807-1808.

Greenspoon, J. The effect of verbal and non-verbal stimuli on the frequency of members of two verbal response classes. Unpublished doctoral dissertation, Univer. of Indiana, 1950.

Haigh, G. V. The role of value and threat in perceptual orientation. Unpublished doctoral dissertation, Univer. of Chicago, 1950.

Haimowitz, M. L. Ethnic hostility-displacement and psychotherapy. Unpublished doctoral dissertation, Univer. of Chicago, 1950.

Halloway, R. S. Sociological theory and analysis of the self: a study of self attitudes as related to the selection of social roles. *Dissertation Abstr.,* 1953, 13, 448.

Hamilton, R. Jane. Generality of personal constructs. *Dissertation Abstr.,* 1958, 18, 656-657.

Hampton, B. J. An investigation of personality characteristics associated with self-adequacy. *Dissertation Abstr.,* 1955, 15, 1203-1204.

Harlow, R. G. The perception of persons: an exploratory study of some of the determinants of self perception and social perception. *Dissertation Abstr.,* 1956, 16, 2220-2221.

Hartley, M. Changes in the self-concept during psychotherapy. Unpublished doctoral dissertation, Univer. of Chicago, 1951.

Hauser, F. S. The relationship of self-concept to security, anxiety, and rigidity. Unpublished doctoral dissertation, Univer. of Rochester, 1953.

Hertz, L. A study of the discriminative efficiency of statements expressing the self concepts of a group of teachers. *Dissertation Abstr.*, 1955, 15, 2469-2470.

Hogan, R. A. The development of a measure of client defensiveness in the counseling relationship. Unpublished doctoral dissertation, Univ. of Chicago, 1948.

Howard, A. R. Psychological change as revealed by self-descriptions. *Dissertation Abstr.*, 1958, 18, 658-660.

Hoyt, D. P. Differential outcomes of counseling with college men. *Dissertation Abstr.*, 1954, 14, 2126.

Isenberger, Wilma E. Self-attitudes of women physical education majors as related to measures of interest and success. *Dissertation Abstr.*, 1957, 17, 2911-2912.

Jesness, C. F. The effects of counseling on the self-perceptions of college men. *Dissertation Abstr.*, 1955, 15, 1553.

Jessor, R. A methodological investigation of the strength and generalization of verbal reinforcement. Unpublished doctoral dissertation, Ohio State Univer., 1951.

Jonietz, Alice K. A study of the phenomenological changes in perception after psychotherapy as exhibited in the content of Rorschach percepts. Unpublished doctoral dissertation, Univer. of Chicago, 1950.

Kaplan, M. J. Unconscious self evaluation and subliminal familiarity: an evaluation of the Wolff-Huntley expressive behavior technique for eliciting self concepts and its relationship to subliminal familiarity. *Dissertation Abstr.*, 1957, 17, 3083-3084.

Kell, B. L. An experimental study of the ability to predict the self-concept of an individual from his therapeutic interview behavior. Unpublished doctoral dissertation, Univer. of Chicago, 1950.

Leuthold, C. A. A study of the perception of self and of others as a function of group experience. *Dissertation Abstr.*, 1956, 16, 998.

Levine, M. The process of judgment and projection in the rating of personality characteristics of others. *Dissertation Abstr.*, 1954, 14, 878-879.

McGehee, T. P. The stability of the self-concept and self-esteem. *Dissertation Abstr.*, 1957, 17, 1403-1404.

McPartland, T. S. D. The self and social structure: an empirical approach. *Dissertation Abstr.*, 1953, 13, 447-448.

Mannheim, Betty F. An investigation of the interrelations of reference groups, membership groups, and the self image: a test of the Cooley-Mead theory of the self. *Dissertation Abstr.*, 1957, 17, 1616-1617.

Mazurkiewicz, J. F. A comparison of the effect of a reflective and of a leading type of psychotherapy on client concept of self, of ideal, and of therapist. *Dissertation Abstr.*, 1957, 17, 1121.

Melniker, R. C. Self-acceptance and the mechanism of identification: a Q-sort investigation of the relationship between levels of self-acceptance, character, parental descriptions and identification patterns in college women. *Dissertation Abstr.*, 1957, 17, 1812-1813.

Mosak, H. H. Evaluation in psychotherapy: a study of some current measures. Unpublished doctoral dissertation, Univer. of Chicago, 1950.

Mulford, H. A., Jr. Toward an instrument to identify and measure the self, significant others, and alcohol in the symbolic environment: an empirical study. *Dissertation Abstr.*, 1955, 15, 1667-1668.

Newman, D. K. A study of factors leading to change within the personal construct system. *Dissertation Abstr.*, 1957, 17, 1597-1598.

Newman, M. Personality differences between volunteers and non-volunteers for psychological investigation; self-actualization of volunteers and non-volunteers for researches in personality and perception. *Dissertation Abstr.*, 1957, 17, 409.

Pock, J. C. The influence of controlled structure and composition upon performance and self-conception in task-oriented groups: a laboratory study. *Dissertation Abstr.*, 1957, 17, 419-420.

Pyne, F. F. The relationship of measures of self concept, motivation and ability to success in competitive athletics. *Dissertation Abstr.*, 1957, 17, 559.

Raymaker, H., Jr. Relationships between the self-concept, self-ideal concept and maladjustment. *Dissertation Abstr.*, 1957, 17, 409-410.

Reeder, Thelma A. A study of some relationships between level of self-concept, academic achievement and classroom adjustment. *Dissertation Abstr.*, 1955, 15, 2472.

Renzaglia, G. A. Some correlates of the self structure as measured by an index of adjustment and values. Unpublished doctoral dissertation, Univer. of Minnesota, 1952.

Robison, R. K. A study of the concept of the idealized image in relation to similar concepts and to certain psychological experiments. *Dissertation Abstr.*, 1954, 14, 398-399.

Roos, D. E. Complementary needs in mate-selection: a study based on R-type factor analysis. *Dissertation Abstr.*, 1957, 17, 426-427.

Ross, E. M. The social sensitivity of college students in judging their parents. *Dissertation Abstr.*, 1957, 17, 1128-1129.

Rubin, S. I. A study of the self-concept of function within the profession of counseling psychology. *Dissertation Abstr.*, 1957, 17, 1587.

Russell, D. L. A comparsion of rating, test, and sociometric methods of personality measurement. *Dissertation Abstr.*, 1954, 14, 552-553.

Scheide, Elizabeth J. Anxiety: its relationship to self-evaluation. *Dissertation Abstr.*, 1955, 15, 880.

Scher, S. C. Some group attitudes related to expressed acceptance of self and others. *Dissertation Abstr.*, 1955, 15, 2579.

Scott, H. A. The empirical assessment of self-acceptance. Unpublished doctoral dissertation, Duke Univer., 1953.

Selzer, S. Relationships between developmental experiences and choice of defensive behavior: Study II, Females. *Dissertation Abstr.*, 1957, 17, 1389-1390.

Shelsky, I. The effect of disability on self-concept. *Dissertation Abstr.*, 1957, 17, 1598-1599.

Short, M. R. Self-esteem: a study of the ethical significance of certain aspects of the dynamics of self-esteem as developed in psychiatry and Gestalt psychology. *Dissertation Abstr.*, 1953, 13, 412-413.

Silver, I. H. Attitudes toward the self and others of a group of psychoanalysands. A determination of the relationship between attitudes toward self and toward others and human and human-like responses on the Rorschach. *Dissertation Abstr.*, 1957, 17, 1815-1816.

Silverman, H. The prediction of consciousness of conflict in the self from the Rorschach. *Dissertation Abstr.*, 1953, 13, 438.

Silverstein, A. B. The expression of acceptable and unacceptable needs in thematic apperception. *Dissertation Abstr.*, 1957, 17, 410.

Solomon, A. Identification, differentiation, and extension of self: a study of perceptions of self; mother, and daughter in a sample of college women. *Dissertation Abstr.*, 1955, 15, 1121.

Stee, Marjorie. Some dimensions and personality correlates of social self-insight. *Dissertation Abstr.*, 1954, 14, 2148.

Stewart, R. L. The self and other objects: their measurement and interrelationships. *Dissertation Abstr.*, 1955, 15, 1668-1669.

Tatum, C. D. The influence of parental acceptance on selected self factors in children. *Dissertation Abstr.*, 1957, 17, 97.

Thorne, R. B. The effects of experimentally induced failure on self-evaluations. *Dissertation Abstr.*, 1954, 14, 1817.

Tolor, A. Rigidity of self-concept as a mechanism in the maintenance of personality equilibrium, and as an expression of this equilibrium. *Dissertation Abstr.*, 1955, 15, 1121-1122.

Torrance, E. P. Self-concepts and their significance in the learning and adjustment of college freshmen. Unpublished doctoral dissertation, Univer. of Michigan, 1951.

Waisanen, C. E. Preference aspect of self-attitudes. *Dissertation Abstr.*, 1957, 17, 2079.

Walker, J. H. The relationship between consistency of attitude toward the self and personal adjustment. *Dissertation Abstr.*, 1956, 16, 796.

Walker, P. D. Pre-retirement problems as related to the self-concept of the individual. *Dissertation Abstr.*, 1956, 16, 1169.

Warrington, W. G. The efficiency of Q-sort and other test designs for measuring the similarity between persons. Unpublished doctoral dissertation, Univer. of Illinois, 1952.

Wilk, R. E. The self perceptions and the perceptions of others of adolescent leaders elected by their peers. *Dissertation Abstr.*, 1957, 17, 1954-1955.

SUPPLEMENTAL BIBLIOGRAPHY

Adams, J. K., & Adams, Pauline A. Realism of confidence judgments. *Psychol. Rev.*, 1961, 68, 33-45.

Adams, J. S., & Hoffman, B. The frequency of self-reference statements as a function of generalized reinforcement. *J. abnorm. soc. Psychol.*, 1960, 60, 384-389.

Allison, J., & Hunt, D. E. Social desirability and the expression of aggression under varying conditions of frustration. *J. consult. Psychol.*, 1959, 23, 528-532.

Altrocchi, J., Parsons, O. A., & Dickoff, Hilda. Changes in self-ideal discrepancy in repressors and sensitizers. *J. abnorm. soc. Psychol.*, 1960, 61, 67-72.

Anderson, C. C. The many voices: a preliminary investigation into the consistency of the self concept. *Alberta J. educ. Res.*, 1959, 5, 7-15.

Arbuckle, D. S. Self-ratings and test scores on two standardized personality inventories. *Personnel Guid. J.*, 1958, 37, 292-293.

Armstrong, Renate G. The Leary Interpersonal Check List: a reliability study. *J. clin. Psychol.*, 1958, 14, 393-394.

Armstrong, Renate G., & Hauck, P. A. Sexual identification and the first figure drawn. *J. consult. Psychol.*, 1961, 25, 51-54.

Armstrong, Renate G., & Wertheimer, M. Personality structure in alcoholism. *Psychol. Newsltr*, 1959, 10, 341-349.

Babladelis, Georgia. Personality and verbal conditioning effects. *J. abnorm. soc. Psychol.*, 1961, 62, 41-43.

Barnett, C. D., & Traver, W. N. Self-rated problems of institutionalized delinquent vs. non-delinquent girls. *Psychol. Rep.*, 1959, 5, 333-336.

Bartlett, C. J. The relationships between self-ratings and peer ratings on a leadership behavior scale. *Personnel Psychol.*, 1959, 12, 237-246.

Becker, W. C. The relationship of factors in parental ratings of self and each other to the behavior of kindergarten children as rated by mothers, fathers, and teachers. *J. consult. Psychol.*, 1960, 24, 507-527.

Beer, M., Buckhout, R., Horowitz, M. W., & Levy, S. Some perceived properties of the difference between leaders and non-leaders. *J. Psychol.*, 1959, 47, 49-56.

Bendig, A. W. Factor analysis of the non-MAS items in Edwards' Social Desirability Scale. *Psychol. Newsltr*, 1959, 10, 336-340.

Berger, E. M. Willingness to accept limitations and college achievement. *J. counsel. Psychol.*, 1961, 8, 140-146.

Berkowitz, L. Anti-Semitism and the displacement of aggression. *J. abnorm. soc. Psychol.*, 1959, 59, 182-187.

Berkowitz, L. The judgmental process in personality functioning. *Psychol. Rev.*, 1960, 67, 130-142.

Berkowitz, L. Some factors affecting the reduction of overt hostility. *J. abnorm. soc. Psychol.*, 1960, 60, 14-21.

Bieri, J., & Lobeck, Robin. Acceptance of authority and parental identification. *J. Pers.*, 1959, 27, 74-86.

Bieri, J., & Lobeck, Robin. Self-concept differences in relation to identification, religion, and social class. *J. abnorm. soc. Psychol.*, 1961, 62, 94-98.

Bieri, J., Lobeck, Robin, & Galinsky, M. D. A comparison of direct, indirect, and fantasy measures of identification. *J. abnorm. soc. Psychol.*, 1959, 58, 253-258.

Bills, R. E. Personality changes during student centered teaching. *J. educ. Res.*, 1956, 50, 121-126.

Bills, R. E. Two questions: a reply to Cowen and Tongas. *J. consult. Psychol.*, 1959, 23, 366-367.

Blizzard, S. W. The parish minister's self-image and variability in community culture. *Pastoral Psychol.*, 1959, 10, 27-36.

Bloom, L. Self concepts and social status in South Africa: a preliminary cross-cultural analysis. *J. soc. Psychol.*, 1960, 51, 103-112.

Bodwin, R. F., & Bruck, M. The adaptation and validation of the Draw-a-Person Test as a measure of self concept. *J. clin. Psychol.*, 1960, 26, 427-429.

Borgatta, E. F. Rankings and self-assessments: some behavioral characteristics replication studies. *J. soc. Psychol.*, 1960, 52, 279-307.

Braaten, L. J. The movement from non-self to self in client-centered psychotherapy. *J. counsel. Psychol.*, 1961, 8, 20-24.

Briggs, P. F., & Wirt, R. D. Intra-Q deck relationships as influences and realities in personality assessment. *J. consult. Psychol.*, 1960, 24, 61-66.

Bronson, G. W. Identity diffusion in late adolescents. *J. abnorm. soc. Psychol.*, 1959, 59, 414-417.

Brophy, A. L. Self, role, and satisfaction. *Genet. psychol. Monogr.*, 1959, 59, 263-308.

Broverman, D. M. Effects of score transformations in Q and R factor analysis techniques. *Psychol. Rev.*, 1961, 68, 68-80.

Burma, J. H. Self-tattooing among delinquents: a research note. *Sociol. soc. Res.*, 1959, 43, 341-345.

Burstin, J. *L'evolution psycho-sociale de l'enfant de 10 à 13 ans. (Psychosocial development of the child from 10 to 13 years of age.)* Neuchatel, Switzerland: Delachaux & Niestle, 1959.

Buss, A. H. The effect of item style on Social Desirability and frequency of endorsement. *J. consult. Psychol.*, 1959, 23, 510-513.

Buss, A. H., & Guerjoy, H. The scaling of terms used to describe personality. *J. consult. Psychol.*, 1957, 21, 361-369.

Calden, G., Lundy, R. M., & Schlafer, R. J. Sex differences in body concepts. *J. consult. Psychol.*, 1959, 23, 378.

Calogeras, R. C. Some relationships between fantasy and self-report behavior. *Genet. psychol. Monogr.*, 1958, 58, 273-325.

Cartwright, Rosalind D., & Vogel, J. L. A comparison of changes in psychoneurotic patients during matched periods of therapy and no therapy. *J. consult. Psychol.*, 1960, 24, 121-127.

Cassel, R. N. Comparing the effectiveness of the ego-strength Q-sort test by use of R- and Q-methodologies. *J. genet. Psychol.*, 1959, 94, 161-168.

Chang, Judy, & Block, J. A study of identication in male homosexuals. *J. consult. Psychol.*, 1960, 24, 307-310.

Chansky, N. M. The self-concept and the perception of values of teachers. *J. hum. Relat.*, 1959, 7, 358-366.

Chase, P. H. A note on projection. *Psychol. Bull.*, 1960, 57, 289-290.

Cleveland, S. E. Body image changes associated with personality reorganization. *J. consult. Psychol.*, 1960, 24, 256-261.

Coelho, G. V. A guide to literature on friendship: a selectively annotated bibliography. *Psychol. Newsltr*, 1959, 10, 365-394.

Coombs, C. H. A theory of data. *Psychol. Rev.*, 1960, 67, 3, 143-159.

Coopersmith, S. Self-esteem and need achievement as determinants of selective recall and repetition. *J. abnorm. soc. Psychol.*, 1960, 60, 310-317.

Corah, N. L., Feldman, M. J., Cohen, I. S., Gruen, W., Meadow, A., & Ringwall, E. A. Social desirability as a variable in the Edwards Personal Preference Schedule. *J. consult. Psychol.*, 1958, 22, 70-72.

Cornell, A. D. An experiment in apparitional observation and findings. *J. soc. Psych. Res.*, 1959, 40, 120-124.

Corsini, R. J. *Standard adjective* Q *sort*. Chicago: Psychometric Affiliates, 1956.

Couch, A., & Keniston, K. Agreeing response set and Social Desirability. *J. abnorm. soc. Psychol.*, 1961, 62, 175-179.

Couch, A., & Keniston, K. Yeasayers and naysayers: agreeing response set as a personality variable. *J. abnorm. soc. Psychol.*, 1960, 60, 151-174.

Cowen, E. L. The Social Desirability of trait descriptive terms: preliminary norms and sex differences. *J. soc. Psychol.*, 1961, 53, 225-233.

Cowen, E. L., Budin, W., & Budin, Florence A. The Social Desirability of trait descriptive terms: a variation in instructional set. *J. soc. Psychol.*, 1961, 53, 317-323.

Cowen, E. L., Budin, W., Wolitzky, D. L., & Stiller, A. The Social Desirability of trait descriptive terms: a factor in the prediction of Q sort. *J. Pers.*, 1960, 28, 530-544.

Cowen, E. L., Staiman, M. G., & Wolitzky, D. L. The Social Desirability of trait descriptive terms: applications to a schizophrenic sample. *J. soc. Psychol.*, 1961, 54, 37-45.

Crook, M. N. The constancy of neuroticism scores and self-judgments of constancy. *J. Psychol.*, 1937, 4, 27-34.

Crook, M. N. A further note on self-judgments of constancy in neurotics in scores. *J. soc. Psychol.*, 1938, 9, 485-487.

Crowne, D. P. A new scale of Social Desirability independent of psychopathology. *J. consult. Psychol.*, 1960, 24, 349-354.

Crowne, D. P., & Stephens, M. W. Self-acceptance and self-evaluative behavior: a critique of methodology. *Psychol. Bull.*, 1961, 58, 104-121.

Crowne, D. P., Stephens, M. W., & Kelly, R. The validity and equivalence of tests of self-acceptance. *J. Psychol.*, 1961, 51, 101-112.

deCharms, R., & Rosenbaum, M. E. Status variables and matching behavior. *J. Pers.*, 1960, 28, 492-502.

de Jung, J. E. Measurement of accuracy of self-role perceptions. In Edith M. Huddleston (Ed.), *The sixteenth yearbook of the National Council on Measurements Used in Education.* Pp. 111-116.

DeSoto, C. B., Coleman, E. B., & Putnam, P. L. Predictions of sequences of successes and failures. *J. exp. Psychol.*, 1960, 59, 41-46.

DeSoto, C. B., Kuethe, J. L., & Wunderlich, R. Social perception and self-perception of high and low authoritarians. *J. soc. Psychol.*, 1960, 52, 149-155.

Deutsch, M., & Solomon, L. Reactions to evaluations by others as influenced by self-evaluations. *Sociometry*, 1959, 22, 93-112.

Dickey, Brenda. Attitudes toward sex roles and feelings of adequacy in homosexual males. *J. consult. Psychol.*, 1961, 25, 116-122.

Dinitz, S., Mangus, A. R., & Pasamanick, B. Integration and conflict in self-other conceptions as factors in mental illness. *Sociometry*, 1959, 22, 44-55.

Doleys, E. J., & Kregarman, J. Construct validity of the Chicago Q-sort: frustration tolerance. *J. clin. Psychol.*, 1959, 15, 177-179.

Dreger, R. M., & Miller, K. S. Comparative psychological studies of Negroes and Whites in the United States. *Psychol. Bull.*, 1960, 57, 361-402.

Dymond, Rosalind F. An adjustment score for Q sorts. *J. consult. Psychol.*, 1953, 17, 339-342.

Edwards, A. L. Social Desirability and the description of others. *J. abnorm. soc. Psychol.*, 1959, 59, 434-436.

Edwards, A. L., & Walker, J. N. A note on the Couch and Keniston measure of agreement response set. *J. abnorm. soc. Psychol.*, 1961, 62, 173-174.

Edwards, A. L., & Walker, J. N. Social Desirability and agreement response set. *J. abnorm. soc. Psychol.*, 1961, 62, 180-183.

Edwards, A. L., Wright, C. E., & Lunneborg, C. E. A note on "Social Desirability as a variable in the Edwards Personal Preference Schedule." *J. consult. Psychol.*, 1959, 23, 558.

Eigenbrode, C. R., & Shipman, W. G. The body-image barrier concept. *J. abnorm. soc. Psychol.*, 1960, 60, 3, 450-452.

Endler, N. S. Changes in meaning during psychotherapy as measured by the semantic differential. *J. counsel. Psychol.*, 1961, 8, 105-111.

Englander, Meryl E. A psychological analysis of vocational choice: teaching. *J. counsel. Psychol.*, 1960, 7, 257-264.

Fagan, J., & Guthrie, G. M. Perception of self and of normality in schizophrenics. *J. clin. Psychol.*, 1959, 15, 203-207.

Feldman, M. J., & Corah, N. L. Social Desirability and the forced choice method. *J. consult. Psychol.*, 1960, 24, 480-482.

Feldman, M. J., & Siegel, S. M. The effect on self description of combining anxiety and hostility items on a single scale. *J. clin. Psychol.*, 1958, 14, 74-77.

Fiedler, F. E., Hutchins, E. B., & Dodge, Joan S. Quasi-therapeutic relations in small college and military groups. *Psychol. Monogr.*, 1959, 73 (3, Whole No. 473).

Fillenbaum, S. How fat is fat? Some consequences of similarity between judge and judged object. *J. Psychol.*, 1961, 52, 133-136.

Fillenbaum, S. Own position in relation to estimates of average standing and desirability for more and less self-comparable objects. *J. Pers.*, 1961, 29, 195-204.

Fisher, S. Body reactivity gradients and figure drawing variables. *J. consult. Psychol.*, 1959, 23, 54-59.

Fisher, S. Extensions of theory concerning body image and body reactivity. *Psychosom. Med.*, 1959, 21, 142-149.

Fisher, S. Front-back differentiations in body image and body reactivity. *J. gen. Psychol.*, 1961, 64, 373-379.

Fisher, S. Head-body differentiations in body image and skin resistance level. *J. abnorm. soc. Psychol.*, 1960, 60, 283-285.

Fisher, S. Prediction of body exterior vs. interior reactivity from a body image schema. *J. Pers.*, 1959, 27, 56-62.

Fisher, S., & Fisher, Rhoda L. A developmental analysis of some body image and body reactivity dimensions. *Child Develpm.*, 1959, 30, 389-402.

Fosmire, F. R. The role of ego defense in academic reputations. *J. soc. Psychol.*, 1959, 49, 41-45.

Foulds, G. A. Attitudes toward self and others of psychopaths. *J. indiv. Psychol.*, 1960, 16, 81-83.

Freudenberger, H. J., & Robbins, I. Characteristics of acceptance and rejection of optical aids in a low-vision population. *Amer. J. Ophthal.*, 1959, 47, 582-584.

Gabriel, J. Self knowledge and the therapeutic process. *Aust. J. Psychol.*, 1959, 11, 215.

Gaier, E. L. Student self estimates of final course grades. *J. genet. Psychol.*, 1961, 98, 63-67.

Gaier, E. L., & Wambach, Helen S. Self-evaluation of personality assets and liabilities of Southern White and Negro students. *J. soc. Psychol.*, 1960, 51, 135-143.

Garner, W. R. Rating scales, discriminability, and information transmission. *Psychol. Rev.*, 1960, 67, 343-352.

Gocka, E. F. The introversion-extraversion factor and Social Desirability. *J. clin. Psychol.*, 1960, 26, 380-383.

Goldfarb, A. Performance under stress in relation to intellectual control and self-acceptance. *J. consult. Psychol.*, 1961, 25, 7-12.

Goldstein, A. P. Patient's expectancies and non-specific therapy as a basis for (un)spontaneous remission. *J. clin. Psychol.*, 1960, 16, 399-403.

Goldstein, A. P. Therapist and client expectation of personality change in psychotherapy. *J. counsel. Psychol.*, 1960, 7, 180-184.

Goldstein, A. P., & Shipman, W. G. Patient expectancies, symptom reduction and aspects of the initial psychotherapeutic interview. *J. clin. Psychol.*, 1961, 17, 129-133.

Gordon, I. J., & Combs, W. The learner: self and perception. *Rev. educ. Res.*, 1958, 28, 433-444.

Gough, H. G. The adjective check list as a personality assessment research technique. *Psychol. Rep.*, 1960, 6, 107-122.

Grater, H. Changes in self and other attitudes in a leadership training group. *Personnel Guid. J.*, 1959, 37, 493-496.

Gray, Susan W. Perceived similarity to parents and adjustment. *Child Develpm.*, 1959, 30, 91-107.

Grigg, A. E. Superiority of childhood account over current account for judging current self impressions. *J. indiv. Psychol.*, 1960, 16, 64-66.

Grigg, A. E. A validity study of the semantic differential technique. *J. clin. Psychol.*, 1959, 15, 179-181.

Grigg, A. E. A validity test of self-ideal discrepancy. *J. clin. Psychol.*, 1959, 15, 311-313.

Grossack, M. M. The "Who Am I Test." *J. soc. Psychol.*, 1960, 51, 399-402.

Gruen, W. Rejection of false information about oneself as an indication of ego identity. *J. consult. Psychol.*, 1960, 24, 231-239.

Guertin, W. H. A factor analysis of geriatric attitudes. *J. consult. Psychol.*, 1961, 25, 39-42.

Guilford, J. P. Factorial angles to psychology. *Psychol. Rev.*, 1961, 68, 1-20.

Hanley, C. Social Desirability and response bias in the MMPI. *J. consult. Psychol.*, 1961, 25, 13-20.

Hersko, M., & Winder, E. Changes in patients' attitudes toward self and others during group psychotherapy. *Group Psychother.*, 1958, 11, 309-313.

Hetzer, Hildegard. Der Körper in der Selbstdarstellung von Kindern im Jahre 1926 und im Jahre 1957 (The body in self-descriptions of children in 1926 and 1957.) *Z. exp. angew. Psychol.*, 1959, 6, 15-21.

Hill, W. F. Learning theory and the acquisition of values. *Psychol. Rev.*, 1960, 67, 317-331.

Hunt, R. G., & Feldman, M. J. Body image and ratings of adjustment on human figure drawings. *J. clin. Psychol.*, 1960, 26, 35-38.

Hunt, Valerie V., & Weber, Mary E. Body image projective test. *J. proj. Tech.*, 1960, 24, 3-10.

Hutchins, E. B., & Fiedler, F. E. Task-oriented and quasi-therapeutic role functions of the leader in small military groups. *Sociometry*, 1960, 23, 393-406.

Imboden, J. B., Canter, A., Cluff, L. E., & Trever, R. W. Brucellosis: III. Psychologic aspects of delayed convalescence. *AMA Arch. intern. Med.*, 1959, 103, 406-414.

Isenberger, Wilma. Self-attitudes of women physical education major students and of women physical education teachers. *Res. Quart. Amer. Ass. Hlth Phys. Educ. Recr.*, 1959, 30, 44-53.

Izard, C. E. Personality correlates of sociometric status. *J. appl. Psychol.*, 1959, 43, 89-93.

Izard, C. E. Personality similarity and friendship. *J. abnorm. soc. Psychol.*, 1960, 61, 47-51.

Jackson, D. M., & Bidwell, C. E. A modification of Q-technique. *Educ. psychol. Measmt*, 1959, 19, 221-232.

Jervis, F. M. The meaning of a positive self-concept. *J. clin. Psychol.*, 1959, 15, 370-373.

Jones, E. E., Hester, S. L., Farina, A., & Davis, K. E. Reactions to unfavorable personal evaluations as a function of the evaluator's perceived adjustment. *J. abnorm. soc. Psychol.*, 1959, 59, 363-370.

Jones, Mary C., & Mussen, P. H. Self-conceptions, motivations, and interpersonal attitudes of early- and late-maturing girls. *Child Develpm.*, 1958, 29, 491-501.

Jourard, S. M. Age trends in self-disclosure. *Merrill-Palmer Quart. Behav. Develpm.*, 1961, 7, 191-197.

Jourard, S. M. Religious denomination and self-disclosure. *Psychol. Rep.*, 1961, 8, 446.

Jourard, S. M. Self-disclosure and other-cathexis. *J. abnorm. soc. Psychol.*, 1959, **59**, 428-431.

Jourard, S. M., & Landsman, M. J. Cognition, cathexis, and the "dyadic effect" in men's self-disclosing behavior. *Merrill-Palmer Quart. Behav. Develpm.*, 1959-60, **6**, 178-186.

Jung, C. G. *AION: Researches into the phenomenology of the self.* New York: Pantheon Books, 1959.

Kagan, J., & Moss, H. A. The availability of conflictful ideas: a neglected parameter in assessing projective test responses. *J. Pers.*, 1961, **29**, 217-234.

Kamano, D. K. An investigation on the meaning of human figure drawing. *J. clin. Psychol.*, 1960, **26**, 429-430.

Kanfer, F. H. Verbal rate, content, and adjustment ratings in experimentally structured interviews. *J. abnorm. soc. Psychol.*, 1959, **58**, 305-311.

Kaywin, L. On the concept of the self. *J. Hillside Hosp.*, 1959, **8**, 86-93.

Kelly, E. L. Marital compatibility as related to personality traits of husbands and wives as rated by self and spouse. *J. soc. Psychol.*, 1941, **13**, 193-198.

Kennedy, Paulina M. *Acceptance of self and acceptance of others as interdependent variables in interpersonal relations.* Washington, D. C.: Catholic Univer. of America Press, 1958.

Kibrick, Anne K., & Tiedeman, D. V. Conception of self and perception of role in schools of nursing. *J. counsel. Psychol.*, 1961, **8**, 62-69.

Kirchner, W. K., & Dunnette, M. D. How salesmen and technical men differ in describing themselves. *Personnel J.*, 1959, **37**, 418-420.

Klett, C. J., & Yawkey, D. W. A cross-cultural comparison of judgments of Social Desirability. *J. soc. Psychol.*, 1959, **49**, 19-26.

Knapp, R. H. A study of the metaphor. *J. proj. Tech.*, 1960, **24**, 389-395.

Kohn, A. R., & Fiedler, F. E. Age and sex differences in the perception of persons. *Sociometry*, 1961, **24**, 157-163.

Kosa, J., Rachiele, L. D., & Schommer, C. O. Psychological characteristics of ethnic groups in a college population. *J. Psychol.*, 1958, **46**, 265-275.

Krider, Mary A. A comparative study of the self-concepts of crippled and non-crippled children. *Rep. Easter Seal Res. Found.*, 1959, **32**.

Krieger, Margery H., & Worchel, P. A test of the psychoanalytic theory of identification. *J. indiv. Psychol.*, 1960, **16**, 56-63.

Kuhn, M. H. Self-attitudes by age, sex, and professional training. *Sociol. Quart.*, 1960, **1**, No. 1.

Larson, C. A., & Bower, E. M. *Thinking about yourself.* Sacramento: Calif. State Dept. of Education (n. d.)

Levitt, E. E. A comparison of parental and self-evaluations of psychopathology in children. *J. clin. Psychol.*, 1959, **15**, 402-404.

Lewis, M. N., & Spilka, B. Sociometric choice status, empathy, assimilative and disowning projection. *Psychol. Rec.*, 1960, **10**, 95-100.

Lieberman, M. A., Stock, Dorothy, & Whitman, R. M. Self-perceptual patterns among ulcer patients. *AMA Arch. gen. Psychiat.*, 1959, **1**, 167-177.

Lipsitt, L. P. A self-concept scale for children and its relationship to the children's form of the Manifest Anxiety Scale. *Child Develpm.*, 1958, **29**, 463-472.

Livson, N. H., & Nichols, T. F. Discrimination and reliability in Q-sort personality descriptions. *J. abnorm. soc. Psychol.*, 1956, 52, 159-165.

Loehlin, J. C. Word meanings and self-descriptions. *J. abnorm. soc. Psychol.*, 1961, 62, 28-34.

Luckey, Eleanore B. Implications for marriage counseling of self perceptions and spouse perceptions. *J. counsel. Psychol.*, 1960, 7, 3-9.

Luckey, Eleanore B. Marital satisfaction and congruent self-spouse concepts. *Soc. Forces*, 1960, 39, 153-157.

Luckey, Eleanore B. Marital satisfaction and its association with congruence of perception. *Marriage Fam. Living*, 1960, 22, 49-54.

Luckey, Eleanore B. Marital satisfaction and parent concepts. *J. consult. Psychol.*, 1960, 24, 195-204.

Lumsden, J. The construction of unidimensional tests. *Psychol. Bull.*, 1961, 58, 122-131.

McClintock, C. G., & Davis, J. Changes in the attribute of "nationality" in the self-percept of the "stranger." *J. soc. Psychol.*, 1958, 48, 183-193.

McPartland, T. S., & Cumming, J. H. Self-conception, social class, and mental health. *Hum. Org.*, 1958, 17, 24-29.

McPartland, T. S., Cumming, J. H., & Garretson, Wynona. Self-conception and ward behavior in two psychiatric hospitals. *Sociometry*, 1961, 24, 111-124.

Madden, J. E. Semantic differential rating of self and of self-reported personal characteristics. *J. consult. Psychol.*, 1961, 25, 183.

Mahone, C. H. Fear of failure and unrealistic vocational aspiration. *J. abnorm. soc. Psychol.*, 1960, 60, 2, 253-261.

Mann, J. H., & Mann, Carola H. Insight as a measure of adjustment in three kinds of group experience. *J. consult. Psychol.*, 1959, 23, 91.

Martin, B. The validity of a self report measure of anxiety as a function of the time interval covered by the instructions. *J. consult. Psychol.*, 1959, 23, 468.

Matteson, R. W. Self-perceptions of students seeking counseling. *Personnel Guid. J.*, 1958, 36, 545-548.

Mayo, G. D., & Manning, W. H. Motivation measurement. *Educ. psychol. Measmt*, 1961, 21, 73-83.

Meissner, W. W. Intervening constructs—dimensions of controversy. *Psychol. Rev.*, 1960, 67, 51-72.

Merenda, P. F., & Clarke, W. V. Factor analysis of a measure of "social self." *Psychol. Rep.*, 1959, 5, 597-605.

Merenda, P. F., & Clarke, W. V. Multiple inferential selves of male and female college students. *J. psychol. Stud.*, 1960, 11, 206-212.

Messick, S. Dimensions of Social Desirability. *J. consult. Psychol.*, 1960, 24, 279-287.

Milgram, N. A., & Helper, M. M. The Social Desirability set in individual and grouped self-ratings. *J. consult. Psychol.*, 1961, 25, 91.

Mitchell, H. E. The interrelatedness of alcoholism and marital conflict: IV. Interpersonal perception theory applied to conflicted marriages in which alcoholism is and is not a problem. Symposium, 1958. *Amer. J. Orthopsychiat.*, 1959, 29, 547-559.

Moses, M., & Duvall, R. Depreciation and the self concept. *J. clin. Psychol.*, 1960, 26, 387-388.

Murstein, B. I., & Pryer, R. S. The concept of projection: a review. *Psychol. Bull.*, 1959, 56, 353-374.

Nakamura, C. Y. Salience of norms and order of questionnaire items: their effect on responses to the items. *J. abnorm. soc. Psychol.*, 1959, 59, 139-142.

Nebergall, Nelda S., Angelino, H., & Young, H. H. A validation study of The Self-Activity Inventory as a predictor of adjustment. *J. consult. Psychol.*, 1959, 23, 21-24.

Norrell, Gwen, & Grater, H. Interest awareness as an aspect of self-awareness. *J. counsel. Psychol.*, 1960, 7, 289-292.

O'Connell, W. E. The adaptive functions of wit and humor. *J. abnorm. soc. Psychol.*, 1960, 61, 263-270.

O'Hara, R. P., & Tiedeman, D. T. Vocational self concept in adolescence. *J. counsel. Psychol.*, 1959, 6, 292-301.

Page, H. A., & Markowitz, Gloria. The relation of defensiveness to rating scale bias. *J. Psychol.*, 1955, 40, 431-435.

Palermo, D. S., & Martire, J. G. The influence of order of administration on self-concept measures. *J. consult. Psychol.*, 1960, 24, 372.

Parloff, M. B. Therapist-patient relationships and outcome of psychotherapy. *J. consult. Psychol.*, 1961, 25, 29-38.

Peak, Helen. Attitude and motivation. In M. R. Jones (Ed.), *Nebraska symposium on motivation, 1955*, Lincoln: Univer. of Nebraska Press, 1955.

Pepitone, A., & Wilpizeski, C. Some consequences of experimental rejection. *J. abnorm. soc., Psychol.*, 1960, 60, 359-364.

Phillips, B. N., Hindsman, E., & Jennings, E. Influence of intelligence on anxiety and perception of self and others. *Child Develpm.*, 1960, 31, 41-46.

Porter, L. W. Self-perceptions of first-level supervisors compared with upper-management personnel and with operative line workers. *J. appl. Psychol.*, 1959, 43, 183-186.

Porter, L. W., & Kaufman, R. A. Relationships between a top-middle management self-description scale and behavior in a group situation. *J. appl. Psychol.*, 1959, 43, 345-348.

Prelinger, E. Extension and structure of the self. *J. Psychol.*, 1959, 47, 13-23.

Radlow, R., & Berger, P. Relationship of degree of self-esteem to gossiping behavior. *J. soc. Psychol.*, 1959, 50, 153-155.

Raskan, E. E. C. I. Zelf-concept en situatie. (Self-concept and situation.) *Ned. Tijdschr. Psychol.*, 1959, 14, 133-149.

Reidy, J. J., & Colvin, R. W. Voice recognition as a measure of self-attitude and relatedness. *AMA Arch. Neurol. Psychiat.*, 1959, 81, 636-638.

Reilly, Mary S., Commins, D. W., & Stefic, E. C. The complementarity of personality needs in friendship choice. *J. abnorm. soc. Psychol.*, 1960, 61, 292-294.

Reynolds, G. S. The effects of stress upon problem-solving. *J. gen. Psychol.*, 1960, 62, 83-88.

Reznikoff, M., & Toomey, Laura C. *Evaluation of changes associated with psychiatric treatment*. Springfield, Ill.: Charles C Thomas, 1959.

Rodgers, D. A. Personality correlates of successful role behavior. *J. soc. Psychol.,* 1957, 46, 111-117.

Rodgers, D. A. Personality of the route salesman in a basic food industry. *J. appl. Psychol.,* 1959, 43, 235-239.

Rodgers, D. A. Relationship between real similarity and assumed similarity with favorability controlled. *J. abnorm. soc. Psychol.,* 1959, 59, 431-433.

Roen, S. R. Personality and Negro-White intelligence. *J. abnorm. soc. Psychol.,* 1960, 61, 148-150.

Rosen, E., & Mink, Shirley H. Desirability of personality traits as perceived by prisoners. *J. clin. Psychol.,* 1961, 27, 147-151.

Rosenbaum, M. E. Social perception and the motivational structure of interpersonal relations. *J. abnorm. soc. Psychol.,* 1959, 59, 130-133.

Rosenbaum, M. E., & deCharms, R. Direct and vicarious reduction of hostility. *J. abnorm. soc. Psychol.,* 1960, 60, 105-111.

Rosenberg, B. G., & Lauber, J. Selected success and failure experiences as factors in Bender Gestalt performances. *J. gen. Psychol.,* 1961, 64, 31-36.

Rothaus, P., & Worchel, P. The inhibition of aggression under nonarbitrary frustration. *J. Pers.,* 1960, 28, 108-117.

Rychlak, J. F. Self-confidence, ability, and the interest-value of tasks. *J. genet. Psychol.;* 1959, 94, 153-159.

Sarason, I. G. Intellectual and personality correlates of test anxiety. *J. abnorm. soc. Psychol.,* 1959, 59, 272-275.

Schultz, K. V., & Knapp, W. E. Perceptual preferences and self descriptions. *Personnel Guid. J.,* 1959, 37, 581-584.

Sears, Pauline S. Problems in the investigation of achievement and self-esteem motivation. In M. R. Jones (Ed.), *Nebraska symposium on motivation, 1957.* Lincoln: Univer. of Nebraska Press, 1957.

Secord, P. F., & Backman, C. W. Personality theory and the problem of stability and change in individual behavior: an interpersonal approach. *Psychol. Rev.,* 1961, 68, 21-32.

Sells, S. B. Structured measurement of personality and motivation: a review of contributions of Raymond B. Cattell. *J. clin. Psychol.,* 1959, 15, 3-21.

Shippee-Blum, Eva M. The young rebel: self-regard and ego ideal. *J. consult. Psychol.,* 1959, 23, 44-50.

Siegel, S. M., & Feldman, M. J. A note on the effect on self description of combining anxiety and hostility items on a single scale. *J. clin. Psychol.,* 1958, 14, 389-390.

Singer, J. L., & Schonbar, Rosalea A. Correlates of daydreaming: a dimension of self-awareness. *J. consult. Psychol.,* 1961, 25, 1-6.

Singer, R. D., & Feshbach, S. Some relationships between manifest anxiety, authoritarian tendencies, and modes of reaction to frustration. *J. abnorm. soc. Psychol.,* 1959, 59, 404-408.

Smith, E. E. Defensiveness, insight, and the *K* scale. *J. consult. Psychol.,* 1959, 23, 275-277.

Smith, Kay H. Ego strength and perceived competence as conformity variables. *J. abnorm. soc. Psychol.,* 1961, 62, 169-171.

Smith, P. A. A factor analytic study of the self-concept. *J. consult. Psychol.,* 1960, 24, 191.

Spilka, B. & Lewis, M. Empathy, assimilative projection, and disowning projection. *Psychol. Rec.,* 1959, 9, 99-102.

Storm, T., Rosenwald, G. C., & Child, I. L. A factor analysis of self-ratings on social behavior. *J. soc. Psychol.,* 1958, 48, 45-49.

Storms, L. H., Mintz, R. S., & Palmer, J. O. Psychologists' predictions and twins' evaluations of self and the paired sibling. *J. proj. Tech.,* 1960, 24, 182-185.

Stotland, E. Determinants of attraction to groups. *J. soc. Psychol.,* 1959, 49, 71-80.

Streitfeld, J. W. Expressed acceptance of self and others by psychotherapists. *J. consult. Psychol.,* 1959, 23, 435-441.

Strong, D. J., & Feder, D. D. Measurement of the self concept: a critique of the literature. *J. counsel. Psychol.,* 1961, 8, 170-178.

Strunk, O., Jr., Relationship between self-reports and adolescent religiosity. *Psychol. Rep.,* 1958, 4, 683-686.

Talland, G. A. Sex differences in self assessment. *J. soc. Psychol.,* 1958, 48, 25-35.

Taylor, J. B. The "yeasayer" and Social Desirability: a comment on the Couch and Keniston paper. *J. abnorm. soc. Psychol.,* 1961, 62, 172.

Todd, W. B., & Ewing, T. N. Changes in self-reference during counseling. *J. counsel. Psychol.,* 1961, 8, 112-115.

Van der Veen, F., & Fiske, D. W. Variability among self-ratings in different situations. *Educ. Psychol. Measmt,* 1960, 20, 83-93.

Videbeck, R. Self-conception and the reactions of others. *Sociometry,* 1960, 23, 351-359.

Warren, J. R. Self concept, occupational role expectation, and change in college major. *J. counsel. Psychol.,* 1961, 8, 164-169.

Weinberg, J. R. A further investigation of body-cathexis and the self. *J. consult. Psychol.,* 1960, 24, 277.

Weinstein, E. A. *The self-image of the foster child.* New York: Russell Sage Foundation, 1960.

Werner, Emmy, & Gallistel, Elizabeth. Prediction of outstanding performance, delinquency, and emotional disturbance from childhood evaluations. *Child Develpm.,* 1961, 32, 255-260.

Wessman, A. E., Ricks, D. F., & Tyl, Mary M. Characteristics and concomitants of mood fluctuation in college women. *J. abnorm. soc. Psychol.,* 1960, 60, 117-126.

Will, O. A., Jr. Paranoid development and the concept of self. *Psychiatry,* 1961, 24, 2(supplement), 74-86.

Winthrop, H. Self-images of personal adjustment vs. the estimates of friends. *J. soc. Psychol.,* 1959, 50, 87-99.

Wittenborn, J. R. Contributions and current status of Q methodology. *Psychol. Bull.,* 1961, 58, 132-142.

Worchel, P. Hostility: theory and experimental investigation. In Dorothy Willner (Ed.), *Decisions, values and groups,* Vol. I. New York: Pergamon Press, 1960. Pp. 254-266.

Worchel, P. Personality factors in the readiness to express aggression. *J. clin. Psychol.*, 1958, 14, 355-359.

Worchel, P., & Hillson, J. S. The self-concept in the criminal: an exploration of Adlerian theory. *J. indiv. Psychol.*, 1958, 14, 173-181.

Young, H. H. A test of Witkin's field-dependence hypothesis. *J. abnorm. soc. Psychol.*, 1959, 59, 188-192.

Zander, A., Stotland, E., & Wolfe, D. Unity of group, identification with group, and self-esteem of members. *J. Pers.*, 1960, 28, 463-478.

Zax, M., & Klein, A. Measurement of personality and behavior changes following psychotherapy. *Psychol. Bull.*, 1960, 57, 435-448.

Zigler, E., & Phillips, L. Social effectiveness and symptomatic behaviors. *J. abnorm. soc. Psychol.*, 1960, 61, 2, 231-238.

Zuckerman, M., & Oltean, Mary. Some relationships between maternal attitude factors and authoritarianism, personality needs, psychopathology, and self-acceptance. *Child Develpm.*, 1959, 30, 27-36.

Dissertation Abstracts, 1958 - June, 1961, Unpublished Dissertations

Adamek, E. G., Jr. The effects of testing and two methods of test interpretation on selected self-perceptions. *Dissertation Abstr.*, 1961, 21, 3697.

Amos, W. E. A study of self-concept: delinquent boys' accuracy in selected self-evaluations. *Dissertation Abstr.*, 1961, 21, 3179.

Aspromonte, V. A. Distortion of the self and others in schizophrenia. *Dissertation Abstr.*, 1959, 20, 746.

Atchison, C. O. A comparative study of the self-concept of behavior problem and non-behavior problem high school boys. *Dissertation Abstr.*, 1958, 19, 1010.

Bassin, A. Effect of group therapy upon certain attitudes and perceptions of adult offenders on probation. *Dissertation Abstr.*, 1958, 18, 2241-2242.

Baxter, L. F. An investigation of the usefulness of self-concept theory in explaining some aspects of the results of chlorpromazine treatment of schizophrenics. *Dissertation Abstr.*, 1958, 19, 565-566.

Belenky, R. L. The relationship between accuracy in self perception and the perception of others: a study of estimates of performance on a test of values and a test of aspiration level. *Dissertation Abstr.*, 1960, 20, 3825-3826.

Billinger, Lois W. Relation of empathy, self image, and social acceptance among gifted and average children of the sixth grade. *Dissertation Abstr.*, 1959, 20, 1222-1223.

Bird, H. R. The relationship between maternal attitudes toward sons, sons' self-attitudes, and maternal awareness of sons. *Dissertation Abstr.*, 1958, 19, 358-359.

Blake, E., Jr. A comparison of intraracial and interracial levels of aspiration. *Dissertation Abstr.*, 1960, 20, 4586.

Blocher, D. H. A study of the relationships between self descriptions and stereotypes of occupations with high and low claimed interests. *Dissertation Abstr.*, 1959, 20, 2139-2140.

Bloom, K. L. Some relationships between age and self perception. *Dissertation Abstr.*, 1960, 21, 670.

Bobgan, M. A comparison of variability in identification and self-acceptance of male delinquents and male socially acceptable school students. *Dissertation Abstr.*, 1961, 21, 3355.

Bodwin, R. F. The relationship between immature self-concept and certain educational disabilities. *Dissertation Abstr.*, 1959, 19, 1645-1646.

Bookbinder, L. J. Self perception, social perception, and response sets in high and low authoritarians. *Dissertation Abstr.*, 1959, 20, 2410.

Bourque, E. J. The construction and evaluation of an instrument based on Q-methodology which measures the relative importance of self-perceived needs of the tuberculous. *Dissertation Abstr.*, 1958, 19, 1289-1290.

Boy, A. V. An experimental study of the effectiveness of client-centered therapy in counseling students with behavior problems. *Dissertation Abstr.*, 1961, 21, 2010-2011.

Bozeman, Alvia L. An analysis of self-concepts of preschool children. *Dissertation Abstr.*, 1959, 19, 2510.

Bramel, D. H. Some determinants of defensive projection. *Dissertation Abstr.*, 1960, 21, 980.

Brown, P. K. A study of the relationship between Social Desirability as a psychological variable and learning performance in a complex verbal task. *Dissertation Abstr.*, 1958, 18, 1488.

Bruck, M. A study of age differences and sex differences in the relationship between self-concept and grade-point average. *Dissertation Abstr.*, 1959, 19, 1646.

Campbell, Mary M. The primary dimensions of item ratings on scales designed to measure 24 of Murray's manifest needs. *Dissertation Abstr.*, 1960, 20, 4161.

Campbell, V. N. Assumed similarity, perceived sociometric balance, and social influence: an attempted integration within one cognitive theory. *Dissertation Abstr.*, 1961, 21, 3516.

Carlson, Betty R. Parent-child relationships and the self-concept of children. *Dissertation Abstr.*, 1958, 19, 1436.

Chickering, A. W. Self concept, ideal self concept, and achievement. *Dissertation Abstr.*, 1958, 19, 164.

Chilman, Catherine S. A comparative study of measured personality needs and self-perceived problems of ninth and tenth grade students: half of the group possessing characteristics associated with early school leaving and the other half not possessing such characteristics. *Dissertation Abstr.*, 1960, 20, 3190-3191.

Christiansen, H. D. The relationship of several self-other indices to claimed and measured interests of vocational high school seniors. *Dissertation Abstr.*, 1959, 20, 4032.

Clark, E. T. A study of the measured and self-perceived outcomes of adult reading training: an investigation of certain outcomes of the training given Air Force and other Department of Defense personnel in a voluntary reading improvement course. *Dissertation Abstr.*, 1959, 19, 1647.

Clark, J. P. Blame acceptance among Ohio prisoners. *Dissertation Abstr.*, 1961, 21, 2396-2397.

Claye, C. M. A study of the relationship between self-concepts and attitudes toward

362　　*THE SELF CONCEPT*

the Negro among secondary school pupils in three schools of Arkansas. *Dissertation Abstr.*, 1958, **19**, 587.

Congdon, C. S. Self theory and chlorpromazine treatment. *Dissertation Abstr.*, 1959, **19**, 2654-2655.

Connor, R. G. The self-concepts of alcoholics. *Dissertation Abstr.*, 1961, **21**, 3871.

Cooper, M. Differences in self-perception among physically dependent drug addicts, alcohol addicts, and controls. *Dissertation Abstr.*, 1959, **19**, 2672.

Corrie, C. C. Aspiration, self acceptance, and acceptance of others in normal and neuropsychiatric groups. *Dissertation Abstr.*, 1958, **18**, 1855.

Creelman, Marjorie B. The C S C Test: Self conceptions of elementary school children. *Dissertation Abstr.*, 1955, **10**.

Crowne, D. P. The relation of self-acceptance behavior to the social learning theory construct of need value. *Dissertation Abstr.*, 1959, **20**, 374.

Davis, A. D. Physiological correlates of the body-image. *Dissertation Abstr.*, 1958, **18**, 2206-2207.

Deitche, J. H. The performance of delinquent and non-delinquent boys on the Tennessee Department of Mental Health Self-Concept Scale. *Dissertation Abstr.*, 1959, **20**, 1437-1438.

Dimmitt, J. S. The congruence of past and ideal self concepts in the aging male. *Dissertation Abstr.*, 1960, **20**, 2933.

Doyle, Mother H. The self-concept studied in relation to the culture of teen-age boys and girls in Canada, England, and the United States. *Dissertation Abstr.*, 1961, **21**, 2981.

Dunbar, D. S. Sex-role identification and achievement motivation in college women. *Dissertation Abstr.*, 1960, **20**, 4161-4162.

Edmiston, A. J. The dimensionality of discrepancies between self and ideal concepts. *Dissertation Abstr.*, 1961, **21**, 1994-1995.

Ehrenberg, O. Concepts of masculinity, a study of discrepancies between men's self-concepts and two different ideal concepts and their relationship to mental health. *Dissertation Abstr.*, 1960, **21**, 1275.

Endler, N. S. Conformity analyzed and related to personality. *Dissertation Abstr.*, 1958, **19**, 1114.

Esterson, H. H. A study of the self attitudes and attitudes towards authority of conservatives and radicals. *Dissertation Abstr.*, 1961, **21**, 3164-3165.

Eynon, T. G. Factors related to onset of delinquency. *Dissertation Abstr.*, 1959, **20**, 2414-2415.

Faeth, H. W., Jr. The discrepancy between self-ideal self concepts as needs projected to Thematic Apperception Test pictures. *Dissertation Abstr.*, 1961, **21**, 1999-2000.

Fagan, Margaret J. Perceptions of self and of normality in schizophrenics. *Dissertation Abstr.*, 1958, **19**, 170-171.

Fairweather, P. D. The appropriateness of field and level of vocational choice as related to self-concepts, intelligence, school achievement, and socioeconomic status. *Dissertation Abstr.*, 1959, **20**, 4032-4033.

Ferson, Jean E. The displacement of hostility. *Dissertation Abstr.*, 1959, **19**, 2386-2387.

Fish, Jeanne E. An exploration of developmental aspects of body scheme and of ideas about adulthood in grade school children. *Dissertation Abstr.*, 1960, **21**, 1253.

Franklin, G. H. The effect of group therapy on the attitudes toward self and others of institutionalized delinquent boys. *Dissertation Abstr.*, 1958, **18**, 1104-1105.

Freeman, B. B. Evaluating W-A-Y technique in relationship to measurement and stability of the self concept. Unpublished doctoral dissertation, Univer. of Denver, 1956.

Freeman, D. An experimental investigation of the construct self-cognition. *Dissertation Abstr.*, 1959, **20**, 4443-4444.

Friedland, D. M. Group counseling as a factor in reducing runaway behavior from an open treatment institution for delinquent and pre-delinquent boys: the evaluation of changes in frustration tolerance, self-concept, attitude toward maternal figures, attitude toward paternal figures, attitude toward other authority figures, and in reality testing of runaway delinquent boys. *Dissertation Abstr.*, 1960, **21**, 237-238.

Garfinkle, M. The relationship between general self concept, role self concept, and role behavior in high school. *Dissertation Abstr.*, 1958, **19**, 897-898.

Gavales, D. Relationships between self-portrayal and psychopathology. *Dissertation Abstr.*, 1961, **21**, 2001.

Gerler, W. Outcome of psychotherapy as a function of client-counselor similarity. *Dissertation Abstr.*, 1958, **18**, 1864-1865.

Goering, J. D. An investigation of the effect of an in-service self-study seminar on the adjustment, concept of self and concept of others of mental hospital employees. *Dissertation Abstr.*, 1960, **20**, 3414.

Goffman, I. W. Self-other differentiation and role performance: a study of professional agents of social control. *Dissertation Abstr.*, 1959, **20**, 1884-1885.

Gourevitch, Vivian P. Motivation and social adequacy. *Dissertation Abstr.*, 1960, **20**, 4170-4171.

Grierson, K. M. A study of the self concepts of a group of adolescent students and the relationship between these self concepts and behavioral ratings. *Dissertation Abstr.*, 1961, **21**, 2588-2589.

Gross, H. W. The relationship between insecurity, self-acceptance, other-direction, and conformity under conditions of differential social pressure. *Dissertation Abstr.*, 1959, **20**, 395.

Hamachek, D. E. A study of the relationships between certain measures of growth and the self-images of elementary school children. *Dissertation Abstr.*, 1961, **21**, 2193.

Harris, J. J. A self concept measure for prisoners and its relation to certain objective indices of criminality. *Dissertation Abstr.*, 1958, **18**, 285.

Hawk, T. L. Concept of self as a variable in adolescent behavior. *Dissertation Abstr.*, 1958, **19**, 1014.

Hayden, R. G. An experimental study regarding the effects of social marginality and authoritarianism on self-esteem. *Dissertation Abstr.*, 1958, **19**, 898.

Heller, K. Dependency changes in psychotherapy as a function of the discrepancy between conscious self-description and projective test performance. *Dissertation Abstr.*, 1960, **20**, 3378.

Hickman, N. W. The role of self-related-concept discrepancies in personal adjustment. *Dissertation Abstr.*, 1959, **19**, 2656-2658.

Hine, Frances D. An investigation of one dimension of personality, self-esteem, and its relationship to a pupil's art experience. *Dissertation Abstr.*, 1961, **21**, 2776-2777.

Hoff, G. R. The use of *Q*-sort technique in investigating changes in self-concept and self adjustment during a general psychology course. *Dissertation Abstr.*, 1960, **21**, 124-125.

Holden, R. H. Changes in body imagery of physically handicapped children due to a summer camp experience. *Dissertation Abstr.*, 1961, **21**, 3165.

Hood, P. D. *Q*-methodology: a technique for measuring frames of reference. *Dissertation Abstr.*, 1960, **20**, 2935-2937.

Hope, L. H. Background of vocational choice in a denominational university. *Dissertation Abstr.*, 1961, **21**, 1847-1848.

Hurlburt, Julia K. Role expectations and the self—an empirical study of their relationship to marital adjustment. *Dissertation Abstr.*, 1960, **21**, 1658-1659.

Iazetta, V. B. Perceptions of mother and daughter as they pertain to certain aspects of the self concept. *Dissertation Abstr.*, 1961, **21**, 3360-3361.

Ibelle, B. P. Discrepancies between self-concepts and ideal self-concepts in paranoid schizophrenics and normals. *Dissertation Abstr.*, 1961, **21**, 2004-2005.

Jasper, H. S. The relationship between two aspects of self-concept and the initial student-teaching experience. *Dissertation Abstr.*, 1959, **19**, 3233-3234.

Katz, I. S. A study of the stability of the self-concept and its relationship to sociometric status and sociometric perception. *Dissertation Abstr.*, 1958, **19**, 877-878.

Kendall, J. S. The concept of the minister—a study of certain relationships between occupational stereotype, self concept, and selected variables. *Dissertation Abstr.*, 1959, **20**, 2377-2378.

Kenney, R. C. An analysis of self perceptions in counselor trainees. *Dissertation Abstr.*, 1960, **20**, 2677-2678.

Kerns, R. D. Changes in concept of self and others as a function of incarceration in a correctional institution. *Dissertation Abstr.*, 1959, **19**, 2171-2172.

Kimmel, J. A comparison of children with congenital and acquired orthopedic handicaps on certain personality characteristics: an evaluation of self-concept, anxiety, defense mechanisms, and adjustment in children with orthopedic handicaps. *Dissertation Abstr.*, 1959, **19**, 3023-3024.

Kinch, J. W. Certain social-psychological aspects of types of juvenile delinquents. *Dissertation Abstr.*, 1960, **20**, 2937-2938.

Knox, Wilma J. Acceptance of self, other people, and social conformity as effects of group therapeutic experiences. *Dissertation Abstr.*, 1958, **19**, 172-173.

Krider, Mary A. A comparative study of the self-concepts of crippled and noncrippled children. *Dissertation Abstr.*, 1959, **20**, 2143-2144.

Landau, Miriam F. Body image in paraplegia as a variable in adjustment to physical handicap. *Dissertation Abstr.*, 1960, **21**, 960.

Leckie, Janet T. Self-image of competence, peer-relations and anomie in a group of 10th grade girls. *Dissertation Abstr.*, 1960, 20, 3872-3873.

Leonard, Julia B. A study of the organization of self-percepts through their susceptibility to change. *Dissertation Abstr.*, 1958, 18, 1492-1493.

Levin, B. L. The use of role playing as a method for producing self-perceived personality change. *Dissertation Abstr.*, 1959, 20, 779.

Levine, Conalee. A comparison of the conscious and unconscious identifications with both parental figures among addicted and non-addicted male adolescent character disorders. *Dissertation Abstr.*, 1960, 20, 3380-3381.

Lively, E. L. A study of teen-age socialization and delinquency insulation by grade levels. *Dissertation Abstr.*, 1960, 20, 4207-4208.

Lumpkin, D. D. The relationship of self-concept to achievement in reading. *Dissertation Abstr.*, 1959, 20, 204-205.

McBrearty, J. F. The effect of self-ideal discrepancy on simple and disjunctive reaction-time. *Dissertation Abstr.*, 1958, 19, 1446.

McCoy, G. F., Jr. Some ego factors associated with academic success and failure of educable, mentally handicapped pupils. *Dissertation Abstr.*, 1961, 21, 2990-2991.

McElvaney, C. T. Recall of positively and negatively affective material related to self-esteem. *Dissertation Abstr.*, 1958, 18, 1495-1496.

McKee, R. C. An evaluation of the relationship between college educational level achieved and self-concept ratings. Unpublished doctoral dissertation. Univer. of Denver, 1958.

Mahan, T. W. The relationship between self perception and school adjustment: a study in pupil assessment. *Dissertation Abstr.*, 1959, 20, 1270.

Marlens, Hanna S. A study of the effect of hospitalization on children in a metropolitan municipal institution: a comparative study of emotional attitudes toward self and the environment of children hospitalized and those non-hospitalized with similar physical complaints. *Dissertation Abstr.*, 1960, 20, 3385-3386.

Marshall, R. J. Variation in self-attitudes and attitudes toward others as a function of peer group appraisals. *Dissertation Abstr.*, 1958, 18, 2239.

Menlo, A. The incarcerated deviated criminal sex offender: his peceptual relationships with himself and his society. *Dissertation Abstr.*, 1958, 19, 483.

Miller, Carrie E. The effect of the home broken by divorce upon the self concept of selected college women. Unpublished doctoral dissertation. Univer. of Denver, 1958.

Miller, R. V. Self and social perception of gifted and typical children. *Dissertation Abstr.*, 1960, 21, 1277.

Mills, R. B. Empathy related to real similarity, group identification and interpersonal attraction. *Dissertation Abstr.*, 1958, 19, 173-174.

Moore, E. J. Concept of vocational personality and occupational values as related to self concept at different stages of vocational maturity. *Dissertation Abstr.*, 1961, 21, 2195.

Moran, M. R. Inmate concept of self in a reformatory society. *Dissertation Abstr.*, 1959, 20, 2418-2420.

Moroney, Frances M. Methods of studying self-concepts of teachers. *Dissertation Abstr.*, 1958, 19, 90.

Morton, A. S. Similarity as a determinant of friendship: a multidimensional study. *Dissertation Abstr.*, 1960, 20, 3857-3858.

Moses, D. L. The relationship of self concept discrepancies to vocational choice, intelligence, school achievement and socioeconomic status. *Dissertation Abstr.*, 1960, 21, 127-128.

Mowers, G. E. Self-judgments and objective measures as related to first semester academic achievement of non-selected college students. *Dissertation Abstr.*, 1961, 21, 1852.

Mueller, W. J. Relationships among self, parental, and teacher behavior descriptions of superior secondary school students. *Dissertation Abstr.*, 1959, 20, 957-958.

Mullen, Esther. An investigation of some aspects of depression and its effect on the perception of the self and others in a non-psychiatric population. *Dissertation Abstr.*, 1959, 19, 2390.

Nardini, W. Criminal self-conceptions in the penal community: an empirical study. *Dissertation Abstr.*, 1959, 20, 397.

Nauss, A. H. Scholastic ability, self-concept, and occupational plans. *Dissertation Abstr.*, 1961, 21, 2596.

Oliensis, D. G. Some correlates of distortion in the perception of self-blindness. *Dissertation Abstr.*, 1959, 20, 761.

Oliner, Marion M. Sex role acceptance and perception of parents. *Dissertation Abstr.*, 1958, 18, 1868-1869.

Overstreet, Phoebe L. Factors associated with the quality of self-evaluations. *Dissertation Abstr.*, 1959, 20, 761-762.

Peck, B. The effect of self-observation on self-awareness: an exploratory study. *Dissertation Abstr.*, 1958, 18, 501-502.

Piety, K. R. The role of defense in reporting on the self concept. *Dissertation Abstr.*, 1958, 18, 1869-1870.

Ravitz, L. A. Teacher self-acceptance related to acceptance-of-pupils in the classroom. *Dissertation Abstr.*, 1958, 18, 459.

Roff, Catherine. The self-concept in adolescent girls. *Dissertation Abstr.*, 1959, 20, 385-386.

Rogers, J. M. Operant conditioning in a quasi-therapy setting: the influence of interviewer reinforcement upon subjects' self-reference verbalizations. *Dissertation Abstr.*, 1959, 20, 763-764.

Rosenzweig, S. The effects of failure and success on evaluation of self and others: a study of depressed patients and normals. *Dissertation Abstr.*, 1960, 21, 675.

Ross, G. R. An exploratory investigation of self concept differences between groups of college students. Unpublished doctoral dissertation, Univer. of Denver, 1955.

Rozynko, V. V. Social Desirability in schizophrenics' reaction to ambiguity and to different sources of conformity pressure. *Dissertation Abstr.*, 1960, 21, 243.

Rubenstein, B. O. Freud and Rogers: a comparative study of two psychological systems. *Dissertation Abstr.*, 1958, 19, 1293.

Rutherford, Jeanne McE. Personality correlates of creativity. *Dissertation Abstr.,* 1959, **20,** 4434.

Sayres, Avivah L. A comparison of attitudes toward child rearing of mothers who differ significantly in self-concepts. *Dissertation Abstr.,* 1958, **19,** 3026.

Schuman, E. P. Self-acceptance as a determinant of the mode of interpretation of problem situations. *Dissertation Abstr.,* 1958, **19,** 358-359.

Schutz, R. A. The relationship of self-satisfaction to stated vocational preferences. *Dissertation Abstr.,* 1959, **20,** 2148.

Seay, L. C. A study to determine some relations between changes in reading skills and self-concepts accompanying a remedial program for boys with low reading ability and reasonably normal intelligence. *Dissertation Abstr.,* 1961, **21,** 2598-2599.

Selden, E. H. A study of self-structure and level of aspiration in delinquent and non-delinquent boys. *Dissertation Abstr.,* 1961, **21,** 2394.

Sharp, W. H. An investigation of certain aspects of the interaction between a group of delinquent boys and their mother-figures. *Dissertation Abstr.,* 1959, **20,** 2391.

Silver, A. W. The self concept: its relationship to parental and peer acceptance. *Dissertation Abstr.,* 1958, **19,** 166-167.

Silverberg, J. A study in body-concept. *Dissertation Abstr.,* 1958, **18,** 1113-1114.

Silverman, Dorothy. An evaluation of the relationship between attitudes toward self and attitudes toward a vocational high school. *Dissertation Abstr.,* 1960, **21,** 1128.

Smith, A. Discrepancy in the meaning of self in a multilevel personality system and emotional disturbance. *Dissertation Abstr.,* 1958, **19,** 1120.

Smith, M. V. Self representations of American and Korean youth. *Dissertation Abstr.,* 1958, **18,** 2064.

Snoek, J. D. Some effects of rejection upon attraction to the group. *Dissertation Abstr.,* 1960, **20,** 4740-4741.

Snoxell, L. F. A self-concept study of university student leaders. Unpublished doctoral dissertation, Univer. of Denver, 1953.

Spicola, Rose F. An investigation into seven correlates of reading achievement including the self-concept. *Dissertation Abstr.,* 1961, **21,** 2199.

Springfield, F. B. Concept of father and ideal self in a group of criminals and non-criminals. *Dissertation Abstr.,* 1960, **21,** 1258-1259.

Steffen, H. H. J. Relationship between self-estimates of occupational competence and *n*-Achievement of high school students. *Dissertation Abstr.,* 1961, **21,** 1860.

Strider, F. D. Self concept factors affecting judgments of others. *Dissertation Abstr.,* 1961, **21,** 3858.

Suinn, R. M. The relationship between self-acceptance and acceptance of others: a learning theory analysis. *Dissertation Abstr.,* 1960, **20,** 3846-3847.

Summers, D. A. Theories of the self: an analytical study of some perspectives. *Dissertation Abstr.,* 1960, **20,** 3419.

Sundland, D. M. Psychotherapists' self-perceptions and patients' perceptions of their psychotherapists. *Dissertation Abstr.,* 1961, **21,** 2373-2374.

Tabachnik, B. R. Some correlates of prejudice toward Negroes in elementary age children: satisfaction with self and academic achievement. *Dissertation Abstr.*, 1958, 19, 2884-2885.

Thompson, V. T. The relationship of self acceptance to the consistency of employment of the vocationally rehabilitated. *Dissertation Abstr.*, 1959, 19, 2012-2013.

Thrash, Patricia A. Women student leaders at Northwestern University: their characteristics, self-concepts, and attitudes toward the university. *Dissertation Abstr.*, 1960, 20, 3638.

Veldman, D. J. Hostility and self-evaluation. *Dissertation Abstr.*, 1961, 21, 2789-2790.

Wallen, V. A *Q*-technique study of the self-concepts of adolescent stutterers and non-stutterers. *Dissertation Abstr.*, 1960, 20, 3392.

Warshay, L. H. Breadth of perspective, culture contact, and self. *Dissertation Abstr.*, 1960, 20, 4201-4202.

Waskow, Irene E. The effect of selective responding by the therapist in a quasi-therapy setting. *Dissertation Abstr.*, 1960, 20, 4180-4181.

Weiner, I. B. The ego-ideal, defensive style, and achievement-related behavior. *Dissertation Abstr.*, 1960, 20, 4727.

Whiteman, P. H. The relation of religious affiliation to parents' opinions concerning child rearing and children's problems, and parents' evaluations of their own personalities. *Dissertation Abstr.*, 1959, 20, 2149-2150.

Wood, E. C. Self-concept as a mediating factor in social behavior. *Dissertation Abstr.*, 1960, 20, 2896.

Wright, J. M. Attribution of social responsibility and self concept. *Dissertation Abstr.*, 1961, 21, 3530.

Zilaitis, V. Relationship of consistency in self-perception to judgment confidence. *Dissertation Abstr.*, 1960, 21, 965-966.

Subject Index

A

ACE, 96, 168-169, 224, 298, 310
Achievement
  aspirations for, 144
  ideal self and, 139
  level-of-aspiration behavior and, 245-247
  n Ach, TAT, 141, 246, 254, 271
  nonphenomenal self and, 218, 257
  in *Q* sort, 64
  in Self-Activity Inventory, 75
  self concept and, 144, 169, 224-225, 245
  [Self—Ideal] discrepancies and, 246
  self-insight concerning, 292, 297-298, 303-304, 309-312
  tests of, 225, 298, 310
Adjective check lists
  listing of, 86-98
  reliability of, 39, 80-81, 86-102
  scaling procedures and, 102-104
  validity of, 27-39, 98, 104-107
Adjustment
  definition of, 202-205, 215, 234-235
  factor in self-concept measure, 97
  Ideal Self and, 57, 77, 211-212
  inferred from:
    diagnosed pathology, 204-218
    peer ratings, 204, 218-221
    projective techniques, 61, 72, 204, 226-229, 300
    self-reports, 94, 204, 229-234
    teacher or authority ratings, 204, 218-219, 224
  parent-child interaction and, 124-127, 134-136
  score for *Q*-sort items, 46, 56
  [Self—Ideal] discrepancies and, 77-78
  self-insight and, 275-276, 286-306
  self-insight re, 87, 287-288, 307-309
  self-regard and, 56-57, 72, 77-78, 83, 94, 118, 161-183, 202-235, 242

Adjustment—(cont.)
  stability of self concept (Brownfain) and, 82-83
Affiliation
  n Affiliation (TAT) and leadership, 141, 254
  in *Q*-sort instrument, 64
  need for Social Approval, 261
  self concept re, 87, 89, 96
Aggression (hostility)
  nonphenomenal
    in photo-judgment, 256, 261
    in Rorschach, 298-300
    in TAT, 141-142, 253-254, 258, 259-260
  phenomenal self concept of
    factors in *Q* sort, 62, 138
    in ratings, questionnaires, etc., 75, 90, 96-98, 256, 298-300
    self-insight re, 298-300
Alcoholism, 207
American Council on Education Psychological Examination, 96, 168-169, 224, 298, 310
Anxiety
  body, 68, 228, 262
  parent-child similarity and, 129, 134-135
  self concept of, 89-90, 96, 303
  self-insight and, 275-276, 303
  self-regard and, 72, 78, 106, 153-154, 194-195, 232
  Social Approval Motive and, 157
  test, 78, 90, 153-154, 157, 194-195, 232
Artifacts, 20-21, 116-118, 154-155, 165, 284-286. *See also* Research design
As-If Test, 148-149
Authoritarianism. *See* California F Scale
Autobiographies, 301-302
Autonomy. *See* Dependency needs

B

Barrier Score. *See* Rorschach Test

Behavior Interpretation Inventory, 156-157, 261

Behavioristic psychology
constructs used in, 11
personality theories and, 318, 320-321
self and, 1-2
stimulus definition and, 14-15
subject variables and, 18-20

Bell Adjustment Inventory, 294

Berger's Self- and Other-Acceptance Questionnaire, 66-67, 71, 98, 145, 223-224, 229, 235-236

Bernreuter Personality Inventory, 169, 176

Bills-Vance-McLean Index of Adjustment and Values, 28, 69-77, 85, 87, 89, 98, 105-106, 201, 225-226, 232-233, 235-236, 244, 246-247, 269

Body-Cathexis. See Jourard et al's Body-Cathexis, Scales

Body characteristics. See under Self-regard

Body image. See under Nonphenomenal self concept

Bonney Sociometric Technique, 219, 238

Bugental's Conceptual Matrix Method, 108, 140

Buss's sixteen-adjective scales, 145, 212-213, 230, 236

Butler and Haigh Q-sort instrument, 30, 41-61, 63, 110, 112, 145, 150-151, 167, 179, 205-206, 212, 220, 222, 224, 227, 231-232

C

Caldwell Pictures, 91, 256, 261

California Achievement Test, 225

California E Scale, 176, 239-243

California F Scale, 174, 176, 232, 239, 240-243

California PEC Scale, 239, 242

California Test of Personality, 57, 96, 134, 177, 219, 232-233, 238, 309

Cause-effect inferences. See under Research designs

Chapin's Social Insight Scale, 279

Chicago Attitude Scale, 91

Child Personality Scale, 87, 307

Children's Test Anxiety Scale, 195

Conceptual Matrix Method, 108, 140

Conformity, 153-159

Construct validity. See Validity, construct

Constructs
in behavioristic psychology, 11-12, 320
nonphenomenal, 4-5, 6-8, 250-251, 275-276, 319-320
phenomenal, 4-5, 6-8, 21-40
research design and, 11-12
in self theories, 6-8, 21, 250-251, 274-276, 317-321
See also Validity, construct

Cooperative English Test, 96, 298, 310

Cooperative Reading Achievement Test, 96, 298

Counseling. See Psychotherapy

Cultural Ideal (stereotype, norm)
ideal self and, 28, 43, 52-53, 57, 64, 71, 74, 76-77, 82-85, 88, 96, 105-106, 133, 143-144, 146-147, 151-152, 225, 245
self-report "intensity" and, 80
See also Social Desirability

D

DAT. See Differential Aptitude Test

De scale. See Gough Delinquency Scale

Defensiveness
failure and, 185-190, 194-199
in interpersonal perception, 226
in learning experiments, 201-202
in level-of-aspiration behavior, 244
measured by:
interviews, 175
inventory, 229-231, 255-256, 297-298
perceptual defense, 300-301
photo judgment, 255-256
projectives, 262, 298
trait attribution, 285, 295-297, 299-300, 301-302
self-overestimation, 310-313, 315
in psychotherapy, 162, 171-172, 174-175, 206, 242
self-insight and, 275-276, 283-284, 286, 295-302, 305

Defensiveness—(cont.)
  self-regard and, 7, 27-31, 203, 206,
    224, 226, 229-232, 242-243, 250-
    251, 256, 310-316
  test-taking, 27-31, 72-73, 77-78, 80,
    85, 172, 203-204, 229-232, 241-
    243
Delinquency, 218-219
Dependency (autonomy) needs
  in Self-Activity Inventory, 75
  in self-concept questionnaire, 96
  in Q sort, 64
Depression
  and self concept, 72, 90, 214, 226
Development. *See under* Self concept
Diagnostic categories. *See* Nosological
  categories
Differential Aptitude Test, 311
Draw-a-Person Test, 223. *See also* Machover Figure Drawing Scales
Driscoll Play Kit, 218, 257, 262
D statistic
  criticism of, 54
  used in studies, 127, 129, 131, 149-
    150
Dual (dyadic) indices
  artifacts and, 116, 127, 129, 130-132,
    134-135, 149-150, 247, 285-306
  discrepancy scores, 41
    derived by experimenter, 54, 104,
      276-277
    reported by S, 54, 65, 69-70, 76-
      83, 104
    problems of interpretation, 36, 50,
      53-54, 57, 73-77, 83-85, 104-106,
      130-132, 135, 149-150, 166, 172,
      192, 212, 220, 231-232, 244-248,
      276-286, 322
  See also Insightfulness of self concept;
    Self-concept stability; Self-regard,
    [Self—Ideal] discrepancies; [Self
    —Other] discrepancy

E

Eavesdropping question, 261
Edwards's Social Desirability Scale, 29
Ego-control scale. *See* Minnsota Mul-
  tiphasic Personality Inventory

Ego strength
  inferred from:
    autobiography, 228-229
    interviews, 228-229
    MMPI, 94, 230
    Scott-Duke Questionnaire, 95
    [Self — Ideal] discrepancies, 78
    [Self — Other] discrepancies, 78
  selective recall and, 78
E-M scores, 55, 57, 167-168
Essays for inferring:
  ideal self, 120, 125, 131, 139, 200
  self concept, 33, 35
  self-insight, 301
Ethnocentrism, 176, 239-243
Existential psychology, 9-10, 178

F

Factor analysis
  in construct validation, 25, 37
  of ideal self, 111
  inverse, 177-181
  item choice and, 39, 64, 89-92, 95
  of PPS Inventory, 34
  R-R designs and, 118
  of self-concept measures, 62, 94, 97,
    138, 241-242, 308
  subregions of self concept and, 37
  of therapy change measures, 168,
    172-174
Failure and self-evaluation, 18, 78, 118,
  184-199
Fey's Acceptance of Self and Others
  Questionnaire, 66-67, 89, 93, 220,
  222, 232, 235
Forced choice
  as irrelevant response determiner, 33-
    34, 52
  item writing and, 58-59
  See also Q sort
Freudian theory, 1-3, 9, 159, 251, 275,
  320
Friendliness, self-insight re, 297-300
Friendship choice, 137, 150-153. *See
  also* Sociometric ratings

G

Galvanic skin response
  and body image, 267
  generalization of, 15
  as index of "subception," 33

GAMIN Inventory, 64, 83, 85, 192, 226, 232
Gestalt
properties of nonphenomenal self, 181, 261, 263
properties of self concept, 7, 44, 51-54, 110-113, 168, 181, 208, 261, 263
psychology, 11, 13, 15, 318
Global scores, obscuring effects of, 52-54, 69, 73-75, 77, 105, 166
Gough Adjective Check List, 94, 142, 144, 205, 289. *See also* Sarbin's Adjective Check List
Gough Delinquency Scale, 289
"Guess Who" Test, 219, 307
Guilford-Zimmerman Temperament Survey, 130, 292

H

Happiness Self-rating Scale, 98, 228, 255, 307, 312
Health (mental). *See* Adjustment
Health (physical), 221-223
Hostility. *See* Aggression

I

IAV. *See* Bills-Vance-McLean Index of Adjustment and Values
Ideal Self
adjustment and, 57, 77, 211-212, 228
cultural ideal and, 28, 43, 52-53, 57, 64, 71, 74-75, 76-77, 82-86, 88, 96, 105-106, 133, 143-144, 146-147, 152, 225, 245
definition of, 41
discrepancies within, 111
essays for inferring, 120, 125, 131-132, 139, 200
friends' characteristics and, 151-152
models for, 125-126, 131-133, 200
negative self concept and, 105-106
of neurotic Ss, 211-212
nonphenomenal, 55, 254
parents' ideals and, 75, 126, 133
psychotherapy and, 57
of schizophrenic Ss, 211-212
sex role stereotypes and, 143-144, 146-147

Ideal Self—(cont.)
social class status and, 139
stability over time, 50, 126, 133
stereotypy of, 57, 74, 77, 82, 105-106, 133, 152, 212, 228
of teachers, 152-153
Taylor Manifest Anxiety Scale and, 105-106
See also Cultural ideal; Social Desirability
Ideal-sort
defined, 41
in diagnostic groups, 212
psychotherapy and, 57
See also Ideal Self
Identification
adjustment and, 124-126
definitions of, 123-126, 128-132
with parent, 125-126, 128-131, 135
Index of Adjustment and Values. *See* Bills-Vance-McLean Index of Adjustment and Values
Initial opinion artifact, 154-155
Ink-Blot Suggestion Test, 271
Insight. *See* Insightfulness of self concept
Insightfulness of self concept, 275-324
"adjustment" and, 275-276, 285-306
anxiety and, 275-276, 303
behavior and, 275-276, 286-306
defensiveness and, 275-276, 283-284, 286, 295-302, 305. *See also* overestimation errors in, below
definitions of, 275-279
descriptive facts re, 306-316
errors in studies of, 285-286, 304-305
intra-S consistency in, 314-315
measures of
classified, 276-279
validity problems in, 36, 278-284
overestimation errors in, 310-313, 315-316
perceptual defense and, 300-301
projection and, 286, 295-301
psychotherapy and, 286, 294-295
psychotherapeutic competence and, 286, 302-303
relationships with other variables, 285-306

Insightfulness of self concept—(cont.)
  research recommendations re, 305-306
  stereotype accuracy and, 280, 304, 308, 310, 315
  theories re, 275-276
  trait characteristics and, 314-316
Intelligence
  ideal self and, 139
  insight re, 297-298, 307-312
  self concept re, 89, 92, 94, 96, 98, 247-248
  tests of, 96, 139, 168-169, 176, 224, 267, 298, 310-311
Interpersonal Check List, 79-82, 90, 214-215
Interviews for inferring:
  defensiveness, 175
  self concept, 71, 107-110, 164-165, 170-176, 183
  self-concern, 183
  Self-regarding Span, 183-184
Item analysis
  in construct validation, 25, 322
  instruments developed with, 66, 69-70, 75, 87, 89, 92
Intuition Questionnaire, 301
Iowa Achievement Test, 224
"I Quest" Inventory, 96, 134

J

Jenkins's Sentiments Inventory, 239, 242
Jourard *et al.'s* Body-Cathexis Scales, 68-69, 90, 126, 160
Jourard *et al.'s* Self-Cathexis Scales, 68-69, 90, 113, 126, 130

K

Kuder Vocational Interest Inventory, 176

L

LA, 72, 94, 118, 243-249
Leadership
  nonphenomenal self concept and, 140-142, 253-254
  self concept and, 136, 140
  self-insight re, 87, 89, 98, 290-291, 310, 312

Learning
  ego-involvement and, 318
  of ideal self, 200
  of self-accepting statements, 164, 200
  of self concept, 121-122, 132-133, 136
  self concept and, 73, 118, 201-202, 251
Level of aspiration, 72, 94, 118, 243-249
Little and Fisher's Denial and Admission Scale, 230
Lobotomy, 118, 183-184

M

Machover Figure Drawing Scales, 157, 261
Marital Happiness Scale, 89, 97, 145, 232
Maslow Security-Insecurity Inventory, 69, 237
Maslow Self-Esteem Scale, 91, 169
Maslow Social Personality Inventory for College Women, 67-68, 91, 169, 224
MAT, 267
Measurement
  extant instruments for
    of insight, 278-279, 286-316
    of nonphenomenal self, 251-274
    of phenomenal self, 39-113
  problems re insight, 275-284, 304-306
  problems re nonphenomenal variables, 250-251, 274
  problems in phenomenological theory, 6-8, 28-39, 322
  See also Reliability; Validity, construct
Michigan Sentence Completion Test, 142, 261
Miller Analogies Test, 267
Minnesota Multiphasic Personality Inventory
  as adjustment measure, 127-129, 131, 229-231, 286-288
  attitude toward self index, 89, 172-174
  Barron's Ego-Strength Scale, 94
  as defensiveness measure, 72-73, 229-231, 255-256

Minnesota Multiphasic Personality Inventory—(cont.)
  diagnostic categories, 131, 217
  Edwards's Social Desirability Scale, 29
  Ego-Control Scale, 230
  Gough's Delinquency Scale, 289
  Little and Fisher's Denial and Admission Scale, 230
  as personality measure, 168-169
  as psychotherapy change measure, 172-173
  and self-acceptance, 72-73
  self-concept index, 91, 93, 105, 128-129, 146, 150, 168-169, 172-173, 177
  self-organization measure, 111
  social interaction measure, 82
  See also Taylor Manifest Anxiety Scale
Minnesota Personality Scale, 169
MMPI. *See* Minnesota Multiphasic Personality Inventory
Multidimensional Scale for Rating Psychiatric Patients, 94, 308
Multi-method, multi-trait matrix
  defined, 25-26
  extent of use, 37
  need for, 38

N

Negative self concept
  nonphenomenal, 141, 253-254, 258, 261
  phenomenal, 71, 83-86, 247
Negroes, self-hatred of, 253
Neo-Freudians
  nomological laws and, 9
  self constructs and, 2
  theories about insight and, 275
Neurosis, 78, 205-209, 211-218
Nomological psychology, 9, 10-21
Nonphenomenal self concept, 4
  behavior and, 251, 319-320
  of body image
    measured with aniseikonic lenses, 264-265
    measured by distorted pictures, 265-266
    measured by Rorschach, 266-273

Nonphenomenal self concept—(cont.)
  of body image—(cont.)
    relationships with other variables, 267-273
  construct validity, 250-251
    problems in, 250-251
    status of, 251, 258, 274
  correlations with self concept, 252-253, 255-257, 266, 269
  defensiveness and, 250-251, 255-256
  definitions of, 6
  ideal self, in TAT, 55, 254
  measures of, 251-274
    doll play, 257
    figure-drawings, 157-158, 160-161, 257, 261, 263-264
    picture-judging techniques, 255-256, 258
    Rorschach test, 85, 158, 181, 248, 251, 259-263, 266-273
    story-telling techniques, 252-258
    TAT, 55, 252-255, 258-261
  negativity of, 141-142, 253-254, 258, 261
  organization of, 181, 261, 263
  phenomenological theories and, 6-8, 38, 250-251, 319-320
  preverbal learning and, 251
  relationships to other variables, 250-274
  of self-acceptance, 248, 259, 263
  of self-adequacy, 248, 254, 258-259, 261, 263
  of self-attitudes, 263
  of self-esteem, 158
  of self-hatred, 253, 258
Nonphenomenal variables. *See* Phenomenological theories; Nonphenomenal self concept
Nosological categories
  ideal self and, 211-212
  self concept and, 78, 81-82, 205-218
  nonphenomenal self and, 210, 252

O

Occupational Interest Inventory (Singer and Stefflre), 177
Otis Higher Intelligence Test, Form A, 176

P

Paranoia, 209-212, 214, 252

Parent-child interaction, 118, 121-136, 257

Perception, research in, 24-27, 32-35, 38

Person I Would Like to Be Like, 120, 125, 131, 139, 200

Personal Preference Schedule (PPS), 33-34, 232

Persuasibility and self-esteem, 153-159

Phenomenal self. *See* Self concept

Phenomenological constructs
  behavior and, 7-8, 38, 319-321
  measurement problems, 6-8, 23-39
  specific measures of, 39-113
  See also Self concept; Self-regard

Phenomenological theories
  ahistorical propositions and, 20-21
  behavior theory and, 19-20
  exponents of, 2-3
  genetic propositions and, 20-21, 115
  meaning of, 3, 6
  nonphenomenal variables in, 4, 7-8, 38, 319-321
  research design and, 6-22
  re self-insight, 275-276
  vagueness of, 3-4, 8, 21-22, 110, 136, 240-241, 243-245, 248, 318-321

Phenomenology, 3
  definition of, 6
  research design and, 3, 6-22
  and self-concept theory, 7

Phillips Self- and Other-Acceptance Questionnaire, 66-67, 71, 92, 138, 221, 236

Positive self concept, 72, 83-84

Postural Sway Test, 271

PPS, 33-34, 232

Private self concept, 83-84, 276, 278, 280, 284, 290, 293, 307-309

Projective measures
  n Ach, 141, 246, 254, 271
  of adjustment, 61, 72, 204, 226-229, 300
  n Affil, 141, 254
  of aggression, 141, 253-254, 256, 258-261, 298-300
  of body image, 223, 264-273
  of nonphenomenal self concept, 251-274

Projection Movement Sequences, 267

Psychogalvanic skin response. *See* Galvanic skin response

Psychophysical methods
  in testing phenomenological theories, 15, 18
  in scaling self-concept dimensions, 102-104

Psychosis, 207, 209-218, 252

Psychosomatic Inventory, 228

Psychosomatic symptoms
  and body image, 267-268
  and self-regard, 72, 83-84, 214-215, 221, 228-229, 233

Psychotherapy
  motivation and self-regard, 82, 167, 172, 174, 206, 217
  research for theory testing, 161-166, 181, 183
  self concept and, 55-58, 107, 118, 161-183
  self-insight and, 286, 294-295

Q

Questionnaires
  re adjustment, 94, 204, 229-234
  reliability of, 39, 66-68, 70, 77, 86-102
  re self-disclosure, 31
  re self-regard, 66-107
  validity of, 98, 104-107

Q sort
  adjustment scores, 29-30, 46-47, 56-57
  Butler and Haigh's instrument, 41-59
  criticisms of, 33, 35-36, 45, 51-56, 59-60
  cultural ideals and, 43
  ideal-sort variance, 57
  index of phenomenal-self organizaation, 51-54
  index of self-regard, 53, 55-58, 60
  instruments listed, 59-64
  item length, 59-60
  procedure in, 41-42
  reliability, 35, 47-51, 59-64
  social desirability and, 29-30
  validity of, 36, 51-60

R

Ranking procedures, 32, 280

Rating scales

Rating scales—(cont.)
  listing of, 86-98
  reliability of, 39, 70, 98-102
  scaling procedures and, 102-104
  types of, 32-33, 65
  validity of, 27-39, 98, 104-107
  See also Semantic Differential scales
Rationalization-Projection Inventory, 237, 297
Recall ratios, 78, 196
Reliability
  of adjective check lists, rating scales, questionnaires, 39, 66-70, 77, 80, 83, 98-102
  general problems of, 47-51, 99-102
  of interview codes, 107-110
  of nonphenomenal self measures, 254, 257, 259-262
  of Q sorts, 39, 47-51, 61-64
Religious affiliation, 142-143
Research designs
  ahistorical, 20-21, 115
  antecedent-consequent, 13-14, 15, 19-21, 115, 322
  Brunswik's representative, 45
  cause-effect inferences and, 13-14, 15, 19-21, 115, 322
  common errors in, 20-21, 114-118, 163-166, 285-286
  existential psychology and, 9-10
  genetic (historical), 20-21, 115
  individual differences and, 17-19
  longitudinal, 119
  in perception and self-concept theories, 24-27
  phenomenal theory and, 6-21, 114-118, 322
  recommendations for, 21, 115-118, 163-166, 322
  Response-response (R-R), 13-14, 15, 19-21, 115, 322
  Stimulus-response (S-R), 13-14, 15, 19-21, 115, 322
  See also Dual indices; Measurement; Variables
Response determiners, irrelevant, 24-39
  content areas, 31
  contextual factors, 32
  instructions, 34-35, 276-277, 280, 284

Response determiners, irrelevant—(cont.)
  instrument form, 32
  known identity of S, 31
  rapport, 31, 229
  response frequency and familiarity, 35
  response sets, 32, 66-67, 81, 101-102, 104
  restrictions of S's responses, 32-34
  scoring and statistical procedures, 35-36
  set or expectation, 34-35
  Social Desirability, 27-30
  test-taking, 181
Role, 136-149, 181
Rorschach Test
  as adjustment measure, 61, 226-227, 300
  as affect measure, 72
  Barrier scores, 266-273
  as depression measure, 226
  as hostility measure, 298-300
  as nonphenomenal self-concept measure, 85, 158, 181, 251, 259-263
  as psychotherapy change measure, 172
  as self-acceptance measure, 248
  as self-adequacy measure, 248
Rosenzweig Picture Frustration Study, 98, 192, 195, 256
Rotter Board, 246
Rotter Incomplete Sentences Blank, 35, 228

S

SAI. See Self-Activity Inventory
SAM Pseudoscope, 271
Sampling of items, 39-40, 44-46, 48-49, 61-64, 68-69, 83, 87-88, 91-92, 95, 96
Sarason Test Anxiety Questionnaire, 78, 153-154, 157, 194-195, 232
Sarbin's Adjective Check List, 94-95, 143-144, 148
Scales. See Rating scales; Semantic Differential scales
Scaling
  of adverbs of degree, 103
  category, 103

Scaling—(cont.)
  need for, 54, 102-104, 166, 182, 198, 306, 322
  psychophysical methods for, 103-104
  ratio, 103
  of Social Desirability, 27
Schizophrenia, 209-212, 216-218, 252
Scott-Duke Questionnaire, 95, 209
Secord Homonyms Test, 228, 262, 267
Security-Insecurity Inventory, 69, 237
Selective recall, 78, 196
Self
  behaviorists and, 1-2
  concept of. See Self-regard; Self concept
  Freud and, 1-2
  functionalists and, 2
  history of interest in, 1-2
  inferred, 277
  Introjecting-Extrojecting, 111
  introspectionists and, 1
  James and, 1
  meanings of, 1, 4, 7
  neo-Freudians and, 1-2
  percept of. See Self concept; Self-regard
  Primitive Construed, 111
  structure, 7
  Social, 111
Self acceptance. See under Self-regard
Self-Activity Inventory, 74, 75-79, 105, 196-197, 211, 213, 232, 236, 246
Self-adequacy. See under Self-regard
Self Approval motive, 156-157, 261
Self awareness, 108, 171, 175, 294-295
Self blame. See under Self-regard
Self-Blame Questionnaire, 195
Self concept (phenomenal or conscious self concept)
  of aggression, 62, 75, 90, 96-98, 138, 256, 298-300
  of anxiety, 89-90, 96, 303
  as antecedent variable(s), 7, 18, 20, 114, 118, 140-141, 150-159, 200-202
  behavior and, 7-8, 114, 118, 250-251
  of beauty, 98, 296-297
  body image and. See Nonphenomenal self
  child's view of parent and, 124-125, 128-132

Self concept—(cont.)
  classification of research on, 118-119
  coded from interviews, 71, 107-110, 164-165, 170-176, 183
  congruence with ideal self. See Self-regard
  as consequent variable(s), 20, 114, 118, 121-200
  consistency of, 7, 110-113, 168
  definition of, 1, 7
  development of, 111, 118-121
  differentiation within, 110, 113
  discrepancies from reality, 7-8. See also Insightfulness of self concept
  drugs and, 64
  evaluative aspects of, 40-41. See also Self-regard
  of executives, 139
  experimental role enactment and, 148-149
  friendship choice and, 137, 150-153
  Gestalt (organizational) properties of, 7, 44, 51-54, 110-113, 168, 181, 208, 261, 263
  of happiness, 98, 228, 255, 307, 312
  hypnotic age regression and, 181
  identification and. See Identification
  insight and, 5. See also Insightfulness of self concept
  re intelligence. See Self-regard
  Introjecting-Extrojecting, 111
  learning and, 73, 121-122, 132-133, 136, 164, 199-202, 251
  lobotomy and, 118, 183-184
  measurement, 6-8, 23-113
  of Naval officers, 63
  negative nonphenomenal. See Nonphenomenal self
  negative phenomenal, 71, 83-86, 247
  nonoperational definitions of, 4
  nonphenomenal self concept. See Nonphenomenal self
  organization within. See Gestalt properties of; consistency of
  positive, 72, 83-84
  Primitive Construed, 111
  private, 83-84, 276, 278, 280, 284, 290, 293, 307-309
  related to other variables, 114-249
  religious affiliation and, 142-143
  role perception and, 181

Self concept—(cont.)
    role playing and, 148-149
    role status and, 136-147
    scaling of, 102-104, 166
    sex differences and, 143-147
    similarity in courtship and marriage
        pairs, 151
    social, 83, 89, 91-92, 95, 111, 276,
        278, 280-284, 290, 294-295
    stability of (Brownfain's), 36, 82-
        85, 220, 247
    stability over time, 50-51, 64, 101-
        102, 120-121
    of supervisors, 139
    teacher adjustment ratings and, 204,
        218-219, 224
    theories. *See* Phenomenological theo-
        ries
    unconscious. *See* Nonphenomenal self
        concept
    unconscious motivation and, 7, 250-
        251, 319-320
    See also Self-regard
Self-concern, 93, 183
Self-confidence, nonphenomenal, 141
Self-consistency. *See* Gestalt; Self concept
Self-continuity, 183
Self-criticality. *See under* Self-regard
Self-depreciation. *See under* Self-regard
Self-differentiation. *See* Gestalt; Self con-
    cept
Self-dislike. *See under* Self-regard
Self-esteem. *See under* Self-regard
Self-Esteem Behavior Rating Form, 224
Self-Esteem Inventory, 88, 224
Self-evaluation. *See under* Self-regard
Self-favorability. *See under* Self-regard
Self-ideal correlation. *See under* Self-
    regard
[Self—Ideal] discrepancies. *See under*
    Self-regard
Self-insight. *See* Insightfulness of self
    concept
Self-Insight Scale, 279
Self-Inventory, 96
Self-organization. *See* Gestalt
Self-Other Attitude Scale, 239-240, 242-
    243
[Self—Other] discrepancy
    as measure of ego strength, 78
    as measure of self depreciation, 76

[Self—Other] discrepancy—(cont.)
    and selective recall, 78, 196
Self-regard
    inclusive listing
        acceptance by others and, 219-221
        acceptance of others and, 66-67,
            118, 130, 145, 147, 170, 212,
            235-243
        achievement in school and, 144,
            169, 224-225, 245
        adjustment and, 55-57, 72, 77-78,
            83, 94, 118, 161-183, 202-235,
            242
        of alcoholics, 207
        anxiety and, 72, 78, 106, 153-154,
            194-195, 232
        authoritarianism and, 118, 174,
            176, 232, 239-243
        body cathexis and, 68-69, 160
        body characteristics and, 118, 159-
            161, 253
        body image and, 269
        conflict and, 73, 225
        defensiveness and, 203, 206, 224,
            226, 229-232, 242-243, 250-
            251, 256, 310-316
        defined, 40
        delinquency proneness and, 218-
            219
        depression and, 72, 90, 214, 226
        development of, 119-121
        ethnocentrism and, 118, 176, 239-
            243
        expectation of success and, 72
        failure and, 78, 118, 184-185
        and friendship choice, 137, 150-
            153
        and "group therapy" teaching, 72
        re intelligence, 88-89, 92, 94, 96,
            98, 247-248
        interviews coded for, 71, 107-110,
            164-165, 170-176, 183
        leader behavior and, 136, 140-142
        re leadership ability, 87, 89, 98,
            290-291, 310, 312
        learning and, 73, 118, 121-122,
            132-133, 136, 164, 201-202
        level of aspiration and, 72, 94,
            118, 243-249
        lobotomy and, 118, 183-184
        marital happiness and, 89, 145, 232

Self-regard—(cont.)
  inclusive listing—(cont.)
    measures of, 39-110
    mental hygiene films and, 169
    motivation for therapy and, 82,
      167, 172, 174, 206, 217
    of Naval officers, 63, 225
    negative self concept and, 71, 83-
      86
    in neuroses, 78, 205-209, 211-218
    nonphenomenal. See Nonphenom-
      enal self concept
    nosological categories and, 78, 81-
      82, 205-218
    of alcoholics, 207
    of Naval officers, 63, 225
    of paranoid Ss, 209-212, 214, 252
    parent-child interactions, 118, 121-
      136
    peer adjustment ratings and, 219
    persuasibility and, 137, 153-159
    physical health and, 221-223
    positive self concept and, 72, 83-
      84
    PPS scores and, 232
    of prison guards, 139
    projectively measured adjustment
      and, 72, 226-229, 300
    psychosomatic symptoms and, 72,
      83-84, 214-215, 221-222, 228-
      229, 233
    psychotherapy and, 55-58, 107,
      118, 161-183, 217
    of psychotic Ss, 207, 209-218, 252
    regard for others and, 235-240
    related to other variables, 114-249
    religious affiliation and, 142-143
    of schizophrenic Ss, 209-213, 216-
      218, 252
    selective recall and, 78, 196
    self-blame and, 72, 194-195
    self-concept stability and, 82-86
    sex behaviors and, 233
    sex differences in, 143-147
    social class status and, 137-139
    Social Desirability and, 28-29, 75
    social interaction and, 118, 136-
      159
    sociometric status and, 133, 219-
      221
    stability over time, 50-51, 64, 101-
      102, 120-121

Self-regard—(cont.)
  inclusive listing—(cont.)
    stress reactions and, 78
    of stutterers, 223-224
    success and, 118, 184-199
    Taylor Manifest Anxiety Scores
      and, 72, 78, 129, 134-135, 232
    teacher adjustment ratings and,
      204, 218-219, 224
    test-taking defensiveness and, 27-
      31, 72-73, 77-78, 85, 172, 203-
      204, 229-232, 241-243
    of volunteers for sex study, 224
    word association and, 73, 225, 228
  self-acceptance (rejection)
    alternate measures compared, 67,
      71-72, 106-107
    definition of, 40, 66, 82
    discriminant validity, 67, 106-107
    measured
      "directly," 65-75, 87-95, 98,
        106-107
      by self-minus-ideal discrepancies,
        79-82, 91, 97, 106-107, 133,
        145, 212
      by interviews, 109
    motivation for therapy, 82, 167,
      172, 174, 206, 217, 242
    nonphenomenal. See Nonphenome-
      nal self concept
    relationships with other variables.
      See Self-regard, inclusive listing
    [Self—Ideal] discrepancies and,
      71, 74, 79, 82, 133, 145, 230
  self-adequacy, 246
  self-blame, 72, 124, 128, 194-195,
    237
  self-criticality, 94
  self-depreciation, 76
  self-dislike questionnaire, 87
  self-esteem
    as aspect of self-regard, 107
    defined, 40
    measures of, 34, 54-60, 64, 67-68,
      88-93
    nonphenomenal. See Nonphenome-
      nal self concept
    relationships with other variables.
      See Self-regard, inclusive listing
  self-evaluation scale, 92
  self-favorability
    defined, 40

Self-regard—(cont.)
  self-favorability—(cont.)
    measurement of, 62, 87, 89, 133, 228
    relationships with other variables. *See* Self-regard, inclusive listing
  self-ideal correlation, 41-60
    contribution of ideal sort, 57
    defined, 41-42
    discriminant validity of, 57-58
    as index of "adjustment," 55-57, 205, 211, 213
    as index of self-concept organization, 44
    as index of self-regard, 43, 51-60
    relationships with other variables. *See* Self-regard, inclusive listing
    stability of, over time, 47-48, 51, 120
  [Self—Ideal] discrepancies
    as aspect of self-regard, 107
    criticized, 36, 53, 70-82, 104-107
    defined, 41, 243
    measures of, 69-82, 87, 89-97
    relationships with other variables. *See* Self-regard, inclusive listing
    "reversed" discrepancies and, 53, 74-75, 77, 105
    self-acceptance and, 71, 74, 79, 82, 133, 145, 230
    as self-acceptance index, 79-82, 91, 97, 106-107, 133, 145, 212
    Social Desirability and, 28-29, 75
    variance of Ideal, 74, 77, 82, 105-106, 133, 212, 228
    variance of Self, 74, 77, 105-106
  self-satisfaction (dissatisfaction)
    defined, 40
    measures of, 46, 61-62, 70, 88-90, 174, 176, 242
  self worth, 91, 137
Self-regarding Span, 93, 183-184
Self report
  and self-concept theory, 5, 11, 23-24
  See also Response determiners, irrelevant; Validity, construct; and Tables I-III
Self-satisfaction (dissatisfaction). *See under* Self-regard
Self-sorts
  defined, 41-42
Self-steering behavior, 271-272

Self-worth. *See under* Self-regard
Semantic Differential scales, 32-33, 89-90, 95, 197, 220, 222
Sensibility Questionnaire, 93, 183-184
Sentence completion, 35, 228-229, 267
Sex
  behaviors, 233
  development, 257
  differences, 143-147
  needs in SAI, 75
S-I, 69, 237
Social Approval motive, 156-157, 261
Social class, 137-139
Social Desirability, 27 ff.
  of Allport and Odbert adjectives, 88
  of Butler and Haigh Q-sort items, 30
  friendship choice and, 152
  of IAV items, 28
  Ideal Self ratings and, 28, 105, 146
  influence on self-reports, 27-31, 34, 204, 234
  meanings of, 29-30
  of MMPI items, 29, 105, 146
  of PPS items, 33-34
  of Q-sort items, 29
  of rating-scale items, 75, 172
  Scale. *See* MMPI
  scaling of, 27
Social Insight Scale, 279
Social Personality Inventory for College Women, 67, 91, 169, 224
Social self concept, 83, 89, 91-92, 95, 111, 276, 278, 280-284, 290
Sociometric ratings
  child-parent similarity and, 133
  as friendship index, 149-151
  of interpersonal behavior, 82
  self-concept similarity and, 150-151
  in self-esteem index, 154-155
  self-insight and, 293
  self-regard and, 219-221
  stability of ideal-self and, 133
Stability of self concept. *See* Self concept, stability
Stereotype accuracy, 117, 134, 280, 304, 308, 310, 315
Stimulus
  contemporary, 13-18
  defined
    in data language, 14
    physicalistically, 13

Stimulus—(cont.)
  defined—(cont.)
    as response-inferred construct, 13-18
    Jessor's analysis of, 14-15
    past, 20
    in phenomenological theory, 16-18, 20
    Verplanck's analysis of, 14
Stress, 78, 267
Strong Vocational Interest Inventory, 169
Stuttering, 223-224
Subception, 33
Subject variables
  in behavioristic research, 18-20
  contemporary, 18-20
  in phenomenological research, 18-20
Success, 72, 184-199
Suicide, 93, 222

T

TAT. *See* Thematic Apperception Test
Taylor Manifest Anxiety Scale, 72, 78, 106, 129, 134-135, 232
Thematic Apperception Test
  adjustment scales, 61, 227, 300
  guilt-feeling index, 192
  nonphenomenal self indices, 55, 62, 141-142, 160, 252-255, 258-261
  n Achievement score, 141, 246, 254, 271
  n Affiliation score, 141-254
  n Aggression score, 141-142, 253-254, 258-260
  other-blame scores, 195
  psychoanalytic mental health scales, 227
  psychotherapy improvement indices, 171-172
  self-blame index, 195
Thorndike-Lorge Word Count, 88, 96, 201
Thorndike Senior Century Dictionary, 48
Two-part indices. *See* Dual indices

U

Unconscious self concept. *See* Nonphenomenal self concept
UPC (Universe of Personal Constructs). *See* Sampling of items

V

Validity
  concurrent, 23
  construct, 4, 23-24
    converging operations and, 24-25
    factor analysis and, 25-26
    of interview codes, 107
    and irrelevant response determiners, 24-39
    item analysis and, 25
    multi-method, multi-trait matrix and, 25-26, 38
    of nonphenomenal self-concept measures, 250-262, 264, 274, 319
    of phenomenal self-concept measures, 27-40, 104-107
      Q-sort procedures, 51-64
      rating scales, etc., 66-98, 104-107
    of self-organization indices, 110-113
    specifications for establishing, 25-27
  discriminant
    of body image measures, 266, 269, 273
    of insight measures, 279, 283-284, 289, 302
    of nonphenomenal self measures, 251
    of self-concept stability, 84-85
    of self-differentiation measures, 113
    of self-regard measures, 57-58, 67, 71, 74, 76, 106-107
  empirical, 38
  face, 38
  predictive, 23
Variables
  antecedent observable (stimulus, environmental), 12-21, 115
  consequent observable (behavioral), 10-11, 15, 115
  contemporary stimulus or environmental antecedents. *See* Stimulus
  demographic, interpretative problems, 116
  inferred, intervening, 11-12, 115
  past stimulus or environmental antecedents. *See* Stimulus; Construct

Variables—(cont.)
  sociological, 116
  subject variables, as independent variables, 115
Vineland Social Maturity Scale, 91, 95, 160-161, 257

W

Warner's Index of Status Characteristics, 138

W-A-Y. *See* Who-Are-You Test
Wechsler-Bellevue Scale, 267
Who-Are-You Test, 87, 96, 142, 151, 207, 219, 223, 238
Willoughby Emotional Maturity Scale, 55, 57, 167-168
Witkin rod and frame test, 271
Word association measures, 73, 225-226, 228-229, 262, 267, 300

Author Index

See Subject Index for proper names associated with particular measuring instruments.

A

Aaronson, L., 342
Abelson, R. P., 90, 154, 156, 334
Abercrombie, J., 265, 330
Abt, L. E., 334
Adelson, D., 342
Adler, A., 3, 159, 211, 325
Aidman, T., 342
Alden, P. J., 342
Alexander, S., 72, 106, 232, 328
Alexander, T., 255, 259, 325
Alfert, E., 87, 237, 325
Algeo, N. B., 184, 325
Allison, S. G., 342
Allport, G., 69, 88, 91
Alm, O. W., 126, 134, 334
Amatora, S. M., 87, 307, 314, 325
Ames, L. B., 119, 325
Angel, E., 336
Angyal, A., 3, 325
Applezweig, M. H., 156, 261, 336
Arnold, F. C., 35, 325
Aronfreed, J. M., 342
Aronson, C. E., 343
Arsenian, S., 277, 292, 310, 312, 325
Asch, M. J., 343
Ax, A. F., 29, 63, 207, 334
Axelrod, H. S., 72-73, 106, 201, 232, 328

B

Baer, M., 97, 145, 212, 236, 342
Baldwin, A. L., 326
Balester, R. J., 343
Bandura, A., 278, 303, 325
Barron, E., 89, 276, 277, 278, 309, 331
Barron, F. X., 343
Barry, J. R., 343
Beardslee, B. A., 343
Beier, E. G., 123, 124, 128, 325
Beilin, H., 87, 307-308, 325
Bellak, L., 334
Bellugi, U., 88, 228, 236, 328

Beloff, H., 259, 325
Beloff, J., 259, 325
Benjamin, J., 198, 325
Berdie, R. F., 168, 325
Berger, E. M., 66-67, 71, 87, 93, 98, 109, 145, 223, 224, 229, 236, 325
Berger, S., 223, 325, 343
Berkowitz, H., 98, 189, 333
Bice, H. V., 223, 326
Bieri, J., 202, 326
Bigbee, L., 89, 276, 277, 278, 309, 331
Bills, R. E., 28, 69-75, 77, 85, 87, 89, 98, 105, 201, 225, 226, 232, 236, 244, 246, 247, 269, 326
Blaisdell, F. J., 62, 150, 330
Blake, R. R., 338
Blane, H. T., 223, 327
Block, J., 59, 61, 213, 229, 326, 343
Block, Jeanne, 343
Blodgett, H. E., 343
Blumberg, A., 30, 342
Bosley, J. J., 29, 329
Bossom, J., 235, 237, 326
Bourestom, N. C., 343
Bowdlear, C., 343
Bower, E. M., 343
Boxer, M., 343
Brandt, R. M., 277, 278, 291, 311, 314-315, 326
Branson, B. D., 343
Brim, O. G., 151, 326
Brodbeck, A. J., 241, 326
Brodney, F. E., 343
Bronfenbrenner, U., 87, 278, 280-283, 326
Brophy, A. L., 343
Brown, E. A., 264, 326
Brownfain, J. J., 72, 82-85, 87, 91, 94, 106, 191, 220, 227, 231, 247, 276, 278, 290, 326
Bruce, P., 343
Brunswik, E., 45, 326
Bryant, N. D., 32, 342

383

Bugental, D., 292, 326
Bugental, J. F. T., 87, 108, 151, 219, 223, 224, 326, 327, 342, 343
Burch, I. A., 343
Burgess, T. C., 343
Butler, J. M., 30, 41-60, 61, 63, 110, 145, 150, 166, 167, 179, 206, 212, 220, 222, 224, 227, 327, 344

C

Caldwell, B. McD., 327
Calkins, M. W., 1, 327
Calogeras, R. C., 344
Calvin, A. D., 87, 167, 276, 277, 278, 284, 286, 313, 314, 327
Campbell, D. T., 24, 25, 26, 37, 115, 116, 117, 322, 327
Candee, B. L., 344
Caplan, S. W., 61, 166, 167, 327
Cartwright, D. S., 112, 168, 170, 201, 202, 239, 241-242, 327, 331
Cartwright, R. D. See Dymond, R. F.
Cath, S. H., 223, 327
Cattell, R., 39, 42, 64, 89, 91, 92
Chase, P. H., 57, 61, 212, 327, 344
Chein, I., 4, 327
Chertok, E., 344
Child, I. L., 87, 252, 259, 278, 327
Chodorkoff, B., 61, 63, 213, 229, 246, 300, 301, 327, 334
Christensen, G. M., 344
Clancy, D. D., 344
Cleveland, S. E., 251, 260, 263, 272, 327, 328, 330, 331, 341
Cliff, N., 103, 328
Coates, C. H., 139, 328
Cohen, A. R., 34, 59, 61, 64, 98, 156, 191, 197, 328, 340, 344
Cohen, H. M., 344
Cohen, L. D., 248, 259, 263, 328
Combs, A. W., 3, 4, 8, 233, 328, 340, 341
Comrey, A., 34, 334
Cooley, C. H., 136, 328
Cooper, A., 30, 342
Coopersmith, S., 88, 219, 224, 328
Costa, L. D., 344
Couch, C. J., 344
Cowen, E. L., 28, 71, 72, 73, 75, 84, 85, 106, 201, 232, 328
Crandall, V. J., 88, 228, 236, 328

Cranston, R., 62, 180, 331
Cromwell, R. I., 91, 150, 335
Cronbach, L. J., 23, 25, 26, 32, 36, 45, 52, 54, 99, 100, 101, 265, 280, 328, 329, 330, 331
Cuadra, C. A., 278, 286, 289, 338
Cureton, E. E., 50, 99, 101, 329

D

Davids, A., 31, 97, 228, 252, 259, 329
Davidson, K. S., 344
Davitz, J. R., 150, 151, 329
Dawkins, P. B. H., 344
DeLisle, F., 344
Dellen, J. E., 344
DeSoto, C. B., 29, 30, 329
Detweiler, J., 92, 150, 151, 337
Diggory, J. C., 88, 185, 192, 193, 329
Diller, L., 33, 88, 194, 240, 259, 262, 329
Dinitz, S., 93, 218, 338
Dittes, J. E., 88, 187, 188, 329
Dodge, J. S., 89, 205, 330
Doleys, E. J., 344
Dolinko, P., 344
Dollard, J., 14, 132
Doris, J., 185, 194, 195, 329
Dornbusch, S. M., 92, 276, 308, 336
Dorr, M., 120, 125, 131, 200, 332
Dudek, F. J., 101, 103, 329
Dunn, M. B., 344
Dymond, R. F., 44, 46, 47, 50, 53, 56, 57, 58, 88, 112, 166, 167, 168, 171, 179, 205, 227, 231, 243, 254, 327, 329, 332, 338, 339, 341

E

Eastman, D., 89, 97, 145, 232, 240, 330
Edelson, M., 59, 61, 180, 330
Edwards, A. L., 27, 28, 29, 33, 163, 330
Ellenberger, H. F., 336
Engel, M., 62, 120, 144, 147, 219, 230, 231, 330
English, A. C., 4, 330
English, H. B., 4, 330
Epstein, S., 210, 260, 330
Eriksen, C. W., 24, 33, 330, 331
Estes, W. K., 341
Ewing, T. N., 89, 170, 330

F

Fabian, W. A., 344
Fagan, E. R., 90, 139, 334
Farberow, N. L., 181, 261, 263, 339
Faust, V., 344
Festinger, L., 97, 191, 330
Fey, W. F., 66, 67, 89, 93, 220, 222, 232, 235, 330
Fiedler, F. E., 62, 89, 150, 205, 220, 221, 222, 223, 224, 232, 234, 330
Field, P. B., 90, 154, 156, 333
Fisher, S., 251, 260, 262-266, 268-270, 272-273, 327, 328, 330, 331, 341
Fishman, S., 344
Fiske, D. W., 24, 26, 37, 293, 327
Fitts, W. H., 345
Flyer, E., 89, 276, 277, 278, 309, 331
Fogelson, H., 345
Force, D. G., 345
Fordyce, W. E., 345
Fox, M., 345
Frank, K. F., 87, 252, 259, 278, 327
Frank, J. D., 176, 337
Freeman, W., 93, 183, 184, 262, 338
Freud, S., 1, 3, 9, 159, 251, 275, 320, 331
Friedman, I., 62, 211, 213, 252, 260, 278, 331
Frisch, P., 62, 180, 331
Froehlich, C. P., 89, 181, 311
Fromm, E., 3, 331
Fruchter, B., 93, 241, 242, 338
Funkenstein, D. H., 272

G

Gage, N. L., 280, 331
Gaines, G. R., 345
Galanter, E. H., 103, 340
Gallwey, M., 87, 280-283, 326
Garner, W. R., 24, 331
Garret, J. F., 325
Gebel, A. S., 136, 140, 141, 331
Gerard, H. B., 97, 313, 331
Gibson, R. L., 89, 172, 331
Gilinsky, A. S., 98, 247, 331
Glaze, J. A., 112, 201
Gleser, G. C., 45, 52, 54, 329
Glud, E., 223, 327
Goitein, P. L., 264, 326
Goldberg, M. L., 345

Goldfarb, A., 345
Goldings, H. J., 98, 228, 255, 260, 276, 307, 331
Goodman, H., 345
Goodrich, E. G., 345
Gordon, E. M., 194, 339
Gordon, T., 170, 239, 241-242, 331
Grace, M., 264-265
Graham, E., 90, 157, 261, 334
Grayson, M., 223, 331
Green, G. H., 98, 277, 290, 311, 314, 332
Green, L. A., 345
Greenfield, N., 93, 221, 222, 338
Greenspoon, J., 345
Gross, L., 279, 332
Grummon, D. L., 227, 254, 260, 332
Guilford, J. P., 103, 332
Gulliksen, H. O., 101, 332
Gunning, E. C., 87, 327
Guthrie, E. R., 14

H

Haigh, G. V., 327, 332, 345 (*see also* Butler, J. M.)
Haimowitz, M. L., 260, 263, 332, 345
Haimowitz, N. R., 260, 263, 332
Hake, H. W., 24, 331
Hall, C. W., 4, 332
Halloway, R. S., 345
Halpern, H. M., 226, 332
Hamilton, R. J., 345
Hampton, B. J., 345
Hanlon, T. E., 57, 62, 206, 232, 332
Harding, J., 87, 280-283, 326
Hardyck, C., 111, 336
Harlow, R. G., 345
Hartley, M., 345
Harvey, O. J., 89, 185, 186, 332
Hauser, F. S., 85, 346
Havighurst, R. J., 120, 125, 131, 138, 139, 200, 332
Hebb, D. O., 11, 12
Heider, F., 12, 332
Heilizer, F., 72, 73, 106, 201, 232, 328
Helper, M. M., 89, 91, 126, 132, 133, 199, 332
Henry, A. F., 97, 124, 128, 236, 237, 252, 259, 329, 332
Hertz, L., 346

Hilden, A. H., 48, 50, 57, 59, 61, 62, 332
Hilgard, E., 1, 277, 332
Hill, T. J., 137-138, 332
Hillson, J. S., 78, 211, 213, 332
Hobbs, N., 173
Hofstaetter, P. R., 57, 62, 63, 111, 151, 206, 232, 332, 335
Hogan, R. A., 346
Holt, R., 291, 333
Holtzman, W. H., 32, 87, 276, 277, 278, 286f., 288, 313, 314, 327, 342
Hornberger, R. H., 91, 146, 335
Horney, K., 3, 333
Hovland, C. I., 328, 333, 334
Howard, A. R., 346
Howard, R. C., 98, 189, 333
Hoyt, D. P., 346
Hull, C. L., 11, 19
Humphreys, L. G., 25, 333
Hutchins, E. B., 89, 205, 330

I

Isenberger, W. E., 346
Israel, J., 89, 276, 310, 312, 314, 333

J

Jackson, D. N., 101, 333
James, W., 1, 333
Janis, I. L., 90, 153, 154, 156, 328, 333, 334
Jenkins, R. L., 94, 335
Jersild, A., 62, 63
Jesness, C. F., 346
Jessor, R., 14, 333, 346
John, E. S., 227, 254, 260, 332
Johnson, D. G., 176, 333
Jones, A., 33, 52, 212, 333
Jones, A. E., 59, 61, 180, 330
Jones, D. S., 94, 148, 339
Jones, M. C., 120, 160, 253, 261, 336
Jones, R. E., 89, 205, 330
Jonietz, A. K., 346
Jordan, R. M., 302, 303, 333
Jourard, S. M., 31, 32, 33, 68, 90, 105, 113, 124, 125, 126, 127, 130, 160, 228, 262, 333, 339

K

Kaplan, M. J., 346

Kardiner, A., 253, 260
Karon, P. B., 253, 260, 333
Kates, S. L., 302, 303, 333
Katkovsky, W., 91, 150, 335
Katz, M. M., 90, 94, 174, 335
Kay, B., 93, 218, 338
Kell, B. L., 346
Kelley, H. H., 89, 185, 186, 293, 332
Kelman, H. C., 62, 175, 278, 294, 333, 337
Kenny, D. T., 27, 334
King, S. H., 272
Kinsey, A. C., 224
Klausner, S. Z., 62, 138, 334
Klein, G. S., 98, 277, 278, 303, 334
Koch, S., 341
Kogan, W. S., 29, 30, 63, 207, 217, 334
Koslosky, J. C., 206
Krasner, L., 164, 334
Kuethe, J. L., 29, 329
Kuhn, M. H., 142, 334

L

LaFon, F. E., 226, 227, 334
LaForge, R., 79, 90, 334
Langford, L. M., 126, 134, 334
Lasakow, P., 31, 33, 333
Lawson, E. D., 90, 139, 334
Lazowick, L. M., 90, 125, 126, 129, 134, 334
Leary, T., 10, 79, 80, 81, 82, 213, 214, 215, 217, 334
Lebo, D., 95, 120, 160, 256, 262, 340
Lecky, P., 3, 334
Lehner, G. F. J., 292, 326
Lepine, L. T., 63, 246, 334
Lesser, G. S., 90, 154, 156, 334
Leuthold, C. A., 346
Levanway, R. W., 90, 188, 334
Levine, M., 346
Levonian, E., 34, 334
Levy, L. H., 58, 63, 334
Levy, S., 157, 262, 334
Levy, W., 34, 334
Lewin, K., 9, 12
Lindzey, G., 4, 332
Linton, H., 90, 157, 261, 334
Lipkin, S., 109, 171, 334
Lodge, H. C., 200, 334
Loevinger, J., 162, 203, 335

Lorr, M., 90, 94, 174, 241, 242, 308, 335, 339
Lundy, R. M., 91, 150, 335
Lynd, H. M., 3, 335
Lynn, D. B., 144, 335

M

McArthur, C. C., 97, 252, 259, 329
McClelland, D. C., 3, 252, 326, 335
MacCorquodale, K., 341
McFarland, R. A., 228, 335
McGeehee, T. P., 346
McIntyre, C. J., 67, 220, 335
McKee, J. P., 91, 95, 143, 144, 335, 339
McKenna, H. V., 63, 111, 150, 151, 206, 335
McLean, O. S., 326 (see also Bills, R. E.)
McNamara, L. F., 97, 252, 259, 329
McPartland, T. S., 142, 334, 346
McQuitty, L. L., 91, 208, 209, 335
Magaziner, D. E., 88, 185, 192, 193, 329
Manis, M., 91, 123, 124, 125, 129, 131, 137, 149, 150, 335
Mannheim, B. F., 346
Martire, J. G., 91, 146, 246, 335
Maslow, A. H., 3, 69, 91, 224, 233, 235, 237, 300, 326, 335, 336
Mason, E. P., 91, 137, 138, 256, 261, 336
Mathews, R., 111, 336
Matteson, R. W., 92, 144, 336
May, R. I., 9, 336
Mazurkiewicz, J. F., 346
Mead, G. H., 3, 136, 336
Meehl, P. E., 23, 25, 26, 265, 329, 341
Melniker, R. C., 346
Mertens, M., 164, 168, 336
Messick, S., 101, 333
Miller, K. S., 78, 196, 246, 336
Miller, N., 14, 132
Mittelman, B., 300
Miyamoto, S. F., 92, 276, 308, 336
Moeller, G., 156, 261, 336
Monashkin, I., 97, 145, 212, 230, 236, 342
Morison, R. S., 324, 336
Mosak, H. H., 347
Moser, W. E., 311, 331

Mowrer, O. H., 42, 45, 51, 52, 56, 328, 336
Mueller, C. G., 341
Mulford, H. A., 347
Murray, E., 93, 218, 338
Murray, H. A., 39, 45, 62, 87, 88, 252, 261, 291
Murstein, B. I., 98, 277, 278, 298-299, 336
Mussen, P. H., 120, 136, 140, 160, 253, 261, 336

N

Nahinsky, I. D., 63, 225, 337
Newman, D. K., 347
Newman, M., 347
Newstrand, M. B., 261, 337
Nishimura, R., 64, 150, 151, 341
Norman, R. D., 92, 277, 293-294, 337
Northway, M. L., 92, 150, 151, 337
Nunnally, J. C., 63, 178, 179, 337
Nuthmann, A., 92, 199, 337

O

O'Connor, J., 57, 62, 63, 111, 151, 206, 232, 332, 335
Odbert, H. S., 88, 91
O'Dea, J. D., 177, 337
Omwake, K., 66, 67, 71, 236, 337
Osgood, C. E., 89, 90, 95, 129, 132, 197, 337
Ossorio, A., 162, 203, 335
Ovesy, L., 253, 260

P

Parloff, M. B., 62, 175, 278, 294, 333, 337
Paul, C., 98, 256, 261, 338
Pearl, D., 63, 176, 241, 337
Pellegrini, R. J., 139, 328
Perkins, H. V., 63, 120, 144, 219, 225, 337
Perlmutter, H. V., 87, 92, 241, 242, 326, 337
Petrullo, L., 36, 329
Phillips, E. L., 66, 67, 71, 92, 138, 221, 236, 337
Pock, J. C., 347
Porter, L. G., 123, 125, 130, 337
Porter, L. W., 136, 140, 253, 261, 336

Powell, M., 307, 337
Precker, J. A., 337
Procter, D., 34, 334
Pullen, M. S., 184, 325
Pyne, F. F., 347

Q

Quinn, R., 29, 63, 207, 334

R

Raimy, V. C., 7, 107, 109, 170, 173, 239, 337
Rafferty, J., 339
Ramsey, G. V., 338
Rapaport, G. M., 105, 337
Raskin, N. J., 109, 176, 337
Rasmussen, G., 92, 95, 150, 152, 233, 338
Ratzeburg, F., 123, 124, 128, 325
Ray, W. S., 89, 172, 331
Raymaker, H., 347
Reckless, W. C., 93, 218, 338
Reed, C. F., 278, 286, 289, 338
Reeder, T., 347
Remy, R. M., 68, 113, 124, 126, 127, 333
Renzaglia, G. A., 72, 347
Rife, D., 90, 153, 154, 156, 333
Riklan, M., 260, 262, 329
Ripley, H. S., 29, 63, 207, 334
Roberts, G. E., 73, 225, 338
Robinson, M. F., 93, 183, 184, 262, 338
Robinson, M. Z., 120, 125, 131, 200, 332
Robison, R. K., 347
Roessler, R., 93, 221, 222, 338
Rogers, A. H., 93, 98, 209, 255-256, 261, 338
Rogers, C. R., 3, 4, 7, 9, 20, 44, 50, 55, 58, 63, 88, 110, 112, 166-168, 171, 179, 201, 205, 243, 254, 275, 327, 329, 331, 332, 338, 339, 341
Rokeach, M., 93, 98, 241, 242, 277, 296, 338
Roos, D. E., 347
Rosen, E., 93, 105, 146, 230, 338
Rosenberg, B. G., 94, 142, 144, 205, 339
Rosenman, S., 109, 170, 239, 338
Ross, E. M., 347

Roth, I., 327
Rotter, J. B., 339
Rubenstein, E. A., 90, 94, 174, 241, 242, 308, 335, 339
Rubin, S. I., 347
Rudikoff, E. C., 57, 58, 170, 239, 339
Rundquist, E. A., 307
Russell, D. H., 309, 312, 339
Russell, D. L., 347

S

Sakoda, J. M., 224, 336
Sarason, S. B., 90, 186, 194, 195, 329, 339
Sarbin, T. R., 91, 94, 111, 142, 144, 148, 181, 205, 261, 263, 289, 336, 339
Sarnoff, I., 142, 236, 237, 261, 339
Schaefer, E., 94, 335
Scheerer, E. T., 66, 109, 170, 238, 339
Scheide, E. J., 347
Scher, S. C., 347
Schoenfeld, W. N., 341
Scott, H. A., 347
Scott, W. A., 203, 339
Sears, P., 94, 245, 339
Sears, R. R., 95, 276, 277, 278, 284, 295, 296, 314, 339
Secord, P. F., 68, 105, 160, 208, 228, 262, 333, 339
Segman, S., 30, 342
Seitz, C. P., 228, 335
Selzer, S., 347
Shapiro, M. M., 89, 185, 186, 332
Sharma, S. L., 95, 186, 192, 339
Sheehan, J. G., 223, 342
Sheldon, W. H., 267
Shelsky, I., 347
Sherriffs, A. C., 91, 95, 143, 144, 335, 339
Shoemaker, D. J., 91, 150, 335
Shontz, F. C., 223, 339
Short, N. R., 347
Silver, I. H., 348
Silverman, H., 348
Silverstein, A. B., 348
Singer, S. L., 177, 340
Skinner, B. F., 14
Sletto, R. F., 307
Smith, G. M., 64, 288, 340
Smith, M. B., 8, 340

Smith, W. D., 95, 120, 160, 256, 262, 340
Snyder, W. U., 89, 172, 331
Snygg, D., 3, 8, 340
Solley, C. M., 95, 197, 340
Solomon, A., 348
Sopchak, A. P., 123, 124, 125, 128, 131, 340
Soper, D. W., 4, 328
Spence, K. W., 10, 13, 340
Stacey, C. L., 123, 125, 130, 337
Stagner, R., 95, 197, 340
Stee, M., 348
Stefflre, B., 177, 340
Steier, L. D., 309
Steiner, I. D., 95, 247, 340
Stephenson, W., 10, 41, 45, 178, 340
Stevens, S. S., 103, 340
Stewart, R. L., 348
Stock, D., 108, 238, 340
Storm, T., 87, 252, 259, 278, 327
Stotland, E., 34, 59, 61, 64, 95, 98, 185, 190, 191, 197, 340
Strodtbeck, F. L., 326
Suci, G. J., 337
Suczek, R., 79, 90, 334
Sullivan, H. S., 3, 340
Swensen, C. H., 157, 264, 340
Symonds, P. M., 4, 340

T

Taba, H., 138, 139, 332
Taguiri, R., 36, 329
Tamkin, A. S., 95, 209, 340
Tannenbaum, P. H., 337
Tarwater, J. W., 96, 126, 134, 294, 341
Tatum, C. D., 348
Taylor, C., 233, 341
Taylor, D. M., 35, 50, 64, 341
Thomas, E., 59, 64, 98, 191, 340
Thomas, H., 59, 61, 213, 229, 326
Thompson, W. R., 64, 150, 151, 341
Thorne, R. B., 348
Thorley, S., 59, 64, 98, 191, 340
Tolor, A., 207, 341, 348
Tongas, P. N., 28, 75, 328
Torgerson, W. S., 103, 341
Torrey, J., 97, 191, 330
Torrance, E. P., 96, 277, 278, 297, 310, 311, 341, 348

Travers, R. M. W., 58, 341
Trieschman, A., 202, 326
Turner, R., 153, 341
Turner, R. H., 145, 205, 206, 220, 222, 224, 231, 341

U

Underwood, B. J., 115, 341

V

Vance, E. L., 326 (*see also* Bills, R. E.)
Vanderlippe, R. H., 145, 205, 206, 220, 222, 224, 231, 341
Vargas, M. J., 108, 171, 341
Verplanck, W. S., 14, 341

W

Wahl, C. W., 206, 341
Wahler, H. J., 96, 167, 172, 206, 341
Waisanen, C. E., 348
Walker, J. H., 348
Walker, P. D., 348
Walsh, A. M., 218, 257, 262, 341
Walsh, T. M., 255, 256, 261, 338
Walter, V. A., 35, 325
Ware, K. E., 272, 341
Warrington, W. G., 62, 150, 330, 348
Webb, W. B., 96, 307, 309, 314, 341
Weider, G. S., 72
Weingarten, E. M., 278, 285, 301, 342
Wepman, J. M., 62, 223, 224, 330
Wiener, M., 30, 46, 342
Wilk, R. E., 348
Willerman, B., 97, 191, 330
Wittreich, W. J., 264-265
Wolff, W. W., 337
Wonderlic, E. F., 267
Wood, N., 151, 326
Worchel, P., 74, 75-78, 96, 105, 196, 211, 213, 232, 236, 332, 336, 342
Wrenn, C. G., 183, 342
Wylie, R. C., 33, 35, 96, 236, 278, 295, 297, 309, 312, 314, 342

Y

Young, H. H., 32, 342

Z

Zander, A., 59, 64, 92, 95, 98, 150, 152, 185, 190, 191, 233, 338, 340
Zelen, S. L., 87, 96, 219, 220, 223, 236, 238, 327, 342

Zeran, F. R., 177, 337
Zimmer, H., 96, 97, 225, 236, 238, 342
Zuckerman, M., 97, 145, 212, 230, 236, 342

A NOTE ABOUT THE AUTHOR

RUTH C. WYLIE was born in Beaver Falls, Pennsylvania, and took her B.S. degree with highest honors at Geneva College (1939). She received her M.A. (1940) and Ph.D. (1943) from the University of Pittsburgh. After teaching at Stephens College and Connecticut College for Women, Dr. Wylie became a Member of the Teaching Faculty at Sarah Lawrence College in 1952, where she established the psychological laboratory of which she is presently director. Dr. Wylie is a member of the American Psychological Association, the Psychonomic Society, and Sigma Xi, and has held grants from the National Science Foundation, the American Philosophical Society, and the National Institute of Mental Health. Articles of which she is author or co-author have appeared in the *Journal of Experimental Psychology*, the *Journal of Abnormal and Social Psychology*, the *Journal of Applied Psychology*, and the *Journal of Personality*.